Hospitality Management Law

Hospitality Management Law

First Edition

Edward Perez

cognella
SAN DIEGO

Bassim Hamadeh, CEO and Publisher
Mieka Portier, Senior Acquisitions Editor
Tony Paese, Project Editor
Jeanine Rees, Production Editor
Emely Villavicencio, Senior Graphic Designer
Greg Isales, Licensing Coordinator
Natalie Piccotti, Director of Marketing
Kassie Graves, Vice President of Editorial
Jamie Giganti, Director of Academic Publishing

Printed in the United States of America.

cognella® ACADEMIC PUBLISHING
3970 Sorrento Valley Blvd., Ste. 500, San Diego, CA 92121

I dedicate this book to Patricia, my loving wife and a great mom to our children. I could not have written this book without her. She left us unexpectedly and too soon, but our paths will cross en futurus *at a unique, predetermined moment.*

RIP "until we meet again."

Brief Contents

Detailed Contents

Introduction

A business cannot operate successfully without a fundamental understanding of applicable business law. The objective of this text is to introduce students to legal concepts that will assist in the appreciation of business law as applied to the hospitality industry. It is intended to help students understand legal principles well enough to take preventive action and, if necessary, know when to contact a lawyer.

Whether you are a student with plans for a career in hospitality, or currently a manager therein, an important first step is to gain an understanding of the sources of law. In the litigious society of America, every person should become familiar with the law and its application because we all will either sue, be sued, or violate a law or an administrative rule sometime in our lives. Understanding the law will assist in dealing with the inevitable foregoing issues.

Law is a body of rules and regulations imposed on denizens through government and its oversight mechanisms, such as the U.S. Congress at the national level and state legislatures at the local level. Violation of law invokes sanctions, such as fines, incarceration, penalties, monetary damages, loss of property, and, on occasion, loss of life. The principle underlying the creation and application of law is to protect society and the various institutions upon which people rely to achieve safe, happy, and productive lives.

The law affects every facet of life. Laws protect people from crime, fraud, pollution, and tyranny. Laws promote the health, welfare, morals, and safety of society, education, freedom, and democracy. The list continues, but it is too voluminous to completely enumerate in the introduction of a textbook. The textbook will focus on substantive areas of the law as applied to hospitality and those who work within the industry. It includes, among other things, contracts, negligence, and government regulation. It also includes discussion of business relations, finance and banking, and international business issues. When students successfully complete instruction using this textbook, they will be prepared to successfully compete in the hospitality industry.

For the foregoing reasons, Chapter 1 begins with a review of the following concepts and general areas of American law:

- the genesis of common law, which commenced with the conquest of England in 1066 CE by William the Conqueror and the creation of English common law under direction of the Normans
- the transition of English common law into American common law after the 13 colonies rebelled against English rule. The starting point was The Declaration of Independence from England in 1776, followed by the adoption of the Articles of Confederation (by the 13 colonies) in 1777, and adoption of the United States Constitution in 1787.
- the sources of American law
- statutory law and its interaction with common law and the pervasive impact of administrative law
- the U.S. court systems, which will help students understand the procedural aspects of a lawsuit

The subsequent chapters in this textbook will explain the procedural components of a lawsuit in more detail and the various substantive areas of business law as applied to the hospitality industry.

Chapter 1

Understanding the Law and Its Application

Introduction

In order to function in the hospitality industry, a person must understand the applicable law. The purpose of this chapter is to lay a foundation for that understanding. The history and derivation of law, including sources of American law, is covered in this chapter. Knowledge of the United States Constitution, federal and state statutory law, common law, and administrative law is essential and will be reviewed.

A discussion of the federal and state court systems as well as administrative agency systems are included. Important terms, most of which will be new to students reading this and subsequent chapters, are set forth in bold print. For ease of reference and as a study guide for review and testing purposes, each term will have a page reference to the chapter.

Chapter Objectives

Upon completion of this chapter, the student will understand:

- common law and its derivation
- constitutional and statutory law
- other sources of law
- separation of powers
- state sovereignty
- the federal and state court systems
- the administrative agency system

Key Terms

Directions: Each of the terms below will be used in this chapter. Before reading, scan the chapter. The terms will appear in bold. Take a moment to see how the term is used so you can understand it in context. The terms are listed in the order in which they will appear in the chapter.

American common law (p. 2)	Specific performance (p. 3)	Federal question (p. 6)
English common law (p. 2)	Precedent (p. 4)	Sovereign power (p. 6)
Common law (p. 2)	Stare decisis (p. 4)	Residual power (p. 6)
King's court (p. 3)	U.S. Constitution (p. 5)	Judicial branch (p. 6)
Courts of Law (p. 3)	Organic law (p. 5)	Interstate commerce (p. 6)
Courts of Equity (p. 3)	States' rights (p. 6)	Judicial branch (p. 6)

Preemption (p. 6)
Police power (p. 6)
Federalism (p. 6)
U.S. Supreme Court (p. 6)
Statute (p. 6)
Ordinances (p. 6)
Rules and regulations (p. 7)
Legislative branch (p. 8)
Executive branch (p. 8)
Separation of powers (p. 8)
Enumerated powers (p. 10)
Federal district court (p. 10)
Circuit court of appeals (p. 10)
Supremacy Clause (p. 10)
Superior court (p. 11)
State court of appeals (p. 11)
State supreme court (p. 11)
Federal policy (p. 13)

Evolution of Common Law

American common law evolved from **English common law** (Figure 1.1). In 1066 CE William the Conqueror led the Norman invasion of England. Upon his arrival he found the country without a formal judicial system. There were no judges, courts, or rules of law generally applicable to all persons living in England. Instead, he found an array of tribes, clans, and loosely organized communities.

Each of the foregoing groups had leaders with their own set of norms to follow and associated local sanctions, such as public beatings, ordered by tribal chiefs. Absent was a judicial system common to all living in England. Hence, William the Conqueror imposed a Norman style judicial system applicable to all persons living in the country, and it was referred to as **common law**.

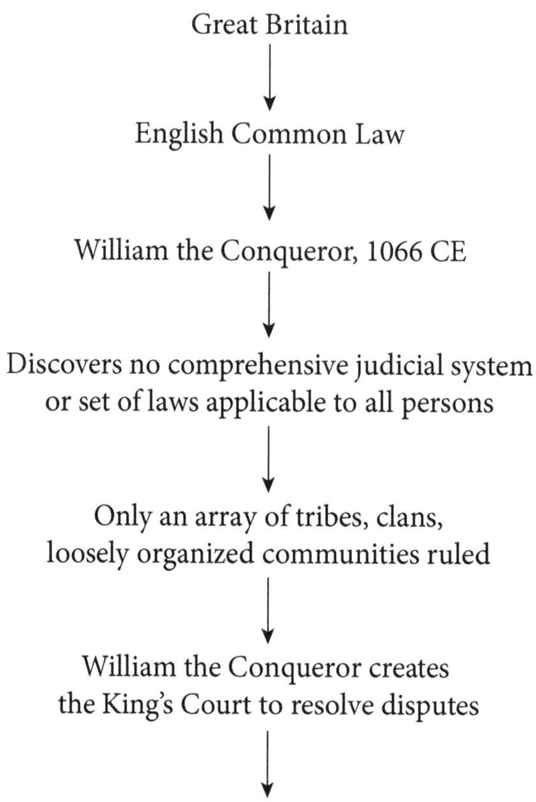

FIGURE 1.1 English Common Law

The **King's Court** was created to handle disputes among denizens of the country. The King's Court was divided into two separate courts: the **Courts of Law**, which heard cases that could be resolved with a monetary award, and the **Courts of Equity**, which provided a remedy other than money, such as specific performance of a contract, contract rescission, and injunctive relief (Figure 1.2). The king appointed friends and close allies to judgeships of his court. A legislative body to promulgate statutory law was nonexistent at this time. The law consisted of edicts from the king and decisions by judges of the King's Court. The judicial decisions were referred to as English Common Law.

Courts of law were primarily concerned with resolving disputes more suitable to money damages. For example, if a person rented a room at an inn and failed to pay upon departure, the innkeeper could seek monetary payment in a court of law. As mentioned above, courts of equity, on the other hand, were concerned with disputes that result in nonmonetary awards, such as specific performance, contract rescission, and injunctive relief.

Assume, for example, a person contracted to purchase a unique parcel of real property upon which to build a restaurant, and the seller breached the contract. The buyer may not be satisfied with money damages because the property was so perfect for the buyer's future business. For that reason, the buyer might choose to go to a court of equity rather than a court of law and attempt to persuade the judge to order the seller to convey the property according to the contract terms. This is an equitable remedy called **specific performance**. Contract rescission and injunctive relief will be discussed in Chapter 5.

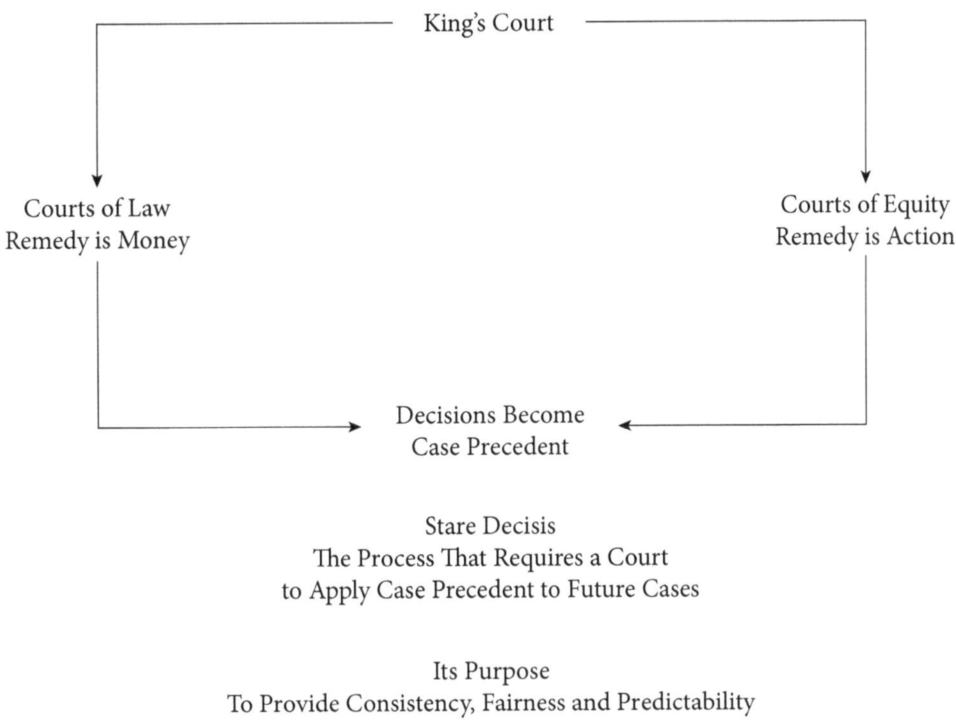

FIGURE 1.2 Courts of Law and Courts of Equity

As decisions of the King's Court were issued, it became apparent a record of the judicial decisions should be maintained to provide guidance for future court decisions. A leading case would be decided and transcribed into a book called a record. Recorded cases became **precedent** for use with future cases. The application of case precedent to a current dispute was known as **stare decisis**, a process that provided consistency, fairness, and predictability to English Common Law.

In the 1500s the Puritans, who were being persecuted in England for their religious beliefs, fled to America and eventually established the 13 American Colonies. At this time, a comprehensive, formal legal system was not established for the colonies. Subsequently, the British conquered the colonies and imposed English Common Law, replete with legal and equitable courts and the substantive English Common Law.

The English system prevailed until the colonies declared independence in 1776. The colonies adopted the Articles of Confederation and established the United States of America in 1777. The United States temporarily continued the British court system but gradually developed its own set of court decisions based upon its societal values. That transformation created and evolved into American Common Law (Figure 1.3).

Development of American Common Law

1. Great Britain conquers the 13 American Colonies.

↓

2. Great Britain imposes English Common Law on the Colonies. Courts of Law, Courts of Equity and English Substantive Law.

↓

3. The Colonies declare independence in 1776 and adopt the Articles of Confederation. The United States of America is formally established in 1777.

↓

4. The 13 United States continue to use the English Common Law.

↓

5. The founding fathers of the United States adopt the United States Constitution in 1787. It, among other things, provided for a national Federal Judicial System headed by the U.S. Supreme Court.

↓

6. The U.S. Constitution provided for the legislative branch to adopt laws, the executive branch to implement laws and the judicial branch to interpret laws. This structure is referred to as "separation of powers" and was designed to prevent any one entity from assuming dictatorial power.

↓

7. The U.S. Supreme Court first convened in 1790 and American Courts commenced issuing court decisions.

↓

8. The above referenced activities spawned the American Common Law.

FIGURE 1.3 American Common Law

Congress was not established until after adoption of the **U.S. Constitution** in 1787 (hereinafter, all references to the Constitution refer to the U.S. Constitution), and therefore, no statutory law existed. Accordingly, English Common Law, with its Courts of Law and Courts of Equity, was continued in the colonies. American common law, like its English counterpart, was created by judicial decisions.

Each time an American judge issued an important decision, it became American common law applicable to all in the United States. As in English Common Law, the American court decision was a precedent that judges could use for guidance in similar lawsuits. As time passed, precedents were transcribed into written opinions and were required by appellate courts to be followed by lower courts. As in English Common Law, this process in American Common Law is also called stare decisis. For example, a decision by a state court of appeals has to be followed by a lower court within its jurisdiction, such as a county superior court. Stare decisis provides the continuity and predictability that is essential for a society to fairly and economically apply the law to all persons.

The Interplay of Law

American law is a dynamic, evolving interplay among sources of law, norms, and mores of society, as well as creative thought by judges, scholars, and lawyers. The creation of English Common Law initiated the process. The King's Court produced decisional laws that were applicable to denizens of England that became English Common Law and were transcribed into judicial opinions that were followed by courts for centuries. Each time an English court issued a decision different from precedent, new English common law was formed.

After the colonies declared their independence from England, they subsequently adopted the United States Constitution. (See Appendix A: U.S. Const., preamble; art. VII.) The Constitution provides for a federal court system (U.S. Const. art. III), and it permits creation of a state system of courts through the authority granted in the Tenth Amendment. Today we have constitutional law, statutory law, judicial law, administrative law, and executive law, at both the federal and state levels, which collectively comprise American jurisprudence. Their interplay is discussed below.

Constitutional Law

As mentioned above, the colonies declared their independence from England in 1776 and shortly thereafter, in 1777, adopted the Articles of Confederation, creating the United States of America. The Articles of Confederation were declared "in force" after the State of Maryland ratified them in 1781.

Under the Articles of Confederation, each state created protective economic barriers for their respective business interests, which interfered with the overall economic growth of the Confederation. This protectionism spawned, in part, the adoption of the U.S. Constitution in 1789. The drafters of the Constitution, in an effort to promote economic growth among the colonies, inserted the Commerce Clause in the constitutional powers delegated to the federal government (U.S. Const. art. I, § 8, cl. 3.) The Commerce Clause empowers the federal government to regulate interstate commerce and promote interstate commerce by dismantling the protective economic barriers imposed by each state.

The Constitution is America's **organic law**, defined as "the body of laws that define and establish a government" (Garner 2005, 928)[1]. Organic law is characterized by a vote of the people, rather than the vote of elected representatives. The Constitution contains an important dichotomy of power. It is the supreme law of the land for **federal questions**, while providing authority for self-government by the states via the Tenth Amendment (also known as **States' Rights**). Federal questions concern U.S. constitutional issues, federal statutes, federal regulations and U.S. treaties.

The Constitution expressly enumerates and limits the power of the federal government (art. I, sec. 8) and provides each state with the power of states' rights. Thus, each state is a **sovereign power** capable of creating binding law for its citizens. The Tenth Amendment does not enumerate states' power but rather provides states with the **residual power** not expressly provided to the federal government. Therefore, the Constitution enables each state to create organic law via a state constitution and amendments thereto by a vote of the people.

The constitution also provides states with the power to create a **judicial branch** to resolve questions concerning states' rights. For example, the federal government has express authority over questions of **interstate commerce**, and it preempts any conflicting state law to the contrary. **Preemption** is defined as "the principle (derived from the Supremacy Clause) that a [valid] federal law can supersede or supplant any inconsistent state law or regulation" (Garner 2005, 987).

The public's health, welfare, and safety (referred to as "police power") is not enumerated in Article I, Section 8, and therefore, **police power** belongs to the states. The federal government may not preempt the state's police power by passing a federal law to the contrary. This dual sharing of power between the federal government and the states is referred to as **federalism.**

The **U.S. Supreme Court** is the final arbiter of disputes between the federal government and the states regarding preemption questions. The high court does not have authority to resolve questions of rights reserved to the states. That power is left to the various state supreme courts by the Tenth Amendment.

Statutory Law

Our country was founded upon a representative form of government. This means that each citizen is entitled to vote for elected officials to represent their interests before legislative bodies. At the federal level it is the Congress of the United States (art. I, § 1), and at the state level, it is a legislature for each state in the union. A **statute** is a law passed by a legislative body of elected officials. Accordingly, the federal government passes federal statutes (e.g., internet companies must register their URL with the federal government), and state governments pass state statutes (e.g., the sale and use of both medical and recreational marijuana is legal in many states).

Ordinances

Local governments (such as counties and cities) pass local laws called **ordinances** that apply to activity within their jurisdictional boundaries. Local governments are not mentioned in the U.S. Constitution and are not sovereigns but are creatures of the state. Their existence and power to legislate is delegated by the state and may be granted and removed at the will of the state legislature.

---

1 Garner, Bryan A. and Henry Campbell Black. 2004. *Black's Law Dictionary*. St. Paul, MN: Thomson/West.

For example, in California, the legislature permitted local citizens to incorporate the city of Vernon on September 22, 1905. On March 25, 2011, because of rampant government corruption, the state legislature introduced a bill (Assembly Bill 46) to disincorporate the City of Vernon, CA. If the bill had been approved, the City of Vernon would have ceased to exist. However, the City of Vernon successfully convinced the state legislature to cease its disincorporation efforts on August 29, 2011. They did so by promising to behave and also by promising to contribute to local charitable organizations.[2]

Constitutional law prevails over statutory law because constitutions are organic law, changeable only by a vote of the people. Statutory law can be changed by a vote of elected officials without direct vote of the people. Accordingly, the provisions of the U.S. Constitution preempt a federal statute, and provisions of the state constitution preempt a state statute.

Administrative Law

Administrative agencies were created to help government implement statutory laws. They exist at the federal, state, and local levels. For example, the Environmental Protection Agency (EPA), was created by Congress to implement laws adopted by Congress that pertain to environmental protection issues, such as the Clean Air Act. State agencies exist to implement state administrative laws in a similar fashion as federal agencies.

For example, the California State Air Quality Department is the parallel state agency that implements state laws adopted in California to regulate state environmental issues, such as clean air. Local agencies (i.e., county/city agencies) are created to implement county and city ordinances. For example, local agencies adopt health codes regulating air quality for local businesses.

Administrative agencies have the power to adopt **rules and regulations** to enforce their decisions. Rules and regulations are not laws, but they carry the force and effect of laws. Agencies impose sanctions for violations of administrative rules or regulations similar to statutory law. A person can be fined, denied the right to conduct business, and even incarcerated for a violation. (Administrative law and the difference between a rule and regulation is discussed in more detail in Chapter 12.)

Executive Orders

The President of the United States has the power to negotiate treaties and conventions, subject to advice and consent of the Senate (U.S. Const. art. II, § 1; § 2, cl. 1 & 2; § 3). The president may also issue orders to various federal departments and agencies to carry out their constitutional duties (U.S. Const. § 3; U.S. Reports: *McCulloch v. State of Maryland*, 17 U.S. 316 (1819)). The governor is the chief executive of each state and possesses the same type of executive power as the president over the state departments and agencies. A mayor of a city is the local chief executive and possesses power similar to the president and state governor to issue executive orders (see "Sources of American Law" below).

2 Sam Allen, "State Senate Rejects Controversial Plan to Disband City of Vernon," *Los Angeles Times*, Aug. 29, 2011, https://latimesblogs.latimes.com/lanow/2011/08/senate-votes-down-controversial-plan-to-disband-city-of-vernon.html/

SOURCES OF AMERICAN LAW

Constitutional Law

- U.S. Constitution: organic law of the United States; all power of the federal government delegated by the U.S. Constitution by way of Article I, Section 8
- State constitutions: organic law of the 50 states created by way of the Tenth Amendment to the U.S. Constitution

Statutory Law

- laws adopted by Congress, the several states, and by local officials as elected representatives of the people
- Federal statutory law
- State statutory law
- local statutory law: created by counties, cities, and special districts; historically referred to as local ordinances

Common Law

- Created by judicial decisions; judge-made laws that create precedents and by which the precedents are made binding on lower courts through the process of stare decisis

Administrative Law

- Rules and regulations created by administrative agencies with legislative powers delegated by Congress to federal agencies and state legislatures to state agencies. Rules and regulations are technically not laws because they are not created by elected officials, but instead by appointed officials. However, they have the force and effect of law, replete with sanctions, such as license revocation and fines.

Executive Orders

- Directives by the elected executive of the federal government (the president of the United States), the state government (the governor), and the elected local government official (e.g., the mayor of a municipality). Unless challenged by the legislative branch, they have the force and effect of law.

Separation of Powers

The drafters of the Constitution created three branches of government; Congress, the **legislative branch**, was designated as the lawmaking branch of government. The president is in charge of the **executive branch**, which implements the laws, and the U.S. Supreme Court is the judicial branch, which interprets the laws. The Constitution is based upon the doctrine that neither one person nor a single entity should control the country.

This doctrine is referred to as the separation of powers doctrine. **Separation of powers** is defined as "the division of governmental authority into three branches of government—legislative, executive, and judicial—each with specified duties on which neither of the other branches can encroach; the constitutional doctrine of checks and balances designed to protect the people against tyranny" (Garner 2005, 1134). This concept was developed largely as the result of tyranny imposed on the American colonies by the king of England. Brutal rule by the monarch fostered abhorrence to a strong centralized form of government. Accordingly, the nation's founding fathers developed a system of checks and balances to prevent one person or entity from acquiring too much power.

The Constitution provides the three independent branches of government with power of approval over the acts of other branches in certain cases. Such approval limits the ability of one branch to acquire tyrannical power. For example, Congress, the legislative branch, is comprised of the House of Representatives (art. I, § 2) and the Senate (art. I, § 3), which have the responsibility of passing all laws. Each time Congress passes a law, it must be approved by the president, who has power to veto the law.

Another example is the executive branch with the power to make appointments to the U.S. Supreme Court. Those appointments must be approved with advice and consent of the Senate. Finally, the U.S. Supreme

Court decides whether a law passed by Congress is constitutional or not and also whether the president has exceeded constitutional authority in the exercise of executive power.

For example, the executive branch, under authority of the president, has the responsibility to enforce and implement all laws (U.S. Const. art. II), and the judicial branch, under authority of the U.S. Supreme Court, interprets the laws (U.S. Const. art. III). In 1970 Congress passed a federal statute that criminalized the use of marijuana (Federal Controlled Substances Act of 1970). The federal statute conflicts with several state statutes that permit medicinal and recreational marijuana (e.g., Col. Rev. Sta. Ann. §18-18-102, amendment 64, (2012)). The Bush administration enforced the federal statute, and that action was challenged in the courts by states that adopted medical and recreational marijuana laws. Several states challenged the Bush administration in court and raised a question of invalid federal preemption.

Preemption occurs when a federal and state statute concern a similar issue and the laws conflict. The U.S. Supreme Court determined, under the power of the Commerce Clause, that the federal statute preempted the state statute and was the law of the land (*Gonzales v. Raich*, 545 U.S. 1 (2005)). However, President Obama's administration refused to enforce the federal statute against individuals, and limited enforcement to growers and sellers of large quantities of marijuana.

Theoretically, Congress or a citizen group could have filed suit against the Obama administration demanding enforcement of the federal statute, and the judiciary would have had to decide if the president's policy was constitutional. The challenge never occurred, and states were permitted to decide whether or not to do so.

Under our system of separation of powers, all three branches of government get involved in certain decisions to prevent one branch from acquiring dictatorial power (see Figure 1.4).

Separation of Powers

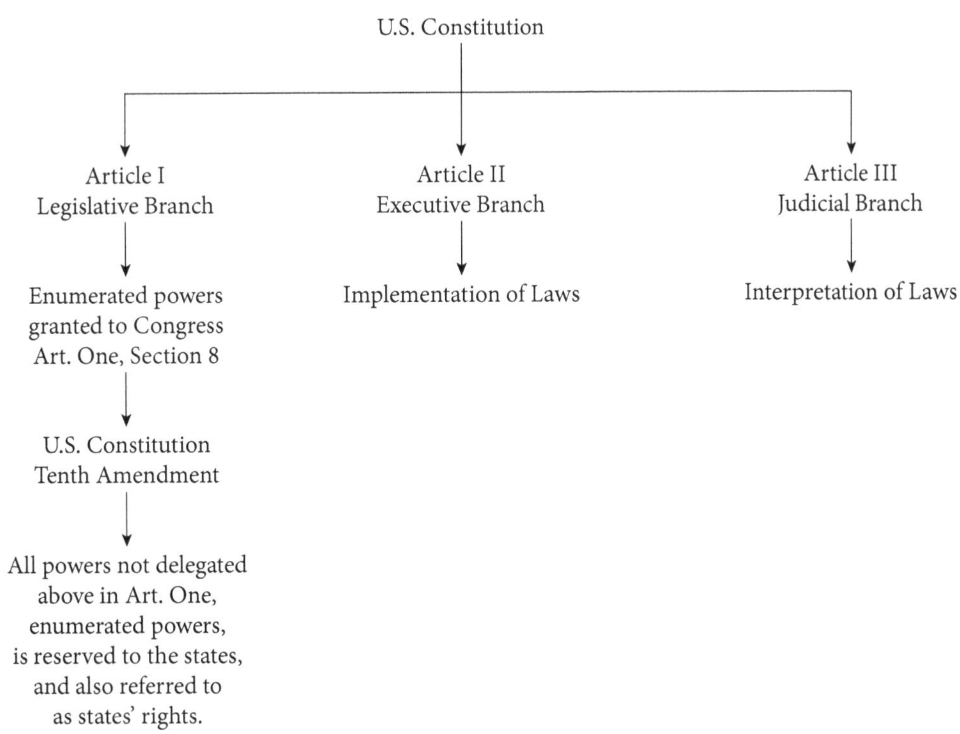

FIGURE 1.4 Separation of Powers

The **enumerated powers** in the U.S. Constitution refer only to those powers expressly provided to the federal government. All powers not enumerated are within the Tenth Amendment power of states' rights.

Statutory Law

The origin of a statutory law can vary. For example, statutory law might be the codification of common law, modified to meet current societal needs, or it might be a new law enacted by Congress or a state legislature. For example, under common law it is unlawful to take the property of another without permission. A statute, on the other hand, may make it lawful to take the property of another if it is of dire necessity (e.g., taking medicine from a neighbor's home to save a person's life).

Statutory law may also be the creation of new law required by changes in American society. For example, as a result of technological innovation, the telephone was invented. A statute passed by Congress (18 U.S.C. § 2511) makes it illegal to listen in on a telephone call without the parties' permission.

Once a statute is adopted and implemented, upon violation and a legal challenge to the statute it may be subject to interpretation in a court of law. Once the court interprets the statute, it will issue a judicial opinion. A judicial opinion is common law, and the judicial opinion is new common law. The process is similar for state court interpretations of a state statute (see Cal. Pen. Code § 632, Prohibition of Eavesdropping).

The Federal and State Court Systems

As previously mentioned, the court system in the United States is a carryover from English common law modified to meet the needs of contemporary America. Consistent with the dichotomy of sovereignty in our federal constitution, there is a federal judicial system and a state judicial system. The federal system consists of the **federal district court**, which is a trial court where the litigation originates, and a trial is conducted by a federal Judge. Appeals from the trial court are heard by a three-judge panel at a **circuit court of appeals**. There are 13 circuit courts of appeal in the federal system. Eleven of these are based upon geography (e.g., the Ninth Circuit Court of Appeals has jurisdiction over most of the continental western United States, Alaska, Hawaii, and the territory of Guam).

Appeals from circuit courts are heard by the nine-member United States Supreme Court, the ultimate arbiter of federal questions. Under the **Supremacy Clause** in the U.S. Constitution, federal law is the supreme law of the land. That means a state law in conflict may be preempted and rendered unenforceable. Federal judges are appointed by the president of the United States, with consent of the Senate, for life terms (Table 1.1 and Figure 1.5).

TABLE 1.1 **METHODS OF JUDICIAL APPOINTMENT**

Federal	President appoints judges for life terms. Senate must approve with two-thirds vote of members.
State	Chief executive appoints judges for a term of years.
Supreme Court	Governor appoints for initial 12-year term. Vote of the people for subsequent term.
Court of Appeals	Governor appoints for initial 12-year term. Vote of the people for subsequent term.
Superior Court	Governor appoints for initial four-year term. Vote of the people for subsequent term.

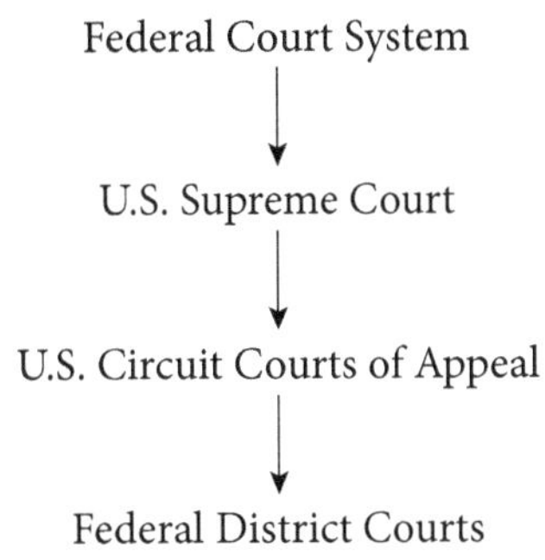

FIGURE 1.5 The Federal Court System

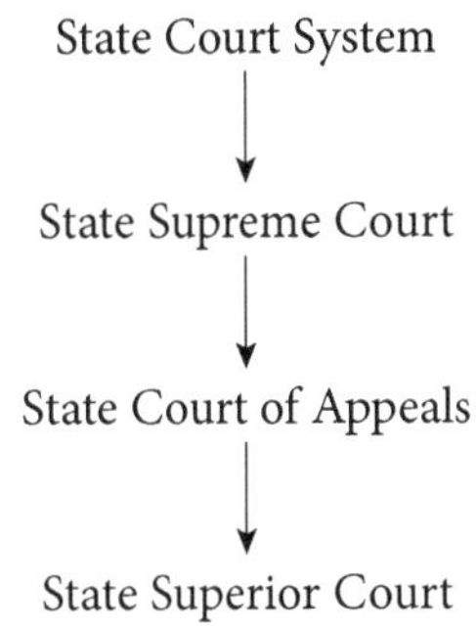

FIGURE 1.6 The State Court Systems

The state court systems are similar to the federal system (Figure 1.6). A judge conducts the trial in a court referred to in most states as the **superior court**. Usually, a three-judge panel hears appeals from the trial court in a **state court of appeals**. Appeals from the state court of appeals are heard by a **state supreme court,** usually consisting of seven members. In most state courts, judges are initially appointed for a certain term of years by the governor and then stand for election by the people for a subsequent term (Table 1.1). The state supreme court is the ultimate arbiter of state legal questions. The Supremacy Clause in the U.S. Constitution does not apply to valid state court issues (Figure 1.6).

An appeal can be made from a state supreme court to the U.S. Supreme Court only if a federal question is raised by the appeal. For example, and continuing the medicinal marijuana issue, a state has authority to pass a law that permits the use of marijuana for medicinal purposes because health of the community is not an enumerated right of the federal government. The health, welfare, and safety of citizens is generally a right left to the states under the Tenth Amendment and commonly referred to as police power. The Tenth Amendment reserves to the states all power not expressly provided the federal government or enumerated in Article I.

However, if marijuana used within a state for medicinal purposes is transported across state borders or from foreign countries, it becomes a federal issue under the Commerce Clause (art. III, § 8, cl. 3). Based upon the power granted to the federal government under the Commerce Clause, the U.S. Supreme Court, in a 5–4 decision (*Gonzales v. Raich*, discussed above), ruled the use of marijuana for any purpose is a federal question, and the state medicinal law is preempted by federal statute.

SUPREME COURT OF THE UNITED STATES

Alberto Gonzales, Attorney General
v.
Angel McClary Raich, et al.
Argued Nov. 29, 2004
Decided June 6, 2005

STEVENS, J. delivered the opinion of the Court

Background: Users and growers of marijuana for medical purposes under California Compassionate Use Act sought declaration that Controlled Substances Act (CSA) was unconstitutional as to them. The United States District Court for the Northern District of California denied plaintiffs motion for preliminary injunction. Plaintiffs appealed to the Ninth Circuit ... reversed and remanded.

Certiorari was granted.

***

California's Compassionate Use Act authorizes limited marijuana use for medicinal purposes. Respondents Raich and Monson are California residents who both use doctor recommended marijuana for serious medical conditions. After federal Drug Enforcement Administration agents seized and destroyed all six of Monson's cannabis plants, respondents brought this action seeking injunctive and declaratory relief prohibiting the enforcement of the federal Controlled Substances Act (CSA) to the extent it prevents them from possessing, obtaining, or manufacturing cannabis for their personal medical use. Respondents claim that enforcing the CSA against them would violate the Commerce Clause and other constitutional provisions.

***

Held: Congress' Commerce Clause authority includes the power to prohibit local cultivation and use of marijuana in compliance with California law.

(a) For the purposes of consolidating various drug laws into a comprehensive statute providing meaningful regulation over legitimate sources of drugs to prevent diversion into illegal channels and strengthening law enforcement tools. Against international and interstate drug trafficking, Congress enacted the [CSA]. [Citations omitted.] To effectuate the statutory goals, Congress devised a closed regulatory system making it unlawful to manufacture, distribute, dispense, or possess any controlled substance except as authorized by the CSA. [Citations omitted.]

***

Marijuana is classified as a Schedule I substance based on its high potential for abuse, no accepted medical use, and no accepted safety for use in medically supervised treatment. This classification renders the manufacture, distribution or possession of marijuana a criminal offense.

(b) Congress' power to regulate purely local activities that are part of an economic "class of activities" that have a substantial effect on interstate commerce is firmly established. [Citations omitted.] If Congress decides that the "total incidence" of a practice poses a threat to a national market, it may regulate the entire class. [Citations omitted.]

***

352 F. 3d 1222, [Ninth Circuit] vacated and remanded.

Federal preemption, however, may not be the final answer. Notwithstanding the high court's decision, states may still permit medical marijuana to be dispensed as a matter of **federal policy**. For example, under the policy of the George W. Bush administration, the federal statute banning the use of marijuana was enforced by the federal government's Drug Enforcement Agency.

President Obama's administration chose not to enforce the federal statute because, among other things, of the belief the country has limited law enforcement resources. Hence, resources would be better spent on more serious drug crimes, such as importation of drugs from foreign sources and the sale of large quantities of the drug for nonmedicinal purposes. Accordingly, states with medical marijuana laws currently are permitted to continue to do so under executive order of the president.

President Trump decided to continue President Obama's policy. However, if Trump's successor, Joe Biden, or any future president wished, that president could decide to re-impose the Federal Preemption and make it a felony once again. That could mean closing the medical marijuana dispensaries in the future. However, many states have adopted statutes that permit medical marijuana and use of small amounts for recreational purposes. That includes states such as California, Colorado, Washington, Nevada, and Oregon. That issue is on the ballot for many other states across the country. If the pattern continues and a majority of the states decide to approve medical marijuana and recreational use of marijuana, Congress or the U.S. Supreme Court may take action that overturns *Gonzales v. Raich.*

Summary

In order to understand law, a student must know the derivation of the law, as well as the policies and rationale for the law. With a proper understanding of the foregoing, a person will be able to navigate the sometimes-murky imposition of the law. The enumerated powers in the U.S. Constitution refer to those powers expressly provided to the federal government for application of our nation's laws. Chapter 1 provides the background necessary to prepare the student for a career in the hospitality industry.

The genesis of American law commenced in England when William the Conqueror imposed Norman law and appointed a king to rule. The King's Bench created English Common Law. Great Britain conquered America and imposed its common law on the Colonies. In 1776 the colonies defeated the British in the Revolutionary War and declared independence.

The colonies adopted the Articles of Confederation in 1776 and established the United States of America, which continued the use of English Common Law until the U.S. Constitution was adopted in 1787. The Constitution created three branches of government: legislative, executive, and judiciary. The three branches of government made laws, implemented laws, and interpreted laws, respectively. The above collective action created American Common Law and statutory law.

The three branches of government also served another very important function, referred to as separation of powers. They served as a check and balance on each branch's activities designed to prevent any one person or branch from acquiring too much power. This process avoids a dictatorship.

In addition to the Constitution and statutory law created by Congress, there are several other sources of law by which all persons and business entities must adhere. The courts can create common law when there is no statutory or judicial precedent and when they interpret the constitution and statutory law. Administrative agencies are created by Congress to implement federal statutes, and they adopt rules and regulations to do so. Finally, the president has executive power to order federal agencies to take action consistent with executive policy.

The Constitution was designed to empower states with the right to adopt and enforce laws consistent with the will of the people in each respective state. The Tenth Amendment to the Constitution reserves all rights not enumerated in the Constitution for the federal government to the states. It's called states' rights and was designed to prevent too much power in the centralized federal government. Each state is a sovereign with its own constitution, legislature, chief executive, and court system.

The U.S. Constitution, as amended (Tenth Amendment), created a dual power structure with a federal government and a state government, collectively referred to as federalism. Each level of government is a sovereign, with its legislative body, chief executive, and judicial system. The federal and state courts may not interfere with the jurisdiction of the other.

Comprehension Check

True/False

Directions: Look at each statement below. Based on what you learned in this chapter, decide if the statement is true or false.

1. The early formation of hospitality law was largely the result of judicial common law, most notably the federal and state constitutions and various government statutes.
2. The Constitution was created with three branches of government in order to prevent any one entity or person from acquiring dictatorial powers.
3. The U.S. system is based upon federalism, which means federal government action will always preempt any conflicting state law.
4. The enumerated powers in the U.S. Constitution refer to those powers expressly provided to the executive branch of government.
5. The Tenth Amendment to the Constitution includes the Commerce Clause, which provides the police power for local government to regulate the hospitality industry.
6. Administrative agencies pass rules and regulations in order to implement the intent of congressional enabling statutes that created the agency and also regulate hotels and restaurants.
7. The ten amendments contained in the Bill of Rights do not apply to the hospitality industry because restaurants and hotels are not persons; they are entities.
8. The U.S. Constitution is a higher source of law because it was created by elected officials rather than a vote of the people.
9. The policy reason for creating administrative agencies is to relieve the legislative and executive branches from the chore of implementing the thousands of laws passed each year.
10. Due process of law means fundamental fairness to persons charged with crimes and civil violations.
11. An executive order of the president is binding law on all citizens of the United States.

Multiple Choice

Directions: Use what you learned in this chapter to choose the best response to each of the prompts below.

1. The number of members on the U.S. Supreme Court is:
   a. 7
   b. 8
   c. 9
   d. none of the above
2. The genesis of U.S. Law is:
   a. Roman law
   b. Spanish law
   c. civil law
   d. none of the above
3. Common law is:
   a. legislative law
   b. constitutional law
   c. judicial law
   d. none of the above
4. Stare decisis is:
   a. prospective application
   b. retrospective application
   c. precedent
   d. a and c
5. The modern sources of U.S. law include all of the following, except:
   a. statutory law
   b. constitutional law
   c. adversary law
   d. common law
6. An initiative is:
   a. lawmaking by the people
   b. making new statutes by the legislature
   c. changing of the state constitution by the people
   d. a and c

7. Public law includes all of the following, except:
    a. civil law
    b. criminal law
    c. administrative law
    d. all of the above
8. With regard to administrative agencies, all the following are true, except:
    a. Rules and regulations are binding laws.
    b. Administrative agencies are the fourth branch of government provided by the U.S. Constitution.
    c. Agencies were created to implement legislative laws.
    d. all of the above
9. All of the following are sources of law, except:
    a. constitutional law
    b. statutory law
    c. referendum law
    d. administrative law
10. The doctrine of separation of powers is in:
    a. the 14th Amendment
    b. the Bill of Rights
    c. the state constitution
    d. none of the above
11. Federalism means:
    a. The federal government is the supreme law of the land.
    b. The federal government is an umbrella power over a union of self-governing states.
    c. The federal government has only enumerated powers.
    d. The 10th Amendment is relatively ineffective.
12. States' rights means:
    a. no federal oversight
    b. Article IV of the Constitution is relevant.
    c. The 10th Amendment is relevant.
    d. all of the above
13. Direct democracy includes:
    a. recall
    b. initiatives
    c. campaign reform
    d. a and b

14. Common law is developed by:
    a. agencies
    b. Congress
    c. judges
    d. referendum of the people

15. All the following are sources of law, except:
    a. agency rules
    b. state constitution
    c. U.S. Constitution
    d. referendum

Scenarios

1. John has terminal cancer and is undergoing chemotherapy. His doctor, in reliance on a state medical marijuana statute, prescribed marijuana to minimize the serious aftereffects. DEA agents raided his doctor's office to obtain evidence for a prosecution of both John and his doctor, alleging a violation of federal law prohibiting use of marijuana. The U.S. Supreme Court has upheld the federal statute. The president's policy is nonenforcement of marijuana for personal use of the drug. What will be the result? Explain your answer and the rationale for the DEA's and the president's policy.
2. The State of Colorado passed a statute permitting same-sex marriage. Mary and Jane married shortly thereafter. They subsequently moved to Alabama to live with relatives. Alabama prohibits same-sex marriage, and it refuses to recognize the marriage by denying employment benefits to the couple. They sue for discrimination. What will be the result? Explain your answer.

Decisional Review

1. Plaintiffs, two delivery truck drivers, sued employer for misclassification of their status to one of independent contractors rather than employees. Plaintiffs allege they are employees for employment considerations such as wages and benefits. Employer alleges federal law controls because of interstate commerce. What will be the result? Explain your answer. See *Bedoya v. American Eagle*, 914 F.3 812.
2. Appellants, a neighborhood family planning group and its director, a physician and Yale medical professor, were prosecuted and found guilty of violating a state law prohibiting sale of contraceptives and for providing educational advice for family planning. State supreme court affirmed lower courts upholding the prosecution. Appellants appealed to the U.S. Supreme Court alleging state's right to regulate medical issues. What will be the result? Explain your answer.

Chapter 2

Anatomy of Litigation

Introduction

A person or business entity in the hospitality industry must understand the basic steps in the litigation process in order to be mentally and physically prepared when they become involved in a lawsuit. The purpose of this chapter is to provide the information necessary to accomplish that goal. Knowledge of what to expect is key to preparation for trial. An understanding of the cost of a trial in terms of money, time demands, and disruption to the business will assist with settlement negotiations. The importance of settlement rather than litigation will become clear after a study of this chapter.

Chapter Objectives

Upon completion of this chapter, the student will understand:

- the litigation process
- pretrial activities
- pleadings/motions
- discovery
- trial Activities
- appeals

Key Terms

Directions: Each of the terms below will be used in this chapter. Before reading, scan the chapter. The terms will appear in bold. Take a moment to see how the term is used so you can understand it in context. The terms are listed in the order in which they will appear in the chapter.

Litigation (p. 20)
In personam jurisdiction (p. 21)
In rem jurisdiction (p. 21)
Subject-matter jurisdiction (p. 21)
State jurisdiction (p. 22)
Federal jurisdiction (p. 22)
Federal question (p. 22)
Diversity jurisdiction (p. 22)
Diversity rationale (p. 22)
Exclusive jurisdiction (p. 22)
Original jurisdiction (p. 22)
Concurrent jurisdiction (p. 22)
Out-of-state jurisdiction (p. 22)
Internet jurisdiction (p. 25)
Pretrial (p. 25)
Answer (p. 26)
Discovery (p. 26)
Motion for summary judgment (p. 26)
Pretrial conference (p. 26)
Defendant (p. 28)
Service of process (p. 28)
Summons (p. 28)
Default judgment (p. 28)
Pleadings (p. 31)

Motion to dismiss a case for failure to state facts sufficient to state a cause of action (p. 31)

Motion to quash (p. 31)

Motion to strike (p. 31)

Motion for judgment on the pleadings (p. 31)

Interrogatories (p. 32)

Depositions (p. 32)

Written transcript (p. 32)

Impeach (p. 32)

Private investigation (p. 32)

Document production (p. 32)

Inspection of physical evidence (p. 32)

Motion to compel discovery (p. 33)

Motion for summary judgment (p. 34)

Pretrial hearing (p. 34)

Voir dire (p. 35)

Opening statements (p. 35)

Case in chief (p. 35)

Closing argument (p. 35)

Motion for a new trial—insufficient evidence (p. 37)

Motion for a new trial because of prejudicial error (p. 37)

Judgment notwithstanding the verdict (p. 37)

Motion to poll the jury (p. 37)

Motion for remittitur (p. 37)

Entry of judgment (p. 37)

Appeal (p. 37)

Hearsay (p. 37)

Judgment (p. 40)

Writ of execution (p. 41)

Judgment debtor (p. 41)

Judgment creditor (p. 41)

Record the judgment (p. 41)

Litigation

The judicial process that resolves a dispute between two or more parties in a court of law is called **litigation.** It is defined as "the process of carrying on a lawsuit" (Garner 2005, 778). It is comprised of the following main components:

1. Pretrial: pleadings, discovery, pretrial conference
2. Trial: jury selection, opening statement, introduction of evidence by the parties, summation, jury instructions, deliberation, the verdict
3. Posttrial: various motions
4. Entry of judgment
5. Appeal

Litigation is the bedrock of American jurisprudence; it is a process designed to effectuate a peaceful resolution of disputes between two or more opposing parties. Although the Constitution permits self-representation, each party is usually represented by an attorney. When a dispute is litigated in a court of law, the parties make a selection to appear before a judge (bench trial) or a jury (jury trial).

A court reporter is present to record the proceedings verbatim and to prepare a written transcript. A court clerk is the administrative aid to the court. The court clerk receives all court filings of the parties and other relevant correspondence, prepares the court calendar, and assists with management of the court proceedings. The bailiff is a sworn police officer, usually from the sheriff's department, who maintains order in the court room. The bailiff also assists the court with management of persons in the court room, such as the parties, criminal defendants, attorneys, jurors, the press, and spectators.

Each party to the lawsuit defines the issues in their court filings from their point of view and presents evidence to the court to support their arguments. The judge makes rulings with regard to the admissibility of evidence and the application of law to the evidence. The judge or jury decides the facts, dependent on whether the case is a bench trial or jury trial.

Jurisdiction

Prior to commencement of pretrial activities, the court must consider whether it has jurisdiction to resolve the dispute. Jurisdiction is "a government's general power to exercise authority over all persons and property within its territory [and] a court's power to decide a case or issue a decree" (Garner 2005, 707). It is an integral part of the complaint and means a court must have jurisdiction before it can resolve a legal dispute among litigants. It also is an essential procedural prerequisite to the filing of a complaint in a state or federal court. If a plaintiff does not assert and prove a court has jurisdiction, the complaint will be dismissed.

English Common Law Jurisdiction

The concept of jurisdiction was created by judges of the king's bench after William the Conqueror installed a monarchy and imposed a feudal system on Great Britain. Jurisdiction for cases with claims for money damages were placed in Courts of Law, and cases with claims for certain requests for court action were placed in Courts of Equity (see previous discussion of common law). Over the course of time, English common law evolved with the following types of jurisdiction: *in personam* (Latin for "against a person"), *in rem* (Latin for "against the thing"), and subject matter.

In personam jurisdiction, also referred to as personal jurisdiction, is a term that refers to a court's power to bring a person into its adjudicative process (i.e., jurisdiction over a defendant's personal rights, rather than a property interest; Garner 2005, 709). For example, suppose a guest in a hotel slips and falls on wet tile in the foyer of the building. In order for the injured party to recover damages, they would have to allege and prove the accident occurred within the geographical boundaries of the court. Otherwise, there is no personal jurisdiction over owners of the hotel. In other words, an injured tourist can't go home and file the lawsuit in a local court. The local court does not have personal jurisdiction over parties to the accident. For purposes of in personam jurisdiction, a business, such as the hotel, is treated as a person.

In rem jurisdiction is "A court's power to adjudicate the rights to a given piece of property, including the power to seize and hold it" (Garner 2005, 709). If there is a dispute over title to the hotel property, the geographical boundaries of the court location where the hotel is located has in rem jurisdiction over the building and its furnishings. Parties who live outside of the geographical boundaries of the court must litigate the matter where the property is located.

Subject-matter jurisdiction is a court's "jurisdiction over the nature of the case and the type of relief sought" (Garner 2005, 710). For example, if the hotel declares bankruptcy, it is asking for special relief that only a bankruptcy court may provide.

American Jurisdiction

American jurisdiction evolved after the Revolutionary War and the independence of the American colonies. In addition to English common law, still used in the United Sates, the following types of jurisdiction evolved in American courts: state jurisdiction, federal jurisdiction, diversity jurisdiction, exclusive jurisdiction, original jurisdiction, appellate jurisdiction, and internet jurisdiction.

State jurisdiction is the jurisdiction required to file a case in the state court system. The Tenth Amendment to the U.S. Constitution provides the states with the authority to make laws regarding subjects not expressly delegated to the federal government in Article I, such as cases involving state constitutional and state statutory law. Each state has unique jurisdictional issues, such as health, welfare, and safety laws. State jurisdiction also refers to common law jurisdiction applicable to activity within its geographical boundaries, such as land use issues.

Federal jurisdiction is the jurisdiction required in the federal court system. It applies to cases involving federal constitutional issues (e.g., free speech), federal statutory law (e.g., Clean Air Act), and international treaties (e.g., NAFTA). In order to obtain federal jurisdiction, the complaint must state the basis for federal jurisdiction, collectively referred to as a **federal question.**

Diversity jurisdiction is a second way to obtain federal jurisdiction and applies to cases that involve litigants from different states with a claim at issue that is $75,000 or greater. The parties may agree to a forum in one of their respective states that meets the usual other requirements of jurisdiction. This is referred to as forum selection and permits the case to be tried in the mutually agreed state court. If that can't be done, the federal court has the power to resolve the dispute. Diversity also applies if there is dispute between two states, which is a federal question.

Diversity rationale is developed because of two important considerations: First, to avoid the tendency of a state court to favor one of its citizens over one from another state. Second, if two states have important considerations at stake, neither may be willing to concede jurisdiction to the other state. Therefore, an arbiter is required to settle legitimate interstate disputes. The federal courts are a natural forum for resolution of such disputes.

Exclusive jurisdiction exists with courts that have a special subject matter authority, such as probate issues in a state court or an issue on the high seas in the federal maritime court. A person with such a claim must file a case in the specialized court of proper jurisdiction.

Original jurisdiction refers to a case that is usually handled for the first time by a trial court. For example, an accident in a hotel occurring within a state superior court's jurisdiction (the state trial court) is not a specialized issue for a court of exclusive jurisdiction. Another example is a violation by a hotel of a federal statute, like the Americans with Disabilities Act, which is in a federal district court's jurisdiction (the federal trial court).

Concurrent jurisdiction occurs when either a federal court or a state court may hear the matter, such as the aforementioned diversity case. For example, in a case that concerns an automobile accident between persons from different states, the federal court where the case is filed has authority to resolve the matter. It will apply the law of the state in which the federal court is located. The same case may be tried in the state courts if the parties agree. If the parties don't agree, a federal court will be the forum if the claim is more than $75,000.

Out-of-state jurisdiction exists for the determination of jurisdiction between litigants in transactions who reside in different states. For example, assume someone purchases a defective oven manufactured in Michigan from a retail outlet in Portland, Oregon. The purchaser files a lawsuit in a Portland court naming the retail outlet and the manufacturer as defendants. A court will have to decide if it has jurisdiction over the manufacturer since the manufacturer is not located in Oregon. The issue will be whether sufficient minimum contacts exist to warrant making the manufacturer appear for litigation in Portland, Oregon.

The Constitution's Due Process Clause requires a fair hearing. Under the minimum contacts test, the court evaluates the extent of business conducted in a state. The court may conclude enough contacts exist by an out-of-state business, and therefore, it is fair to order it to defend in the state where the lawsuit is filed. For example, if a business has retail outlets, advertises, has an active sales force with hundreds of sales each year in the state, and provides a toll-free number for sales and service, the court will likely find minimum contacts to warrant jurisdiction.

The following case, *International Shoe v. Washington*, explains the concept of out-of-state jurisdiction and minimum contacts.

INTERNATIONAL SHOE V. STATE OF WASHINGTON, 326 U.S. 310 (1945).

66 S. Ct. 154
INTERNATIONAL SHOE CO.
v.
STATE OF WASHINGTION
No. 107
Decided Dec. 3, 1945

Proceeding by the State of Washington against International Shoe from a judgment of the Supreme Court of Washington affirming a judgment for the plaintiff, the defendant appeals.

Mr. Chief Justice STONE delivered the opinion of the court.

The questions for decisions are (1) whether, within the limitations of the due process clause of the Fourteenth Amendment, appellant, a Delaware corporation, has by its activities in the State of Washington rendered itself amenable to proceedings in the courts of that state to recover unpaid contributions to the state unemployment compensation fund. ... and (2) whether the state can exact those contributions consistently with the Due Process Clause of the Fourteenth Amendment.

***

The facts as found by the appeal tribunal and accepted by the state Superior Court and Supreme Court are not in dispute. Appellant is a Delaware corporation, having its principal place of business in St. Louis, Missouri, and is engaged in the manufacture of shoes and other footwear.

***

Appellant has no office in Washington and makes no contacts either for sale of purchase of merchandise there, it maintains no stock of merchandise in that state and makes there no deliveries of goods in intrastate commerce. During the years in question ...

appellant employed eleven to thirteen salesmen under direct supervision and control of sales managers located in St. Louis. These salesmen resided in Washington, their principal activities are confined to that state, and they were compensated by commissions based upon the amount of their sales.

***

The authority of the salesmen is limited to exhibiting their samples and soliciting orders from prospective buyers. The salesmen transmit the orders to appellant's office in St. Louis for acceptance or rejection, and when accepted the merchandise for filling the orders is shipped f.o.b. from points outside Washington to the purchasers within the state.

***

The Supreme Court of Washington was of opinion that the regular and systematic solicitation of orders in the state by appellant's salesmen, resulting in a continuous flow of appellant's product into the state, was sufficient to constitute doing business in the state so as to make appellant amenable to suit in its courts.

***

The court also held that the statute as applied did not invade the constitutional power of Congress to regulate interstate commerce and did not impose a prohibited burden on such commerce.

***

Appellant also insists that its activities within the state were not sufficient to manifest its "presence" there and that in its absence the state courts were without jurisdiction, that consequently it was a denial of due process for the state to subject appellant to suit.

***

But now that ... due process requires only that in order to subject a defendant to a judgment in personam, if he be not present within the territory of the forum, he have certain minimum contacts with it such that the maintenance of suit does not offend "traditional notions of fair play and substantial justice." [Citations omitted.]

***

Applying these standards, the activities carried on in behalf of appellant in the State of Washington were neither irregular nor casual. They were systematic and continuous throughout the years in question. They resulted in a large volume of interstate business, in the course of which appellant received the benefits and protection of the laws of the state, including the right to resort to the courts for the enforcement of its rights. The obligation is here sued upon arose out those very activities. It is evident that these operations establish sufficient contacts or ties with state of the forum to make it reasonable and just according to our traditional conception of fair play and substantial justice to permit the state to enforce obligations which appellant has incurred there. Hence we cannot say the maintenance of the present suit in the State of Washington involves an unreasonable or undue procedure.

***

Affirmed.

Internet jurisdiction poses a special problem because it is a relatively new technology that makes it difficult to determine location for jurisdiction. The courts have developed a sliding scale to determine where location of jurisdiction may be most appropriate based upon a concept of minimum contacts that justifies bringing a defendant to a distant venue for a trial (see *International Shoe* case above for discussion of minimum contacts).

With regard to e-contracts generated by websites, the court will make its determination by evaluating the interactivity of the website. The courts developed a sliding scale to determine where location of jurisdiction may be most appropriate based upon a concept of minimum contacts that justifies bringing a defendant to a distant venue for a trial (see *Zippo Manufacturing Co. v. Zippo Dot Com, Inc.*, 952 F. Supp. 1119 (W.D. Pa. 1997)).

A website that provides only informational data is not interactive and would probably not subject the manufacturer to personal jurisdiction. On the other hand, if the website is fully interactive and provides a toll-free number for ordering products, accepts credit card purchases, provides delivery service and technical support, and the number of direct sales to a state was in the hundreds each year, a court could justify jurisdiction.

Not all factual patterns will be identical, so the court must (on a case-by-case basis) evaluate the number and quality of the contacts to make its decision. Use of a sliding scale helps the court decide if the facts show a level of activity closer to full interactivity or lesser activity. The closer to full interactivity, the more likely in personam jurisdiction will be present. The closer to a passive website, the less likely in personam jurisdiction will be present.

There are many other types of jurisdiction (see Garner 2005, 707–710), but the aforementioned types of jurisdiction are some of the most commonly used in business disputes, such as those found in the hospitality industry.

Pretrial

Activities of each party to the lawsuit from the filing of the complaint until commencement of the trial with jury selection is considered **pretrial**. The activities are the pleadings, discovery, summary judgment, and the pretrial conference. They are discussed below.

The Pleadings

A complaint is defined as "the initial pleading that starts the basis for the court's jurisdiction, the basis for the plaintiff's claim and the demand for relief" (Garner 2005, 239). The purpose of the complaint is to put the defendant on notice that a claim has been filed, alleging the defendant is liable and alleging facts such as the defendant's specific actions that caused the injury and a request for damages to be paid.

The answer is filed in response to the complaint by the defendant denying liability and alleging facts in support of the denial. The **answer** is defined as "a defendant's first pleading that addresses the merits of the case, usu. by denying the plaintiff's allegations" (Garner 2005, 77). In addition, a defendant has the right to file a counterclaim. A counterclaim is defined as "a claim for relief asserted against an opposing party after an original claim has been made; esp. a defendant's claim in opposition to or as a setoff against the plaintiff's claim" (Garner 2005, 299).

For example, a counterclaim may assert the plaintiff is liable instead of the defendant. As such, in a lawsuit for negligence, the defendant may claim the plaintiff is the person responsible for the incident and that the plaintiff owes the defendant damages. Analytically, the defendant becomes the plaintiff in a separate lawsuit, and the plaintiff becomes the defendant. This requires the plaintiff to answer the counterclaim. In some states, such as California, the counterclaim is referred to as a cross-complaint.

Discovery

After the pleadings, discovery takes place. **Discovery** is defined as "compulsory disclosure, at a party's request, of information that relates to the litigation" (Garner 2005, 393). It is the process by which litigants obtain evidence from each other, and it is discussed more fully below. After discovery is complete, the parties usually file a **motion for summary judgment**, also discussed below. The final step in pretrial is the **pretrial conference** where the court and the parties discuss the details of the trial procedure. The court will also make a concerted effort to obtain a settlement of the dispute in order to avoid a trial. The pretrial conference is discussed below.

Pretrial Activities

1. Plaintiff files a complaint.
2. Defendant files an answer.
3. File various relevant motions regarding 1. & 2.
4. Court holds hearings on each motion.
5. Pleadings are complete.
6. Discovery is initiated and completed.
7. Motion for Summary Judgment filed and heard by court.
8. Pretrial conference held.
9. Pretrial is complete.

FIGURE 2.1 Flow Chart of Pretrial Activities

Commencement of a Lawsuit

The following factual pattern applies to a hypothetical lawsuit. For example, consider a dispute between Seafood Restaurant ("Seafood") and Linen Restaurant Supply Co. ("Linen") after Seafood ordered 200,000 red napkins from Linen at a cost of $1.00 per napkin. Linen delivered 190,000 red napkins and 10,000 pink napkins. Linen's invoice states the napkins are $2.00 each, and the total bill is $400,000. Seafood accepts

PLD-PI-001

ATTORNEY OR PARTY WITHOUT ATTORNEY *(Name, State Bar number, and address):* TELEPHONE NO.: FAX NO. *(Optional):* E-MAIL ADDRESS *(Optional):* ATTORNEY FOR *(Name):*	*FOR COURT USE ONLY*
SUPERIOR COURT OF CALIFORNIA, COUNTY OF STREET ADDRESS: MAILING ADDRESS: CITY AND ZIP CODE: BRANCH NAME:	
PLAINTIFF: DEFENDANT: ☐ DOES 1 TO ________	
COMPLAINT—Personal Injury, Property Damage, Wrongful Death ☐ **AMENDED *(Number):*** Type *(check all that apply):* ☐ **MOTOR VEHICLE** ☐ **OTHER *(specify):*** ☐ **Property Damage** ☐ **Wrongful Death** ☐ **Personal Injury** ☐ **Other Damages *(specify):***	CASE NUMBER:
Jurisdiction *(check all that apply):* ☐ **ACTION IS A LIMITED CIVIL CASE** Amount demanded ☐ does not exceed $10,000 ☐ exceeds $10,000, but does not exceed $25,000 ☐ **ACTION IS AN UNLIMITED CIVIL CASE (exceeds $25,000)** ☐ **ACTION IS RECLASSIFIED by this amended complaint** ☐ **from limited to unlimited** ☐ **from unlimited to limited**	

1. **Plaintiff** *(name or names):*
   alleges causes of action against **defendant** *(name or names):*
2. This pleading, including attachments and exhibits, consists of the following number of pages:
3. Each plaintiff named above is a competent adult
   a. ☐ **except** plaintiff *(name):*
      (1) ☐ a corporation qualified to do business in California
      (2) ☐ an unincorporated entity *(describe):*
      (3) ☐ a public entity *(describe):*
      (4) ☐ a minor ☐ an adult
         (a) ☐ for whom a guardian or conservator of the estate or a guardian ad litem has been appointed
         (b) ☐ other *(specify):*
      (5) ☐ other *(specify):*
   b. ☐ **except** plaintiff *(name):*
      (1) ☐ a corporation qualified to do business in California
      (2) ☐ an unincorporated entity *(describe):*
      (3) ☐ a public entity *(describe):*
      (4) ☐ a minor ☐ an adult
         (a) ☐ for whom a guardian or conservator of the estate or a guardian ad litem has been appointed
         (b) ☐ other *(specify):*
      (5) ☐ other *(specify):*

☐ Information about additional plaintiffs who are not competent adults is shown in Attachment 3.

Page 1 of 3

Form Approved for Optional Use
Judicial Council of California
PLD-PI-001 [Rev. January 1, 2007]

COMPLAINT—Personal Injury, Property Damage, Wrongful Death

Code of Civil Procedure, § 425.12
www.courts.ca.gov

FIGURE 2.2 Complaint

delivery of the 190,000 red napkins, rejects the 10,000 pink napkins, and issues a check for $190,000, or $1.00 per red napkin.

Linen alleges its invoice is correct, and Seafood disputes the claim. Unless the parties can amicably settle the dispute, one of the parties will commence legal action. Settlement, if possible, is always recommended because of the high cost in money, time, and anxiety levels associated with litigation.

Since Linen believes its invoice is correct and it was not fully paid by Seafood, it will file the complaint. Linen will be the plaintiff seeking recovery of the difference in the amount it claims Seafood owes. Seafood will be the defendant and will file the answer denying it owes anything further to Linen.

A complaint serves two functions. It formally initiates the lawsuit and places the **defendant**, Seafood, on notice of the claims asserted in the complaint. Notice to Seafood is accomplished with service of process. **Service of process** is the procedure designed to provide the defendant with the requisite legal notice of the complaint. It includes a document generated from the court referred to as the summons. A **summons** is legal notice the complaint has been filed and is a court order to appear within 30 days. It is accompanied with a copy of the complaint (Figure 2.3).

The summons informs the defendant a lawsuit has been filed and that the defendant has 30 days to respond. If Seafood does not respond in 30 days, the court will issue a **default judgment** against Seafood. That means Seafood must pay the claims asserted by the plaintiff in the complaint. Seafood will probably respond by filing an answer (see Figure 2.4 below, a copy of an answer).

PRACTICUM

If you are a defendant and you get served with a summons and complaint, you must act quickly to ensure you respond within 30 days and avoid a default judgment. A default judgment may subject you to liability for all damages requested in the complaint. CONTACT AN ATTORNEY immediately. Even if you are unsure of retaining a particular attorney after interviewing them, that lawyer can file a request to continue the time within which to file an answer to the complaint (at a minimal cost) and avoid a default judgment.

Once served, Seafood will probably respond by filing an answer. The answer is a legal document that, among other things, rebuts the claims of the complaint. The answer admits and denies allegations of the complaint. In the Linen example, Seafood would admit certain allegations, such as its name, address, the purpose of the contract, and so on but would deny it breached the contract when it paid an amount Linen claims is incorrect. Seafood will claim Linen is incorrectly overcharging in its invoice.

The answer is also used by a defendant to assert a counterclaim against the plaintiff. In California, the defendant's claim is referred to as a cross-complaint. Once the answer is filed with the court and served on Linen, a lawsuit has formally commenced (Figure 2.4).

An answer contains numbered responses to the allegations in the complaint and any affirmative defenses available to Seafood. An affirmative defense is "a defendant's assertion of facts and arguments that, if true, will defeat the plaintiff's or prosecution's claim, even if all the allegations in the complaint are true" (Garner 2005, 356). For example, in the Linen case, Seafood might assert Linen filed its claim two weeks late, and therefore, the claim is barred by the statute of limitations.

SUM-100

SUMMONS
(CITACION JUDICIAL)

FOR COURT USE ONLY
(SOLO PARA USO DE LA CORTE)

NOTICE TO DEFENDANT:
(AVISO AL DEMANDADO):

YOU ARE BEING SUED BY PLAINTIFF:
(LO ESTÁ DEMANDANDO EL DEMANDANTE):

NOTICE! You have been sued. The court may decide against you without your being heard unless you respond within 30 days. Read the information below.

You have 30 CALENDAR DAYS after this summons and legal papers are served on you to file a written response at this court and have a copy served on the plaintiff. A letter or phone call will not protect you. Your written response must be in proper legal form if you want the court to hear your case. There may be a court form that you can use for your response. You can find these court forms and more information at the California Courts Online Self-Help Center (*www.courtinfo.ca.gov/selfhelp*), your county law library, or the courthouse nearest you. If you cannot pay the filing fee, ask the court clerk for a fee waiver form. If you do not file your response on time, you may lose the case by default, and your wages, money, and property may be taken without further warning from the court.

There are other legal requirements. You may want to call an attorney right away. If you do not know an attorney, you may want to call an attorney referral service. If you cannot afford an attorney, you may be eligible for free legal services from a nonprofit legal services program. You can locate these nonprofit groups at the California Legal Services Web site (*www.lawhelpcalifornia.org*), the California Courts Online Self-Help Center (*www.courtinfo.ca.gov/selfhelp*), or by contacting your local court or county bar association. NOTE: The court has a statutory lien for waived fees and costs on any settlement or arbitration award of $10,000 or more in a civil case. The court's lien must be paid before the court will dismiss the case.

¡AVISO! Lo han demandado. Si no responde dentro de 30 días, la corte puede decidir en su contra sin escuchar su versión. Lea la información a continuación.

Tiene 30 DÍAS DE CALENDARIO después de que le entreguen esta citación y papeles legales para presentar una respuesta por escrito en esta corte y hacer que se entregue una copia al demandante. Una carta o una llamada telefónica no lo protegen. Su respuesta por escrito tiene que estar en formato legal correcto si desea que procesen su caso en la corte. Es posible que haya un formulario que usted pueda usar para su respuesta. Puede encontrar estos formularios de la corte y más información en el Centro de Ayuda de las Cortes de California (www.sucorte.ca.gov), en la biblioteca de leyes de su condado o en la corte que le quede más cerca. Si no puede pagar la cuota de presentación, pida al secretario de la corte que le dé un formulario de exención de pago de cuotas. Si no presenta su respuesta a tiempo, puede perder el caso por incumplimiento y la corte le podrá quitar su sueldo, dinero y bienes sin más advertencia.

Hay otros requisitos legales. Es recomendable que llame a un abogado inmediatamente. Si no conoce a un abogado, puede llamar a un servicio de remisión a abogados. Si no puede pagar a un abogado, es posible que cumpla con los requisitos para obtener servicios legales gratuitos de un programa de servicios legales sin fines de lucro. Puede encontrar estos grupos sin fines de lucro en el sitio web de California Legal Services, (www.lawhelpcalifornia.org), en el Centro de Ayuda de las Cortes de California, (www.sucorte.ca.gov) o poniéndose en contacto con la corte o el colegio de abogados locales. AVISO: Por ley, la corte tiene derecho a reclamar las cuotas y los costos exentos por imponer un gravamen sobre cualquier recuperación de $10,000 ó más de valor recibida mediante un acuerdo o una concesión de arbitraje en un caso de derecho civil. Tiene que pagar el gravamen de la corte antes de que la corte pueda desechar el caso.

The name and address of the court is:
(El nombre y dirección de la corte es):

CASE NUMBER: *(Número del Caso):*

The name, address, and telephone number of plaintiff's attorney, or plaintiff without an attorney, is: *(El nombre, la dirección y el número de teléfono del abogado del demandante, o del demandante que no tiene abogado, es):*

DATE: *(Fecha)* Clerk, by *(Secretario)* , Deputy *(Adjunto)*

(For proof of service of this summons, use Proof of Service of Summons *(form POS-010).)*
(Para prueba de entrega de esta citatión use el formulario Proof of Service of Summons, *(POS-010).)*

[SEAL]

NOTICE TO THE PERSON SERVED: You are served

1. ☐ as an individual defendant.
2. ☐ as the person sued under the fictitious name of *(specify)*:
3. ☐ on behalf of (specify):

   under: ☐ CCP 416.10 (corporation) ☐ CCP 416.60 (minor)
   ☐ CCP 416.20 (defunct corporation) ☐ CCP 416.70 (conservatee)
   ☐ CCP 416.40 (association or partnership) ☐ CCP 416.90 (authorized person)
   ☐ other *(specify)*:
4. ☐ by personal delivery on *(date)*

Page 1 of 1

Form Adopted for Mandatory Use
Judicial Council of California
SUM-100 [Rev. July 1, 2009]

SUMMONS

Code of Civil Procedure §§ 412.20, 465
www.courts.ca.gov

For your protection and privacy, please press the Clear This Form button after you have printed the form.

Print this form | Save this form | Clear this form

FIGURE 2.3 Summons

PLD-PI-003

ATTORNEY OR PARTY WITHOUT ATTORNEY *(NAME AND ADDRESS)*: TELEPHONE NO.: ATTORNEY FOR *(NAME)*:	***FOR COURT USE ONLY***
Insert name of court, judicial district or branch court, if any, and post office and street address:	
PLAINTIFF:	
DEFENDANT:	
ANSWER—Personal Injury, Property Damage, Wrongful Death ☐ **COMPLAINT OF (name):** ☐ **CROSS-COMPLAINT OF *(name)*:**	CASE NUMBER:

1. This pleading, including attachments and exhibits, consists of the following number of pages: __________
2. **DEFENDANT OR CROSS-DEFENDANT *(name)*:**
3. a. ☐ DENIES each allegation of the following numbered paragraphs:

   b. ☐ ADMITS each allegation of the following numbered paragraphs:

   c. ☐ DENIES, ON INFORMATION AND BELIEF, each allegation of the following numbered paragraphs:

   d. ☐ DENIES, BECAUSE OF LACK OF SUFFICIENT INFORMATION OR BELIEF TO ANSWER, each allegation of the following numbered paragraphs:

   e. ☐ ADMITS the following allegations and generally denies all other allegations:

Page 1 of 2

Form Approved for Optional Use
Judicial Council of California
PLD-PI-003 [Rev. January 1, 2007]

ANSWER—Personal Injury, Property Damage, Wrongful Death

Code of Civil Procedure, § 425.12
www.courts.ca.gov

FIGURE 2.4 Answer

Both parties will also file various motions related to the complaint and answer, such as a motion to dismiss the complaint, motion to strike portions of the complaint, and a motion for judgment on the pleadings. See Key Concept Focus 2.1 for a list of the various pretrial motions with a short explanation.

The complaint, answer, and the related motions are collectively referred to as the **pleadings**.

KEY CONCEPT FOCUS 2.1. TYPICAL MOTIONS ASSOCIATED WITH PLEADINGS

A motion is "a written or oral application requesting a court to make a specified ruling or order" (Garner 2005, 852). Motions are made to clarify the pleadings, clear up ambiguities, streamline the issues, and, in some cases, end the litigation. They can be very effective tools to assist a party in litigation. The nomenclature and description of pretrial motions will vary according to each state's code of civil procedure, but the general purpose of the following motions is similar. Some of the most important pretrial motions are listed below.

Motion to dismiss a case for failure to state facts sufficient to state a cause of action. A complaint must state a cause of action, such as negligence, and allege sufficient facts to prove the elements of a cause of action exists. Such a motion is usually made pursuant to various states and federal rules of civil procedure with a motion to dismiss (see Chapter 4 for detailed discussion of negligence elements).

For example, if the case is a slip and fall caused by a wet floor on the premises of a hotel, the plaintiff must allege the defendant Hotel (a) had a duty to provide safe premises (e.g., had notice the floor was wet), (b) breached that duty (e.g., did nothing to warn guests), (c) the breach caused an injury, (d) the failure to warn was the proximate cause of the injury, and (e) identify compensable damages. Failure to prove each element will lead to a dismissal of the complaint.

Motion to Quash. This is "a party's request that the court nullify process or an act instituted by the other party, as in seeking to nullify a subpoena" (Garner 2005, 855). It may be used to dismiss the case for such defects as lack of jurisdiction by the court, defective service of process, and improper venue. For example, in each state there is a requirement that service of process must be completed within a statutory time. If not, the motion to quash will be granted, and the case will effectively be over.

Motion to strike. This is "a party's request that the court delete insufficient defenses or immaterial, redundant, impertinent, or scandalous statements from on opponents pleading" (Garner 2005, 855). For example, a plaintiff in a slip-and-fall case may allege the defendant is known for fraudulent behavior with its vendors. Even if true, that conduct may be immaterial to a claim for negligence.

Motion for judgment on the pleadings. This is "a party's request that the court rule in its favor based on the pleadings on file, without accepting evidence" (Garner 2005, 853). This motion is filed after the complaint, answer, and any relevant motions have been considered (i.e., after the pleading stage is complete). It is filed as a matter of law and without consideration of any evidence. It is often erroneously referred to as a motion for summary judgment, which is filed after discovery with consideration of all the evidence available at that time.

Discovery

After the pleadings phase is complete, each party will attempt to obtain as much evidence as it can from the other to support their respective position. This process is called discovery, and it is utilized by the parties to learn as much about the facts of the case as possible. In litigation, it is defined as "the act or process of finding or learning something [from the opposing party] that was previously unknown" (Garner 2005, 392).

Pretrial discovery is conducted before trial to obtain information and develop admissible evidence. The objective is to provide the parties with the knowledge to either settle the case or go forward with a trial. The parties to a lawsuit are required by law to cooperate with each other and to provide all relevant information requested by the opposing party. Failure to provide relevant information may result in sanctions (a form of punishment).

A sanction in a tort case is referred to as "a means of recovery for another party's discovery abuse, whereby the judge orders the abusive party to pay a fine to the injured party for the discovery violation" (Garner 2005, 1112). Sometimes, a judge may order a nonmonetary penalty, such as issue sanctions or termination sanctions.

Issue sanctions means the court may rule in favor of the party that requested certain information but did not receive it from the other party. It means the requesting party will not need to prove that issue in the trial. For example, an issue in the case may be whether or not the defendant had prior incidents similar to the instant case, such as failing to maintain safe premises. Failure to disclose that information during discovery could cause the judge to conclude, as a matter of fact, that there were prior accidents. Accordingly, that issue is resolved in favor of the party seeking that information.

Termination sanctions occur with serious cases of noncooperation, such as where one party does not act in good faith regarding numerous requests for discovery. The court may impose a ruling that awards the entire case to the party that requested but failed to receive its discovery requests.

Discovery Methods

Civil discovery procedures vary by state jurisdiction. The methods listed below are some of the most frequently used in most states to obtain relevant information from the opposing parties. They are interrogatories, depositions, private investigations, inspection of physical evidence, and document production.

Interrogatories are written questions parties to a lawsuit are permitted ask of each other. They can be very technical in nature and are designed to elicit incriminating evidence. Any question that seeks information of admissible evidence or that may lead to admissible evidence may be asked. Accordingly, great care must be taken in their preparation, and therefore, they are prepared by each respective party's attorney. Because of the foregoing, witnesses are not required to respond to interrogatories. They don't have a stake in the case, and it would be unfair and too costly to require a witness to obtain an attorney.

Depositions are oral questions taken under oath outside the courtroom (usually in the law office of the lawyer requesting the deposition) and transcribed by a court reporter into a **written transcript**. A transcript is defined as "a handwritten, printed, or typed copy of testimony given orally; esp. the official record of proceedings in a trial or hearing, as taken down by a court reporter" (Garner 2005, 1253).

The transcript may be used by the parties at trial if the witness is unavailable or to **impeach** a witness if the deposition testimony differs from the trial testimony of the witness. The transcript may also be required for an appeal of a court ruling or a final judgment in the case.

Private investigation is the process, without court supervision, whereby the parties hire professional investigators to find relevant information. The various state codes of civil procedure do not regulate private investigation, but relevant information obtained this way is admissible at trial just as any other form of fact-finding process.

Document production is the legal process that requires parties to produce relevant documents in their possession to the opposing side. This would include items such as incident reports, medical records, financial ledgers, correspondence, contracts, invoices, cancelled checks, pictures, and emails.

Inspection of physical evidence includes items such as personal property, real property, visual inspection of a scene of an accident, and items relevant to an accident, such as vehicles, staircases, defective equipment, and so on.

Motion to compel discovery is "a party's request that the court force the party's opponent to respond to the party's discovery request (as to answer interrogatories or produce documents)" (Garner 2005, 854). Despite the threat of sanctions, many attorneys don't cooperate with the request. Accordingly, this is a motion frequently filed to move the discovery stage along expeditiously.

KEY CONCEPT FOCUS 2.2. DISCOVERY

Discovery commences informally at the scene of the incident. For example, assume a female guest at a hotel slips and falls while descending a staircase. She spent several hours in the second-floor bar. The guest (plaintiff) will probably file a lawsuit against the hotel (defendant) for negligence. Allegedly, the cause of the incident was a loose hand railing that separated from the wall when the guest grabbed it while walking down the stairs.

At the scene, the hotel's staff will commence discovery by taking statements from the guest and any witnesses and placing them in the hotel files. The hotel's attorney will review the reports and conduct follow-up interviews with the witnesses. This initial information will be helpful in determining how to respond to a potential lawsuit.

Informal discovery for the guest commences when the guest seeks the services of and is interviewed by an attorney. At this time, the attorney is eliciting key facts to determine if the plaintiff has a triable cause of action. If the attorney takes the case, they will probably request the hotel reports (at this point the hotel is not obligated to release the reports but, in the interest of early settlement, may wish to do so).

The attorney will likely hire a private investigator to independently research the incident to determine what may have happened. If the guest's information is corroborated, a complaint will subsequently be filed (action that formally commences the lawsuit). The defendant hotel will file an answer and perhaps a cross-complaint. Both parties will file related motions (see pretrial motions above), and the pleading stage is complete.

After the pretrial stage, the formal discovery begins. Each state has its own set of civil procedures applicable to discovery rules. In order to obtain as much information as possible regarding the incident, the parties' respective attorneys will engage in the most common methods described below. The discussion below is premised upon the facts of the woman falling down the hotel's stairwell expressed above.

Interrogatories. An interrogatory may be used by the plaintiff's attorney to ask how many accidents occurred in the hotel the last year in order to determine a pattern of negligent conduct. The hotel's attorney may ask how many previous lawsuits the plaintiff has filed to determine if the plaintiff is a vexatious litigant.

Depositions. The attorneys will want to ask questions of any witness present at the time of the incident. That would include the plaintiff, other guests, and hotel staff. The hotel may wish to depose the plaintiff's doctor. If expert witnesses (such as a surgeon or a construction engineer) are retained by either party, they too may be deposed.

Document production is the process available for the parties who seek relevant documentation of the incident. For example, the plaintiff will want to see maintenance reports of the staircase, especially of the handrail. They will also likely want relevant files of other accidents or complaints by guests about safety of the hotel. The hotel will want to see the medical reports of the plaintiff's injuries, interviews of bartenders, servers, friends of the plaintiff present at the time, or other guests in the bar to determine if the plaintiff was drinking alcoholic beverages in excess at the time of the incident.

Inspection of physical evidence. The plaintiff may request the court to order the jury to visit the hotel and see the staircase and handrail at issue. If the handrail was replaced, the plaintiff may want to see the old one if it was not discarded. The hotel may want the court to order the shoes worn by the plaintiff at the time of the incident be available for inspection by the jury. Perhaps the style or worn condition may be a contributing factor to the incident. For example, the plaintiff may have been wearing stiletto high heels.

Motion for summary judgment (MSJ) is made after discovery is complete, when all the evidence has been obtained by the parties. It is the most important pretrial motion because, if granted, the case is usually over, which means a costly, time-consuming trial is avoided, and the movant usually wins the case. However, there are times when the motion for summary judgment will only be used to eliminate certain causes of action or only some of the major issues.

A motion for summary judgment is defined as "a request that the court enter judgment without a trial because there is no genuine issue of material fact to be decided by a fact-finder—that is, because the evidence is legally insufficient to support a verdict in the non-movant's favor" (Garner 2005, 854).

A motion for summary judgment requires evaluation of all relevant evidence, pleadings, court filings, and court rulings to determine if a triable issue of material fact exists. If a proponent of a MSJ can convince the judge that none exists, the court will decide the case as a matter of law without a trial.

In the above staircase incident, if the plaintiff has not presented sufficient facts to prove each and every element of negligence, the court will rule as a matter of law that the defendant hotel is not guilty of negligence. For example, if the facts show that the plaintiff fell because she was intoxicated, was wearing high heels, and the hand rail dislodged because of her heavy weight as she grasped it during the tumble down, legal causation (a crucial element) may be absent.

After the motion for summary judgment has been resolved, and if denied, the court will convene the last step in the pretrial phase of the litigation, which is the **pretrial hearing**. At this hearing, the judge will make an effort to obtain a settlement from the parties. If that fails the court will do the following: (1) set the trial date; (2) confirm jury instructions; (3) obtain a list of witnesses to be called; (4) obtain a list of the relevant evidence, such as physical evidence, charts, and graphs; and (5) identify the issues to be resolved and resolve any other questions the parties may raise concerning the trial.

A successful motion for summary judgment saves the taxpayers, the court, and the parties the time, cost, and stress of a trial.

PRACTICUM

A motion for summary judgment is expensive and time consuming because the attorney filing one must review the entire record developed at the time the motion is filed. Courts are not tolerant of mischaracterization of the evidence, so Counsel must be thorough and accurate with the summary of the evidence. That will include all the pleadings, responses thereto, and all discovery, such as the interrogatories, depositions, investigative reports, document production, and so on. Plus, the attorney for the nonmoving party must do likewise in order to respond.

If a motion for summary judgment is successful, both parties stand to save huge sums of money by avoiding a costly trial, and the movant saves itself from a large judgment. Finally, with the current problem of congested courts and long wait times to obtain a trial date, courts have been granting more motions for summary judgment than historically has been the case. The courts do so in order to reduce congestion of court calendars. Unless it is clear that such a motion will fail, it is wise to do one.

The Trial

Jury Selection

The trial commences with the selection of people from a cross-section of the community to decide the factual issues in the case, referred to as the jury. County officials in charge of the courts select names from voter registration lists and Department of Motor Vehicles lists. The lawyers in the case, with advice of their clients and direction from the judge, select those who will sit on the jury. This process is called ***voir dire***, a French term for "to speak the truth" (Garner 2005, 1309).

Usually, the jury is comprised of 12 people from a jury pool in which the court is geographically situated. Some states permit fewer than 12 jurors depending on the type of case, but criminal cases are usually always 12. Minor civil cases may provide for as few as six jurors.

Once the jury is selected, lawyers for each party present their **opening statements**. The purpose of the opening statement is to provide the jury with a roadmap for the case. The lawyers will explain what evidence will be presented and what they believe such evidence will show. At this point, each side is presenting the most favorable picture of their respective case for the jury to consider.

After opening statements are completed, the evidentiary stage of the trial begins. The plaintiff presents its **case in chief**, which consists of all evidence it possesses and that it obtained during discovery that supports the plaintiff's claim for relief. This includes testimony from the parties and witnesses, plus any physical evidence (e.g., documents, photos, inventory, motor vehicles, tools, etc). The defendant has the right to challenge the testimony of the plaintiff, cross-examine the witnesses, and object to the introduction of any evidence the defendant believes is not probative.

After the plaintiff's case in chief is complete, the defendant will present its case in chief, which consists of all evidence it possesses and that it obtained during discovery that supports the defendant's cause. The plaintiff has the right to cross-examine the defendant's witnesses and object to the introduction of any evidence the plaintiff believes is not probative.

After all the evidence is presented, each party presents a closing argument (also referred to as summation). The **closing argument** "is a lawyer's final statement to the judge or jury before deliberation begins, in which the lawyer requests the judge or jury to consider the evidence and to apply the law in his or her client's favor" (Garner 2005, 212). The lawyers summarize their client's respective position with regard to evidence admitted into the record and encourage logical inferences to be drawn from that evidence.

Lawyers are limited to discussing only the evidence admitted in the record during trial. For example, if the testimony of a witness is deemed unreliable, a judge may not admit it in the official record. Consequently, a lawyer in closing arguments is prohibited from mentioning such testimony, and the jury will be instructed not to consider that testimony in their deliberations.

After closing arguments, the judge will instruct the jury on its duties during deliberations, which, among other things, is to decide the case based only upon evidence admitted into the record by the judge, to follow the jury instructions, to be impartial, and to render a fair verdict. The verdict is "a jury's finding on the factual issues of a case" (Garner 2005, 1298). After the verdict is rendered, the judge will decide any posttrial motions that may be filed. Posttrial motions are filed by the litigants asking the court for relief from an alleged defect in the trial. Examples of posttrial motions are:

- a defendant's request to dismiss the case because of insufficient evidence to support the verdict
- a request for a new trial because of prejudicial error
- a motion for remittitur
- a judgment notwithstanding the verdict

Trial Activities of a Jury Trial

Jury selection

↓

Opening statement by attorneys

Plaintiff's case-in-chief

↓

Direct exam of each witness by plaintiff's attorney

↓

Cross exam of each plaintiff witness by defendant's attorney

↓

Defendant's case-in-chief

↓

Direct exam of each witness by defendant's attorney

↓

Cross exam of each defendant's witness by plaintiff's attorney

↓

Plaintiff's rebuttal to defendant's case-in-chief

↓

Closing statements by attorneys

Court provides jurors with instructions

↓

Jurors retire for deliberations

↓

Jurors reach a verdict

↓

Attorneys file relevant post-trial motions

↓

Hearings held for post-trial motions

↓

Court enters the verdict in the record
The trial is completed

FIGURE 2.5 Trial Activities of a Jury Trial

A more detailed explanation of each may be found in the following text box.

POSTTRIAL MOTIONS

After the conclusion of the evidentiary phase of the trial and after the jury renders a verdict, the litigation is not over. The case becomes ripe for appeal only after the court enters a final judgment. Prior to entry of judgment, the parties have the option to file posttrial motions. The following are the most common:

Motion for a new trial—insufficient evidence. Either party may believe the jury verdict is inconsistent with the evidence and request a new trial.

Motion for a new trial because of prejudicial error. The judge will not grant this motion unless it can be shown there was prejudicial error by the judge or the jury, and as such, it would not be in the interest of justice to accept the judgment (e.g., jury selection is successfully challenged on the grounds of unconstitutional exclusion of a certain minority group).

Judgment notwithstanding the verdict. This is "a party's request that the court enter a judgment in its favor despite the jury's contrary verdict because there is no legally sufficient evidentiary basis for a jury to find for the other party" (Garner 2005, 853). This motion, also known as a motion for judgment notwithstanding the verdict, or j. n.o.v., asks the trial judge to reverse the jury's verdict and rule in favor of the losing party. It is justified when the jury clearly misunderstood or ignored the jury instructions. For example, the judge may have instructed the jury to decide the case based upon a preponderance of the evidence, and the jury used a higher standard, such as clear and convincing evidence.

Motion to poll the jury. This motion is used to ensure each juror agrees with the verdict as submitted to the court. Sometimes, a juror may recant a vote when outside the pressure of jury deliberations. If so, the jury may be ordered back for further deliberations, and sometimes, a different outcome results.

Motion for remittitur. This motion is used to challenge the amount of the jury's award in the case. It may be used by either party to challenge the amount as unreasonably low (typically by the plaintiff) or unreasonably high (typically by the defendant). This is a good motion to file if the case is destined for appeal. It will give the court of appeals a starting point for consideration of the issue.

After the posttrial motions are resolved, the court enters the verdict in the record. This process is called **entry of judgment** and it signifies the formal completion of the trial. Until this happens, the trial is not over, and the appeals process cannot commence.

The Appeal

An **appeal** is "a proceeding undertaken to have a decision reconsidered by a higher authority; esp., the submission of a lower court's or agency's decision to a higher court for review and possible reversal" (Garner 2005, 80). Most states have an intermediate court of appeals between the trial court and the state supreme court. Once the trial judge enters the judgment in the record, the trial stage of the case is over, and the matter is ripe for appeal.

An appeal commences when one of the parties in the trial files a notice of appeal with the court of appeals along with a copy to the trial court. The trial court will then assemble the record in the case and forward it to the appellate court. The record consists of all pleadings and documents filed testimony of witnesses, and any evidence admitted into the record.

The function of an appeals court is to rule on matters of law, not fact. The trial court is the forum for determinations of fact, which are usually not disturbed on appeal absent an abuse of discretion. For example, a trial court may decide that a witness is competent to testify in court because that person was at the scene of an incident and therefore has relevant direct evidence for the record. However, that same witness may state facts in a reply to question that was not direct evidence but, instead, was obtained by overhearing someone else discussing the issue. Such evidence is referred to as **hearsay** and is inadmissible in court, absent some exception to the hearsay rule.

Admissibility of hearsay is a legal question that the appellate court will decide if a party challenges a trial court's ruling. An appellate court's decision to overrule the trial court could be the basis for overturning a judgment. If either party is unhappy with the appellate court's ruling, that party may appeal the ruling to the state supreme court, which will be the final forum in the state. A similar process exists in the federal court system.

Figures 2.6 and 2.7 depict the appellate process for both the federal court and the state court of appeals, respectively. The time frames for the steps in the state appellate process may vary by jurisdiction. The time frame for the federal appellate process is the same throughout the federal court system.

There is no appeal from a U.S. Supreme Court decision.

↑

After oral arguments, the court will render a decision.

↑

The U.S. Supreme Court will set a date for oral argument before the full nine members of the court.

↑

If the court accepts the appeal it will order the record and evidence transmitted to the court and it will set a schedule for submission of briefs.

↑

The U.S. Supreme Court has 180 days to accept or deny the appeal.

↑

If a party is unhappy with the decision, there is a right to appeal to the U.S. Supreme Court.

↑

After oral arguments, the court of appeals will render a decision.

↑

The court of appeals will set a date for oral arguments before a three-judge panel.

↑

If the court of appeals accepts the appeal it will order the trial court to transmit the transcript and evidence of the trial to the court of appeals and set a date for submission of written briefs.

↑

The circuit appellate court has 90 days to accept or reject the appeal.
Loser of the trial files an appeal with the circuit court of appeals.

↑

Completion of a federal district court trial.

FIGURE 2.6 The Appellate Process: Federal Court System

There is no appeal from the decision of the State Supreme Court unless a party can show a valid federal question.

↑

After oral arguments, the State Supreme Court will render a decision.

↑

The State Supreme Court will set a date for oral arguments before the full seven members of the court.

↑

If the court of appeals accepts the appeal it will order the trial court to transmit the transcript and evidence of the trial to the State Supreme Court and set a date for submission of written briefs.

↑

The State Supreme Court has 90 days to accept or reject the appeal.

↑

If a party is unhappy with the decision, there is a right to appeal to the State Supreme Court.

↑

After oral argument, the court of appeals will render a decision.

↑

The court of appeals will set a date for oral argument before a three-judge panel.

↑

If the court accepts the appeal it will order the trial court to transmit the transcript and evidence of the trial to the court of appeals and set a date for submission of written briefs.

↑

The state court of appeals has 60 days to accept or reject the appeal.

↑

Loser of the trial files an appeal with the state court of appeals.

↑

Completion of a state superior court trial.

FIGURE 2.7 The Appellate Process: State Court System

Courts of appeal have options for deciding a case. They may affirm the decision, reverse the decision, modify a lower court ruling, or remand the case to the lower court for further action (e.g., dismiss the case, affirm in part or reverse in part, modify the decision, or some combination of the aforementioned options; see Key Concept Focus 2.3).

KEY CONCEPT FOCUS 2.3. ACTION BY COURTS OF APPEAL

The overall role of a court of appeals (COA) is essentially the same for both the state court and federal court system. That role is to review the legal decisions of the trial courts, not its factual decisions. For example, hearsay (i.e., testimony not within the direct knowledge of the witness but, instead, obtained from another person's observations) is a legal question, not a factual question. If the trial court rules that certain testimony is inadmissible hearsay, the COA can decide the legal question of whether an exception to the hearsay rule exists. But it can't rule on the factual question of whether or not the witness is credible.

The rationale for this limitation is that a court of appeals usually does not take live testimony from witnesses. It only has a transcript from the trial court to review. Without a live witness to question, a COA has no way to observe demeanor of the person testifying. Demeanor has historically been recognized as a reliable way to judge credibility, and that usually occurs only at the trial court level. The exception to the above referenced limitation would be if the COA finds an abuse of discretion concerning a factual determination. In addition, the COA has the option to take any of the following actions:

Affirm the decision. This means the COA concurs with the rulings of the court below, and this usually ends the litigation. A small minority of cases are appealed to state courts of appeal or to the U.S. Supreme Court.

Reverse the decision. This means the COA disagrees with the court below, and the case will be sent back to the lower court for further action. A typical instruction to the lower court is that "the case is reversed and remanded to the lower court for further action not inconsistent with this decision." Such an instruction gives the lower court flexibility to remedy the COA's reason for reversal.

Remand the decision. This means the COA disagrees with a specific ruling, issue, or particular action but is not reversing the entire judgment of the lower court. It may include special instructions as to what it wants the lower court to do. For example, if the COA disagrees with admissibility of certain evidence, the instruction may be to exclude the evidence and reevaluate the judgment without inclusion of the evidence.

Dismiss the case. In rare situations, the COA may find the judgment so inconsistent with the evidence that it will overrule the lower court and find for the opposing party.

Affirm in part or reverse in part. This means the court will state which issues it agrees with and affirm them. It will also state which issues it will reverse and provide instructions on how the lower court should proceed.

Modify the decision. This means the COA will change the judgment in some fashion but not send it back for further proceedings. This typically happens when the damage award is excessive, and the court changes the amount.

Until the appellate process is complete, the litigation is generally not over, and the judgment is not binding or enforceable by the parties. In our Linen example, if the plaintiff supplier wins a monetary judgment from Seafood, payment will not be required until Seafood exhausts its available appeals.

Enforcement of the Judgment

A **judgment** is "a court's final determination of the rights and obligations of the parties in a case" (Garner 2005, 699). Judgments are often difficult to collect and require further court and other legal action. In our above example, if the court determined Linen was owed \$2.00 for each red napkin but nothing for the pink ones, the contract price would be \$380,000 (190,000 × \$2 each). If Linen accepted and deposited the \$190,000 that Seafood initially paid to Linen, the judgment would be for \$190,000 (\$380,000 – \$190,000), the amount Linen initially accepted. After entry of judgment and exhaustion of appeals, Seafood is legally bound to pay the judgment upon demand.

If Seafood does not pay the judgment in a timely manner, the supplier may have to return to court and get an order for payment. This may come in the form of a **writ of execution**, an order instructing the sheriff to seize Seafood's property and sell it at a public auction and pay the judgment. The writ of execution must be served on Seafood (the **judgment debtor**) on behalf of Linen (the **judgment creditor**) to provide notice of the public auction. Once served, the sheriff will seize Seafood's available assets, such as real or personal property and money in bank accounts. The real and personal property will be sold at a public auction, and the proceeds will be used to satisfy the judgment.

Sometimes the judgment debtor (Seafood) will have insufficient assets to satisfy the judgment. In that case, the judgment creditor (Linen) may **record the judgment** (i.e., file it) with the county recorder's office in the jurisdiction where the judgment was entered. Recording the judgment provides notice to the public that Linen has priority to any future assets that may be acquired by Seafood. For example, if Seafood subsequently became financially solvent and tried to acquire assets, it would be required to pay off the judgment first.

The recorded judgment would preclude Seafood from buying property, purchasing a business or inventory, or acquiring some form of formal credit (e.g., bank loan, credit cards, etc.). In each of the forgoing situations, Seafood would have to pass a credit check, which includes a review of the judgment rolls in the county recorder's office. Linen's judgment against Seafood would be found by the credit check, and the purchase would not be permitted until the judgment is paid in full.

The entire process from filing a lawsuit, conducting a trial, appealing the judgment, and attempting to collect a judgment can take many years. Often the best resolution is to agree to a reasonable settlement as soon as practicable and save the time, money, and frustration that accompanies a lawsuit.

PRACTICUM

America is one of the most litigious countries in the world. It is likely that every person owning a business or involved in the management of business will be sued, initiate a lawsuit, or become significantly involved in a lawsuit at some time in their career. A person planning employment in the hospitality industry is no exception.

In order to function successfully, a basic understanding of a lawsuit is extremely important. The businessperson will be called upon to participate in the lawsuit, know what to expect, and how to prepare. In addition, an appreciation of the cost, time requirements, disruption to business operations, and the stress and anxiety created by a lawsuit is mandatory for settlement negotiations.

After a lawsuit, whether or not there is negative judgment, a business may be forced to close or at least will experience a severe negative impact on its viability because of the cost and time required to litigate. After completion of this chapter, not only will the student understand this huge problem, but the student will be sensitive to the best practice, which is avoidance of costly trials. The way to do so is to obtain a reasonable settlement of the case as soon as possible or find some form of alternative dispute resolution to minimize the serious negative effects of litigation.

Summary

Litigation is the process used to resolve legal disputes. It is very time consuming, costly, and disruptive to business operations. It commences with a plaintiff filing a complaint for damages against the defendant. The purpose of the complaint is to provide legal notice to the defendant that a lawsuit has commenced, and it also explains the reasons for the lawsuit.

The defendant will file an answer to the complaint admitting and denying the various allegations. The defendant may also file a separate complaint against the plaintiff, which is called a cross-complaint or counterclaim. In addition, each party may file relevant motions to the complaint and answer. The complaint, answer, and relevant motions are collectively called the pleadings.

After the pleadings are complete, each party will seek relevant information the other side may possess. This is called discovery, and all parties are required by law to provide such information. At this point, a motion for summary judgment may be filed by either party to avoid the need for a full trial. If the motion for summary judgment is denied, a trial will commence.

If a trial is held, the first step is the selection of a jury, followed by opening statements by the attorneys. The opening statement is where the lawyers present a roadmap of what they think the evidence will show. After opening statement each party will present its case in chief, which means each party presents the evidence supporting their respective positions. After the case in chief is completed, the lawyers present closing arguments that represent their view of what the evidence in the case shows.

If the case is a jury trial, the court explains the jury instructions and sends the jury to a private room to deliberate. The jury will decide the guilt or innocence of the parties, and a verdict will be reached. The judge will consider any posttrial motions that may be filed. If the motions do not require a change in the verdict, the judge will formally enter the judgment into the record. This is the final formal step in the trial.

After entry of judgment, each party has a right to appeal the trial court's judgment to the state court of appeals and ultimately to the state supreme court. An appeal is another time consuming, costly process. The federal court system has a similar appellate process. If there is an appeal, the trial court judgment is usually not enforceable until after the appellate process is complete. If there is no appeal or after the appellate process is complete, the judgment, if upheld, will become enforceable.

However, often a defendant may not timely pay or refuse to pay. This will require more legal effort by the plaintiff. The plaintiff may have to get a court order for a writ of execution to seize the defendant's assets and sell them to satisfy the judgment. If the defendant does not have sufficient assets, the plaintiff will have to record the judgment with the county recorder located in the jurisdiction of the court.

Recordation will provide notice to the public that the plaintiff has a legal priority to the defendant's assets. Such recording of judgments often leads to payment of the judgment, another very time consuming, stressful process. The lesson to be learned from studying the litigation process is to avoid it by settling the case or using alternative dispute resolution.

Comprehension Check

True/False

Directions: Look at each statement below. Based on what you learned in this chapter, decide if the statement is true or false.

1. In order to qualify for federal jurisdiction, you must have either diversity of jurisdiction or have a federal question for the court.
2. Service of process means the plaintiff must have the complaint and the summons physically delivered to the defendant.
3. If the defendant fails to respond to the summons, the plaintiff will not have to engage in the formal discovery process.
4. The defendant may respond to the complaint by filing an answer and any counterclaims that are available.
5. Once the pleadings are completed, the trial judge will conduct a pretrial conference to ensure evidence is properly preserved for trial.
6. If you have a technical issue to be resolved, such as an infringement of intellectual property, it is best to have a bench trial rather than a jury trial.
7. After a jury verdict has been offered into evidence at a trial, a posttrial motion may be to overrule the jury with a judgment notwithstanding the verdict.
8. A citation of a case that reads "476 U.S. 488" means the case will be found in volume 476 of the *United States Reports* at page 488.
9. A witness may be required to answer interrogatories just as a party to the lawsuit must.
10. Before a judge will accept a case for litigation, the plaintiff must prove the court has proper jurisdiction.

Multiple Choice

Directions: Use what you learned in this chapter to choose the best response to each of the prompts below.

1. In order to obtain federal jurisdiction a plaintiff must show all the following, except:
   a. diversity of citizenship
   b. a claim for at least $ 100,000
   c. a federal question exists
   d. all of the above

2. The purpose of the pretrial conference is to:
   a. set ground rules for the trial
   b. settle the case
   c. review jury instructions
   d. all of the above

3. The best method of discovery is:
   a. interrogatories
   b. depositions
   c. a simple telephone call
   d. all of the above
4. The answer serves the following purpose:
   a. admits or denies allegations
   b. sets forth the possible damages
   c. permits default judgments
   d. none of the above
5. All the following are major parts of the trial process, except:
   a. plaintiff's case in chief
   b. summation
   c. in camera review of evidence
   d. a and b
6. All the following are true, except:
   a. Before a trial is complete, the judge must enter the judgment in the record.
   b. A popular form of attorney compensation for both plaintiff and the defendant is the contingency fee.
   c. Service of process means the defendant has successfully completed the answer.
   d. In personam, in rem, and diversity are three types of state jurisdiction.
7. All the following are true, except:
   a. A civil litigation is not over until the judgment has been entered into the record.
   b. Interrogatories are questions posed, under oath, to a prospective witness.
   c. Depositions are oral questions posed outside the courtroom.
   d. The California State Supreme Court is comprised of seven justices.
8. All the following are true, except:
   a. Prior to challenging an agency rule, you must exhaust all administrative remedies.
   b. A trial is officially commenced after the opening statement to the jury.
   c. A typical action an appellate court can take is to call for rebuttal witnesses.
   d. ADR stands for alternative dispute reconciliation.
9. All the following are appellate court actions, except:
   a. advance
   b. affirm
   c. deny
   d. overrule

10. All the following are true for the trial phase of litigation, except:
    a. Summation is the step that that immediately precedes jury deliberation.
    b. Voir dire means jury selection.
    c. The plaintiff has a right to rebuttal, but the defendant does not.
    d. Defendant has the right to cross-examine Plaintiff's witnesses.

Scenarios

1. John filed a lawsuit in the state court for racial discrimination. He lost the trial and all his appeals in state courts, including the state supreme court. He decides to try his luck with an appeal to the U.S. Supreme Court. What will be the result? Explain your answer.
2. Mary, a New York resident, purchased a car from a dealership in Arizona. She ordered the vehicle based upon information on the dealership website. The car turned out to be a "lemon," and she sued in the New York Superior Court. The dealership filed a motion to quash the complaint for lack of in personam jurisdiction. What will be the result? Explain your answer.

Decisional Review

1. Plaintiff, a Pennsylvania manufacturing corp., in a trademark infringement case seeks personal jurisdiction over Defendant, a California internet company, for allegedly using Plaintiff's trademark in its domain name. Defendant provides memberships in an internet news service. Payment is by credit card over the internet or by telephone. It has all its offices and employees in California. The website provides information and advertisements regarding Defendant's internet products. Out of its 140,000 internet memberships, 3,000 are Pennsylvania residents. Will Plaintiff succeed? Explain your answer. See *Zippo Manufacturing Co. v. Zippo Dot Com, Inc.*, 952 F. Supp. 1119 (1997).
2. Plaintiff, a judgment creditor, filed suit against a major national bank asserting the bank was in violation of the Enforcement of Judgments Law. At issue was a lien placed on several certificates of deposit held by a client of the bank. The bank refused to honor Plaintiff's request for the lien, alleging it was not subject to the Enforcement of Judgments Law. The trial court granted the bank a judgment on the pleadings, and Plaintiff appeals. What will be the result? Explain your answer. See *Grayson Services v. Wells Fargo Bank*, 199 Cal. App. 4th 563 (2011).

Credits

Fig. 2.2: Source: https://www.courts.ca.gov/documents/pldpi001.pdf.
Fig. 2.3: Source: https://www.courts.ca.gov/documents/sum100.pdf.
Fig. 2.4: Source: https://www.courts.ca.gov/documents/pldpi003.pdf.

Chapter 3

Torts

Introduction

A tort is an act or failure to act that is committed by a person or entity against another person or entity. The person committing the tort is referred to as a tortfeasor. It is a civil cause of action usually remedied by payment of monetary damages. Torts are a very common occurrence in the hospitality industry and can be intentional or unintentional.

An intentional tort is an act that a tortfeasor knowingly commits. Intent to injure is not required. It can be a playful act, such as pushing someone to gain attention. This chapter will discuss intentional acts as opposed to unintentional acts. Unintentional torts occur because the tortfeasor has been careless in their behavior and a person is injured as a result. Unintentional torts are referred to as negligent acts and will be discussed in Chapter 4.

Chapter Objectives

Upon completion of this chapter, the student will understand:

- the nature of a cause of action in tort
- the various types of torts and their elements
- the defenses to the various types of torts
- how to recognize the torts common to the hospitality industry and ways to avoid them
- the usual types of damages associated with a tort cause of action

Key Terms

Directions: Each of the terms below will be used in this chapter. Before reading, scan the chapter. The terms will appear in bold. Take a moment to see how the term is used so you can understand it in context. The terms are listed in the order in which they will appear in the chapter.

Tort (p. 48)
Intentional tort (p. 48)
Damages (p. 48)
Assault (p. 49)
Battery (p. 49)
Consent (p. 50)
Self-defense (p. 50)
Defense of others (p. 50)
Defense of property (p. 50)
False imprisonment (p. 50)
Intentional infliction of emotional distress (p. 53)
Negligent infliction of emotional distress (p. 54)
Defamation (p. 54)
Libel (p. 54)
Slander (p. 55)
Public figure (p. 55)
Privileged speech (p. 58)
Privilege (p. 58)
Absolute privileged speech (p. 58)
Legislative privilege (p. 58)
Qualified privilege (p. 59)
Misrepresentation of fact (p. 62)

The Basis of Tort Law

A **tort** in law is "a civil wrong, other than breach of contract, for which a remedy may be obtained, usually in the form of damages; as such, a tort represents a breach of a duty that the law imposes on persons who stand in a particular relation to one another" (Garner 2005, 1247). It is an act or failure to act committed by a person or entity against another person or entity. A tort differs from a criminal act because the sanction is usually money damages rather than incarceration in a jail. Accordingly, the wrong is resolved in a civil litigation rather than a criminal proceeding.

Tort law is premised upon societal recognition that certain personal interests, such as personal safety, require protection (protected interests). The law holds those responsible for wrongful conduct liable for the damages they cause. "Tortfeasor" is legalese for the wrongdoer. For the purposes of this text, the term "defendant" will be used instead of tortfeasor because it is more commonly understood. Tort law provides the means by which a remedy is obtained for a violation of the protected interests of a person or an entity. Chapter 4 discusses unintentional torts, commonly referred to as "negligence."

Intentional Torts

An **intentional tort** is one committed by someone acting with general or specific intent. This action is also termed "willful torts" (Garner 2005, 1247). General intent means the defendant intended to do the act that caused the injury. Specific intent means the defendant also intended to do the injury. Some examples of intentional torts include battery, false imprisonment, and trespass to land. Engaging in business activity always carries a risk something may go wrong and someone may be injured. The injury will usually result in a lawsuit for damages unless the matter is settled outside of court (see "Anatomy of a Litigation" discussed in Chapter 2).

An example of an intentional tort related to the hospitality industry is the consumption of spoiled food at a restaurant. A guest who orders food at a restaurant expects to receive a meal that is safe to eat. This expectation creates a legal duty for the restaurant to provide a safe, edible meal. Assume a restaurant knowingly serves food, despite its spoiled condition, and the guest becomes ill. The restaurant has breached the above-referenced duty, caused the illness, and is liable for any **damages** that result from serving the spoiled food. Damages could be medical expenses, lost wages if the person is unable to go to work, and even emotional distress caused by the incident.

An intentional tort is based on a defendant's intentional action (as opposed to unintentional action, called "negligence"). The requisite intent need not be malicious, and the defendant does not need specific intent to injure the plaintiff. The act may have been perceived by the defendant as beneficial. For example, consider the waiter in a restaurant who pulls a chair from the table to assist seating a guest. In doing so, however, the waiter fails to ensure the guest is positioned safely to sit, and the guest falls and suffers an injury. In this instance, the waiter was without malice and was well-intentioned; however, the act to assist the guest was intentional. That intent is referred to as general intent, and that is the requisite intent to qualify as an intentional tort.

Now assume the guest is a frequent patron of the restaurant who is routinely verbally abusive to the wait staff. The waiter has been waiting for an opportunity to get even with the patron, and in this instance, he intentionally pulled the chair back before the patron could safely sit down. This incident is an example of specific intent because the waiter intended for the patron to fall.

Using the same example, let us suppose that the chair in question had defective legs, and the chair collapsed when the guest sat down. In this instance, the restaurant would be liable for not checking and ensuring that the chair was safe to use. This unfortunate situation is considered an unintentional tort, called negligence, which will be discussed in Chapter 4.

In this chapter we will discuss the intentional torts most often encountered in business, the elements of each, and we will consider proactive ways to avoid or mitigate the problem. Intentional torts are separated into two groups: torts against a person and torts against property.

The most common intentional torts against a person are assault, battery, false imprisonment, intentional infliction of emotional distress, defamation, invasion of privacy, appropriation, and fraudulent misrepresentation.

Assault is an intentional act that is "the threat or the use of force on another that causes that person to have a reasonable apprehension of imminent harmful or offensive contact" (Garner 2005, 92). It is placing a person in fear or apprehension of a battery. The person guilty of the assault must have the capability of causing the threatened harm. For example, a thin, short 12-year-old boy who threatens to beat a tall, 200-pound, muscular man to death probably would not create the requisite fear to be guilty of assault. But the same boy pointing a gun at the same man could certainly create fear.

A **battery** is "an intentional and offensive touching of another without lawful justification" (Garner 2005, 125). It does not have to cause physical injury and may only be an unwanted touching. It can be an unconsented touch on the shoulder of a person, a slight kiss on the cheek, or an arm around the waist. For example, a stranger may see a person of the opposite sex that is attractive. In an attempt to flirt, the stranger may approach the person, place an arm around the person's shoulders, and make a suggestive remark. This action is technically a battery, although in reality, without more, this would probably not lead to a lawsuit or a criminal prosecution.

KEY CONCEPT FOCUS 3.1. ASSAULT AND BATTERY

The tort of assault and battery is often referred to as one incident. Technically, however, they are two separate torts, each of which occurs independent of the other. Assault creates a fear of an immediate harmful and unconsented touching, but it falls short of the physical touching.

For example, assume a restaurant patron disputes a bill and insults a restaurant employee in the process. The employee becomes enraged and attempts to punch the patron in the face but misses. The patron was not hit but did experience fear that the punch might have landed. This is an instance of assault because physical contact was not made. If the employee connected with the punch, it would be an assault and battery. Keep in mind the patron experienced fear prior to the landing of the punch. If the punch had been thrown and connected when the patron was not looking, only a battery would occur. The patron did not see the punch and could not have experienced the necessary fear of an assault.

KEY CONCEPT FOCUS 3.2. DEFENSES TO THE TORT OF ASSAULT AND BATTERY

The law recognizes that certain action is reasonably necessary to protect one's self or one's property. Such action is referred to as a "defense to the torts of assault and battery." The following are common defenses:

Consent. If a person consents to the act that causes injury, there generally is no liability. For example, participants in a "Ladies Night Boxing Match" at a local bar expect to be punched, and they would not have a cause of action for assault or battery against each other.

Self-defense. In the example involving the restaurant billing dispute above, assume the patron threw and connected with the first punch, and the employee returned the punch to protect himself. Since the employee was not the aggressor and was only protecting himself, the employee would not be liable in a cause of action for assault and battery. However, the patron who threw the first punch would be liable for assault and battery.

Defense of others. If a patron starts a fight in the restaurant/bar with another patron, an employee may take reasonable action to restrain the aggressor, without fear of liability, since the employee defended the attacked patron.

Defense of property. If the patron in the bar fight (mentioned above) becomes enraged and decides to pick up a chair and start to break it on the bar, the employee may take reasonable action to restrain the patron from damaging the chair or the bar without fear of liability.

False imprisonment is the intentional confinement or "restraint of a person in a bounded area without reasonable justification or consent" (Garner 2005, 508). Assume a patron consumes a meal that costs $44.00, plus the patron adds a $6.00 gratuity. He leaves a 50-dollar bill on the table to pay for the meal. The patron gets up, puts on his coat, and leaves the table. As he placed his arms in the sleeves and swings the coat over his shoulders to secure it, the movement creates a breeze that knocks the bill to the floor.

The waiter goes to the table and finds no payment and also sees the patron leaving. The waiter believes the patron is "dining and dashing" (restaurant parlance for leaving without paying the bill). The employee becomes infuriated, detains the patron at the door, and demands payment. The patron tries to explain that he left the money on the table, but the waiter will not listen. Instead, the waiter forces the patron into the restaurant office and calls the police.

In this case, the waiter will be guilty of false imprisonment for being unreasonable and failing to check for the missing 50-dollar bill and also for restraining the patron's movement without reasonable justification. As a consequence, both the waiter and the restaurant owner would be liable for false imprisonment.

The owner of the restaurant would be liable under the theory of *respondeat superior* (Latin for "Let the master answer"; discussed below) for the acts of his employee during the course of employment. In addition, a charge of assault would be viable because the waiter accosted the patron at the door (creation of fear). Finally, a charge of battery would also lie because the waiter physically forced the person into the office (offensive touching).

FALSE IMPRISONMENT

False imprisonment is the unreasonable restraint of a person's movement without justification. It is commonly found in retail operations when poorly trained loss-prevention personnel attempt to prevent a suspected thief from leaving the premises until police arrive. The best practice is for loss prevention to wait until the suspected thief passes the cash register or exits the door. Until that occurs, a person can always say they are still shopping and intended to pay upon departure. The following case is an example of alleged false imprisonment by police officers.

[I504 SO.2D 1205]

Supreme Court of Mississippi.
David THORNHILL
v.
Terry WILSON, John Pittman, W.R. Selman and City of Columbia.
No. 56474.
April 8, 1987.

Facts: David Thornhill was camping with his family. The police department received a call regarding a person shooting excessively in the area. The police were dispatched to investigate. They encountered Mr. Thornhill with his family and commenced an inquiry. Mr. Thornhill denied firing a weapon and his wife corroborated his denial. Mr. Thornhill was slightly inebriated and became verbally confrontational. The officers placed Mr. Thornhill in their police vehicle for further interrogation. He was released after approximately five minutes. Mr. Thornhill filed a lawsuit alleging, among other things that he was arrested without probable cause and that the police officers and the City of Columbia were guilty of false imprisonment. The trial court found defendants not guilty and Mr. Thornhill appealed.

The Court of Appeals:

"Our law respects the individual's interest in freedom from confinement. The decision to afford this respect proceeds from long felt notions of the inviolability of the person. [Citations omitted.] Correlative to each person's duty to respect this interest in each other is the right of recovery of and from one who falsely confines another. [Citations omitted.] The tort of false imprisonment involves two elements: detention of the plaintiff and the unlawfulness of such detention; imprisonment and the falsity thereof. [Citations omitted.] Here there can be no question but that Thornhill was detained by Officers Pittman and Wilson acting at the behest of Alderman Selman and as officers of the City of Columbia. Our focus is upon the legality vel none [Latin "or not"] of Thornhill's detention. This leads in turn to an inquiry into the reasonableness of the actions of Officers Pittman and Wilson. [Citations omitted.] Thornhill presents an excessively formalistic approach. If the detention was technically an "arrest," he argues Pittman and Wilson were without probable cause. If the detention was a "stop and frisk" detention, he argues that the officers exceeded their limited authority in that regard.

***

Eschewing formalistic jurisprudence, our concern is whether the actions of Pittman and Wilson in detaining Thornhill were objectively reasonable in their nature, purpose, extent and duration. We make this inquiry by reference to the totality of the circumstances reasonably apparent to persons situated as were Pittman and Wilson at the time.

***

It may well be that David Thornhill was in effect under arrest. [Citations omitted.] Nothing turns on the point, for in the present context our law affords a defense to one sued for false imprisonment that the plaintiff was temporarily detained for reasonable investigative purposes. [Citations omitted.]

On the basis of these principles, this Court has in other contexts authorized a number of reasonable detentions, justified by reasonable suspicion, short of probable cause. Griffin v. State, *339 So.2d 550 (Miss. 1976) (suspected shoplifter held for questioning);* Singletary v. State, *318 So.2d 873 (Miss. 1975) (suspected bank robber and store burglar stopped in auto);* Chapman v. State, *284 So.2d 525 (Miss. 1973) (speeders held for identification in connection with other crime);* Dotson v. State, *260 So.2d 839 (Miss. 1972) (suspected post office box burglary held by reason of peculiar gait and furtive movement);* Williams v. State, *210 So.2d 780 (Miss. 1968) (suspected house burglar held for fingerprinting).*

The law allows, indeed commands, that its officers investigate possible criminal activity. Reasonable opportunities therefor are conferred consistent with and without unnecessary sacrifice of the individual's interest in freedom from confinement. [Citations omitted.] A detention reasonable at its inception, however, may become unreasonable, and the imprisonment thus false, when it continues past the point where the officers' objectively reasonable needs for the detention cease to exist. [Citations omitted.]

Our review of the facts, of course, is undertaken in the context of a jury's verdict having been rendered for all defendants. In this context we are required to consider all of the evidence—not just the evidence which supports Defendants' case—in the light most favorable to the Defendants, who must also be given the benefit of all favorable inferences that may reasonably be drawn from the evidence. ... On the other hand, if there is substantial evidence in the record consistent with the verdict, that is, evidence of such quality and weight that reasonable and fair-minded men in the exercise of impartial judgment might have reached different conclusions one from the other, it follows that the motion for directed verdict and its post-trial renewal were correctly denied and that the jury's verdict should be allowed to stand. [Citations omitted.]

***

Beyond that, counsel argues vigorously that upon receiving Mrs. Thornhill's advice that there was no trouble, Pittman and Wilson should have released Thornhill. After that moment the detention became unreasonable and actionable, or so we are told. The record suggests that Thornhill's detention continued approximately five minutes after the officers' conversation with Mrs. Thornhill. The officers kept Thornhill in the police vehicle and drove back out to the point where his vehicle was situated. They there conducted a search for weapons. Considering the reports received from the never-identified woman who called the Columbia Police Department dispatcher, coupled with the fact that Thornhill was agitated and at least somewhat intoxicated, we are not prepared to second-guess the jury's obvious determination that it was reasonable for Officers Pittman and Wilson, rather than accepting Mrs. Thornhill's report that there was no trouble and releasing Thornhill, to make a further investigation for a weapon or weapons, perhaps recently fired. Having in mind the standards enumerated above, we certainly cannot say that the jury disregarded its oath in finding this additional five minutes detention reasonable both in its purpose, duration or extent. [Citations omitted.]

***

We hold that the jury's verdict in favor of all Defendants on the false imprisonment claim is, on this record, beyond our authority to disturb. This being the case, all other issues tendered by the parties, and these are several, fall by the wayside.

The tort of emotional distress can be caused by either intentional or negligent conduct. **Intentional Infliction of Emotional Distress** (IIED) is "the tort of intentionally or recklessly causing another person severe emotional distress through one's extreme or outrageous acts" (Garner 2005, 671). For example, suppose a restaurant employee, recently disciplined by the manager, decides to place the head of a rodent in the vegetable soup. The soup is served to a patron who commences dining. After consuming some of the otherwise delicious soup, the head starts to become visible. The patron scoops it up, realizes what it is, screams, and immediately starts to regurgitate, spewing the ingested soup over the table and on members of his dinner party. He passes out, and an ambulance takes him to the hospital where his stomach is pumped. Fragments of rodent skull and strands of rodent hair are retrieved. As a result of the incident, the patron cannot eat for a week. He loses 30 pounds and is unable to work for a month. He suffers from nightmares and decides to consult with a psychiatrist, who treats him for six months.

Under this scenario, the employee intentionally placed the head of the rodent in the soup. It does not matter if the employee intended the consequences that occurred. He may have thought the soup would not be sold because someone in the kitchen would find it before it was served. The important point is that he performed the act of placing a rodent head in the soup and is therefore guilty of IIED. The restaurant may also be guilty under the theory of respondeat superior.

INTENTIONAL INFLICTION OF EMOTIONAL DISTRESS

This intentional tort is very hard to prove. The conduct must be outrageous, malicious, and intended to cause severe emotional distress. A repeated threat, with perceived present capability to cause serious physical harm to a member of a person's family, would be an example of IIED. For example, suppose a neighbor is irate with your children crossing his front yard daily on the way to school. After months of such conduct and numerous requests for the children to stop, the neighbor decides to take matters in his own hands. He threatens the children with a baseball bat, and on occasion, he rushes toward them swinging the bat horizontally, but at a safe distance. Such conduct could induce enough fear in the children and you as well.

Now assume the same set of foregoing facts, except there is no evidence the rodent head was intentionally placed in the soup by any person. Without proof of an intentional act, the proper cause of action is negligent infliction of emotional distress. **Negligent infliction of emotional distress** is "the tort of causing another [person] severe emotional distress through one's negligent conduct" (Garner 2005, 873) rather than through a deliberate act. Negligence in this context is a breach of a duty of due care that causes the extreme emotional distress. The defendant would be the restaurant for its negligent failure to ensure its fare was edible. (Negligence is discussed further in Chapter 4.)

Defamation is making false factual statements about someone with the intent to harm their reputation. The statements may be written (libel) or verbal (slander) and must be heard by third parties (referred to as "publication"). Making such statements only to the intended victim is not actionable, because under that scenario there cannot be damage to one's reputation. Likewise, if the statement is true, there is no damage to one's reputation. Finally, if the statements are a matter of opinion, a cause of action may not be available. It has to be a statement of fact.

The First Amendment is not absolute, and defamation is an exception to that constitutional right. Defamation is defined as "the act of harming the reputation of another by making a false statement to a third person" (Garner 2005, 354). The elements of defamation include the following:

- a false statement of fact about another person
- publication of the statement to a third person
- statement damages another person's reputation

Truth is a defense to defamation, so the statement must be false. The statement must also be presented as one of fact, as opposed to an opinion. Assume a food critic, in a newspaper article, alleges that the food served at Wolfgang Puck's restaurants are not original creations, but created and catered by several local chefs.

The statement is one that can be proved or disproved by an investigation. It is a statement presented as fact and not the food critic's opinion. Therefore, the statement is subject to a defamation lawsuit and liability if proven false. Assume the critic also states the following: "Wolfgang Puck's food tastes lousy, like it was prepared with butcher scraps and more suitable to be served to wolves not people." Arguably, this latter statement is one of opinion, and it may not subject to a defamation lawsuit.

Assessing damages is often difficult in defamation cases. In our example above, several factors come into play. First, defamation comes in two general forms: written and verbal. Written defamation, such as the newspaper article referenced above, is called **libel** and it does not require the plaintiff to prove general damages.

Written defamation has certain permanence and is easily republished by recipients of the damaging statements. Therefore, the law presumes general damages, such as emotional distress, have occurred. The trier of fact need only decide the appropriate amount.

Verbal defamation is called **slander** and is less permanent and, as such, not as harmful to the plaintiff. Therefore, the law requires that special damages as well as general damages be proven for slander to lie. In the Wolfgang Puck example, loss of business is something that can be measured and assessed as special damages. If loss of business is shown, special damages as well as general damages are recoverable (see Key Concept Focus 3.4).

Second, Wolfgang Puck is a public figure. A **public figure** "is a person who has achieved fame or notoriety or who has voluntarily become involved in a public controversy" (Garner 2005, 1027). A public figure (or public official) suing for defamation must prove the defendant acted with actual malice. Actual malice is defined as "knowledge (by the person who utters or publishes a defamatory statement) that a statement is false, or [with] reckless disregard about whether the statement is true" (Garner 2005, 799).

The lives of public figures are deemed by the law as worthy of public discussion; thus, a higher standard of proof is required to find liability. Moreover, society feels public figures differ from the average person, and because of their notoriety, they are deemed to voluntarily call for public scrutiny, which invites comment about their lives. Also, a public figure can easily call a press conference to rebut false statements, a capability unavailable to the average citizen (see *New York Times v. Sullivan*, 376 U.S. 254 below). If the food critic was repeating statements they heard through general industry gossip, the requisite malice may be absent, and Wolfgang Puck may not have a cause of action.

---

84 S.CT. 710

Supreme Court of the United States
The NEW YORK TIMES COMPANY, Petitioner,
v.
L. B. SULLIVAN.
Ralph D. ABERNATHY et al., Petitioners,
v.
L. B. SULLIVAN.
Nos. 39, 40.
Argued Jan. 6 and 7, 1964. Decided March 9, 1964.

Synopsis

A New York newspaper published an "editorial" advertisement communicating information, expressing opinion, reciting grievances, protesting claimed abuses, and seeking financial support on behalf of the Negro right-to-vote movement and the Negro student movement. An elected commissioner of the City of Montgomery, Alabama, brought a civil libel action against the publisher of the newspaper and against Negro and Alabama clergymen whose names appeared in the advertisement. The Circuit Court, Montgomery County, Alabama, entered a judgment on a verdict awarding $500,000 to the plaintiff and the defendants appealed. The Supreme Court of Alabama [Citations Omitted] affirmed, and certiorari was granted. The Supreme Court, Mr. Justice Brennan, *held that the rule of law applied by the Alabama courts was constitutionally deficient for failure to provide the safeguards for freedom of speech and of the press that are required by the First and Fourteenth Amendments in a libel action brought by a public official against critics of his official conduct, and that under the proper safeguards the evidence presented in the case was constitutionally insufficient to support the judgment for the plaintiff.*

This proposition [libel against government] has disquieting implications for criticism of governmental conduct. For good reason, no court of last resort in this country has ever held, or even suggested, that prosecutions for libel on government have any place in the American system of jurisprudence.

***

The second contention is that the constitutional guarantees of freedom of speech and of the press are inapplicable here, at least so far as the Times is concerned, because the allegedly libelous statements were published as part of a paid, "commercial" advertisement.

***

The publication here was not a "commercial" advertisement in the sense in which the word was used in Chrestensen. It communicated information, expressed opinion, recited grievances, protested claimed abuses, and sought financial support on behalf of a movement whose existence and objectives are matters of the highest public interest and concern.

***

*Under Alabama law as applied in this case, a publication is "libelous per se" if the words "tend to injure a person *** in his reputation" or to "bring (him) into public contempt"; the trial court stated that the standard was met if the words are such as to "injure him in his public office, or impute misconduct to him in his office, or want of official integrity, or want of fidelity to a public trust ***." The jury must find that the words were published "of and concerning" the plaintiff, but where the plaintiff is a public official his place in the governmental hierarchy is sufficient evidence to support a finding that his reputation has been affected by statements that reflect upon the agency of which he is in charge. Once "libel per se" has been established, the defendant has no defense as to stated facts unless he can persuade the jury that they were true in all their particulars. [Citations omitted.]*

***

The question before us is whether this rule of liability, as applied to an action brought by a public official against critics of his official conduct, abridges the freedom of speech and of the press that is guaranteed by the First and Fourteenth Amendments.

***

The maintenance of the opportunity for free political discussion to the end that government may be responsive to the will of the people and that changes may be obtained by lawful means, an opportunity essential to the security of the Republic, is a fundamental principle of our constitutional system. [Citations omitted.] It is a prized American privilege to speak one's mind, although not always with perfect good taste, on all public institutions. [Citations omitted.]

***

We hold today that the Constitution delimits a State's power to award damages for libel in actions brought by public officials against critics of their official conduct. Since this is such an action, the rule requiring proof of actual malice is applicable. While Alabama law apparently requires proof of actual malice for an award of punitive damages, where general damages are concerned malice is "presumed." Such a presumption is inconsistent with the federal rule. [Citations omitted.]

***

Applying these standards, we consider that the proof presented to show actual malice lacks the convincing clarity which the constitutional standard demands, and hence that it would not constitutionally sustain the judgment for respondent under the proper rule of law.

***

The judgment against them is thus without constitutional support.

This proposition has disquieting implications for criticism of governmental conduct. For good reason, "no court of last resort in this country has ever held, or even suggested, that prosecutions for libel on government have any place in the American system of jurisprudence." [Citations omitted.]

***

Raising as it does the possibility that a good-faith critic of government will be penalized for his criticism, the proposition relied on by the Alabama courts strikes at the very center of the constitutionally protected area of free expression. We hold that such a proposition may not constitutionally be utilized to establish that an otherwise impersonal attack on governmental operations was a libel of an official responsible for those operations.

***

The judgment of the Supreme Court of Alabama is reversed and the case is remanded to that court for further proceedings not inconsistent with this opinion.

Reversed and remanded.

KEY CONCEPT FOCUS 3.3. DEFAMATION

Consider the hypothetical assertion in a magazine that "the food served at Wolfgang Puck's restaurants are not original creations, but created and catered by several local chefs":

Since the statement is one of fact concerning Wolfgang Puck's culinary abilities, the statement's truth is in dispute. If it is a false statement, it could be actionable.

Since the statement is about Wolfgang Puck, it meets the requirement of another person.

Publication, in the context of defamation, means communicating the statement to other persons. It does not mean it has to be published in a newspaper. It can be just an oral statement to another person. If the statement of fact was made by the critic directly to Wolfgang Puck and no one else, it would not be actionable even if it was false. Without a third-party hearing or reading the statement, there is no publication. If it is published in a magazine, it would be libelous and general damages presumed.

Unless it can be shown that the statement damaged Wolfgang Puck's reputation, there is no cause of action for a defamation suit. For example, suppose Wolfgang Puck could show he lost revenues at his restaurants because of reduced patronage shortly after the statement. The loss in revenue could be proof of the damage caused by the statement.

Privileged Speech

As mentioned above, truth is a defense to defamation. Another defense to defamation is **privileged speech.** In certain circumstances, in order to promote free and uninhibited speech, the law permits certain persons to make statements normally considered libelous or slanderous. **Privilege** is defined as "a special legal right, exemption, or immunity granted to a person or class of persons; an exception to a duty" (Garner 2005, 1004). As to speech there are two types: absolute privileged speech and qualified privileged speech.

Absolute privileged speech is "a privilege that immunizes an actor from suit, no matter how wrongful the action might be, and even though it is done with an improper motive" (Garner 2005, 1004). It is applied to officials during certain government proceedings referred to as **legislative privilege**, which is defined as "the privilege protecting (1) any statement made in a legislature by one of its members, and (2) any paper published as part of the legislative business" (Garner 2005, 1004). For example, in Congress elected officials may call each other slanderous names during legislative hearings and not be subject to defamation lawsuits. References to each other as cheats, liars, and frauds is common lexicon during congressional debates.

It also exists in judicial proceedings. Judges and lawyers in a court of law enjoy absolute privileged speech. For example, prosecutors in the court room proceedings and reporters covering the O.J. Simpson murder trial openly called him a murderer. Even though he was subsequently found not guilty, he can't sue for defamation, because of the absolute privilege.

The law recognizes such exceptions to defamation because it is in the public interest to promote unfettered speech in those venues. Otherwise, people would refrain from thoroughly pursuing their responsibilities or perhaps not accept careers fraught with potential legal liability.

Qualified privilege "is a privilege that immunizes an actor from suit only when the privilege is properly exercised in the performance of a legal or moral duty" (Garner 2005, 1004). It exists in situations when a person shares confidential information

- in good faith,
- to a limited audience, and
- with those who have a legitimate interest in the information.

An example would be written evaluations of employees circulated within a business entity for a legitimate business purpose, such as a promotion. Assume John Smith, the manager for the department of food and beverage in a golf country club, is vying to become the replacement general manger. He was written up several times by the former general manager for enjoying too many samples of alcohol with his favorite vendors. The reports are in his personnel file.

The director of human resources may share those records with the search committee for their consideration of John as a nominee to replace the outgoing general manager. The information is normally confidential, but the search committee is a limited audience with a legitimate interest in the information. The information is relevant to the fitness of John Smith for the position of general manager, and the director of human resources provides it in good faith.

A different result would occur if John Smith was not seeking to become the general manager and the director of human resources just did not like him. In this case, the director of human resources was circulating the information for the purpose of trying to get John fired. This situation would not be protected by the qualified privilege. Our society places a high value on a person's reputation and their privacy. Hence, there is a very active legal practice in defamation law.

Fraudulent Misrepresentation

This tort requires the defendant to make false material factual statements with the intent to cause a person to take action they would not ordinarily do. It also is usually in the context of business transactions, such as selling a house or car and promises to prospective employees. For example, often with real estate sales, the owner fails to disclose a major defect in the property, such as a severely cracked foundation. After several years from the date of the purchase, the new owner discovers the home has slipped partially off the foundation. It takes $25,000 to repair. The seller will likely be subject to damages for fraudulent misrepresentation.

Fraudulent misrepresentation is defined as "the act of making a false or misleading assertion about something, usually with the intent to deceive" (Garner 2005, 838). It occurs when a person or entity makes an untrue statement that is known to be false or a statement made recklessly without knowing or caring whether it is true or false, and it is intended to induce a party to detrimentally rely upon it. The elements are as follows:

- a misrepresentation of material fact
- intent to deceive a person
- justifiable reliance by the deceived person
- causation
- damages to the deceived person

In the restaurant business, a menu is an area where fraudulent misrepresentation occurs frequently. Unscrupulous restaurateurs may list an item on the menu incorrectly in order to attract customers. The vast majority of restaurant patrons can't tell the difference between the food fraudulently misrepresented and the dish served. Therefore, the practice is often used because the likelihood of a challenge is very low.

Many states have adopted truth-in-menu statutes that require disclosure of calories and other nutritional information. The purpose of such statutes is to prevent unscrupulous restaurateurs from intentionally distorting the contents of their menus to lure unsuspecting diners into ordering food at their establishment.

Hotels often make false claims concerning the availability of rooms. The following case demonstrates the consequences for making a false representation regarding room availability at a hotel for a convention.

---

157 GA.APP. 497

Court of Appeals of Georgia.
MARRIOTT CORPORATION
v.
AMERICAN ACADEMY OF PSYCHOTHERAPISTS, INC.
No. 60844.
Feb. 11, 1981.

Synopsis

Plaintiff, an association of psychotherapists, brought suit against hotel where it was to hold a convention alleging willful misrepresentation of material fact and breach of contract. The State Court, Fulton County, Moran, J., entered judgment in favor of association, and hotel appealed. The Court of Appeals, McMurray, P. J., held that: (1) evidence, which indicated that defendant was aware of its having overbooked its hotel to such an extent as to create a substantial likelihood that it would be unable to meet plaintiff's needs during its convention and that defendant continued to represent to plaintiff that plaintiff's convention could and would be handled by defendant as planned by plaintiff, was sufficient to present jury question as to whether defendant was guilty of willful misrepresentation of fact;

***

Affirmed on condition.

Opinion

**497 McMURRAY, Presiding Judge.*

*In the Fall of 1973, American Academy of Psychotherapists, Inc. (the "Academy"), entered an agreement with Marriott Corporation ("Marriott") whereby it was to hold a convention at Marriott's downtown Atlanta motor hotel during the Fall of 1975. Marriott confirmed by letter that it was "definitely holding space for the 1975 convention," **787 initially projecting 100 guest rooms and various conference rooms for workshops, meetings and meals. Marriott further indicated that it was "open to some flexibility" but requested the Academy to finalize its program at least six months prior to its "arrival date."*

During the months that followed, the Academy made various arrangements for its convention and frequently communicated with Marriott regarding revisions in its original plans. In April, 1974, Marriott reconfirmed the convention reservations. In April, 1975, following another "update" by the Academy, Marriott wrote that there may be some difficulties in handling certain of the requirements for meeting rooms, but concluded, "It appears that you will fit perfectly, and that you can expect good attendance and a good show on our part."

***

Two weeks prior to the convention's opening day, the Academy's planning committee chairman, a Dr. Brown, became aware that Marriott might not have enough room for its convention. The Academy contends that following a series of telephone calls and meetings over the next three days it was learned that Marriott had booked another much larger convention at its hotel for dates that overlapped with the Academy's convention, and that Marriott consequently might be unable to handle the convention.

Eventually, Dr. Brown spoke with Marriott's resident manager and was advised that if the Academy's attendees arrived on the dates they had intended, "they would just stack up in the lobby; that there were no rooms available, and they could not evict the tenants (from the other convention)."

***

The Academy filed suit against Marriott on two counts, Count One for willful misrepresentation of fact and Count Two for breach of contract. In accordance with the jury's verdict, judgment was entered in plaintiff's favor in the amount of $1,500 in special damages and $5,000 in punitive damages. Defendant appeals.

Held:

"The five elements of fraud and deceit in Georgia are: (1) false representation made by the defendant; (2) scienter; (3) an intention to induce the plaintiff to act or refrain from acting in reliance by the plaintiff; (4) justifiable reliance by the plaintiff; (5) damage to the plaintiff." [Citations omitted.] Having reviewed the record and transcript, we find that the jury could reasonably conclude from the evidence presented that defendant was aware of its having overbooked the hotel to such an extent as to create a substantial likelihood that it would be unable to meet plaintiff's needs during its convention, and yet defendant continued to represent to plaintiff that plaintiff's convention could and would be handled by defendant as planned by plaintiff. The jury could also find that defendant continued to make such representations with an intent to induce plaintiff's reliance, and that plaintiff did justifiably rely thereon to its damage. "Fraud may not be presumed, but, being in itself subtle, slight circumstances may be sufficient to carry conviction of its existence."

Affirmed for Plaintiff

KEY CONCEPT 3.4. FRAUDULENT MISREPRESENTATION

Assume a seafood restaurant intentionally lists red snapper on its menu when in fact it is rockfish, a less desirable and cheaper species of fish. When cooked it is difficult for the average person to discern the difference. The following discussion applies the elements of misrepresentation to the restaurant menu example.

Misrepresentation of fact. The menu falsely asserts the fish served is red snapper when it is rockfish. This is a material fact for a seafood patron.

Intent. The intent to deceive is clearly present because the owner knows it is rockfish and lists it on the menu as red snapper at the higher price.

Justifiable reliance. The patron is a seafood fan but not an expert capable of appreciating the difference.

Causation. This is present because the restaurateur intentionally served the rockfish as red snapper, and the patron consumed and paid an inflated price for an inferior fish.

Damages. The patron is damaged because they purchased a cheaper fish at a higher price.

Torts Against Business Interests

The foundation of American business is competition and free enterprise. Accordingly, businesses devise many creative strategies to woo employees and customers away from their competition. Such conduct is encouraged and favored in American society and is referred to as "capitalism." The rationale for support of capitalism is that it creates competition, which reduces prices to consumers and increases product quality and service.

Elected officials and the courts aggressively protect capitalism through statutory and case law. However, there is a limit to what legislators and the courts will tolerate and what is considered fair competition and unlawful business practice. The two most commonly occurring unfair business practices are tortious interference with contracts and tortious interference with prospective advantage, discussed below.

Tortious interference with contractual relations is defined as "a third party's intentional inducement of a contracting party to breach a contract, causing damage to the relationship between the contracting parties" (Garner 2005, 1248). The elements for unlawful interference with contract relations are as follows:

- An existing contract must be in place.
- The third party must know of the contract.
- The third party must intentionally act to cause a breach of the contract.

For example, assume a very prominent chef has an existing contract with a five-star restaurant ("Five Star"), with several years left before contract expiration. Superior Restaurant ("Superior") knows of the contract and actively pursues the chef to leave and work for Superior. The CEO of Superior meets with the chef, offers to double his salary, pay moving expenses, and to pay any legal costs the chef may incur for breach of contract.

The chef realizes he has nothing to lose and a lot to gain and immediately leaves and joins Superior. As a result, Five Star suffers a serious decline in business. The conduct of Superior will likely be viewed by a court as unlawful interference because Superior went too far with its inducements to cause the chef to breach the contract with Five Star.

Superior's promise to double the salary and pay moving and legal expenses may exceed the normal competitive encouragement to switch employment. Accordingly, Superior may be liable for all associated damages caused by the breach of contract. Lost business profits of Five Star will probably be the major issue for the determination of monetary damages.

Now, assume the same facts as above, except Superior offers the chef a position only when his contract expires and he becomes available. Superior does not actively pursue the chef but merely encourages him to make contact when he is available. Under this scenario, if the chef leaves immediately, active interference is not present, and Superior may not be liable for tortious interference with contract relations. But the chef would be liable to Five Star for breach of contract.

Interference with contract is distinguishable from normal competition in business by its excessive activity with the existing contract that causes the breach.

Tortious Interference with Prospective Advantage (TIPA) is "an intentional damaging intrusion on another's potential business relationship, such as the opportunity of obtaining customers or employment" (Garner 2005, 1248). TIPA prohibits acts that unfairly interfere with businesses that share a market. It is the opposite of business competition and creates an anticompetitive restraint of trade through unfair competition.

Unfair competition is "dishonest or fraudulent rivalry in trade and commerce; especially, the practice of endeavoring to pass off one's own goods or products in the market for those of another by means of imitation or counterfeiting the name, brand, size, shape, or other distinctive characteristics of the article or its packaging" (Garner 2005, 1277). It is not fair competition, because the practices are attempts to solicit only those customers who have shown an interest in a similar product or service of a specific competitor rather than competitors in general. The elements for the tort of TIPA are as follows:

- The plaintiff must be an established business.
- The defendant engages in some form of unfair business practice.
- The plaintiff suffers damages as a result of the unfair business practice.

For example, assume two eateries are located relatively close on the second floor in a shopping mall. Restaurant A advertises on the radio for a special surf-and-turf lunch at an attractive discount price on a specified day. Restaurant B sends its employees to walk in front of the elevators on the designated date distributing leaflets with a similar advertisement reminding mall shoppers that the location for the surf-and-turf special is at Restaurant B.

Shoppers are now confused and believe that the surf-and-turf special is at Restaurant B and they go there to dine. The intent of Restaurant B is to divert patrons from Restaurant A to Restaurant B with a promise of the same special lunch without paying for the cost of the advertisement. Restaurant B's action is unfair and could be found to be a TIPA violation.

Intentional Torts Against Property

Intentional torts may also be committed against real and personal property. **Real property** is "land and anything growing on, attached to, or erected on it, excluding anything that may be severed without injury to the land" (Garner 2005, 1019). For example, a hotel constructed on a parcel of land is considered real property because it is affixed to the property and cannot be easily removed.

On the other hand, a mobile home used for business offices located on the same parcel is not real property, because it is relatively easily removed. It therefore is personal property, not real property. Personal property is "any movable or intangible thing that is subject to ownership and not classified as real property" (Garner 2005, 1018). A mobile home, because of its mobility, is treated like a motor vehicle rather than a building.

Common intentional torts against property include trespass to land, trespass to personal property, conversion, and disparagement of property. The first three of the foregoing can also be criminal violations.

Trespass to land occurs with "a person's unlawful entry on another's land that is visibly enclosed" (Garner 2005, 1258). The purpose of this tort is to protect a landowner's exclusive right to possession. A physical injury need not occur to have a violation, only the wrongful interference with the use of the land, such as entering the land or remaining on the land without permission. Assume a patron enters a bar to enjoy a couple of alcoholic beverages. He has one too many and becomes unruly. The bartender orders him out, but he refuses to leave and becomes combative. A fight ensues, and tables, chairs, bottles, and drinking glasses are broken.

When he entered the bar, he was a business invitee with permission to be on the property. Once he became unruly and ordered out, he lost his permission to remain on the property and became a trespasser. A trespass occurs when a person has permission to enter the land but later loses the right to remain. The patron may be ordered to leave the premises. If the guest refuses to leave, reasonable force may be used to ensure his departure.

A call to the police department may be required, which could subject the guest to an arrest for violating local trespass laws. Such an arrest is a criminal violation. In addition, if the guest destroys property on the premises, a civil lawsuit for trespass to personal property may also be available. His continued presence on the property will be a trespass to land. The fight will subject him to ejection and perhaps a criminal prosecution for assault and battery and/or a civil lawsuit for damages.

Society places special deference to possessors (owners and lessors) of land. The trespass includes the land and anything permanently affixed to the land, such as a building, trees, or agricultural crops. Physical damage to the property is not required for a trespass to land. Any unconsented interference with its use and possession or entrance onto the land will result in legal sanctions.

Trespass to personal property (also referred to as trespass to chattels) "occurs with the act of committing without lawful justification, an act of direct physical interference with a chattel possessed by another" (Garner 2005, 1258). The interference can be destruction of the property or anything that diminishes the value or quality of the property. In the example above, the broken tables, chairs, bottles, and drinking glasses are the personal property of the bar. The destruction of those items by the unruly patron is a trespass to personal property and liability for the replacement costs.

Anything not classified as real property is personal property. It is characterized as property readily moveable from the land. It includes furniture, fixtures, kitchenware, automobiles, and equipment. Agricultural crops become personal property when they are severed from the land. Trespass to personal property is an interference with or destruction of personal property.

Conversion occurs when a person takes an item of personal property without permission. It is "the wrongful possession or disposition of another's property as if it were one's own; an act or series of acts of willful interference, without lawful justification ... whereby that other person is deprived of the use and possession of the property" (Garner 2005, 282).

Conversion may also be a trespass to personal property because it is an interference with the use of that property. The basic difference between the two is that conversion usually occurs "with the intention to exercise permanent or temporary dominion over it" (Garner 2005, 282). In the example above, if a bar patron takes crystal drinking glasses home for personal use, a conversion rather than trespass to personal property has occurred. Such a conversion may also be a theft, which is a criminal violation.

Conversion may also occur with the innocent taking of the property of another. For example, a patron at a bar may mistakenly pick up a cell phone that belongs to the person sitting next to him and leave the premises. He may be liable for conversion because he took possession without permission. But he will not be guilty of the crime of theft, because he did not have criminal intent to steal. He mistakenly took the item.

Conversion is similar to a trespass to personal property except it is more than an interference or destruction to the property. It is an intentional act that deprives the owner of the personal property without permission. It is a theft that may be prosecuted criminally or civilly to obtain payment for its value. For example, a hotel guest who takes glassware or towels home as a souvenir is guilty of conversion.

Disparagement of property ("disparagement") occurs when "a person makes a false and injurious statement that discredits or detracts from the reputation of another's property, product, or business ... that caused a third party to take some action resulting in specific pecuniary loss to the plaintiff" (Garner 2005, 397). It is similar to defamation, which is making false and injurious statements about a person (see discussion of defamation). Disparagement includes slander of title and slander of goods.

Slander of title occurs when a person makes "a false statement, orally or in writing, that casts doubt on another person's ownership of property" (Garner 2005, 1156). Assume you own a successful hotel, and a competitor circulates flyers in the community suggesting you don't own the hotel but are just a front for the mafia. As a result, business declines, you lose income, and the bank forecloses the property. Your competitor is guilty of slander of title because you are the true owner. For another example, assume Quality Meats, a successful meat processing business, sells restaurants quality meat at a relatively low price. A competitor starts a false rumor stating that Quality Meats purchases some of its product from a wholesaler with a reputation for distributing stolen meat.

Slander of goods is "a false and injurious statement that discredits or detracts from the reputation of another's property, product, or business" (Garner 2005, 397). Assume you have a successful restaurant, and a competitor distributes a flyer alleging meat you serve is not the top quality you advertise, but it is instead "pink slime" (pink slime is the derogatory term associated with a low quality beef product comprised of a butcher's scrap meat). As a result, regular patrons go elsewhere for lunch or dinner, and business declines badly. Your competitor is guilty of slandering the quality of your beef and will be liable for your loss of business. It could also be **slander of quality**. For example, suppose a competitor makes a false statement that Quality Meats was recently cited by the health department for selling spoiled meat. This competitor would be guilty of slander of quality.

Many people rely on social media to decide where to dine. An emerging internet tactic used by unscrupulous business owners is to use social media to destroy a competitor's business. This is especially important if the restaurant or hotel is in a tourist area because out-of-towners do not have any other reasonable way to decide where the good eateries are located. For example, Mary owns a restaurant in a neighborhood that includes several competitors in close proximity. She decides to enlist her family and friends to access social media, such as Yelp, to falsely rate her competitor's food as being of poor quality and very expensive. This can be a very pernicious form of product disparagement because of the difficulty in ferreting out false ratings. There is no reasonable way to determine if the Yelp ratings are legitimate or contrived.

Special Tort Causes of Action

Invasion of privacy occurs when a person intentionally learns of private matters of another person. The U.S. Constitution, the various state constitutions, and statutory and common law have historically protected the privacy of individuals. Invasion of privacy is defined "as the unjustified exploitation of one's personality or intrusion into one's personal activities, actionable under tort law and sometimes under constitutional law" (Garner 2005, 685). It occurs when a person's solitude or personal affairs are invaded. American society places a very high value on privacy rights, and the courts vigorously enforce violations of those rights.

Unless you become a public figure, you have the right to be left alone. Assume a neighbor looks into your bedroom through a window and learns of your personal habits. If your neighbor teases you about your personal habits, they can be held liable for damages. Moreover, the neighbor cannot disclose the information publicly, even if the disclosure is truthful. In America, every person has a right to be left alone.

The U.S. Constitution does not expressly mention privacy rights, but the founding fathers clearly had them in mind when writing and amending the U.S. Constitution. The courts have held that the right to privacy is implicit in the Bill of Rights (see U.S. Const., Bill of Rights, see amendments 1–10). For example, the Constitution guarantees the right of people to be secure in their persons, houses, papers, and effects against unreasonable search and seizures (see U.S. Const., amend. IV). It requires a warrant based upon probable cause for the government to enter your home and search it and/or place you under arrest.

The Third Amendment prohibits the government from using private homes to house soldiers except in times of war. The Fifth Amendment prohibits self-incrimination and the right to remain silent when interrogated by police. It also prevents the taking of private property without due process of law. The aforementioned amendments adopted in 1791 were intended to protect persons from intrusion of privacy rights by federal officials.

The Bill of Rights has been judicially applied to the states by way of the Incorporation Clause of the 14th Amendment. Most states have expressly adopted privacy clauses in their state constitutions (see Cal. Const., Art. I, § 1, Inalienable Rights). As result, American jurisprudence has developed a large body of jurisprudence concerning privacy rights consisting of America's constitutional, statutory, and common law.

As mentioned earlier, privacy is a precious right held in high regard by Americans. It was an English common law protection passed on to America. Since the adoption of the U.S. Constitution (which is replete with provisions designed to protect our right to privacy), to modern statutory law, America has not wavered from this seminal bedrock constitutional principle.

The invasion of privacy consists of four separate causes of action: appropriation, invasion of seclusion and private affairs, portraying a person in a false light, and public disclosure of private facts.

Appropriation is "an invasion of privacy where one person takes the name or likeness of another for commercial gain" (Garner 2005, 84). It occurs when a person's name, likeness, or other identifying characteristic is used without permission. Assume a restaurant publishes an advertisement that states, "Magic Johnson loves our food and is a regular customer." The advertisement shows a picture of him devouring a huge plate of food at the restaurant taken when he dined there on one occasion. That was the only time he dined there, and the restaurant never asked his permission to use the picture or informed him the picture would be used in the advertisement. Magic Johnson could sue the restaurant for the tort of appropriation and obtain an injunction prohibiting further use and also damages for the wrongful use of his likeness.

Appropriation usually occurs in a business context when a name or likeness of a person is used without permission to promote a business, such as a picture or likeness of a famous person used in an advertisement. But sometimes, it is used in a different way that may just be invasion of privacy. For example, several members of the Los Angeles County Sheriff's Department reportedly took pictures of the Kobe Bryant crash site and also of Kobe Bryant's remains. If they were to sell those pictures to the media, they would be guilty of appropriation. If they just showed the pictures to friends, as reported, then that would be an invasion of privacy.

This privacy right protects one's identifiable characteristics from unconsented use by another for commercial gain. A person's name, likeness, picture, and motto are examples of the types of characteristics protected by this tort. But sometimes, the name, picture, or motto is not explicitly used. For example, Samsung Corporation was successfully sued by television personality Vanna White of *Wheel of Fortune* fame. They used a robot caricature of her in a setting similar to that of the *Wheel of Fortune* in a commercial. Even though neither her name nor the program's name were mentioned, the court felt the likeness was sufficient to justify liability under the tort of appropriation.

Portraying a person in a **false light** is "an invasion-of-privacy action in which the plaintiff alleges the defendant attributed views that he or she does not hold, and thus, placed the plaintiff before the public in a highly offensive and untrue manner" (Garner 2005, 508). It often occurs when untrue actions about a person are published. The advertisement that "Magic Johnson loves our food and is a regular customer" would qualify for this tort as well as appropriation. In this example, Magic Johnson only dined at the restaurant once and may actually hate the food and the service.

Publication of information that is intentionally attributed to a person and that is untrue, degrading, and unflattering may be portraying a person in a false light. A newspaper article printed a story of conservative evangelist Oral Roberts stating that he conceived a child with his mother in an outhouse while intoxicated. The court concluded that, outrageous as the article was, it was so unbelievable that it was not actionable.

Public disclosure of private facts is defined as "the public revelation of some aspect of a person's private life without a legitimate public purpose" (Garner 2005, 391). Disclosure of private facts may be acceptable for a public figure because the information is newsworthy (see discussion of defamation). However, the disclosure of the same type of information of a private citizen, even if true, could be actionable under this tort.

Also, the Fourth Amendment to the U.S. Constitution protects a person's right to be safe in their homes from illegal searches for information. Permitting such disclosure, even if true, would create incentives for pursuit of such information and is bad social policy. For example, the U.S. Supreme Court held that the right to privacy "is broad enough to encompass a woman's decision whether or not to terminate her pregnancy" (*Roe v. Wade*, 93 S. Ct. 705 (1973)).

Similarly, it occurs when a person obtains details of a very personal nature of another who is not a public figure and discloses the details publicly. For example, a talk show host decides to jokingly mention that his female neighbor seems to entertain a different man almost every night of the week. He states the men arrive carrying flowers around 8:00 p.m. in the evening and he sees them leave at 8:00 a.m. in the morning. It is irrelevant that his report is true. His neighbor has the right to do as she pleases, and the public has no right to know about her private affairs. If, on the other hand, his neighbor was a prominent movie star, it may be "newsworthy" and considered fair media disclosure.

Intrusion into a person's private life or seclusion is defined as "a highly offensive invasion of another person's seclusion or private life" (Garner 2005, 684). It occurs when, among other things, a private person invades another person's home, office, car, or briefcase. It is the parallel privacy right to the Fourth Amendment's prohibition of government from illegal search and seizure. This tort applies to private people, such as private investigators eavesdropping or wiretapping homes and gathering information without permission. It also applies to paparazzo chasing public figures to obtain photos for newspapers and magazines.

Internet Torts

Internet torts are not new torts with a unique set of elements. Instead, they are traditional torts committed online via the internet, such as, but not limited to, defamation, invasion of privacy, appropriation, interference with contract, and fraudulent misrepresentation. Plaintiffs in cyber tort cases have problems proving their cases when suing for damages because of difficulty identifying the defendant and difficulty determining what court location has jurisdiction (see discussion of jurisdiction in Chapter 2).

First, there is difficulty naming a defendant because it is hard to prove who was at the keyboard when the tort was committed. For example, a hotel may decide to portray a competitor in a false light by alleging the competitor recently experienced an infestation of bed bugs. Rather than attach its name as the sender, the hotel instead creates a phony news article as the source and has it sent to various websites, such as the local convention center. Such a process makes it difficult to ascertain the identity of the sender. Finding the originator of the news article may be even more difficult if the hotel hires a third party in a different state or country to send the phony news article.

Second, internet service providers (ISPs) provide forums for subscribers on social media networks to communicate with each other. Many defamatory statements are made by users of social media networks without the approval of the ISP. Under defamation tort law, republishers of defamatory statements are also liable for the false statements.

Should the ISP be held liable for permitting defamatory statements to be published on its network? The Communications Decency Act of 1996 (CDA) helped resolve that question. It provides that an ISP is not a publisher if it only provides retransmission and, therefore, is immune from a lawsuit (47 U.S.C. § 230). However, if the ISP creates documents and asks discriminatory questions of applicants, rather than just providing a retransmission of information, the ISP could be liable (see *Fair Housing Council of San Fernando Valley v. Roommate.com*, 666 F.3d 1216 (9th circ. 2012)).

A related problem occurs when the ISP knows who sent the statement because it has the names of all its subscribers in its electronic data base. A defamed person may try to obtain that information from the ISP without success. Under certain conditions, such as in a defamation lawsuit, a court may order disclosure of the name of the sender (see discussion of discovery in Chapter 2).

Summary

A tort is a civil wrong committed by a person or entity against another person or entity. The usual remedy is monetary damages, but an equitable remedy, such as an injunction, is also available.

Torts are either intentional or unintentional. Intentional torts are those committed with specific intent to act. They are not necessarily malicious or intended to cause harm. Unintentional torts are those that are not done with specific intent to act but are usually accidental and are referred to as negligent torts (the subject of Chapter 4). Intentional torts are classified as either torts against a person or torts against property. An intentional tort may also be subject to criminal sanctions. For example, conversion may be prosecuted as a criminal theft as well as a civil tort.

The two general categories of intentional torts are torts against a person and torts against property. The most common torts against a person are assault, battery, false imprisonment, defamation, intentional infliction of emotional stress, invasion of privacy, appropriation, and fraudulent misrepresentation.

The most common torts against property are wrongful interference with business relations and wrongful interference with contract relations. Torts against property include trespass to land, trespass to personal property, conversion, and disparagement of property, such as slander of title and slander of goods.

Intentional torts can be internet torts, which are generally not new torts but traditional torts that are committed over the internet. They pose special legal problems because of unique technological characteristics. The law is still evolving as the courts grapple with the new type of cases, such as anonymous defamation experienced by litigants.

Comprehension Check

True/False

Directions: Look at each statement below. Based on what you learned in this chapter, decide if the statement is true or false.

1. The difference between the tort of assault and the tort of battery is the unlawful touching.
2. The theory of tort law is that people should be free from an unwanted invasion of their person and property.
3. An intentional tort is committed by a person only if the wrongdoer wants to inflict harm.
4. Assault and battery is a single consolidated cause of action.
5. If a fight ensues in a restaurant, employees may use reasonable force to intervene only if there exists an attack on a person not for property breakage.
6. False imprisonment can occur either by intentional or negligent conduct.
7. Emotional distress can occur only by an intentional tort.
8. Wrongful interference with contract relations is a breach-of-contract issue.
9. Wrongful interference with a business relationship is a tort and not a breach-of-contract issue.
10. A tort is classified into two general categories: intentional and unintentional.
11. Defamation is the unintentional publication of false statements that damage a person's reputation.
12. Appropriation is the intentional tort of taking someone's property without permission.
13. Fraud is the intentional making of a false material statement with the intent to deceive justifiably relied upon by the victim.
14. Public figures cannot be defamed, because the law considers their notoriety as a matter of public interest.
15. Any person's private life is fair public commentary if it violates statutory or common law.

Multiple Choice

Directions: Use what you learned in this chapter to choose the best response to each of the prompts below.

1. Regarding fraud all the following are true, except:
   a. It must be of a material fact.
   b. It may be unintentional.
   c. It must cause measurable damage.
   d. There must be justifiable reliance by the victim.

2. All of the following are intentional torts against a person, except:
   a. portraying a person in a false light
   b. intrusion in a person's seclusion
   c. conversion
   d. appropriation

3. All the following are true, except:
   a. Slander of title is not an intentional tort.
   b. Slander of goods refers to false statements about a person's product.
   c. Disparagement of property refers to false statements about a person's property, product, or business.
   d. The slandered party must prove damages.

4. Invasion of privacy is a general tort that includes all the following, except:
   a. appropriation
   b. portraying a person in a false light
   c. peeping into your neighbor's window
   d. public disclosure of private facts

5. Intentional torts against property includes all the following, except:
   a. trespass to land
   b. trespass to personal property
   c. conversion
   d. disparagement of property

6. The elements of wrongful interference with business relations include all the following, except:
   a. fair competition
   b. an established business
   c. damages
   d. violation of an unfair business practices statute

7. The elements of wrongful interference with contract relations include all the following, except:
   a. an existing contract
   b. The third party must be engaging in competition with the plaintiff.
   c. The third party must be aware of the contract.
   d. The third party must intentionally act to cause a breach of contract.

8. Privileged speech includes all the following, except:
   a. absolute speech
   b. qualified speech
   c. malicious speech
   d. an attorney's untrue accusations in a public trial

9. The elements of defamation include all the following, except:
   a. a false statement
   b. publication to others
   c. innuendo
   d. damage to a person's reputation

10. Damages for tort causes of action include all the following, except:
    a. compensatory
    b. special
    c. unforeseeable
    d. general

Scenarios

1. John lived in an apartment next door to a very good friend, Peter. They were used to just walking into each other's home after knocking on the door without waiting to be formally welcomed into each other's apartment. One afternoon John entered Peter's apartment in the usual manner. He was surprised to find Peter and a young lady whom he didn't know engaging in sexual foreplay on the couch. He laughed heartily, apologized, and excused himself from the apartment.

   The next day Peter went to the local bar for happy hour, which he, Peter, and multiple friends ritually did. When he walked in, the patrons erupted in laughter and made such comments as "Atta boy!" and "Peter, we understand that you are quite the ladies' man!!" John chimed in, "You deserve a drink on me!!" What cause of action might Peter have, if any? Would there be a different result if Peter had informed John the previous day that he would be entertaining a lady friend?

2. Bill and Steve were teammates on a baseball team. Bill would disregard the hitting coach's instructions, and as a result, the team lost several straight games. Steve would constantly argue with Bill when Bill disregarded the hitting coach's instructions, and it was costly to the team. The last time an argument occurred, Bill took a swing with his baseball bat at Steve as he was walking away, just missing his head, but making contact with Steve's shoulder. Steve filed a complaint with the police alleging assault and battery. What will be the result? Explain your answer.

Decisional Review

1. A contract existed between a restaurant and a vending machine company. The vending machine company provided soft drinks and snacks, such as potato chips and candy. A competitor of the vending machine company contacted the restaurant and convinced the restaurant to break its contract and enter a contract with it. The competitor promised to convert the restaurant into a sports bar, with multiple television sets and sports programing plus more sophisticated vending machines. The competitor also physically removed the existing vending machines and placed them in storage. The competitor promised to pay any legal fees the restaurant might incur for breaking its contract. The vending machine company sued the competitor. What will be the result? See *Melo-tone v. Sherry*, 656 N.E.2nd 312 (Mass. 1995).
2. Plaintiff, a building maintenance company, sued Defendant, a convention center, for interference with contract and economic interests. Plaintiff and Defendant were parties to a contract for maintenance. Defendant changed its policy and sought to require its employees be used for separate contracts with

decorators of exhibits. It also required all maintenance contracts share profits with the convention center. Jury found for Plaintiff, but trial court granted a motion by Defendent for judgment as a matter of law. Ruling that Plaintiff could not sue, because it had an economic interest in the contract in question. As such, the facts do not cover the elements for interference with contractual relations. Plaintiff appealed. What will be the result? Explain your answer. See *United Nat'l Maintenance v. San Diego Convention Center*, 766 F. 3d 1002.

Chapter 4

Negligence

Introduction

Negligence is a tort that occurs without the general or specific intent described in Chapter 3 regarding intentional torts. Negligence is the result of careless behavior that a defendant accidentally causes. It is based upon the breach of a duty created by notice, common law, or statutory law. Negligent torts occur far more often than intentional torts. Therefore, it merits a separate chapter of study. Chapter 4 describes the nature, purpose, damages, and defenses associated with negligence.

Chapter Objectives

Upon completion of this chapter, the student will understand:

- the purpose of negligence law
- the elements of a negligent cause of action
- the negligence causes of action that affect the hospitality industry
- defenses for negligence claims
- damages applicable to negligence

Key Terms

Directions: Each of the terms below will be used in this chapter. Before reading, scan the chapter. The terms will appear in bold. Take a moment to see how the term is used so you can understand it in context. The terms are listed in the order in which they will appear in the chapter.

Negligence (p. 76)
Proximate cause (p. 77)
Duty (p. 77)
Breach (p. 77)
Causation (p. 77)
Injury (p. 77)
Damages (p. 77)
Societal interests (p. 78)
Business invitee (p. 79)
Duty of due care (p. 79)
Actively vigilant (p. 79)
Negligence audit (p. 79)
Licensee (p. 84)
Trespasser (p. 84)
Underaged person (p. 84)
Reasonable person standard (p. 85)
Trier of fact (p. 85)
Bench trial (p. 85)
Jury trial (p. 85)
Intervening event (p. 86)
Compensatory damages (p. 88)
Special damages (p. 88)
General damages (p. 88)
Loss of consortium (p. 88)
Punitive damages (p. 88)
Summary of damages (p. 88)
Assumption of the risk (p. 89)
Contributory negligence (p. 90)
Comparative negligence (p. 91)
Res ipsa loquitur (p. 91)
Prima facie (p. 91)
Rescue doctrine (p. 95)
Good Samaritan laws (p. 96)
Negligence per se (p. 96)
Strict liability (p. 97)

The Nature of Negligence

Negligence is defined as an injury due to "the failure to exercise the standard of care that a reasonably prudent person would have exercised in a similar situation" (Garner 2005, 871). In legal parlance it is also referred to as a "tort," which is defined as "a civil wrong, other than breach of contract, for which a remedy may be obtained, usu. in the form of damages" (Garner 2005, 1247). In other words, it refers to personal injury cases. Examples of such an injury are physical harm (e.g., broken limbs), property damage, damage to reputation, loss of consortium, emotional distress, and pain and suffering.

Negligence is a cause of action by persons against other persons, a business, a government agency, or other form of entity. The remedy for those injured by another's negligence is usually a monetary award for damages. The plaintiff in negligence cases is the injured party, usually not the government, as is the case in criminal law.

For example, a negligence case would be referred to as *John Anderson v. Thomas Smith*. While a criminal case might be referred to as *People of the state of California v. Thomas Smith*. However, the government can be the plaintiff where its civil law interests are at stake. For example, if a motorist crashed into a municipal power pole, the city would sue the motorist for negligence and damages to replace the pole. The case would be referred to as *The City of Chicago v. Thomas Smith*.

Negligence lawsuits are among the most prevalent types of lawsuits that occur in the hospitality industry. Accordingly, owners, managers, and employees in the hospitality industry must understand negligence and take precautionary and mitigating measures wherever practical. This chapter will help prepare students for that task.

The Elements of a Negligent Act

The basic difference between negligence and intentional torts is the state of mind possessed by the person committing the act at the time of the incident. In committing a negligent act, the person does not wish to cause the incident or the consequences. In a court of law, negligence occurs when the defendant is found to have created an unreasonable risk of harm for the injured party. With intentional torts the defendant intended to do the act that injured a person. With negligence the defendant was careless or reckless.

The first element of negligence is creation of a legal duty. Historically, the law of negligence was created with common law through judicial decision. More recently a legal duty is created by acts of government, such as state legislatures and local governments regarding health and safety matters. Such matters, created by the Tenth Amendment to the Constitution, are within sole power of local government and are known as police power.

Notice creates a legal duty owed to another for which a person must comply. Failure to do so will subject a person to a lawsuit for damages. Violation of a legal duty is referred to as a breach. For example, a breach may be a failure to correct a known dangerous condition on one's property that results in an injury to a person entering the property.

A duty may concern the status of persons entering real property of owners/occupiers (this term collectively refers to others, such as lessees as well as property owners) who are required to be "actively vigilant" and seek out safety problems. Upon discovery of dangerous conditions, owners/occupiers must provide notice to business invitees that a dangerous condition exists on their property. A duty may also be created through contract agreements between private parties.

An injury can be physical, such as food poisoning, or it can be psychological, referred to as emotional distress, such as that caused by finding a human finger in a bowl of soup. The injury must be directly related to the breach of the duty. For example, if a restaurant patron eats a meal, contracts food poisoning, becomes ill, and requires medical care, the restaurant could be liable for any damages. The cause of the injury is the consumption of unwholesome food, and it is referred to as the **proximate cause**, which is explained in greater detail below.

Damages can be pain and suffering, cost of the ambulance or medical care, lost wages, and any other costs that may be related to the incident. Moreover, the injury must be directly related to the damages incurred by the injured party. For example, if the restaurant can prove its food was wholesome and the patron who consumed the soup became ill because of stomach flu, the causation cannot fairly be attributable to the restaurant, and there would not be liability (see Key Concept Focus 4.1).

The five elements of a negligent act are (1) the existence of a duty, (2) a breach of the duty, (3) causation, (4) an injury, (5) and the resultant damages. All elements must be present for an injured party to recover. For example, assume a vendor enters a restaurant and slips on a water spill. The restaurant staff was unaware of its presence. Under common law, a vendor is a licensee who is not entitled to a landowners duty of due diligence. Since the danger was not known, there is no duty to warn a licensee of a danger it does not know exists.

KEY CONCEPT FOCUS 4.1. THE ELEMENTS OF A NEGLIGENCE CAUSE OF ACTION

Duty. A duty is an obligation imposed by society on persons and business entities in order to protect the public. For example, a restaurant offers food to the public for a certain sum of money. The public expects the food served to be wholesome, safe to eat, and free from toxic contaminants and disease. Because the restaurant offers food to the public for a profit, society imposes a duty on restaurants to provide customers with food that meets the aforementioned requirements. Unless a duty is imposed, many restaurants would not be diligent in food preparation, and people would get sick without legal recourse.

Breach. If a restaurant fails to provide wholesome food and a patron becomes ill, the restaurant may be liable for the consequences. This is referred to as a breach of its duty. Likewise, if a hotel violates a health or safety code by failing to install an adequate sprinkler system in its guest rooms, as required by the fire code, that would be a breach of their statutory duty.

Causation. The breach of the duty may be the direct cause of the injury, but it may not be the proximate cause of the injury. The proximate cause is the legal cause of the injury as decided by the trier of fact in a lawsuit. If the injury is not reasonably foreseeable, it is not the responsibility of the defendant. For example, if person driving a vehicle faster than the legal speed limit crashes into another vehicle, the driver is both the direct cause and the proximate cause of the accident. The driver is liable for any injuries and damages that flow from the accident. On the other hand, imagine a pedestrian with a weak heart witnesses the accident and dies from a heart attack at the sight of the impact. The driver is the direct cause of the death but not the proximate cause. It may not be reasonably foreseeable that someone would die of a heart attack just from seeing an accident occur. The heart attack is as an intervening event that severs proximate cause.

Injury. The injury caused by a breach of a duty may be physical, such as broken bones, property damage, or emotional injury, such as pain and suffering or simple embarrassment from slipping and falling in a public area of a hotel.

Damages. Although emotional injury, such as simple embarrassment, is arguably an injury, as a practical matter it is not an injury that will usually lead to a lawsuit. Why hire an attorney to file a lawsuit if a reasonable amount of damages is not likely? Moreover, an attorney would not enter into a contingency fee case if a substantial amount of a damages award is not likely.

Creation of a Duty

Duties are created in a variety of ways, such as expressed governmental action by way of adoption of statutes, ordinances, and administrative regulations along with those created by the courts through common law.

Statutory Duty

A statutory duty is a duty "of or related to legislation" (Garner 2005, 1180). A statutory duty is one created by the government to protect certain important **societal interests**. For example, cars are inherently dangerous instrumentalities and must be driven with care. The government determines, by statute, that a posted speed limit is the maximum speed permitted on a street within its jurisdiction. This determination creates a duty not to exceed that speed limit.

As a matter of law, driving above that maximum speed limit is unsafe and creates an unreasonable risk of harm to others. If a motorist exceeds the speed limit and an accident occurs that injures a pedestrian or a person in another vehicle, the driver would be liable for the consequences. Other important societal interests include:

- Health: A local government, such as a city, has police power to protect the health of its residents (Figure 4.2). Most cities adopt ordinances that require meat to be cooled to a minimum temperature in order to prevent spoilage. The ordinance creates a duty on all entities that serve food to the public to maintain the minimum temperature. Violation of the ordinance can result in a fine or loss of a business license. Of particular concern to the restaurant industry is the need ensure food is safe for consumption by restaurant patrons. If a patron consumes spoiled food and becomes ill, an expensive lawsuit could follow in addition to government fines for violation of relevant ordinances (Key Concept Focus 4.2).
- Safety: One of the most important legal duties imposed on landowners/occupiers of facilities open to the public is a duty to provide safe premises. For example, a hotel, restaurant, or sports stadium open to public access has a duty to maintain their property in a safe condition. This duty will vary according to the status of the person entering the property.

CATEGORIES OF PERSONS ON THE PREMISES

Business invitee. A paying customer on the premises for its intended purpose, such as a hotel guest or a restaurant patron. The duty owed to each is a duty of due care, a high standard that requires active vigilance to seek out safety problems and ensure the premises are safe for guests and patrons.

Licensee. A person on the premises primarily for their own benefit (e.g., a vendor who enters the premises to sell supplies to the owner/occupier, a meter reader for a utility company, or an independent contractor performing work on the premises). The owner/occupier only owes a duty to warn of known dangers.

Trespasser. Someone on the premises without permission of the owner/occupier and for which duty of safety is not owed.

Underaged person. A person not of legal age and who may not possess the maturity to protect one's self. The owner/occupier owes a duty to anticipate the underage and make the premises safe. For example, a hotel pool needs to be fenced in order to keep children from falling into it.

Common Law Duty

A common law duty is one imposed by judicial decision. The hospitality industry must be sensitive to one in particular: the duty owed by landowners to persons that enter their premises. The courts created four categories of persons who enter the premises and imposed a different duty of care for each (summarized in Text Box and discussed in further detail below).

Business Invitee

A **business invitee** (also referred to as "business visitor" or "hotel guest") is defined as "A person who is invited or permitted to enter or remain on another's land for a purpose directly or indirectly connected with the landowner's business dealings" (Garner 2005, 165).

A hotel owes of **duty of due care** to its business invitees to ensure the property is safe for their use. For example, a guest with a room at a hotel or a patron eating a meal at a restaurant are using the premises for its intended purposes. They are paying the owner money for use of the room or for the meal, respectively.

The law imposes a duty of care on the landowner for the associated use. The duty of due care requires the landowner to be **actively vigilant** in securing the safety of the guests. Active vigilance means the landowner must make a reasonable effort to find and remove known dangers or to adequately warn of their existence (*Montes v. Betcher*, 480 F.2d 1128 (Minn. 1973).

Maintaining safety should be a major policy for every hospitality organization. For example, a hotel or restaurant employee should be assigned the responsibility for safety of the premises. The employee must ensure periodic inspection of the premises for possible safety hazards are regularly conducted. For example, if floor tile is cracked, it must be promptly replaced to prevent a guest from injury. Until replaced, warning signs or cones must be placed at the site of the danger. If handrails are loose in the stairwells or in the bathroom showers, they must be secured promptly upon notice.

Hospitality employees must be trained to look for such problems, and a procedure must be in place to facilitate reporting and correcting a problem as soon as possible. For example, an independent **negligence audit** (described below) should be periodically conducted. The results should be reported to management and reviewed by all employees.

Further, employee training sessions should be convened on a regular basis, and a safety checklist should be provided to assigned employees to conduct routine inspections. The results of the routine inspections should be dated and signed by the employee assigned the safety responsibility. The potential consequence for failing to do so is an injury to a guest, a possible lawsuit, the payment of damages, and possible damage to the business's reputation.

The following case discusses the duty an innkeeper owes for the safety of the guest. The guest was assaulted by an employee, and since the employee was operating within the scope of his duties, the hotel is liable for the injury to its guest.

94 GA. APP. 385

Court of Appeals of Georgia, Division No. 1.
G. L. NEWTON
v.
CANDACE, Inc.
No. 36278.
Sept. 20, 1956.

Synopsis

Action against hotel proprietor for injury suffered by patron when allegedly assaulted without provocation by hotel clerk. The Superior Court, Fulton County, Ralph H. Pharr, J., rendered judgment of nonsuit, and plaintiff brought error. The Court of Appeals, Quillian, J., held that the evidence was sufficient to take case to jury on question of whether hotel clerk, when making alleged assault, was acting within scope of his employment or in the prosecution of hotel proprietor's business.

***

QUILLIAN, Judge.

1. Like other masters, a hotel proprietor or innkeeper is liable for the torts of his servant committed in the performance of the duties the servant is employed to discharge and that could be reasonably expected of him in the prosecution of the proprietor's business.

2. It is the duty of an innkeeper not only to furnish his guest or patron with shelter and comforts but also to exercise ordinary care to protect him from danger. [Citation omitted.]

3. Hotels customarily transact business with patrons through the medium of clerks. It is within the scope of a hotel clerk's employment, when representing the proprietor of the establishment, to courteously reply to polite requests of the patron for accommodations of a lawful and moral nature irrespective of whether he or the hostelry is under any duty or can reasonably be expected to grant such requests.

***

4. Where, as in the instant case, there was a conflict in the evidence, but some evidence supporting the contention of the plaintiff patron, that, when he tendered the necessary money for the purpose and politely requested of the defendant hotel proprietor's clerk *that he arrange credit for his wife at another hotel, the clerk without provocation committed a violent assault upon him, thereby personally injuring and humiliating him, it was error to grant a nonsuit on the assumption that the clerk when making the attack was not acting within the scope of his employment or **741 in the prosecution of the hotel proprietor's business.*

Judgment reversed.

Often the status of a person on the premises will change depending upon where the person goes and what the person is doing on the premises. For example, a person may be invited to a hotel to visit a guest of the hotel. The person with the room is a business invitee and is owed a duty of due care. The person visiting the guest is treated as a business invitee, like the paying guest, as long as the visitor is there during visiting hours. Once the visitor exceeds visiting hours, the person becomes a trespasser and is owed no duty.

If the guest is not available at the time the visitor arrives, the visitor may wait in the lobby area until the hotel guest is located. However, the visitor may decide to explore hotel premises and wander into an area generally restricted to hotel guests only. The visitor may fall into two different statuses as a licensee or a trespasser during this time. The hotel only owes a licensee a duty to warn of known dangers and it owes no duty at all to a trespasser.

In the case of *Steinberg v. Irvin Operating Co.*, a visiting guest wandered down a hallway away from the waiting area. The guest went into a movie room, which was dark and had a four-inch drop to the movie room floor. There was no signage indicating the floor levels were different and no strips of warning lights on the stairs or aisle. The visiting guest tripped and injured herself.

The court concluded the visitor was a licensee and should have been warned. It also considered whether the visitor was a trespasser and felt it could have been either (see *Steinberg v. Irwin Operating Co.*, 90 So.2d 460 (Fla. 1956)).

The owner of a restaurant must ensure ample space exists among the tables so wait help and patrons may move comfortably through the restaurant. Otherwise, collisions could occur and cause dishes or trays of food to spill on guests or on the floor. Spills of hot coffee or tea can cause serious injury to a person and result in an expensive lawsuit.

Restaurant and hotel kitchens are another source of frequent injury, and as such, they must be regularly inspected for safety of employees. Precautions must be taken to ensure that ovens, burners, hot plates, and toasters are operating correctly and positioned at safe distances from each other and away from the flow of traffic (see *Griffin Industries, Inc. v. Foodmaker, Inc.*, 2000WL 714604 (Tex. 2000)). Fire extinguishers must meet local codes and be positioned in accessible areas and routinely tested for use in case of a fire. The following case, which seeks indemnification for a restaurant's negligence, discusses some of the dangers in the kitchen.

22 S.W.3D 33

Court of Appeals of Texas,
Houston (14th Dist.).
GRIFFIN INDUSTRIES, INC., Appellant,
v.
FOODMAKER, INC., d/b/a Jack in the Box, Appellee.
No. 14-98-00881-CV.
May 11, 2000.

Synopsis

After restaurant employee was injured while pouring spent cooking oil into servicing company's vat, servicing company brought suit against restaurant to determine whether it had to indemnify restaurant for attorney fees and money paid by restaurant to the employee. The 122nd District Court, Galveston County, Frank T. Carmona, J., entered judgment on jury verdict in favor of restaurant, and servicing company appealed. Reverse.

Even assuming that servicing company, which picked up and disposed of spent cooking oil from restaurant, failed to respond to one or more requests to service pump on grease vat, such conduct was not evidence of negligence; duty to pick up the grease stemmed solely from the parties' contract.

Opinion

RUBY SONDOCK, Justice (Assigned).

The principal question in this appeal is whether Griffin Industries, Inc. ("Griffin") owes indemnity to Foodmaker, Inc., d/b/a Jack in the Box ("Foodmaker") for attorney fees and $12,000.00 paid by Foodmaker to one of its employees injured in the course and scope of his employment.

***

The vat supplied by Griffin was 6'10" high and had a 2'x2' covered opening at the top for ventilation. The vat was designed to be filled by Foodmaker personnel with a pump at the bottom of the vat. Griffin's general manager testified the company instructed Foodmaker on the proper operation of the pump, but did not warn against filling the vat through the ventilation opening because it never thought that would be attempted. He also testified that he believed putting the ventilation opening 6'10" high was far enough out of the way so it would not be used for anything else, but "if someone wants to climb up, take the lid off and pour the grease in that is something we (Griffin) can't stop them from doing. ..."

***

On September 13, 1996, one of Foodmaker's employees, with the help of the acting manager, successfully maneuvered himself and a heavy, unlidded container of hot grease up a ladder and emptied the grease into the 2'x2' opening at the top of the vat without wearing any of the protective clothing required by Foodmaker's policy. Part of the supervisor's duty was to make sure the employee was wearing protective clothing when handling hot grease. The acting manager later told the employee to make a second trip up the ladder (which the employee had reported as greasy and wobbly) to dispose of more hot grease. On this trip, without the help of the manager who was then busy elsewhere, the employee fell and was injured.

***

One of Foodmaker's employees testified that he had made two or three calls for service but no one from Griffin responded before the accident. Griffin's general manager testified that untimely response for service was not acceptable.

***

Assuming, without deciding, that Griffin did not respond to one or more service requests in a timely manner, such conduct might constitute a breach of its service contract with Foodmaker but it is not evidence of negligence. The duty to pick up the grease stems solely from the parties' contract.

***

The indemnity clause must meet both prongs of the express negligence rule. We hold that the service agreement purporting to secure indemnity for Foodmaker for its own conduct at least fails to meet the conspicuous requirement of the express negligence rules and the trial court erred in permitting the jury to determine the issue of indemnity. [Citations omitted.] Further, we find that the evidence does not support the jury's negligence finding. Accordingly, we reverse the judgment entered by the trial court and render judgment that Foodmaker take nothing.

Licensee

A **licensee** is "one who has permission to enter or use another's premises, but only for one's own purposes and not for the landowner's benefit" (Garner 2005, 765). For example, a vendor of hotel supplies enters the premises in order to negotiate the sale of pillowcases and sheets. The primary benefit of the entry flows to the vendor, who is attempting to consummate a sale. Society imposes less of a burden on the landowner in this instance since the vendor is the party seeking to make the profit. Active vigilance is not required of the landowner, only a duty to warn the vendor of any known safety hazards.

In contrast, assume the tile in the hotel foyer was recently cracked when a guest dropped his laptop while waiting for the airport shuttle. The guest is in a hurry and does not report the problem to hotel management. Minutes after the incident, the vendor enters the hotel, trips, and falls, injuring himself. Since hotel management was unaware of the problem, it would be unable to warn of the danger. The hotel would not be liable for the injury to the vendor, because it was unaware of the cracked tile and thus had no duty to warn the licensee. On the other hand, if the injured party is a hotel guest, there might be liability if the tile was not repaired promptly or a safety sign was not conspicuously displayed. Active vigilance is required for the safety of a business invitee.

Similarly, in a crowded restaurant, assume a vendor selling tablecloths and napkins walks through the restaurant to an office in the rear of the building to meet the manager. Unbeknownst to the manager and the vendor, an employee has just spilled food on the floor. The vendor slips and falls, causing serious injury to his back. The restaurant may not be liable, because it was unaware of the danger. However, if a business invitee, instead of a salesperson, slips and falls because of the spilled food, the restaurant might be liable if the injured patron can show lack of active vigilance required for a business invitee.

A **trespasser** is "one who commits a trespass; one who intentionally and without consent or privilege enters another's property" (Garner 2005, 1259). In tort law, a landowner owes no duty to unforeseeable trespassers. Absent a legal reason for the trespasser to be on the premises, society does not impose liability on the landowner, even if the landowner was aware of the safety hazard and failed to place a warning sign.

For example, signage at the entrance of a hotel says the restrooms are for patrons only. A passerby sees the sign but ignores it and proceeds to try and find a restroom to use. Upon entering the hotel, the passerby trips on an area of cracked tile, falls, and is injured. The passerby is not a business invitee of the hotel but instead is a trespasser. The hotel may not have liability for the trespasser's injuries, even if management was aware of the safety problem and took no action to repair it or place a warning sign by the tile.

Similarly, assume a passerby enters a restaurant with signage that says restrooms are for patrons only, but in the search for a restroom, ignores the sign. Food has spilled on the floor, and the passerby slips, falls, and is injured. In this instance, as well as in the hotel example, the restaurant may not be liable for the injury, even if management was aware of the problem and delayed in its correction. There is no legal duty to protect a trespasser.

In both of the above examples, if the person injured was a business invitee of the hotel or the restaurant, there would be liability for failing to be actively vigilant and to warn of the danger.

As a general rule, the law treats **underage persons** differently than adults in a variety of ways. One is commonly referred to as the "attractive nuisance doctrine," which is "the rule that a person who owns property on which there is a dangerous thing or condition that will foreseeably lure children to trespass has a duty to protect those children from the danger" (Garner 2005, 105). The doctrine recognizes that younger persons may be too immature to recognize dangerous conditions. Therefore, landowners must be actively vigilant when they are aware underage persons may enter the premises. The duty of care is equal to and in many instances greater than the duty of care to adult business invitees. Examples include the following typical dangerous conditions:

- Unattended swimming pools or open trenches on the land may attract underage persons who don't fully appreciate the danger. A hotel that provides its guests with a pool and/or a spa must ensure gates surround the area to prevent underage guests from entering without supervision. Lifeguards should be present at all times the pool is accessible to such guests. The gates to the pool/spa area should be locked at all other times, and hotel personnel should patrol the area to prevent unauthorized use.
- A restaurant decides to offer a flambé meal to its guests, so special care must be taken to ensure that underage patrons do not come near the flames. Proper signage must be prominently displayed explaining the dangers and reminding parents to supervise their children. An employee should be assigned to monitor the lines and ensure that young patrons don't approach too close to the flames. The person serving and cooking must be properly trained to ensure that the flames do not get out of control.

PRACTICUM

Negligence cases are one of the most voluminous in number and are very costly legal problems experienced in the hospitality industry. Slips and falls are a common problem that could lead to "nuisance lawsuits" (in the $5,000–$15,000 range) and those that incur major personal injury with large claims for a variety of compensatory damages.

Every business should focus on improving safety. It should be part of the establishment's mission statement, with employees dedicated to recognizing potential safety problems and taking quick action to remedy them (i.e., active vigilance). Every business should consider retaining help from experienced professional consultants in the building safety industry.

They should retain a consultant to perform a safety audit. The consultant will recommend safety improvements and assist in implementing necessary changes at reasonable costs. They will also provide training for executives and employees. Yes, they will charge a fee, which may at initial glance cause some businesses to shy away. But think of the consequences for ignoring the value of their expertise (see the discussion of the cost of litigation in Chapter 2). Industry trade associations, such as restaurant, hotel, and entertainment organizations, can also be of help with this issue.

Breach of Duty

The next element of negligence is the breach of a duty. If society imposes a duty and a hospitality facility does not adhere to that duty, liability and an expensive lawsuit may follow. The standard for determining negligence is the reasonable person standard.

The **reasonable person** is "A hypothetical person used as a legal standard, especially to determine whether someone acted with negligence; specifically, a person who exercises the degree of attention, knowledge, intelligence, and judgment that society requires of its members for the protection of their own and of others' interest" (Garner 2005, 1050). The reasonable person standard is based on the idea of what a reasonable person would have done under the same or similar circumstances. The **trier of fact** in each case sits as the hypothetical reasonable person. In a **bench trial** it is the judge, and in a **jury trial** it is the jurors empaneled for the case. The reasonable person theoretically acts in a manner that will prevent or avoid an occurrence of a breach of duty.

The reasonable person concept is difficult for many persons to understand. The judge in a jury trial provides instructions to the jury defining a reasonable person in the context of each case. The reasonable person is, as the saying goes, "a moving target," and an understanding of the term's use often depends on the composition of the jury or the judge assigned to the case. Every person, even seasoned judges, harbors certain biases that may influence the outcome of a case. The practical effect of this truism is that the "reasonable person," for purposes of a lawsuit, will vary according to the trier of fact in the case.

In the hotel example above concerning a licensee, a reasonable person in the position of hotel manager (i.e., a reasonable hotel manager), once informed of the cracked tile, would immediately place signs around the tile warning guests of the danger. The reasonable hotel manager would also take the steps to repair the tile as soon as practicable. If facts show employees knew of the cracked tile but did not inform management or if management was informed but took no corrective action, the hotel could be found liable to any guest who may be injured.

Causation

Causation consists of two types for the purpose of imposing liability in a negligence case. They are direct causation and proximate causation. Direct causation means the injury would not have occurred but for the negligent act. Direct cause may or may not create liability for the defendant. The decision rests upon whether or not the injury was foreseeable. If it was foreseeable the direct cause also is the proximate cause of the injury. The proximate cause is what creates liability.

In the hotel example above, assume the cracked tile was reported to management, and the problem was not fixed nor were danger cones placed around the tile. Two hours later a person enters the hotel to register as a guest, trips on the unmarked cracked tile, and is injured. The injury would not have occurred but for the cracked tile, and therefore, the breach of the duty (that is, the failure to fix the tile or to adequately warn of the danger) is the direct cause of the injury.

The direct cause, if it is foreseeable, is also referred to as the proximate cause. In this case a reasonable hotel would have at least placed danger cones around the problem tile to warn of its existence. Since that did not occur, the direct cause is also the proximate cause, and the hotel will be liable for the injury.

If the cracked tile occurred minutes before the accident, it may not have been foreseeable and therefore was not the proximate cause. If the person was talking on a cell phone and not paying attention to where they were walking, the necessary causation also might not be present. The person's inattention could be an **intervening event** that breaks the chain of causation.

A classic case used to illustrate proximate cause occurred at a Long Island Railway Station. The facts of the case are as follows. A man was having difficulty trying to board a train at a railway station as it was starting to exit the station. Two attendants on the ground and one on the train were assisting him. He had an unmarked bag in his arm that slipped from his possession. It contained high explosive fireworks that ignited when the bag hit the ground.

A huge explosion occurred that injured several people in close proximity. The explosion also shook the railway station and caused a "vertical customer weight station" to fall on a patron and injure her. She was located a substantial distance away at the other end of the train station. She sued the Long Island Railway Co. for damages. The court concluded the injured woman was too far away from the incident, and therefore, her injury was not foreseeable. Accordingly, the explosion was not the proximate cause of her injuries (see *Palsgraf v. Long Island Railway Co.*, 162 NN.E. 99 (1928)).

For another example of foreseeability and proximate cause, assume the following facts. A passenger van is driven by a resort employee at least four round trips a day to pick up guests at the airport. The employee has become very familiar with the road to the airport. On this occasion he is returning from the airport with a group of female college students spending a vacation at the resort. The young ladies become flirtatious with the driver, who chats playfully with his passengers. He becomes distracted, and as a consequence, he veers off the road and strikes a power pole. The power pole falls and the power lines snap. The wires are "hot" and very dangerous.

The downed power line was the direct cause of a series of events that inflicted injury. The trier of fact must decide how far liability should reasonably be imposed. At some point an injury may be so remote that imposing liability would not be reasonable. In other words, it is an event that is not foreseeable and for which legal liability should not attach. The point at which the trier of fact imposes liability (the "cutoff point") is referred to as the proximate cause. Any injury past the cutoff point is too remote, and liability will not be imposed. Any injury before the cutoff point is deemed foreseeable, and liability is imposed.

In the following text box, there are four events that illustrate the concept of proximate cause in the case of the resort employee driving the hotel passenger van.

PROXIMATE CAUSE

Destruction of the Power Pole by the Resort Van Driver

Knocking over the power pole located close to the road is something a reasonable person should foresee would occur by driving off the road. Especially the driver of this van because he drives the road so often. If it is foreseeable, then it is an event for which a negligent driver should be responsible.

Death of the Boys under The Power Pole

Three young boys, ages 8, 9, and 10 trespass on utility property and play directly under the power pole in an unfenced area without signs warning of high voltage power lines. The power lines fall and strike the boys, incinerating them.

Arguably, this is an event a reasonable person would not expect after a vehicle veers off the road and strikes a power pole. If the trier of fact finds the incineration of the boys under this specific set of facts is not foreseeable, liability will not attach to the negligent driver. Knocking over the power pole may be the direct cause of the deaths, but it is not the proximate cause.

More than likely the power company will be subject to a lawsuit and potential liability if it is found negligent for permitting access to the area by the young boys. Thus, if the power company did not fence off the area and did not place signage warning of the danger, they would be liable. It would be foreseeable to the power company that three young boys might wander underneath to play.

Effect on Homes in the Area

The downed power lines also attach to a group of homes in the neighborhood and cause a loss of power. The lost power causes refrigerators in the homes to warm and food spoils. Loss of power from a downed power line causing food to spoil would not be a foreseeable event to the driver of the van. But such a loss of power is foreseeable to the power company, and liability will likely attach for the spoiled food.

A Person Dies on an Operating Table in a Hospital Five Miles Away

The power lines are also the power source for the hospital. Just after the surgeon opens the patient's chest for heart surgery, the power goes out, and the patient dies. The power outage is a direct cause of the death, but arguably, it is not the proximate cause of the death as to the power company or the van driver. Neither would have the knowledge that active surgery was being performed. Therefore, the death is not a foreseeable event as to them. Moreover, the hospital is too far away from the scene of the accident.

The hospital should know that at some point in time power may be lost. They should have backup power precisely for such purposes. Therefore, it is foreseeable as to the hospital. As such the hospital will likely face a negligence lawsuit for failing to provide a backup source of power.

Injury

It is axiomatic that without an injury or damages, there usually is no good reason to sue. For example, if a person slips and falls in a restaurant and is just embarrassed, it is not reasonable to sue the restaurant. The injury needs to be physical, such as a broken arm, lacerated head, or death. Why hire a lawyer to litigate if there is not an injury with the possibility of a reasonable monetary recovery? Moreover, a lawyer would not take a case on a contingency fee basis if there is no injury and there is low to no possible damage award.

Damages

Damages come in two major forms in negligence cases: compensatory damages and punitive damages.

Compensatory damages are intended to pay the injured person for any calculable loss. Such damages are split into two categories: special damages and general damages. **Special damages** are those items relatively easily calculable, such as property damage, lost wages, and medical expenses. **General damages** are items that are not easily calculable, such as pain and suffering, mental distress, or **loss of consortium.**

Punitive damages are defined as "Damages awarded in addition to actual damages when the defendant acted with recklessness, malice, or deceit; specif., damages assessed by way of penalizing the wrongdoer or making an example to others" (Garner 2005, 335). They are not intended to compensate a person for injury but, instead, are intended to punish the wrongdoer and to set an example to deter others from engaging in similar offensive conduct.

The conduct must be egregious and outrageous for a punitive award to be granted. They are discretionary and generally disfavored by the courts. Assume in the power outage example the resort employs several drivers. They have a history of accidents to and from the airport. No corrective action has ever been imposed by the resort on the drivers of its airport van. The courts could assess punitive damages against the resort under the doctrine of respondeat superior. The rationale would be to punish them for gross negligence for not taking corrective action and also to deter others from similar reckless conduct.

Summary of damages. In the above hypothetical negligent airport van example, the power pole knocked over is referred to as special damage because its replacement is easily calculated. The death of the boys would be both special damages for costs of the funeral and also general damages for pain and suffering, mental distress, and loss of consortium. A fence should have been erected to keep anyone away from its high voltage power lines. The loss of food in the neighborhood homes would be special damages.

The death of the patient in the hospital operating room would include both special and general damages. Special damage would include such things as lost wages of the deceased and medical expenses. General damages would include loss of life, pain and suffering, mental distress, and loss of consortium for the family. If the hospital had a history of losing patients in surgery because of faulty power sources, it could be liable for punitive damages as well as compensatory damages.

KEY CONCEPT FOCUS 4.2. DAMAGES

Compensatory damages. The purpose of compensatory damages in tort cases is to pay for injuries incurred by the plaintiff. They are designed to make the injured party whole. They are composed of two types: special damages and general damages.

Special damages. These are "Damages that are alleged to have been sustained in the circumstances of a particular wrong. To be awardable, special damages must be specifically claimed and proved" (Garner 2005, 335). They are characterized by their relative ease of calculation. For example, medical bills (from the hospital), lost wages (from your employer), property value (estimated replacement cost), and future profits (from your business) are relatively easy to determine.

General damages. These are "Damages the law presumes follow from the type of wrong complained of; specifically, compensatory damages for harm that so frequently results from the tort for which a party has sued that the harm is reasonably expected and need not be alleged or proved" (Garner 2005, 334). General damages are characterized by the difficulty in calculation. For example, pain and suffering, emotional distress, and loss of consortium don't lend themselves to ease of calculation.

How do you measure the value of pain and suffering from a broken back? How do you measure the value of the emotional loss of a spouse killed in an automobile accident? How do you measure the value of the loss of consortium (the love and comfort of the deceased spouse)? No formula exists for use to determine the general damages calculation. It depends to a large extent on case precedent, the facts of each case, and the persuasiveness of the trial attorney.

Punitive damages. These are "Damages awarded in addition to actual damages when the defendant acted with recklessness, malice, or deceit; specifically, damages assessed by way of penalizing the wrongdoer or making an example to others" (Garner 2005, 335). The usual method of imposing punitive damages is by way of some form of multiplier. Most states use a range between three and five times compensatory damages. For example, if total compensatory damages total $100,000 and the court decides to make a punitive award using the multiplier of five, the punitive award would be $500,000. That amount would be added to the $100,000 compensatory award for a total award of $600,000.

Defenses for Negligence Lawsuits

Defendants have a variety of ways by which to defend against a claim of negligence. The most prevalent way is to demonstrate the plaintiff has not alleged or proven sufficient facts showing all the elements for a cause action exist. This can be accomplished at the pleading stage of litigation with a motion to dismiss the case for failure to state sufficient facts to constitute a cause of action. It may also occur after discovery is complete with a motion for summary judgment (see Chapter 2). Both motions assert a failure to prove the case because of insufficient facts or supporting evidence. In addition, several legal defenses are available to avoid full or partial liability. They are assumption of the risk, contributory negligence, and comparative negligence.

Assumption of the Risk

Assumption of the risk is "The principle that one who takes on the risk of loss, injury or damage cannot maintain an action against a party that causes the loss, injury, or damage" (Garner 2005, 101), The elements of assumption of the risk are as follows:

- The plaintiff is aware of the risk.
- The plaintiff understood the risk.
- The plaintiff voluntarily participated in the activity.
- The plaintiff was injured.

Assume a long-time season ticket holder attends a baseball game and sits in a seat along the left field sidelines outside the home plate area, which is not protected by a safety net. The person has attended countless baseball games and is well aware that baseballs are often hit into the stands, especially down the sidelines where his seat is located.

One afternoon a foul ball is hit into the stands and strikes him in the face, dislodging his eyeball. He sues both the baseball stadium and the baseball team, alleging negligence for failing to provide a protective safety net in the area where his seat is located. The defendants will probably successfully allege this person assumed the risk because of the following reasons:

- He is a longtime season ticket holder and knew of the risk.
- He understood the risk since he observed many foul balls enter the stands where he sits.
- He voluntarily attended the games.
- He was injured by a foul ball of which he was well aware.

Assumption of the risk will not be successful if all the elements are not present. Assume the same season ticket holder attends a baseball game and sits in the same seat as he always does. Instead of a player hitting a foul ball, the bat breaks in half, and a portion of the broken bat sails into the stands and impales him in the chest.

Assumption of the risk would probably not be successful in this case, because baseball bats do not generally break sending a portion into the stands. It would be difficult to convince the trier of fact the season ticket holder was aware of the danger of a bat breaking in half and sailing into the seats. Foul balls sailing into the stands are routine at baseball games. Broken bats are not.

Contributory Negligence

Contributory negligence is "The principle that completely bars a plaintiff's recovery if the damage suffered is partly the plaintiff's own fault" (Garner 2005, 279). It is an outdated theory abandoned in most states because of its harsh results. All the defendant has to do is prove the plaintiff was partially at fault for the incident, no matter how slight the amount of fault.

For example, assume two vehicles collide in an intersection. The plaintiff was struck by a shuttle operated by a hotel on its way to the airport to pick up guests. The plaintiff sues for negligence because the defendant hotel's employee was talking on a cell phone and was distracted. The defendant counters with proof the plaintiff was traveling one mile per hour in excess of the posted speed, and therefore, the plaintiff was part of the reason for the collision.

Under the contributory negligence theory, the defendant could be relieved of any responsibility for the accident and injury suffered by the plaintiff. There is no recovery for the plaintiff, even though the plaintiff's actions only slightly contributed to the accident. Contributory negligence is legally moribund. Most states have developed some form of comparative negligence, which is discussed below.

Comparative Negligence

"The principle that reduces a plaintiff's recovery proportionally to the plaintiff's degree of fault in causing the damage, rather than completely barring recovery" (Garner 2005, 237) as does contributory negligence. It is the doctrine adopted by most states to counter the potentially harsh results often present under contributory negligence law.

Under comparative negligence, the trier of fact assesses a percentage of responsibility when both parties share fault for the accident. Assume in the vehicle accident discussed above, 90% of the fault is assessed to the defendant, and only 10% of the fault is assessed to the plaintiff. If damages suffered by the plaintiff are $100,000, the court would award $90,000 to the plaintiff. This theory ensures that the relatively innocent plaintiff receives some compensation for the injury caused by a defendant who is mostly at fault. A summary of special defenses is provided in the following text box.

DEFENSES TO CLAIMS OF NEGLIGENCE

Defenses to claims of negligence are fourfold.

The general rule. The plaintiff must state sufficient facts upon which relief may be granted. This means the plaintiff must allege, supported by facts, in the complaint that all the elements of negligence exist. If that fails, the plaintiff must assert in a motion for summary judgment, after discovery is complete, that the evidence shows no triable issue of fact exists, and therefore, a trial is unnecessary. If the case goes to trial, the following are the usual defenses to negligence.

Assumption of the risk. This defense asserts the plaintiff knew of the risk, understood the risk, and voluntarily chose to take the risk. For example, a sky diver knows of the danger involved and voluntarily decides to jump. That sky diver has assumed the risk of injury.

Contributory negligence. This defense is outdated, but it is acknowledged in a dwindling minority of the states. Its premise is that any contribution of fault by the plaintiff in lawsuit negates any recovery at all. It is a harsh doctrine, which has lost support from courts and legislatures. For example, assume a person falls down a staircase in a hotel because they were talking to a friend and did not pay attention to a broken stair. The trier of fact decides the plaintiff was ten percent at fault. Because of the plaintiff's fault, there would be no recovery for the plaintiff.

Comparative negligence. This defense is the majority rule in America. It is fairer than contributory negligence and its harsh result. Under this theory, the trier of fact apportions the fault according to the facts and assigns a percentage fault to each party. Then the percentage fault assessed is applied to the total damage awarded, and each party receives a proportional share of the amount.

Special Doctrines and Statutes

The discussion below concerns several defenses used to avoid liability for negligence created because of special policy considerations designed to avoid a societal injustice. They are *res ipsa loquitur*, the rescue doctrine, Good Samaritan statutes, negligence per se, and strict liability.

Res Ipsa Loquitur

Res ipsa loquitur (*res ipsa*) is a Latin term that means "the thing speaks for itself." **Res ipsa** is "The doctrine providing that, in some circumstances, the mere fact of an accident's occurrence raises an inference of negligence that establishes a *prima facie* case" (Garner 2005, 1085). It is a common law doctrine applicable in situations where negligent conduct exists, but through no fault of the plaintiff, there is insufficient opportunity for the plaintiff to prove their case.

Res ipsa was created to avoid that injustice and assist an innocent third party to recover damages. With res ipsa the court presumes negligence occurred and shifts the burden to the defendant to make a *prima facie* (Latin for "at first sight") showing of an absence of negligence. **Prima facie** case means "2. A party's production of enough evidence to allow the fact-trier (i.e., the judge) to infer the fact at issue and rule in the party's favor" (Garner 2005, 999).

If the defendant is unable to meet the burden, the plaintiff proceeds without having to prove a breach of the duty of due care or that the defendant was negligent. If the defendant meets the burden, the burden reverts back to the plaintiff to prove the case under normal negligence procedure.

For example, assume a pedestrian is walking in front of a flour processing plant and a barrel of flour falls somewhere from the building. It strikes and injures the pedestrian. The pedestrian is the plaintiff and, as such, has the burden of proof for a negligence damage claim in court. Unfortunately, the pedestrian will probably be unable to satisfy the burden because there is no way of knowing how or who caused the barrel to fall. Res Ipsa assists such a plaintiff by shifting the burden to the defendant (the flour processer) to prove it was not negligent (see *Byrne v. Boadle*, 2H & C 722, 159 Eng. Rep. 229 (1863)).

The following case explains how res ipsa works and demonstrates that the plaintiff was unable to prove that the defendant was in exclusive control of the vehicle's wheel mounts.

---

452 F.3D 639

United States Court of Appeals,
Seventh Circuit.
Christine MAROULES, Plaintiff—Appellant,
v.
JUMBO, INC. and James E. Windsor, Defendants—Appellees.
No. 04–3248.
Argued Sept. 20, 2005. Decided June 20, 2006.

Synopsis

Background: Motorist brought action against owner of trucking company and truck driver for injuries incurred when wheel broke free from truck, flew through air, and crashed through front passenger side of car. The United States District Court for the Northern District of Indiana, Andrew P. Rodovich, J., granted summary judgment in favor of defendants. Plaintiff appealed.

Holdings: The Court of Appeals, Rovner, Circuit Judge,

Affirmed.

Opinion

ROVNER, Circuit Judge.

Ordinarily we count on gravity to keep heavy items in place; and so when flour barrels, armchairs, and truck wheels become airborne we assume first that something has gone wrong. Such events, lawyers say, speak for themselves, or in Latin, "res ipsa loquitur," and the blame for any resulting injury can be imputed to the person who had control of the item before it became a dangerous projectile. Christine Maroules asks the court to adopt this view to delegate to the owner of Jumbo, Inc. trucking company and Jumbo's driver, James E. Windsor (together, "Jumbo"), blame for injuries she sustained when a wheel broke free from the truck upon which it was mounted, flew through the air, and crashed through the front passenger side of her car. Because she has failed to demonstrate the elements necessary for res ipsa loquitur to apply, however, we affirm the decision of the district court granting summary judgment to Jumbo.

***

I.

At that point he inspected his truck and determined that five or six of the ten studs upon which the wheel unit was mounted were broken and sheared off, although the thread of the portions of the studs that had remained on the trailer did not appear to be worn. ... According to Windsor's affidavit, he had inspected the nuts just a few hours prior to the accident, as part of his routine walk-around inspection which he conducted at the beginning and end of each day and every time he started the vehicle. ... He testified that upon his inspection, the studs and nuts were not loose in any way. Philip Simonsen, testified that the trailer had received a full annual inspection ... just five weeks before the accident. Simonsen also testified that Jumbo hires a third-party company to inspect, maintain, and repair its trailers and all of their parts, including the wheel studs, which it had done on numerous occasions prior to the accident.

***

II.

In response to Jumbo's summary judgment claim, Maroules asked the district court to apply the doctrine of res ipsa loquitur. Res ipsa loquitur is a shortcut to a negligence claim. Although negligence may not be inferred from the mere fact that an injury occurred, it may be inferred from the circumstances surrounding the injury. [Citations omitted.] The doctrine recognizes that in some situations an occurrence is so unusual that, absent a reasonable justification, the person in control of the situation should be held responsible. [Citations omitted.] In other words, as the Latin describes, "the thing speaks for itself." See Byrne v. Boadle, 2 H & C 722, 159 Eng. Rep. 299 (1863) (the original res ipsa loquitur case involving a flour barrel falling out of a warehouse window). The central question in any res ipsa loquitur case is whether the incident more probably resulted from the defendant's negligence than from some other cause. Deuitch v. Fleming, 746 N.E.2d 993, 999 (Ind.Ct.App.2001). To establish this inference of negligence, the plaintiff must demonstrate: (1) that the injuring instrumentality was within the exclusive management and control of the defendant, and (2) that the accident is of the type that does not ordinarily happen if those who have the management and control exercise proper care. Balfour v. Kimberly Home Health Care, Inc., 830 N.E.2d

145, 148 (Ind.Ct.App.2005) ... Once the plaintiff has met the burden of demonstrating the control and due care prongs of res ipsa loquitur, the doctrine operates to permit an inference of negligence based upon the circumstantial evidence. [Citations omitted.]

***

A successful res ipsa loquitur showing simply creates an inference which the trier of fact may choose to accept or not.

The defendants begin by denying that they had exclusive control. To support this proposition, they contend that they had no role in manufacturing the trailer or its wheel studs; they had no control over the inspection and maintenance of the trailer or its wheel studs prior to the time that Jumbo purchased the trailer in 1999; and that Jumbo does not maintain, service, or repair its trailers and their parts, but instead relinquishes control every time it sends its trailers to an outside third party maintenance company to do this work.

***

To invoke the doctrine a plaintiff must "present evidence that ... the accident is one which in the ordinary course of things does not happen if those who control the instrumentality use proper care." [Citations omitted.] And although a plaintiff may rely upon common sense and experience or expert testimony, the plaintiff still has the burden of showing that the injury was one that would not ordinarily occur in the absence of proper care on the part of those controlling the instrumentality. Ross, 825 N.E.2d at 894.

***

Consequently, summary judgment must be granted for Jumbo, and the judgment of the district court is Affirmed.

The required elements for use of res ipsa are the following:

- The event must have been one most likely caused by negligence.
- The instrumentality that caused the injury must be in sole control of the defendant.
- The plaintiff must not have provoked the cause of the event.

In the flour barrel case, element one is met because the barrel falling from somewhere in the building was probably caused by a negligent act. If the defendant can prove it was intentionally pushed, res ipsa would not stand. Element two is present because the barrel of flour clearly belongs to and was in the sole control of the defendant. Finally, the pedestrian was innocently walking on the sidewalk in front of the building and did nothing to provoke the barrel's fall. Accordingly, all three elements are present, and the burden shifts to the defendant to show it was not negligent. Failure to do so will result in a judgment for the plaintiff.

To illustrate when res ipsa would not apply, assume that the building is a six-story apartment building with 12 units. Instead of a barrel of flour, a potted plant falls and strikes the pedestrian. Elements one and three above are similar to the flour barrel case. However, element two would not be present, because there are 12 suspects (each apartment dweller rather than the owner of the building) who potentially could be guilty of negligence. Although the flowerpot is the instrumentality that caused the injury, it would require an investigation to determine which apartment was in sole control.

The Rescue Doctrine—A Conundrum: To Help or Not to Help? That Is the Question!

Society, as a matter of policy, does not require a person to risk injury or loss of life for the sake of someone in peril. The law does not impose a legal duty on people to rescue a person in distress. Consequently, a very difficult decision must be made when a person encounters someone who needs help. Most people believe a moral duty exists to aid a fellow human being in need of assistance. If the call for help is heard, usually someone heroically attempts to respond.

There are consequences for such noble behavior. First, an attempt to rescue a person can place the rescuer in the same or similar peril. For example, an attempt to save a drowning person may result in both drowning if the rescuer tires in the effort.

Second, the law imposes a duty on rescuers to provide reasonable care during the attempt to help. The good faith rescuer may, through excitement, inexperience, or negligence, aggravate the condition of the victim. This could lead to a lawsuit by the victim against the rescuer; as often mused by philosophers, "No good deed goes unpunished." Third, even if the rescuer is medically trained, such as a doctor or nurse, the medical environment available at the site of the accident may be less than desirable and certainly is not the choice of the rescuer.

Effective first aid may not be possible, and aggravation of an injury may be unavoidable, and the doctor or nurse may be subject to a lawsuit. As a result, different doctrines developed to respond to the above problems premised upon the policy of encouraging people to help in time of peril, such as the rescue doctrine and Good Samaritan doctrine.

The Rescue Doctrine

The **rescue doctrine** is "The principal that a tortfeasor [defendant] who negligently endangered a person is liable for injuries to someone who reasonably attempted to rescue the person in danger" (Garner 2005, 1082–1083). It is designed to encourage people to aid someone in distress. "Thus, if the tortfeasor [defendant] is negligent toward the rescuee, the [law holds the] tortfeasor ... also negligent toward the rescuer" (Garner 2005, 1082–1083).

With this doctrine in mind, assume a hotel has a swimming pool without a lifeguard on duty. A young girl is playfully pushed into deep water by her uncle; she (the rescuee) panics and screams for help. People in the pool are not legally required to save the girl, and consequently, she may drown. Assume another guest, Bill, who is lounging at poolside, yells, "Don't worry I got her!" and he jumps in the pool to save the girl. Bill tires halfway to the sinking girl and decides to turn back. Others watching the event jump in to save her, but it is too late, and she drowns.

The other potential rescuers delayed their effort because they believed the girl was going to be rescued by Bill. Despite his good intentions it appears Bill did not act reasonably, and he may be held liable for the girl's death. Bill should have known his physical capabilities and realized that he probably would tire. Consequently, his unfortunate statement and actions may have delayed others from making a timely response. By his words and actions, Bill created a duty to continue, breached it by failing to do so, and his actions were the proximate cause of the young girl's death and therefore his negligence.

The possibility of injury and/or a lawsuit for the rescuer discourages people like Bill from attempting to aid others. The foregoing example illustrates why many people will not attempt to rescue a person in peril (i.e., the fear of being sued or for fear they may also suffer an injury).

The policy of the rescue doctrine is to encourage others to help a person in distress. Consequently, the person whose negligence caused the rescue attempt is held liable to the rescuer for any injuries and/or lawsuit sustained trying to effectuate the rescue. Under the rescue doctrine and the facts of this case, the playful uncle (the negligent person) could be liable for Bill's (the rescuer) expenses.

Under the rescue doctrine there must be an injury caused by a physical attempt to rescue a person. For example, in one case the alleged rescuer was involved in a car accident with a bus on a street covered with ice and snow. He exited his vehicle to exchange information with the bus driver. As they were talking another vehicle was sliding towards them. The plaintiff yelled at the bus driver to get out of the way, which she did.

He, however, was injured by the second vehicle, which crashed into the bus. He sued the bus company for his injuries, asserting the rescue doctrine. The court denied the claim and ruled that a physical attempt to rescue someone and a resulting injury by the alleged person who caused the injury was required. In this case the bus company was not the tortfeasor, and the plaintiff only verbally warned the bus driver of the impending crash (see *Schwartzman v. Delaware Coach,* 264 A.2d 519).

Good Samaritan Laws

Good Samaritan laws are "... statute(s) that exempt from liability a person (such as an off-duty physician) who voluntarily renders aid to another in imminent danger but negligently causes injury while rendering the aid" (Garner 2005, 576). Such statutes generally apply only to trained and certified persons, such as doctors, nurses, lifeguards, and persons with special EMT training. They were adopted to protect from liability a good faith effort by a trained person, not the lay person. Most such laws provide immunity for a trained person who exacerbates an injury in an attempt to complete a rescue for an ordinary negligence allegation.

Good Samaritan laws usually do not provide liability for gross negligence. In the facts above, attempting to save a drowning person and failing to continue may be viewed as a good-faith failed effort and thus worthy of immunity. However, the statement "Don't worry I got her" may be viewed as gross negligence because it delayed others from making a timely response, which may have cost the young girl's life. The policy is to encourage medical professionals and those with first aid training to respond. In the above case, an off-duty certified lifeguard would be protected by the Good Samaritan doctrine.

Negligence per Se

Negligence per se is "negligence established as a matter of law, so that [neither duty] nor breach of the duty is a jury question" (Garner 2005, 872). It occurs when a statute, ordinance, or administrative rule (government law) is violated, and the violation is the proximate cause of the injury. The purpose of negligence per se is to relieve the injured person of the burden to prove all elements of negligence and also to punish the defendant for violating a government law.

The government law creates a legal duty that must be followed. Accordingly, the injured party (the plaintiff) need not prove elements of duty and breach of duty if there was a violation of the statute. Only the last three elements of causation, injury, and damages will be at issue in a lawsuit.

For example, assume a restaurant violated a health code provision that required meat be maintained at a certain temperature to prevent spoilage. A customer consumed a steak dinner, contracted food poisoning, and was hospitalized for one week. The plaintiff produced evidence the meat became contaminated as a result of a faulty thermostat, which failed to properly cool the refrigerator. In order to recover damages, the plaintiff need only prove the following:

- The thermostat was not operational and did not cool the refrigerator to the proper temperature, so the food spoiled (violation of the statute).
- He ate the spoiled meat and became ill (causation).
- He contracted food poisoning (injury).
- He was hospitalized, incurring medical expenses, lost wages, and pain and suffering (damages).

PRACTICUM

A government law is the minimum requirement for conduct and may not be a safe harbor, in and of itself, to protect the restaurateur. A general common law duty to serve edible food is still available. Failure to serve wholesome meat even with government law compliance may still result in tort liability. In the above example, assume records show the proper temperature was maintained at all times, but the meat still spoiled.

The plaintiff can still sue the restaurant, but it will have to prove all elements of negligence. For instance, perhaps the food was purchased with harmful bacteria present, and the meat was spoiled notwithstanding the proper government-mandated temperature. The restaurant cannot use the statute as a shield. It will be liable for damages if the plaintiff proves the meat was the cause of the food poisoning.

In addition, adhering to a statute does not necessarily absolve a motel for a fire that occurred and injured several guests. There was conflicting evidence as to what caused the fire. The trial court provided a jury instruction that said adherence to a statute is evidence of meeting a motel's duty of due care. The jury rendered a verdict in favor of the motel. The plaintiffs appealed. The court of appeals reversed the trial court, stating that adherence to a statute is the floor for determining due care and that other factors could and should be considered. The common law duty of due care may warrant greater care than merely meeting the standards of the fire code (see *Miller v. Warren*, 390 S.E.2d 207. (W.Va. 1990)).

Strict liability refers to "Liability that does not depend on actual negligence or intent to harm, but is based on the breach of an absolute duty to make something safe" (Garner 2005, 762). It applies in certain situations, such as ultrahazardous acts and product liability, where society holds a defendant liable without the need to prove fault. Normally, all elements of negligence have to be proven for a plaintiff to recover for injuries caused by the defendant. But if an establishment engages in ultrahazardous activity, liability will be imposed without the need to prove the elements of negligence and regardless of any extra precautionary steps imposed by the defendant.

For example, assume a hotel decides to destroy a high-rise structure on its premises in order to build a state-of-the-art hotel facility. It contracts with a demolition company to implode the building. All usual safety precautions are taken. A zone of danger calculated by engineering safety standards is set for a radius of 500 feet. In addition, the hotel set the time for implosion at 5:00 a.m., when pedestrian and motor traffic is minimal. In an abundance of caution, the hotel fenced the entire zone of danger an extra 50 feet further from the building than required by safe engineering standards.

After detonation, a fist size chunk of rock flies farther than anyone would ever expect and strikes a morning jogger in the face, causing serious injury. Negligence would not need to be proven, and the hotel (as well as the demolition company) will be liable under the strict liability doctrine.

The law permits the implosion process because it is a useful, economically proven method to destroy a building, and it is generally a safer practice than historical methods, such as using a crane and a demolition ball. However, as a price for such permission, the hotel must pay for any injury caused by the implosion. Any damage or injury caused by the implosion becomes a cost of doing business and is usually covered with adequate insurance.

Similarly, strict liability may also be imposed in the food industry. A patron of a restaurant expects to be served wholesome food and reasonably relies on the restaurant to provide safe food. Public patrons do not have a reasonable way to check the quality of food at a restaurant. Therefore, the law imposes a duty on the restaurateur to provide wholesome food. If a patron becomes ill after consuming a meal or finds some unexpected ingredient, such as metal in a meatball, the restaurant could be strictly liable for any damages. The policy for strict product liability is fourfold:

- Patrons at restaurant have no way to protect themselves from bad food. They arrive expecting to consume wholesome food.
- The restaurant is in the best position to ensure food is wholesome even if it purchased the product rather than created it in house.
- In the event a product is purchased in defective state, the manufacturer may be judgment proof. The innocent patron requires a remedy for their injury.
- The restaurant can spread the cost of the medical expenses and lawsuit by way of insurance and allocate the expense to its cost of sales.

Defective products can include a wide range of equipment as well as food items. A faulty fire suppression system, an oven, an electric heating product, and an automatic meat slicer are just a few examples. The restaurant need only prove it received the product in a defective condition. Then it will be able sue the manufacturer under the strict liability doctrine for any injury or damage the product caused without having to prove negligence.

SPECIAL DOCTRINES AND STATUTES

Over the years the courts and legislatures have carved out special rules to avoid injustices and to encourage behavior that society wishes to advance. The following concepts are a summary of some of those viewed most important.

Res ipsa loquitur. The courts recognized certain unique circumstances where it is too difficult and sometimes impossible to prove the defendant was negligent. The doctrine of res ipsa loquitur was developed to provide a remedy for that dilemma. For example, res ipsa loquitur was successfully argued in a case where a patient suffered unexplained paralysis in her legs after abdominal surgery (*Gubbins v. Hurson*, 885 A.2d 269 (D.C. 2005)). She alleged the injury could not have occurred without negligence of the doctor.

The rescue doctrine. This is a common law doctrine intended to compensate people injured while assisting someone in distress. Before this doctrine was established, rescuers in attempts to help were left without a remedy for their injuries. Under this doctrine, the person that created the dangerous condition would be liable to an injured rescuer. For example, assume a careless camper throws a cigarette in the brush and starts a fire. Several campers are in their tents, unaware of the pending danger. Other campers in the area see the fire and attempt to rescue those threatened and are injured as a result. The rescuers would have a claim against the careless camper.

Negligence per se. This is a doctrine designed to make it easier for a plaintiff to recover for a violation of a statutory duty. The statute creates the duty and violation of the statute is evidence of the breach. Once a violation of the statute occurs, the plaintiff only need prove causation, injury, and damages. For example, assume a hotel owner fails to comply with government-mandated elevator safety rules, and an elevator drops suddenly, injuring a guest. The hotel will be liable for the injuries without the need to prove a duty exists or breach of duty occurred. Those elements are established as a matter of law (see *Golden Shoreline Limited v. McGowan*, WL 387737 (Fla. 2001)).

Assumption of the risk. This is a principle that denies tort recovery to a person that knew of the risk, understood the risk, and voluntarily chose to take the risk. For example, a young lady volunteered to drive a golf cart used to dispense beverages to the contestants at a golf tournament. She was struck in the mouth by an errant ball, causing injuries to jaw and teeth. The court denied recovery and held she was aware of the danger, understood it, and voluntarily chose to drive the cart and therefore assumed the risk (see *Pfenning v. Lineman*, 922 N.E.2d 45 (2010), Court of Appeals of Indiana).

PRACTICUM

The author disagrees with the conclusion of the court in the *Pfenning v. Lineman* case. The plaintiff was only 16 years old and, arguably, did not appreciate the danger. Moreover, the thrill of participating in a golf tournament, driving a cart dispensing beverages, arguably, is an attractive nuisance. Further, the golf course permitted her to participate, which means comparative negligence should have been applied by the court.

Summary

Negligence is the failure to exercise the standard of care that a reasonably prudent person would have exercised in a similar situation. The law permits a person to recover the cost of an injury from the person that caused the injury. It's society's way to protect people, and it provides an orderly way to do so that tends to negate self-help and breach of the peace. Under negligence theory the defendant does not intend to cause the injury.

The elements of negligence are as follows: creation of a duty, breach of the duty, causation, injury, and damages. A duty is created by statute and common law. Under common law, landowners of property that conduct a business, such as a hotel or restaurant, owe a duty of due care to their business invitees. They must be actively vigilant and inspect the property, fix any dangerous condition, and warn of existing dangers that have yet to be corrected.

Licensees are those on the premises with permission, but they are there for purposes other than to obtain a room or a meal. Vendors are good examples. They are only owed a duty by the landowners to warn of known dangerous conditions. Trespassers have no permission to be on the premises and generally are not owed any duty by the landowner.

A breach of a duty that causes an injury will subject the defendant to various types of monetary damages. Damages are usually compensatory to pay special damages, those easily calculable, such as lost wages, medical bills, and property damages. They also can be general in nature, those difficult to calculate, such as emotional distress, loss of consortium, and pain and suffering. Punitive damages are available for egregious conduct by the defendant.

Common defenses used by the hospitality industry are assumption of the risk, comparative negligence, and the open and obvious doctrine. Several special doctrines and statutes exist to encourage or discourage certain behavior. They include res ipsa loquitur, the rescue doctrine, Good Samaritan statutes, negligence per se, and strict liability.

Comprehension Check

True/False

Directions: Look at each statement below. Based on what you learned in this chapter, decide if the statement is true or false.

1. In order to invoke res ipsa loquitur, the defendant must prove the plaintiff was at fault.
2. Res ipsa loquitur requires the plaintiff establish by clear and convincing evidence that the defendant caused the injury.
3. A breach of a duty is required in order to prove strict liability.
4. Proximate cause must also be the direct cause to provide the plaintiff with requisite causation for recovery of damages.
5. Owners of the resort where a person dove into the water and broke his neck would prevail if they were able to show active vigilance that warned of shallow water.
6. Negligence is based upon the unreasonable person theory.
7. The duty owed to a licensee is a warning of any existing dangers and to refrain from willfully and wantonly inflicting injury.
8. Under the negligence per se theory, once the statute is violated, the plaintiff does not have to prove proximate cause.
9. A person 17 years old is too old to invoke the attractive nuisance doctrine after suffering a life threating injury at a neighbor's pool.
10. It is not legally required for a hotel or restaurant to try and anticipate dangers that may exist on the premises.

11. It is a good idea to train employees how to detect dangerous conditions and to include inspection checklists.
12. If there is a known dangerous condition on the premises, a hospitality manager has a legal duty to warn all people that enter the premises.
13. If someone is choking in a restaurant, you should call 911 and hope they do not die before the paramedics arrive.
14. Active vigilance means you should inspect each meatball you serve to ensure it is safe to eat.
15. Compensatory special damages are difficult to calculate as opposed to general damages.
16. Under strict liability theory, a plaintiff does not have to prove causation.
17. A fundamental question to be answered in negligence cases is the defendant's intent.
18. Assumption of the risk requires the plaintiff to prove the defendant knew of the risk.

Multiple Choice

Directions: Use what you learned in this chapter to choose the best response to each of the prompts below.

1. A person that drives off a road and knocks over a power line is liable for all the following, except:
   a. the replacement of the pole
   b. frying the young boys playing underneath the pole
   c. the loss of pink slime in the refrigerators of the neighboring homes
   d. all of the above

2. If someone gets a piece of chicken stuck in their throat in a restaurant, you should do the following, except:
   a. stick your fingers in their throat and carefully remove the item
   b. give the guest water to wash it down
   c. perform the Heimlich maneuver (being careful you don't crack their ribcage)
   d. none of the above

3. All the following are true, except:
   a. Res ispa loquitur means the burden of proof shifts from the plaintiff to the defendant.
   b. The attractive nuisance theory provides protection to children even if they are trespassers.
   c. Negligence per se provides protection for the plaintiff in a cross-complaint by the defendant.
   d. Strict liability renders the defendant liable without proof of fault.

4. Legal doctrines that aid the defendant are all of the following, except:
   a. choking laws, which relieve a restaurant from liability for failing to perform the Heimlich maneuver if they first call 911
   b. assumption of the risk
   c. respondeat superior
   d. contributory Negligence

5. All the following are elements of negligence, except:
   a. a duty
   b. foreseeability
   c. breach
   d. exclusive control of the instrumentality
6. All the following are true, except:
   a. Res ipsa is a doctrine designed to favor the plaintiff.
   b. Negligence per se means the facts are undisputed and the defendant is liable.
   c. The rescue doctrine permits a lawsuit by the injured rescuer against the defendant causing the rescue.
   d. Contributory negligence is no longer a viable cause of action.
7. The purpose of proximate cause is to:
   a. set the level for assessing damages
   b. settle the case
   c. determine liability
   d. increase the defendant's liability
8. The elements of negligence include:
   a. a duty
   b. proximate cause
   c. damages
   d. all of the above
9. The elements of res ipsa loquitur are:
   a. An injury was caused that would not normally happen without negligence.
   b. The plaintiff did not provoke the defendant.
   c. The injury was not foreseeable.
   d. only a and b
10. Which of the following is not true?
    a. A higher duty of care is owed to children.
    b. Negligence per se means you are strictly liable.
    c. Choking laws relieve a restaurant from liability for failing to perform the Heimlich maneuver.
    d. d. none of the above
11. All the following are true, except:
    a. A statute adopted to protect hotels from installing expensive state of the art glass doors is adequate if the hotel meets the statutory requirements.
    b. Proximate cause is different than direct cause.
    c. Strict liability is an outdated doctrine because insurance is very easy to acquire.
    d. Res ipsa is imposed as an equitable remedy.

12. The following are all false, except:
    a. Res ipsa loquitur may not be used against a hotel.
    b. Comparative negligence may not be used against a hotel.
    c. Contributory negligence may be used against a hotel.
    d. Assumption of the risk can't be used against a hotel.
13. In order to assess damages under comparative negligence, you must do one of the following:
    a. assess a percentage of fault to the defendants
    b. determine whether the cause of action is one that is compensable
    c. determine how much to assess the plaintiff
    d. only a and b
14. Under the attractive nuisance doctrine, all the following are true, except:
    a. The landowner must be aware that the dangerous condition is one likely to attract underage persons.
    b. The reasonable person theory will be applied.
    c. The landowner must be aware that underage persons will likely be in the area.
    d. Due to the child's immaturity, the child does not appreciate the danger.

Scenarios

1. Assume John is driving a used car he just purchased from Slick Sales Used Car, Inc. When he accelerated past 50 miles per hour, the engine fell out of bottom of the vehicle. His crashed into a truck, seriously injured himself, and totaled his car. What legal theory should John advance in his lawsuit?
2. Mary owns a vacant lot upon which many old machines, cars, bricks, and general junk has accumulated over the years. She often sees local children peering through a screen fence talking and pointing to articles inside. Unbeknownst to her a 15-year-old entered and was injured tripping over a piece of metal. The child's parents sue Mary, alleging the attractive nuisance doctrine. What will be the result? Explain your answer.

Decisional Review

1. A restaurant patron went to an eatery and ordered a plate of meatballs and spaghetti. She bit into a meatball and, allegedly, encountered a metal object. It cracked her teeth, and she sued under the theory of res ipsa. The court held res ipsa was not available, because the restaurant was not in sole possession of the meatball. It was purchased from an independent manufacturer. However, there still was a cause of action for common law negligence (*Jones v. GERI Inc.*, 2001 WL 747812 (N.C. 2001)).
2. A seventeen-year-old on vacation signed up to attend a cruise called the "Booze Cruise." Plenty of alcohol was served, and he became inebriated. He subsequently jumped off the boat and was mortally injured by the boat's propellers. His parents sued the owners of the boat. What will be the result? See *Smith v. West Rochelle Travel Agency, Inc.*, 656 Y.Y.S. 2D 340 (2nd Dept. 1997).

Chapter 5

Contracts

Introduction

This chapter introduces the student to business contracts as applied in the hospitality industry. The purpose and importance of a contract is explained. As a general rule both oral and written contracts are enforceable. Some contracts are required to be in writing in order to minimize fraud. However, to the extent possible, all contracts should be in writing to assist with enforcement and litigation. The required elements of an enforceable contract are discussed as well as contract interpretation and enforcement.

Chapter Objectives

After completion of this chapter, the student will understand:

- the purpose of contract law
- the elements of an enforceable contract
- the various types of contracts
- contract interpretation
- contract enforcement

Key Terms

Directions: Each of the terms below will be used in this chapter. Before reading, scan the chapter. The terms will appear in bold. Take a moment to see how the term is used so you can understand it in context. The terms are listed in the order in which they will appear in the chapter.

Mutuality of agreement (p. 107)
Genuine assent (p. 107)
Legal capacity (p. 107)
Consideration (p. 107)
Legality (p. 107)
Form (p. 107)
Express contract (p. 107)
Implied contract (p. 108)
Implied-in-law contract (p. 109)
Quantum meruit (p. 109)
Mechanic's lien (p. 109)
Unjust enrichment (p. 109)
Bilateral contract (p. 109)
Obligor (p. 109)
Obligee (p. 109)
Unilateral contract (p. 110)
Formal contract (p. 110)
Informal contract (p. 111)
Affirmative defenses (p. 112)
Statute of limitations (p. 112)
Voidable (p. 112)
Void contract (p. 112)
Contract of adhesion (p. 112)
Executed contract (p. 113)
Executory contract (p. 113)
Partially executed (p. 113)
Mutual assent (p. 116)
Specific performance (p. 116)
Capacity (p. 116)
Reasonable foreseeable damages (p. 118)
Mitigation of damages doctrine (p. 118)

Contracts in the Hospitality Industry

Hospitality is like any business venture. It offers a product or service the public needs, requires a location and suppliers for its operations, hires employees, advertises, and complies with government regulations. The foregoing are all dependent on enforceable contracts. Therefore, understanding the nature of contracts and learning how to negotiate enforceable contracts is a fundamental necessity.

This chapter provides a basic understanding of negotiating, forming, interpreting, and enforcing business contracts. For example, a restaurant requires, among other things, supplies such as meat, potatoes, bread, milk, spices, and vegetables to prepare meals for its menu.

The restaurant must negotiate enforceable contracts with suppliers for such products to ensure sufficient quantity, quality, and timely delivery. A restaurant must also know how to enforce a contract and how to respond in the event of a breach. Chapter 5 and subsequent chapters (Chapters 6–11) provide information necessary to achieve an understanding of contracts and how to enforce them.

What Is a Contract?

A contract is "an agreement between two or more parties creating obligations that are enforceable or otherwise recognizable at law" (Garner 2005, 271). It is an agreement to perform or forebear performance of a legal right to act. It may concern an immediate act or one to be completed in the future. In a contractual agreement between two or more parties, if one of the parties fails to honor an obligation, recourse for the other party or parties to the contract will be available in a court of law for damages. The court may also order the contract to be performed as originally negotiated, with an equitable remedy, such as specific performance (discussed below).

Judicial interpretation and enforcement of contract elements is achieved through application of the objective theory of contracts (discussed below). Accordingly, owners, executives, agents, and employees in the hospitality industry (hereinafter collectively referred to as "industry personnel") must understand the basic elements of a contract to properly function in performance of their respective jobs.

Historically, some contracts were honored simply because the parties each wanted something in order to conduct business. Other contracts would be breached for a variety of reasons, such as poor cash flow, a shortage of raw materials, a change of mind regarding the need for the contract item, and perhaps just plain fraud.

A potential consequence of the latter scenario is that parties may resort to self-help or a breach of the peace. Therefore, an organized and predictable method of doing business had to be created. The contract concept evolved to provide the stability necessary for reasonable commerce to thrive. The following discussion concerns the more common types of contracts used in the United States.

Contract law provides stability, predictability, and continuity for business transactions. It encourages parties to negotiate and enforce contracts in a lawful and orderly manner, which promotes business and a healthy economy, two important societal policies.

Contract Elements

Contracting parties may agree to any lawful objective; however, the following six elements must be present, or the contract will not be enforceable in a court of law. The elements are as follows:

- Mutual assent—Chapter 6
- Genuine assent—Chapter 7

- Consideration—Chapter 8
- Capacity—Chapter 9
- Legality—Chapter 10
- Proper form—Chapter 11

For a brief explanation of each of these elements, see Key Concept Focus 5.1 below. Refer to Chapter 6 through Chapter 11 for a more detailed discussion of each element.

KEY CONCEPT FOCUS 5.1. ELEMENTS OF A CONTRACT

Mutuality of agreement. The parties must intend to form a contract, and they must willingly agree to all the terms and conditions of the contract. This element is often referred to as a "meeting of the minds."

Genuine assent. A contract must be formed through a voluntary agreement and with a complete understanding of the facts. A contract signed under duress or because of fraudulent representations is not enforceable, because the agreement was not willfully executed. It lacks genuine assent.

Legal capacity. Each party to the contract must have the legal capacity to form a contract. Legal capacity means the ability to understand both the terms and conditions of the contract and the consequences for failing to comply with the terms and conditions.

Consideration. A party must provide some form of value that is bargained for in exchange for value offered by the other party (e.g., hotel service by one party for the promise of payment of money by the recipient hotel guest).

Legality. The subject matter of the contract must not be an illegal activity, such as a promise to violate a government regulation or to sell illegal items.

Form. A contract may be formed verbally or through a written agreement. Pursuant to the Statute of Frauds, certain contracts must be in writing to be enforceable, such as a contract for the purchase of real estate. Other formal contracts, such as a power of attorney, must be in written form as prescribed by law.

Types of Contracts

Contracts can be categorized into various types of agreements. They may be express or implied, bilateral or unilateral, formal or informal, valid or void, or quasi contracts. Each type of contract is discussed below.

Express Contract

An **express contract** is one "whose terms the parties have explicitly set out" (Garner 2005, 273). They are formed by words, either written, oral, or some combination thereof. For example, a hotel general manager calls a painting contractor on the phone and asks for a bid to repaint 100 rooms. The contractor gives a standard bid over the telephone but says he must inspect the rooms to determine if there are any unique qualities that may require extra labor, such as crown moldings. After an inspection of the rooms, the contractor increases the estimated cost by ten percent and submits a written offer. The hotel general manager reviews the offer and calls the contractor one week later and accepts the offer. The combination of telephone calls and the written offer constitutes a binding express agreement.

For another example, assume the vendor of a product, such as cutlery, offers to sell steak knives to a restaurant for $10 each. The restaurant orders 100 of them and pays $1,000 upon delivery with a cashier's check. The terms are clear, and parties each have performed their respective obligations.

Implied Contract

An **implied contract**, also referred to as an implied-in-fact contract, is "a contract that the parties presumably intended by their tacit understanding, inferred from their conduct and other circumstances" (Garner 2005, 274). It is dependent on the conduct of the parties rather than express words.

In the above painting example, assume the contract called for all change orders to be approved in advance and made in writing. After completing the first room, the hotel general manager verbally asked the contractor to darken the white color to a more expensive beige. The contractor did as requested, and the hotel general manager verbally approved.

Next, assume the general manager asks the contractor to add a different, more expensive crown molding in the rooms, and the contractor complies with the request. Spurred by the general manager's insistence in completing the job within two weeks, the contractor commenced painting all the rooms with the revised color and he added the more expensive crown molding.

The general manager periodically checked the completed work and made no other alterations in the specifications of the job. After completion, corporate offices reviewed the contract and refused to pay for the more expensive beige color and the more expensive crown molding because those change orders were not made in writing. Based upon the general manager's conduct, the contractor will likely prevail in a lawsuit because the court would view the verbal changes as an implied waiver of the written requirement.

For another example, a hotel places an order for 200 comforters for some of its beds, at the manufacturer's wholesale price, with a fax on hotel stationery to the vendor's corporate offices. The previous five purchases have all been ordered from the same vendor in the same manner, and each time the product was delivered within 30 days.

Once a new order is received with a fax on hotel stationary, the vendor does not have to fax a formal acceptance to create a contract. It is implied by the previous course of conduct between the two parties. Acceptance is the delivery within 30 days at the manufacturer's wholesale price. Assume the vendor decides not to accept the purchase, because it is short on materials. That decision would have to be communicated to the hotel within a reasonable period of time to permit the hotel to find a substitute source. If not, the vendor may be liable for a breach of contract.

An implied contract is not a legally enforceable negotiated contract containing all six elements required by law. Instead, it is one that the court creates in order to prevent an injustice. For example, assume the facts above regarding the order of hotel comforters, except there has never been any business relations between the two. The hotel verbally places the same order at the same price deliverable within 30 days. The vendor complies as instructed by the hotel.

The statute of frauds requires that if sale of goods exceeds the value of $500 dollars, it must be in writing to be enforceable. The order for comforters will surely exceed $500, and therefore, the verbal contract is unenforceable. The hotel retains the comforters and refuses to pay for them, citing the statute of frauds as a defense. A court would probably require the hotel to pay the vendor for the retained comforters in order to prevent an unjust enrichment by the hotel.

Most states have adopted the Uniform Commercial Code § 2-201(3)(c) and § 2-606, which are codifications of the common law statute of frauds. The aforementioned sections are express exceptions to the writing requirement for a contract. Since the goods in such a contract are totally or partially retained, they are viewed by the courts as an acceptance and indicia of intent to contract.

Implied-in-Law Contract

Under certain circumstances courts will exercise equitable power and create a contract when one or more elements do not exist. Such action is called an **implied-in-law contract** (also referred to as a quasi contract) and is defined as "an obligation created by law for the sake of justice; specifically, an obligation imposed by law because of some special relationship between them [the parties], or because one of them would otherwise be unjustly enriched" (Garner 2005, 274).

It is intended to prevent an unfair result to a party if an implied contract were not created by the court. The measure of damages is referred to as **quantum meruit**, a Latin term that means "the reasonable value of the services; damages awarded in an amount considered reasonable to compensate a person who has rendered services in a quasi-contractual relationship" (Garner 2005, 1036).

For example, suppose a hotel solicits a bid from a contractor to install hardwood floors in its entryway. Several bids are received, and the award of a contract requires corporate approval. The general manager of the hotel is a recent hire and is unfamiliar with contract policy. He erroneously believes he has authority to award the contract and signs an agreement. The contractor reasonably relies upon the general manager's authority and completes the installation.

The corporate office refuses to pay for the services because the general manager lacked proper authority to award the contract. Unfortunately, without corporate approval, an enforceable contract does not exist, and the corporation technically is not liable to pay the contractor. The contractor may sue the hotel for quantum meruit, the value of the services rendered with a contract implied in law. Most states also provide a statutory remedy, usually referred to as a **mechanic's lien**.

Relief with an implied-in-law contract does not always exist when a benefit has been conferred on a party. The court must be convinced the situation is an **unjust enrichment**. In our example above, the contractor performed a benefit because of a misunderstanding regarding the hotel general manager's authority to approve the contract. The fault resided with the hotel that received a benefit, not with the contractor who reasonably relied on the authority of the general manager. It would be patently unfair for the hotel to benefit from the mistake of its employee.

The result would be different, however, if the contractor had performed work for the hotel in the past and knew corporate approval was required. Knowingly accepting the approval of an inexperienced general manager may not meet the requirements for unjust enrichment. In the second example, the contractor would be unfairly taking advantage of a recent hire unfamiliar with corporate requirements. A court might conclude the hotel was not unjustly enriched. It might instead order the contractor to remove the tile or agree to a reasonable amount to the hotel.

Bilateral Contract

A **bilateral contract** is one "in which each party promises performance, so that each party is an obligor on that party's own promise and an obligee on the other's promise" (Garner 2005, 272). It is formed when two or more parties promise to perform certain acts for each other. The party that promises a product or a service is the **obligor**, and the party who accepts the promise is the **obligee**.

A promise to perform by the obligor is consideration because it creates reliance by the obligee, and that reliance creates a legal duty on the obligor to perform. In return, the obligee accepts the offer with a promise to pay a sum certain to form a bilateral contract. The former obligee now becomes the obligor for the return promise to pay the amount due. The promise to pay by the obligee creates reliance by the obligor to perform and creates in the obligee a legal duty to pay. The mutual promises create a bilateral contract between the parties.

Assume a representative of Superior Linens calls Beach Hotel's purchasing agent on April 25, 2016, and offers to sell 2,000 beach towels for $4.00 each. The purchasing agent agrees and indicates the towels must be delivered within one month, but no later than June 1, 2016, the start of the summer tourist season. An agreement is drafted that contains the following provision: Superior Linens promises to deliver 2,000 beach towels to Beach Hotel no later than June 1, 2016, and Beach Hotel promises to pay $8,000 within 30 days of delivery. Note that each party promised future action, thereby creating a bilateral contract via mutual promises.

The contract is binding upon completion of the promises, even though the bargained for exchange (i.e., the product) was not delivered and the contract price was not paid at the time of negotiation. Beach Hotel could have negotiated the same contract with another vendor, but instead, it relied on the promise of Superior Linens.

If Superior Linens fails to deliver the beach towels by June 1, 2016, a breach of contract occurs, and Superior Linens will be liable to Beach Hotel for any damages incurred. Likewise, if Beach Hotel fails to pay within 30 days, Superior Linens will not have money to use for business operations, and Beach Hotel would be liable for the contract price and any consequential damages Superior Linens incurs (see Figure 5.1, a diagram of the bilateral contract between Beach Hotel and Superior Linens).

Unilateral Contract

A **unilateral contract** is one "in which only one party makes a promise or undertakes a performance" (Garner 2005, 277). It is formed when one party promises certain action that calls for performance, rather than a mutual promise in return. In the above example, assume Beach Hotel, in order to ensure it has enough towels for the busy summer season, offers several companies the opportunity for acceptance of its offer to purchase sufficient beach towels. The offer states, "Beach Hotel offers to pay $8,000 for 2,000 beach towels to the first company that delivers the 2,000 beach towels on or before June 1, 2016."

If Superior Linens is the first company to deliver the towels to Beach Hotel on or before June 1, 2016, a contract is formed when Beach Hotel accepts the 2,000 towels. Analytically, Superior Linens would not suffer a legal consequence for failure to deliver the 2,000 beach towels, because it never promised to deliver them. Likewise, Beach Hotel will not have an obligation to pay Superior Linens, unless the towels are delivered on or before June 1, 2016.

Formal Contract

A **formal contract** is one "made through the observance of certain prescribed formalities" (Garner 2005, 273). For example, as mentioned above, some contracts must be written (e.g., statute of frauds) in order to be enforceable in court. In the above beach towel example, the contract concerned the sale of goods in an amount greater than $500. The Uniform Commercial Code (U.C.C.) requires all contracts in excess of $500

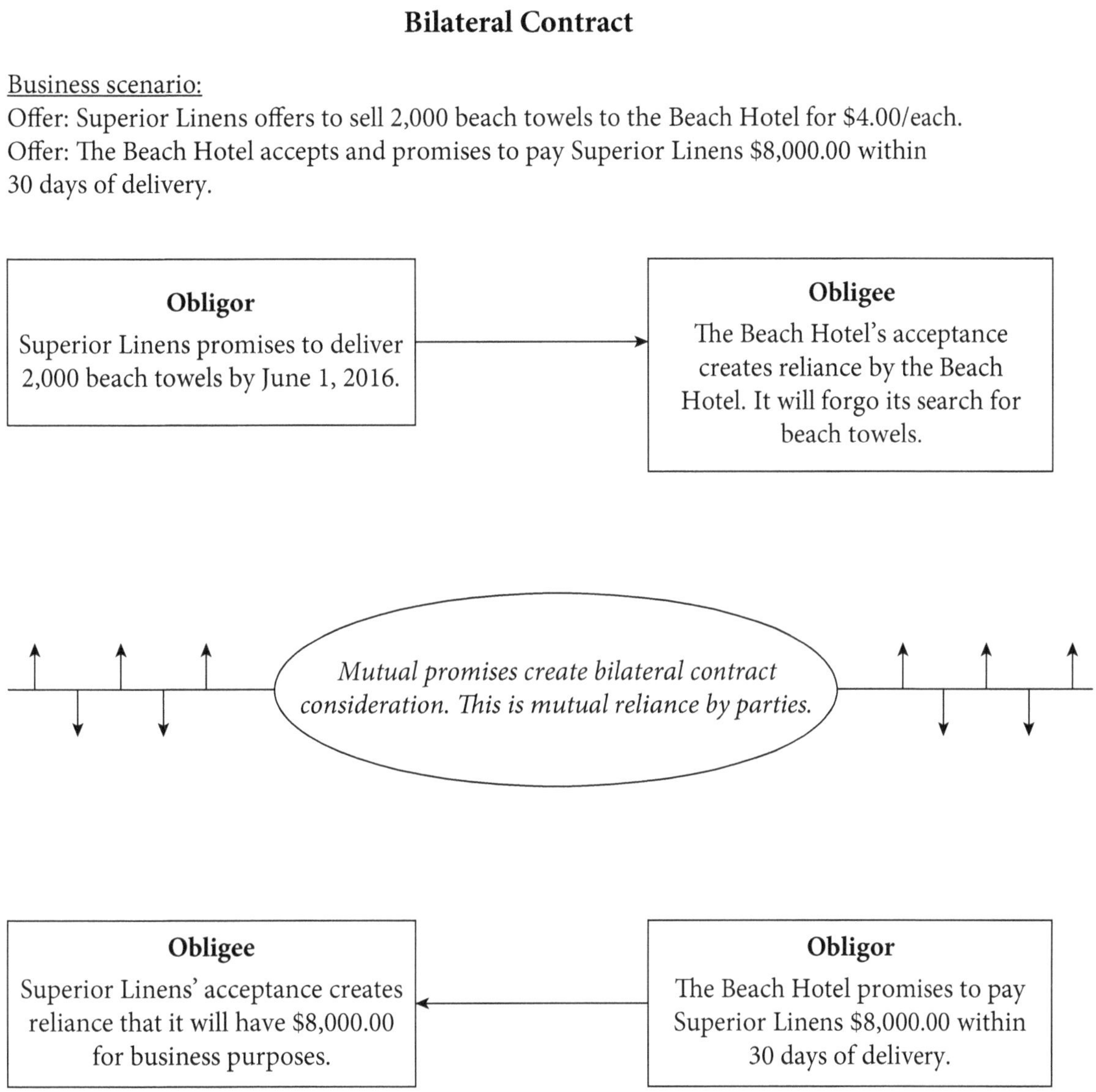

FIGURE 5.1 Bilateral Contract

to be in writing in order to be enforceable in a court of law (U.C.C., § 2-201). Consequently, if the bilateral agreement for the beach towels was verbal, it would be unenforceable in a court of law.

Other examples of formal contracts that must be in writing are real estate contracts, contracts that cannot be performed within one year, and contracts of guarantee (see discussion of statute of frauds, Chapter 11).

Informal Contract

An **informal contract** is one that is "other than one under [formalities] ... specif., that derives its force not from the observance of formalities but because of the presence in the transaction of certain elements that are usu. present when people make promises with binding intent namely—mutual assent and consideration" (Garner 2005, 274). It is a contract not required to meet special written requirements; but it may be in writing or it may be verbal. An informal contract will be enforceable in court as long as it contains the six required elements of a contract (see Key Focus 5.1 above).

For example, if Beach Hotel contracted with Superior Linens for cleaning its existing beach towels rather than purchasing new ones, the contract is for a service and not a sale of goods. Therefore, U.C.C. § 2-201 is not applicable, and a written contract is not required. The vast majority of business contracts are informal contracts.

PRACTICUM

Even though an enforceable contract need not be in writing, it is always wise to prepare it in that manner. It is easier to prove a contract exists in a court of law with physical evidence, such as a writing. For example, memories fade, people move or pass away, evidence may be lost, or the unscrupulous may lie. Without a written contract, enforcement of a contract could devolve into a he-said-she-said scenario and rely only on credibility of the witnesses, if there are any. Without solid witnesses on your behalf, you will have difficulty meeting your burden of proof.

Valid or Void Contracts

In addition to the six elements, a valid contract must also be free from **affirmative defenses**, such as the expiration of time covered by a statute of limitations. A **statute of limitations** is "a law that bars claims after a specified period; specif., a statute establishing a time limit for suing in a civil case, based on the date when the claim accrued (as when the injury occurred or was discovered)" (Garner 2005, 1179).

Statutes of limitation vary by state. In California, the statute of limitations for an oral contract is two years from the date of the breach, and for a written contract, it is four years from the date of the breach. In the above hotel linen example, if the contract was formed orally and the breach was discovered June 5, 2016, the lawsuit would have to be filed before June 6, 2018. If the contract is in writing, the lawsuit would have to be filed before June 6, 2020.

Sometimes, a contract "can be affirmed or rejected at the option of one of the parties" (Garner 2005, 277) and is referred to as **voidable**. For example, if one party to the contract is a minor, contract law provides the minor with the option to void the contract or accept the benefits.

A **void contract** is "a contract that is of no legal effect, so that legally there is really no contract in existence at all. A contract may be void because it is technically defective, contrary to public policy or illegal" (Garner 2005, 277). For example, a person may enter into a contract at an extreme bargaining disadvantage and the terms of the contract do not provide a fair or reasonable choice. As such, a court may void the contract for public policy reasons as a **contract of adhesion** (see also U.C.C. § 2-302 for a statutory provision).

For example, consider a person on welfare with little or no education or one who does not speak the language very well or not at all. They sign a contract for a home refrigerator not fully understanding the monetary consequences. A court can declare the contract void as one of adhesion.

MOST COMMON TYPES OF CONTRACTS

As stated previously, a contract is an agreement between two or more parties creating obligations enforceable in a court of law. A contract is a vehicle for individuals and businesses to conduct their contractual affairs. Without enforceable contracts the business world would be chaotic and unpredictable.

Express contract. One in which the terms of the contract are stated explicitly, in writing, verbally, or a combination of the two.

Implied contract. One in which the parties tacitly intend from their conduct and other relevant circumstances to be bound contractually. It may be implied in fact or implied in law.

Bilateral contract. One in which the parties each make a binding promise to perform certain contract terms. It consists of an obligor who initiates the contract by promising to perform some act and the obligee who in return promises to do something in exchange. See Figure 5.1 for an illustration of a bilateral contract.

Unilateral contract. One in which one person makes a promise (an offer) and the other party accepts by action rather than a return promise as with a bilateral contract. For example, a hotel needs to remodel its dining area and publishes a request for bids from contractors in the local newspaper. The request for bids is not a promise, but instead, it is only an offer to negotiate for work at stated specifications. The respondent contractors submit specifications committing to do so at a stated price. This is an offer and a promise to perform according to the specifications. The hotel accepts the one of its choice, and a contract is formed. It is not a promise, but it is unilateral action that binds the parties.

Formal contract. A contract made through the observance of certain prescribed formalities. Some examples of formal contracts are a contract under seal, a negotiable instrument, a recognizance (an agreement before a judge in a court of law), and a letter of credit (Garner 2005, 273). In addition to the writing requirement, formal contracts may require signatures of witnesses and notarized signatures of some or all the parties. Examples of such formal contracts are wills, trusts, and a power of attorney.

Informal contract. "A contract other than one under seal, a recognizance, or a negotiable instrument" (Garner 2005, 274). It may be oral or written. However, as mentioned previously, it is good practice to require all contracts be written in order to have evidentiary proof for litigation. The vast majority of the contracts entered into are informal contracts.

Executed/Executory Contracts

Contracts are also analyzed according to the extent of performance. A contract is either executed, partially executed, or executory. An **executed contract** is one "that has been fully performed by both parties" (Garner 2005, 273). An **executory contract** is one "that is wholly unperformed or for which there remains something still to be done on both sides [such as a partially executed contract]" (Garner 2005, 273).

For example, suppose a restaurant orders 300 steaks from a meat packing house at $1.00 per steak, delivery at the restaurant in 10 days, full payment in 30 days. After the aforementioned agreement is reached, it is an executory contract until both parties fulfill their obligations. If the steaks are delivered but not paid for, the contract is **partially executed**. After the restaurant pays the packing house $300 at delivery, the contract is fully performed by both parties, and it is an executed contract. The following text box summarizes the stages of contract performance.

STAGES OF CONTRACTS BY PERFORMANCE

Executory contract. A bilateral contract that lacks performance by both parties to the contract (i.e., between the offeror and the offeree). Once the offer is accepted with a promise to perform, the nomenclature changes (see Figure 5.1). In the example above, the meat packing company is the obligor for delivery of the meat, and the restaurant is the obligor for payment of the meat.

Partially executed contract. When only one side of the promise is performed, the contract is partially executed. In the above example, if the meat packing company delivers the meat ordered by the restaurant but the restaurant has not yet paid, the meat packing company fulfilled its promise to deliver, and the contract is partially executed until the restaurant pays for the meat.

Executed contract. A contract fully performed by both parties. After delivery of the meat, the restaurant pays the invoice. Both parties have fully performed, and the contract is executed.

Contract Interpretation

The courts have developed rules for interpreting contracts to assist in the determination of a party's intent. The following is a discussion of the rules most often used.

The Objective Theory of Contracts

Contract theory is based upon "the doctrine that a contract is not merely an agreement, in the sense of a subjective meeting of the minds, but it is instead a series of external acts that give the objective semblance of agreement" (Garner 2005, 906). It is an interpretation of a contract based upon the reasonable person concept, similar to tort law. If a dispute arises with performance, the trier of fact must decide the objective intent of the parties at the time of contract formation and, in particular, what a reasonable person objectively was thinking when the contract was negotiated.

It is impossible to determine a person's subjective intentions at the time of contract formation; therefore, contract law employs the objective theory of interpretation to resolve disputes. Intent is determined by looking at the contract terms and the actions of the parties in developing and responding to the terms rather than guessing what the parties were thinking. Intent will be determined by objective facts.

Typical objective facts are what the parties said to each other, what the terms of the contract state, how the parties responded to the terms, and other objective determinable circumstances related to the contract. Also important in determining the parties' intent and for settling a contract dispute is reliance on trade usage and prior practices between the parties (trade usage and prior transactions are discussed below).

A classic case for determining intent of the parties using the objective theory of contracts is that of *Lucy v. Zehmer*, described in more detail below. The court in *Zehmer* found that despite years of unsuccessful negotiations and an acceptance of a contract offer after consumption of a large amount of alcohol, the parties legally agreed to a contract for the sale of a farm.

LUCY V. ZEHMER

Supreme Court of Appeals of Virginia
196 Va. 493 (1954)

Key Facts: *W.O. Lucy (Lucy) plaintiff had been trying for about eight years to buy a farm from his friends A.H. and Ida Zehmer. They started to drink whisky and engaged in friendly small talk. While there Lucy tried again to buy the farm for $50,000. He stated to Zehmer that "I'll bet you won't take $50,000 for that place." Zehmer replied, "Yes, I would too; you wouldn't give fifty." They continued to visit and consumed more whisky. Eventually Lucy convinced Zehmer to write up an agreement for the sale of the farm for $50,000. The contract was rewritten, at the request of Lucy, to include Ida Zehmer and to clarify specifics of the agreement. All three parties signed the agreement. Subsequently, Mr. Zehmer refused to honor the contract alleging that he was drunk, didn't understand what he was doing and his offer to sell was made in jest.*

BUCHANAN, J., delivered the opinion of the court.

In his testimony, Zehmer claimed that he "was high as a Georgia pine," and that the transaction "was just a bunch of two doggoned drunks bluffing to see who could talk the biggest and say the most." That claim is inconsistent with his attempt to testify in great detail as to what was said and what was done.

****

The appearance of the contract, the fact that it was under discussion for forty minutes or more before it was signed; Lucy's objection to the first draft because it was written in the singular, and he wanted Mrs. Zehmer to sign it also; the rewriting to meet that objection and the signing by Mrs. Zehmer; the discussion of what was to be included in the sale, the provision for the examination of the title, the completeness of the instrument that was executed, the taking possession of it by Lucy with no request or suggestion by either of the defendants that he give it back, are facts which furnish persuasive evidence that the execution of the contract was a serious business transaction rather than a casual, jesting matter as defendants now contend.

****

In the field of contracts, as generally elsewhere, we must look to the outward expression of a person as manifesting his intention rather than to his secret and unexpressed intention. The law imputes to a person an intention corresponding to the reasonable meaning of his words and acts.

The Decision—Comment

The court of appeals reversed the trial courts' decision in favor of Lucy. The rationale cited in this case demonstrates a very clear application of the objective theory of contracts.

This case also demonstrates three other very important legal concepts: mutual assent, specific performance, and capacity:

- **Mutual assent**: Mutual assent is a necessary element of an enforceable agreement between the parties. The court in *Lucy* concluded the objective actions of the parties' demonstrated intent to form a contract. That intent showed an agreement had been formed and is sufficient "meeting of the minds" to conclude the element of mutual assent was present.
- **Specific performance**: There are times when monetary damages are an insufficient contract remedy. If the property is so unique that the plaintiff is dissatisfied with an award of money, the court may order the defendant to honor the contract terms. The *Lucy* court must have felt the eight-year quest by Lucy demonstrated, as to him, that the property was unique enough and it ordered the specific performance.
- **Capacity**: As stated previously, capacity is the ability to understand the terms and conditions of the contract and the consequences for failing to perform as agreed to by parties. Gross intoxication is a defense used to argue lack of capacity to form a contract, but it is a defense that is hard to prove. In this case, the parties had been drinking for several hours, and Zehmer alleged he was "high as a Georgia Pine." But because of the objective conduct of the parties, the court apparently did not believe that the Georgia Pine Zehmer metaphorically referred to was quite high enough.

THE PLAIN MEANING RULE

The plain meaning rule is "the rule that if a 'writing' (contract), or a provision in a writing, appears to be unambiguous on its face, its meaning must be determined from the writing itself without resort to any extrinsic evidence" (Garner 2005, 966). Not all writings are contracts, but the rule does apply to contract interpretation. It is one of the most important rules employed by a court to interpret the terms contained in the four corners of the contract.

If no ambiguities exist, the court will enforce the contract as written and as understood by the court using the obvious meaning of the words. Evidence not contained in the contract (referred to as extrinsic evidence) but that which is offered to show a meaning contra to the unambiguous words in the contract will be excluded.

The following case shows how a court resolved the dispute using trade usage for its interpretation of the contract. Assume a buyer orders chicken from a supplier, which it intends to be used as high-grade chicken to be prepared as chicken cordon blue; however, the buyer instead receives a lower grade, which is normally used as stewing chicken. The issue surfaces because in industry parlance (trade usage), the term "chicken," without qualification, refers to stewing chicken, the lowest grade of chicken.

Unless the buyer specifies it wants a high-grade chicken for baking, the seller may believe the term "chicken," as used in the contract, is the trade usage description intended for the lower grade of stewing chicken. A court sees the term "chicken," and that word does not appear ambiguous. Chicken is chicken. However, the court may permit extrinsic evidence offered by the supplier to show that according to trade usage it sent the proper grade of chicken for the contract at issue (see *Frigaliment Importing Co. v. B.N.S. International Sales Corp.*, 190 F. Supp. 116 (N.Y. 1960)).

ADDITIONAL RULES OF INTERPRETATION

The following rules have been developed over the years by American contract jurisprudence to assist in determining the meaning of a contract.

- The contract will be interpreted as a whole rather than by its subparts. Viewing a contract piecemeal could result in missing the overall intent of the contract.
- Negotiated terms will take precedence over "standard form" terms. Negotiated terms require separate thought and more closely indicate intent of the parties. For the same reason, handwritten words will take precedence over typed words.
- Technical terms will be given their technical meaning unless otherwise indicated by the parties.
- Ambiguous terms will be construed against the author of the contract since that party had control of the contract and its drafting.
- Specific wording will be given precedence over general wording. For example, assume the introductory language of a purchase order says, "50 lbs. of baking chicken parts to be delivered in individual sections." If, in a subsequent paragraph, the purchase order specifies an equal number of legs and thighs but no wings, the more specific later statement "equal number of legs and thighs" will control "baking chicken parts."
- Trade usage, custom, and prior dealings may be used to clarify ambiguities. With the example above, if only the introductive language is stated in the purchase order, prior dealings between the parties may indicate that only drumsticks and thighs are included in the term "baking chicken parts."

Contract Damages

Damage assessment for contracts is different than tort damages. Tort damages include calculation of general damages, such as emotional distress and pain and suffering. Sometimes, when the conduct of a defendant is egregious, courts apply punitive damages to punish the defendant and also as exemplary damages to deter others from similar conduct.

Damages for breach of contract does not include general damages nor does it usually include punitive damages. Contract damages include compensatory damages, which is defined as "damages sufficient in amount to indemnify the injured person for the loss suffered" (Garner 2005, 333).

The contract compensatory damage is measured by the "benefit of the bargain," defined as "damages that a breaching party to a contract must pay to the aggrieved party, equal to the amounts that the aggrieved party would have received, including profits, if the contract had been fully performed" (Garner 2005, 333). That means in addition to actual loss in terms of labor and materials, the expected profit will be awarded if the breach of the contract is foreseeable and the amounts requested are reasonable.

The purpose of the benefit of the bargain theory is to place the nonbreaching party in the position they would have been in had the contract been fully performed. In the example of the hotel contracting to paint 100 rooms, assume the contract called for completion at a certain date because the hotel was scheduled to host a seven-day convention, and all 100 rooms were reserved for the event. Further assume the contractor failed to complete on time. After notification by the hotel of failure to complete the rooms, the sponsors cancelled the convention.

Under the benefit of the bargain theory, the hotel would likely sue for damages, which would include the profits lost from the cancellation of the convention. This would also include administrative costs and any consequential damages, such as minimum fees associated with entertainment contracts, the purchase of food and beverages, and valet service planned for the event.

Damages must be calculable with reasonable certainty and they must be reasonably foreseeable. **Reasonable foreseeable damages** are defined as "damages directly, immediately, and naturally flowing from the act complained of" (Garner 2005, 335). For example, alleged damages based upon a state legislature's failure to provide necessary government authorizations was found not reasonably foreseeable. The court felt such government action is too speculative (*Casino Resorts, Inc. v. Monarch Casinos, Inc.*, 1997 WL 793134 (Minn. 1997)). By contrast, lost profits were recoverable when a restaurant could not open its doors as scheduled. The lessor's failure to complete installation of a heating, ventilation, and air conditioning system caused the delay (see *Ibiza, Inc. v. Samis Foundation*, 131 Wash. App. 1055 (2006)).

Mitigation of Damages

Based upon the public policy to minimize economic waste, courts developed the mitigation of damages doctrine. The **mitigation of damages doctrine** is "the principle requiring a plaintiff, after an injury or breach of contract, to make reasonable efforts to alleviate the effects of the injury or breach. If the defendant can show that the plaintiff failed to mitigate damages, the plaintiff's recovery may be reduced" (Garner 2005, 840).

For example, continuing the hotel contractor case above, assume the contractor completed the painting contract on schedule, but the sponsors canceled the reservations for business reasons a week before the scheduled convention. Under the mitigation of damages doctrine, the hotel cannot just close its doors for the week and then claim lost profits because of the breach of contract by the convention sponsors.

The hotel must make a reasonable effort to find replacement reservations. For example, they might advertise a special room rate to encourage people to fill as many rooms as possible. Otherwise, a court of law may reduce the lost profit damage claim by an amount the court feels is fair and reasonable.

Summary

The hospitality industry is like most types of business with heavy reliance on negotiated contracts. Therefore, a fundamental knowledge of contract negotiations and contract enforcement is a must for all industry personnel. The foregoing persons have to understand what a contract is and be certain that all requisite elements are present. Otherwise, the contract entered into may not be enforceable in a court of law.

Various types of contracts, such as express, implied, bilateral, unilateral, void, valid, executory, or partially executed, were discussed in this chapter. Also discussed was the necessary form of contracts. Most contracts are informal and are not required to be in writing, although it is always best to do so. The statute of frauds and other statutes, such as the Uniform Commercial Code, may require a written contract in certain circumstances.

Contract interpretation was discussed to provide the student with insight into how a court of law views certain contract questions. The general rule is that the courts will use the objective theory of contract interpretation, which means the court will look at the objective actions of the parties, such as what was said and how the parties reacted to the contract. No attempt will be made to try to guess what the parties subjectively thought. Only the objective facts will be considered.

An important judicial tool is the plain meaning rule, which states that unless otherwise required, the courts will look to the common understanding of each word. Exceptions will be made if there is an ambiguity in the language and in certain circumstances where trade usage or a past pattern of prior dealings is present.

Finally, the difference between contract damages and tort damages was explained. Contract damages are based upon the benefit of the bargain theory, and a plaintiff must make a good faith effort to mitigate damages.

Comprehension Check

True/False

Directions: Look at each statement below. Based on what you learned in this chapter, decide if the statement is true or false.

1. Genuine assent means the parties genuinely agree to the contract terms without such outside factors as fraud.
2. Contracts are a very important part of a hospitality executive's knowledge because of the numerous agreements that have to be made with vendors, employees, business invitees, and so on.
3. Capacity is an element of a contract and refers to the ability of a person to understand whatever is mutually agreed upon.
4. An underage person may void a contract for food because it is a necessity of life.
5. The statute of frauds requires full performance as the exception to the required writing if the sale of goods exceeds $500 in value.
6. Consideration means you should always think of others when you negotiate a contract.
7. A plaintiff seeking damages for breach of contract must prove the damages were unforeseeable.
8. In a breach of contract case, the defendant may defend on the grounds that the damages are too speculative.
9. A forum selection clause contained in an internet contract is unenforceable.
10. An appellate court usually rules only on the issues of law.
11. The duty to mitigate contract damages means the plaintiff must make an effort to prevent the defendant from incurring damages.
12. The six elements of a contract are not all present in hotel contracts, because of the temporary nature of room occupancy.
13. In order for a court to award damages, the loss must be foreseeable and calculable in dollars and cents.
14. Genuine assent concerns contract agreements entered into only because of threats of violence and duress.
15. In order for mutuality to exist, the acceptance must be definite.
16. A change in the terms by the offeree constitutes a counteroffer.

Multiple Choice

Directions: Use what you learned in this chapter to choose the best response to each of the prompts below.

1. The elements of a contract include all the following, except:

   a. mutuality of patience
   b. genuine assent
   c. consideration

d. legality

2. What is the definition of a "chicken"?
    a. It usually means stewing chicken.
    b. It is the lowest grade of chicken.
    c. It is better quality than "free-range chicken."
    d. If not defined in your chicken contract, trade industry usage will apply.
3. The elements of a contract include:
    a. legality
    b. consideration
    c. genuine assent
    d. all of the above
4. The statute of frauds applies to the following:
    a. a contract that can be completed within one year
    b. real estate transactions
    c. contracts for the sale of goods over $500
    d. only b and c
5. Breach of contract requires:
    a. an agreement
    b. foreseeability
    c. damages
    d. all of the above
6. Consideration can be:
    a. love and affection
    b. forbearance
    c. an inheritance
    d. only a and b
7. Absence of genuine assent includes all the following, except:
    a. fraud
    b. mitigation of damages
    c. duress
    d. blackmail
8. The parol evidence rule:
    a. precludes the use of oral evidence
    b. encourages the use of an integration provision in a contract
    c. permits the use of intrinsic evidence
    d. permits the use of written evidence

9. With regard to damages, which is true?
   a. Profit history is unimportant.
   b. Consequential damages are always recoverable.
   c. Punitive damages are not easily obtained.
   d. You can get specific performance if the defendant is judgment proof.
10. With regard to a voidable contract, all the following are true, except:
   a. It may be canceled at the option of one party.
   b. The right to cancel is referred to as revocation.
   c. The right to cancel exists for a reasonable amount of time.
   d. none of the above

Scenarios

1. Accurate Publishing has been ordering paper from Affordable Paper Co. for 10 years. The purchase order used provides that Affordable make deliveries to Accurate's warehouse every three months on the first day of the month. The business relationship was excellent. After the sixth year, Accurate stopped expressly including that delivery requirement in its purchase order. Nonetheless, Affordable continued to make the deliveries every three months. The last order was not delivered. Accurate called to complain, and Affordable replied they were under new management and their policy changed. All purchases must be picked up at Affordable's business offices. Accurate sued for damages resulting from the delay in receipt of the last shipment. What will be the result, and why?
2. William and Peter were business partners for ten years, and in their partnership agreement, they expressly agreed to share profits equally. They subsequently began to mistrust each other and decided to terminate their partnership. At the partnership liquidation hearing, Peter claimed he was entitled to 60% of the profits because he was more involved in the business. He claimed that William agreed to the increase in profit sharing the last five years of the business. He produced his profit-sharing paychecks as proof. Is Peter entitled to the 60% profits after liquidation? Explain your answer.

Decisional Review

1. A husband and wife, welfare recipients, purchase a home freezer for a total price of $1,439. Its maximum market price was $300. They could not keep up with the payments and sought legal aid to file suit. The complaint alleged the contract was unconscionable. Defendant's alleged legal time finance costs and other charges comprised the difference and had been explained to plaintiffs. What will be the result? Explain your answer. See *Jones v. Star Credit*, 298 N.Y.S.2d 264 (1969).
2. Plaintiff was riding a bicycle and was rear-ended by a motor vehicle. The driver of the motor vehicle did not have insurance. Plaintiff filed an uninsured motorist claim with his father's insurance company to recover damages. Defendant denied the claim because the insurance policy did not cover bicyclists. It did cover pedestrians. Trial court rule for Plaintiff, concluding the term "pedestrian" was ambiguous and therefore covered the Plaintiff. Defendant appealed. What will be the result? Explain your answer. See *Cole v. Auto-Owners Ins. Co.*, 272 Mich. App. 50 (2006).

Chapter 6

Mutual Assent

Introduction

Mutual assent is referred to as a meeting of the minds. It symbolizes that a contract has been formed. This conclusion is based upon the objective evidence of the intent demonstrated by the parties. Without this element a legal contract does not exist. An offer is made by the offeror in clear terms, and it is communicated to the offeree who then accepts the offer. This chapter explains the steps that take place to create an enforceable contract.

Chapter Objectives

Upon completion of this chapter, the student will understand:

- mutual assent
- the importance of intent
- the importance of clear terms
- communication of the offer
- acceptance of an offer
- termination of an offer
- problems with e-contracts

Key Terms

Directions: Each of the terms below will be used in this chapter. Before reading, scan the chapter. The terms will appear in bold. Take a moment to see how the term is used so you can understand it in context. The terms are listed in the order in which they will appear in the chapter.

Meeting of the minds (p. 124)
Offer (p. 125)
Offeror (p. 125)
Offeree (p. 125)
Counteroffer (p. 125)
Opinion (p. 127)
Future intent (p. 127)
Preliminary negotiations (p. 127)
Sarcasm (p. 127)
Auctions (p. 127)
Auctioneer (p. 127)
Auction with reserve (p. 128)
Auction without reserve (p. 128)
Course of dealing (p. 129)
Trade usage in the industry (p. 129)
The mailbox rule (p. 129)
The mirror image rule (p. 130)
Silence as acceptance (p. 130)
Course of dealing (p. 131)
Trade usage (p. 131)
Revocation (p. 132)
Rejection (p. 132)
Definite time (p. 133)
Reasonable time (p. 133)

Death of a party (p. 134)
Incapacity of a party (p. 134)
Destruction of the subject matter (p. 134)
Supervening illegality (p. 134)
Lapse of time (p. 134)
Formation (p. 134)
Enforcement (p. 135)
Forum selection clause (p. 136)
Choice of law clause (p. 136)

Mutual Assent

The first of the required six elements necessary for the formation of a contract is mutual assent. It is defined as "a mutual assent by both parties to a contract, usu. in the form of offer and acceptance" (Garner 2005, 94). Two or more parties must intend to agree to do something in exchange for something in return, often referred to as a **meeting of the minds**. The following case explains the concept of mutual assent.

---

539 SO.2D 459

Supreme Court of Florida.
James GIBSON, Petitioner,
v.
Garth COURTOIS and Sally Courtois, Respondents.
No. 70921.
March 2, 1989.

KOGAN, Justice.

***

On April 5, 1984, Gibson submitted an offer to purchase Courtois' home. The offer was in the form of a written contract. The next day, before acceptance by Courtois, Gibson revoked the offer and demanded the return of his escrow deposit. The agent holding the escrow brought an interpleader action to determine each party's rights to the deposit funds. The trial court ruled that, because the offer was revoked prior to acceptance, there was no contract and the deposit should be returned to Gibson. On appeal, the district court affirmed the ruling. Courtois v. Gibson, 485 So.2d 429 (Fla. 2d DCA 1986).

Gibson moved the trial court to award him attorney's fees pursuant to a provision in the same contract offer that Gibson revoked. The court denied the motion, and the district court affirmed the ruling. Gibson v. Courtois, 509 So.2d 962 (Fla. 2d DCA 1987). The court held that because Gibson revoked the offer before it was accepted, the attorney's fees provision of the contract was not enforceable. Gibson petitioned this Court to review the district court's decision.

The contract upon which Gibson bases his claim for attorney's fees states:

Attorney's Fees and Costs: In connection with any litigation arising out of the contract, the prevailing parties shall be entitled to recover all costs incurred, including reasonable attorney's fees.

Clearly, if enforceable, this provision allows Gibson to recover his attorney's fees because he was the prevailing party in the underlying action.

***

The trial court held in the underlying action that no contract came into existence and no legal obligations attached. A mere offer not assented to constitutes no contract, for there must be not only a proposal, but an acceptance thereof. So long as a proposal is not acceded to, it is binding upon neither party, and it may be retracted.

***

He [Courtois] never accepted Gibson's offer. Mutual assent is an absolute condition precedent to the formation of the contract. Absent mutual assent, neither the contract nor any of its provisions come into existence. [Citations omitted.]

It is so ordered. [Affirmed.]

That something being exchanged is called consideration and will be discussed in Chapter 8. A meeting of the minds requires each contracting party to demonstrate an intent to be bound by the contract terms. Intent is a key ingredient for contract enforcement and is determined by the trier of fact using the objective theory of contracts.

The parties must agree to the terms of the contract, initially communicated with an **offer** by the proponent (**offeror**) to the party targeted (**offeree**). It is action that initiates contract negotiations. The offeror states the terms, which must clearly show intent to become bound by the offer, and the terms must be communicated to the offeree, who must unequivocally accept them.

If the offeree's acceptance varies any of the material terms, the offer is deemed rejected, and the intended acceptance becomes a **counteroffer**. A counteroffer will switch the designations of the parties. The offeree who makes the counteroffer becomes the new offeror and the offeror becomes the new offeree (Figure 6.1).

The elements for mutual assent are:

- There must be an objective intent by the parties to be bound.
- The terms of the contract must be definite and reasonably clear.
- The offer must be communicated to the offeree.
- The acceptance must be unequivocal.

Offer & Acceptance

In these scenarios, John is looking for a new vehicle. His neighbor Bill has a vehicle he is willing to sell. They make offers and/or accept in order to satisfy both parties.

Straight Sale

Bill offers to sell his car to John for $10,000.

Offeror	**Offeree**
Bill	John
Bill offers a price of $10,000 for his vehicle.	John accepts his offer.

**Bill is the offeror and John is the offeree. John accepts. Sale is consummated.*

Counteroffer 1

Bill offers to sell his car to John for $10,000. John agrees to purchase but will only pay $9,000.

Offeror	**Offeree**
John	Bill
John becomes offeror. John accepts but makes counteroffer for $9,000.	Bill becomes offeree. Bill rejects counteroffer.

**Bill rejects John's counteroffer and makes new counteroffer to John's original counteroffer.*

Counteroffer 2

Bill makes a new counteroffer of $9,500.

Offeror	**Offeree**
Bill	John
Bill counters with a price of $9,500.	John accepts. Sale is consummated.

**John accepts Bill's counteroffer. Sale is consummated.*

FIGURE 6.1 A Diagram of the Offer, Acceptance, and Counteroffer Concept

Intent

Intent of the parties is a crucial point of focus for a court in its analysis of a contract dispute. Several concepts come to play in the court's determination regarding intent; they are opinion, future intent, preliminary negotiations, sarcasm, and auctions. The following discussion explains each one.

Opinion. Courts do not view a person's opinion as legal intent to make a binding offer. As with fraud and puffing, an **opinion** is not a fact-based representation sufficient to bind a reasonable person to a contract. It is one person's belief regarding a product or service.

For example, a salesman who sells Cajun powder designed specifically for seafood dishes meets with the owner of a restaurant. He tells the owner it is the absolutely best Cajun powder on the market, and its use will easily double sales. The owner purchases a year's supply and uses the Cajun powder on all his fish dinners. Sales improved only slightly.

The owner sues for breach of contract and false misrepresentation. He would likely lose a breach of contract suit if he bases the claim on the salesman's misrepresentation that sales would double. A court would likely hold the statement as the salesman's opinion, not a reliable fact that becomes part of the offer. If the salesman produces data, such as a line graph, with gross sales figures demonstrating what other seafood restaurants experienced with the product, the issue may change. The matter is no longer opinion, but instead, it's a representation of fact and, if fraudulent, could be grounds for a lawsuit.

Future intent is an offer to sell something in the future; it is not a present offer that may be accepted to form a binding contract. For example, assume a restaurateur, in a discussion with an investment banker, says he will sell his restaurant in a couple of months for the appraised value of $250,000.

The investment banker cannot accept that statement as an offer to sell by tendering a cashier's check for $250,000 the next day. It is not a present offer to sell the restaurant, but merely an expression to sell some time in the future. More definite terms, such as a date certain when the offer becomes operational, is required.

Assume the restaurateur told the investment banker to help him sell the restaurant, as is, to the first person to present him with a cashier's check for $250,000. The next day the investment banker presents him with a cashier's check in an amount of $250,000, with a handwritten notation on the check stating, "As is." A court of law would likely treat the statements of the restaurateur as a legal offer and the acts of the investment banker as a legally binding acceptance.

Certain statements are not viewed as offers, but only invitations to negotiate. These are called **preliminary negotiations**. In the above example, assume the restaurateur states he will sell his restaurant for at least $250,000. He is not offering to sell at that price, but instead, he is inviting the investment banker to make an offer of no less than $250,000. The words "at least" are not definite and they are intended to be a minimum threshold to initiate a bidding war.

Statements made using **sarcasm** are not legally binding. Assume the restaurateur tells the investment banker that he is sick of all the operational problems with his restaurant and he would sell it immediately to the first person to provide him a check for $50,000. The investment banker can't reach into his pocket, pull out his check book, write a check for $50,000, and accept the offer. A reasonable person would not expect a restaurant worth $250,000 to be sold for $50,000, within the context of that statement.

Auctions are a special type of sales negotiation treated differently from the standard offer/acceptance rules. In an auction, an item is offered for sale through an intermediary called an **auctioneer**. Placement of an item "up for auction" is not an offer by the owner of the goods to sell the item. Instead, it is a request for bidders to make an offer, which the owner may accept or reject. Analytically, the bidder is the offeror, and the owner of the item for sale is the offeree. Bidders make offers until the auctioneer announces the sale is consummated, usually, when the gavel falls for a third time. Each higher bid operates as a rejection of the last lower bid. Whoever makes the last and highest offer will be declared the winner by the auctioneer.

Generally, auctions are either with reserve or without reserve. An **auction with reserve** permits the seller to withdraw the goods from sale at any time before the auctioneer announces the sale to the highest bidder. Upon proper notice to bidders, a seller may reserve the right to withdraw a sale even after the gavel has fallen for the last time and the auctioneer has announced a sale. An **auction without reserve** prohibits withdrawal of an item for sale once bidding commences, and it requires the auctioneer to sell to the highest bidder.

For example, assume a hotel chain files for bankruptcy protection under Chapter 11 of the Bankruptcy Code. Chapter 11 of the Bankruptcy Code is referred to as a "business reorganization" where a business is permitted to remain operational, subject to certain requirements (see Bankruptcy Code in Chapter 11).

The hotel hires an auctioneer to sell furnishings from several of its hotels at an auction, with reserve. As long as the hotel provides legally sufficient notice, it retains the flexibility to change its mind and not agree to the sale. If the auction is without reserve, the sale of the furnishings becomes final upon the last fall of the gavel.

The following classic case was presented in Chapter 5. It was included there and now here because of its discussion of several important legal concepts. The relevant portions concerning intent are repeated below for ease of reference.

EXCERPTS OF *LUCY V. ZEHMER* DISCUSSING INTENT

> *"The appearance of the contract, the fact that it was under discussion for forty minutes or more before it was signed; Lucy's objection to the first draft because it was written in the singular, and he wanted Mrs. Zehmer to sign it also; the rewriting to meet that objection and the signing by Mrs. Zehmer; the discussion of what was to be included in the sale, the provision for the examination of the title, the completeness of the instrument that was executed, the taking possession of it by Lucy with no request or suggestion by either of the defendants that he give it back, are facts which furnish persuasive evidence that the execution of the contract was a serious business transaction rather than a casual, jesting matter as defendants now contend.*
>
> ****
>
> *In the field of contracts, as generally elsewhere, we must look to the outward expression of a person as manifesting his intention rather than to his secret and unexpressed intention. The law imputes to a person an intention corresponding to the reasonable meaning of his words and acts."*

The Importance of Clear Terms

In order to have an enforceable contract, the terms, as well as the offer and acceptance, must be reasonably clear. Otherwise, a court will be unable to determine the objective intent of the parties. If a court is unable to discern intent of the parties, the plaintiff in a contract lawsuit will probably lose the case. Required terms will vary by the type of contract at issue, but the most common terms usually are:

- identification of the parties
- the subject of the contract
- consideration to be paid
- performance requirements, such as quantity, delivery terms, and product specifications
- procedure in case of a dispute (e.g., mediation)

Communication of the Offer

The offer must be communicated to the offeree in order to create a legally binding acceptance. It is unreasonable to conclude a meeting of the minds exists unless the offer has been communicated in clear understandable terms. Without knowledge of a definite, clear offer, a contract cannot be formed.

However, on occasion certain terms may be inadvertently omitted. A court may conclude sufficient information exists to establish a clear overall intent of the parties to enter into a contract. If so, it may supply the missing terms. For example, if the contract execution date was inadvertently left open, the court could supply that date based upon evidence from the parties.

Also, some legal exceptions exist, such as when **course of dealing** between the parties or **trade usage in the industry** permits the court to supply missing terms (see discussion below of those concepts).

Acceptance of the Offer

Acceptance is "an offeree's assent, either by express act or by implication from conduct, to the terms of an offer, in a manner authorized or requested by the offeror, so that a binding contract is formed" (Garner 2005, 10). It is the agreement by the offeree to be bound in contract according to the terms of the offer. It must be voluntary, unequivocal, and mirror the essential terms of the offer. The acceptance may be expressed by words or acts and must follow any special terms for acceptance contained in the offer.

Since intent is the linchpin of an enforceable contract, any variation of the material terms of the offer is viewed as a rejection of the offer. The courts view the variation of the terms in the offer as a failure to attain a meeting of the minds. Analytically, the courts treat such an acceptance, with the varied terms, as a rejection of the offer. Instead, it is treated as a counteroffer, which must be accepted by the former offeror without further material variation.

The mailbox rule is defined as "the principle that an acceptance becomes effective and binds the offeror once it has been properly mailed" (Garner 2005, 795). It is a legal presumption that acceptance becomes effective when the offer is deposited in the U.S. mail system rather than upon receipt by the addressee. The mailbox rule is based upon the rationale that once a letter is deposited in the mail system, its probabilities of being received are very high. Also, it prevents the recipient of the acceptance (i.e., the offeror) from falsely claiming the acceptance was never received.

The general rule is the offer must be accepted in the manner described in the offer, such as by the United States Postal Service (USPS). If not described in the offer, an acceptance may be made in the same or similar manner as the offer. Assume the offer is sent by USPS and states, "Acceptance must be by USPS within 15 days." The offeree must follow that instruction, and an acceptance by email within 15 days will not bind the offeror. If the instruction is that the acceptance must be made within 15 days but USPS is not specified, the offer should be acceptable if delivered within 15 days by USPS or a similar method, such as Federal Express.

A legal problem may arise if the offeree accepts the offer in the manner directed in the offer, but because of timing the mailbox rule prevents the legality of the acceptance. In the above example, assume the acceptance is made by deposit of the acceptance via the USPS on the 14th day. According to the mailbox rule, acceptance is effective upon deposit on the 14th day after receipt of the offer. Also assume the offeror mails a letter of revocation on the ninth day after the offer was made and received on the 15th day after the offer was made. Consequently, the revocation of the offer is received by the offeree in the mail after the offeree dispatched the acceptance as requested, by USPS.

The issue under these facts becomes, is there a contract via the acceptance, or is there not a contract because of the revocation? The courts would probably conclude the revocation takes precedence because the offer was revoked well in advance of the acceptance. The revocation should have been received a day or two before the 14th day of acceptance.

The legal presumption under the mailbox rule has the effect of stabilizing contract negotiations conducted through the U.S. mail system, an important social and business policy. The mailbox rule is not limited to the USPS and is applicable to other similar authorized modes of communication, such as UPS and FedEx. The mailbox rule does not apply to instantaneous communications, such as fax, telephone, Skype, and so on.

However, if the stated method of acceptance is not used, acceptance may still be effective and honored if the offeror so desires. In such an instance, the mailbox rule will not apply, and the acceptance will be deemed effective upon receipt rather than upon dispatch. The mailbox rule is usually a defense to an allegation that a contract is legally binding (e.g., if the offeror decides not to honor the acceptance and claims it was never received).

The mirror image rule is "the doctrine that states the acceptance of a contractual offer must be positive, unconditional, unequivocal, and unambiguous and must not change, add to, or qualify the terms of the offer" (Garner 2005, 835–836). In practice, the material terms as opposed to minor terms of the offer must not be varied by the acceptance.

Assume the offer states, "Green Grocer will sell 100 bushels of potatoes at $20/bushel, delivery at your restaurant, within 10 days, payable in full within 15 days." The acceptance must mirror the offer in all material respects. The acceptance cannot say, "Accepted, 100 bushels of potatoes at $20/bushel, delivery at your restaurant, within 10 days, full price within 30 days." The change of deadline for full payment from 15 to 30 days varies an essential term of the contract and will be viewed as a counteroffer. It may be accepted or rejected by Green Grocer. However, if the only change is adding an extra day for delivery (11 days for delivery instead of ten), it may be viewed as a nonessential variation that does not prejudice Green Grocer (the offeror) and is not violative of the mirror image rule.

Silence as acceptance refers to the fact that proper communication is a requirement of a valid, enforceable contract. Normally, silence is not understood to be an acceptance. There must be an unequivocal assent to be bound. Public policy will not permit unscrupulous sellers of an unsolicited product to force a party to say no or otherwise be bound.

Moreover, silence may simply mean the offer was not communicated properly to the offeree. Such a practice would create chaos in business and clog the courts with unnecessary litigation. There are several exceptions to that rule. If silence is the course of dealing between the parties or is accepted trade usage in the industry (see discussion below), a party may be bound unless it affirmatively rejects an offer.

Course of Dealing and Trade Usage

Course of dealing means "an established pattern of conduct between parties in a series of transactions (e.g., multiple sales of goods over a period of years)" (Garner 2005, 301). This practice may be introduced in a court of law as evidence to show intent of the parties in a contract dispute. In the preceding example, the omission of the acceptance terms "delivery at your restaurant" can be viewed as a material term that ordinarily would require the parties to express it in a contract. But if delivery at the purchaser's restaurant has been the practice for several years, failure to express it in an invoice may not be necessary.

Continuing the above example, assume Green Grocer and a restaurant have been doing business for years, with delivery of supplies at the restaurant by Green Grocer. Executing contracts without the need for an expressed acceptance would create a course of dealing between the two. A simple invoice followed by a restaurant delivery would bind the restaurant and could make a formal acceptance unnecessary. This might occur with a large chain restaurant that requires replenishment of supplies quickly and where it would normally reject an offer in advance if it did not need supplies.

Moreover, the cost of delivery by Green Grocer versus a pickup by the restaurant at Green Grocer's place of business can be significant. Assume delivery and acceptance of supplies between Green Grocer and the restaurant in the past has been consistent, with the restaurant picking up at Green Grocer's place of business. A court may consider this pattern of conduct as the usual course of dealing between the parties. Failure of Green Grocer to designate "pick up by the restaurant" and failure to deliver them would not be a breach of contract by Green Grocer.

For another example of course of dealing, assume a restaurant and its supplier of condiments have been doing business for ten years. Their relationship is characterized by trust and confidence between the restaurant's purchasing agent and the supplier's sales force. The supplier often offered large discounts to its regular customers if a purchase was made within a specified time.

However, express terms in their written contract calls for "rejection of the discount offer if acceptance is not communicated in writing within ten days of the offer." Because of their mutual trust and years of good business relations, the rejection provision was not enforced by the supplier for the past five years. The supplier's sales force, with approval from the supplier's management, permitted the restaurant to obtain the discounts after the deadline.

Unless the supplier expressly communicates to the restaurant that discounted late acceptances would no longer be allowed, a discount rejected because of a late acceptance would have to be reinstated. The restaurant could challenge the failure to receive the discount as a breach of contract based upon course of dealing. The legal argument is that the express language in the contract has been waived by the course of dealing between the restaurant and supplier.

Trade usage is a similar but broader concept than course of dealing. It pertains to all restaurant suppliers and restaurants in a large geographical metropolitan business area. In the interest of business convenience, such establishments may omit destination and acceptance terms in purchase orders. As a matter of standard practice, delivery and acceptance is customarily made at the premises of the restaurants. The courts may conclude this is a common restaurant business practice and trade usage for the industry.

In addition, accepting the benefits of an order (in the absence of course of dealing and trade usage practices) could make the restaurant liable under unjust enrichment theories. For example, if supplies are shipped by Green Grocer and the restaurant uses them without acceptance or rejection of the offer, a court could find a binding contract implied in law exists. This means the restaurant would be required to pay for what it used in order to avoid unjust enrichment by unscrupulous restaurants.

Termination of an Offer

An offer may be terminated by action of the parties or by operation of law. Termination by action of the parties occurs by revocation, rejection, and, as mentioned above, by a counteroffer.

Action of the Parties

Revocation is one form of termination by action. The offeror may expressly revoke the offer any time before a party accepts the offer. For example, assume a restaurant offers a special steak dinner for $11.95 available for a specified two-week period. Any person that enters the restaurant to dine during the two designated weeks may order that meal for $11.95. The restaurant may change the price on its menu any time (i.e., revoke its original offer) before the two week expires and communicate a new price to its customers.

PRACTICUM

In an abundance of caution, many restaurants that make an offer for a special dinner may add a qualifier, such as "Prices are subject to change at the discretion of the management."

Another termination by action is in the form of **rejection**. In the above example, a customer rejects the offer by deciding not to order the steak dinner, ordering a different menu item instead. Likewise, leaving the restaurant without ordering any meal is a rejection of the offer.

The last termination by action is a **counteroffer**. A customer may wish to pay less for the steak dinner and offer the restaurant $11.00 for the meal. Since the customer has varied the terms, the $11.00 is a counteroffer the restaurant may accept or reject.

For another example of a counteroffer, assume a cruise line (the offeror) advertises in the local newspaper for a trip to the Greek Islands for seven days at an "all-inclusive fare," excluding alcohol, for $3,000. All-inclusive means lodging, food, and other stated activities are included for one price. A traveler (the offeree) reads the offer and unequivocally accepts by making a reservation and paying a deposit. At this point, the parties have a meeting of the minds with a mutually expressed objective intent to form a contract. The failure of either party to fulfill the terms of the contract results in a breach of the contract, subject to enforcement in a court of law.

If the offeree responds with an acceptance that states, "I agree to the seven-day cruise for $3,100, alcohol included," the offer will be deemed rejected. With the addition of new consideration, the alcohol requirement, the acceptance is treated as a counteroffer. The traveler, the initial offeree, is now the offeror, and the cruise line, the initial offeror, is now the offeree, which must accept or reject the pending counteroffer.

Operation of Law

An offer may also terminate as a matter of law in several different ways. They are lapse of time, destruction of subject matter, death, or incompetence of either the offeror or offeree, and superseding causes such as illegality of the subject matter.

Lapse of Time

If the offer provides a **definite time** period for acceptance, the offer terminates at the end of the stated time without further action by the offeror. For example, the offer may say, "This offer remains open until Friday, October 15, 2019." At midnight October 15, 2019, the offer will expire, and the offeree may no longer accept the proposed terms and conditions.

If the offer states, "It will be open for 30 days," the offer will remain open for the stated period, but the counting of time does not commence until the offer is received by the offeree, not when it was sent. Assume a supplier sends a letter containing an offer to sell certain goods for 30 days at a stated price. The 30 days will not start to run until the offer is received by the offeree through the mail. It may take two to three days after deposit in the mail system to be received. This issue becomes important if the offeror decides to revoke the offer and the acceptance has already been mailed.

If the offer does not state a definite time, it will expire after a reasonable time. A **reasonable time** will vary according to the circumstances of each offer. For example, if the offer is for fresh fish, the offer may expire in a few days because the subject matter of the offer may spoil. If the offer is for potatoes, the offer may last several weeks or longer because potatoes won't spoil as fast as fresh fish. If the offer is for cookware, the offer may last for a year in accordance with industry trade usage.

Destruction of Subject Matter

If the subject matter of an offer is destroyed, it obviously cannot be sold. Assume a hotel chain offers to sell one of its hotels for a stated period of time at a minimum specified price. The offer to purchase a hotel will immediately terminate if the hotel is destroyed by fire.

There is no need to communicate the loss of the hotel to potential purchasers. As a matter of law, you cannot accept an offer and create a contract for something that does not exist. Consideration, a vital element, is no longer available. If acceptance is in the mail, the contract cannot be consummated unless the risk of loss passed to the buyer in contract negotiations. For example, the offer may state that formal written acceptance also constitutes acceptance of the risk of loss (the statute of frauds requires a contract for the sale of real estate to be in writing).

Death or Incompetence of Either Party

If either of the parties to the contract dies, performance cannot be achieved. If either party becomes unable to understand the nature of the contract due to mental incompetence, a meeting of the minds can no longer be achieved. The element of mutuality of contract is no longer possible, and the element of contractual capacity no longer exists.

Superseding Cause

A superseding cause is an unforeseen event the law considers legally sufficient to void a contract that was originally lawful. Assume a commercial fisherman offers to sell shark fins to restaurants for use in shark fin soup. Before acceptance, the government places sharks on the endangered species list and promulgates a rule prohibiting the sale of shark fins to restaurants. Upon adoption of the rule, the offer is terminated automatically by law. The new rule is a superseding cause that makes it illegal to sell or use shark fins (see the text box below on offer termination).

TERMINATION OF AN OFFER—SUMMARY

Termination by the parties:

Revocation. The offer may expressly revoke the offer any time before a party accepts. The revocation is usually made with the same method of communication used for the offer. However, any other reasonable method, such as USPS, FedEx, or telephone, may suffice and is effective upon receipt. A formal withdrawal sent return receipt requested is probably the best way to revoke. It provides a signature that is strong evidence of receipt of the revocation. Conduct by the offeror may also suffice for revocation. For example, the sale of real estate to another person will eliminate the offer.

Rejection. The offeree may reject the offer by written notice or by conduct. For example, in the above example, the offeree may purchase a different property. Once the offer is rejected, the offeree may not accept the original offer, but it can make a counteroffer that the offeror may or may not accept.

Counteroffer. By making a counteroffer, the offeree automatically rejects the original offer and may no longer accept it. However, the offeree may make a counteroffer (as new offeror) that may or may not be accepted.

Termination by operation of law:

Death of a party. If either party dies, mutual assent is no longer possible, and the offer is null and void.

Incapacity of a party. If either party becomes mentally incapacitated, the requisite understanding of the terms and conditions and the consequences for failure to adhere to the foregoing is not possible.

Destruction of the subject matter. If the subject of the contact is no longer in existence, you can't buy it. Formal notice need not be made to the offeree (e.g., a building is offered for sale but is destroyed by fire before an acceptance is received by the owner).

Supervening illegality. A statute adopted by the state legislature or an ordinance passed by a city council that prohibits the action contemplated in an offer will automatically terminate the offer. Similarly, a decision by a court of competent jurisdiction will do likewise.

Lapse of time. When an express deadline contained in the offer passes, so does the offer. If a deadline is not expressed, then a reasonable amount of time will terminate an offer. What is reasonable will depend on the nature of the subject matter.

E-Contracts

An electronic transaction (i.e., a contract consummated via the internet) is "a transaction formed by electronic messages in which the messages of one or both parties will not be reviewed by an individual as an expected step in forming a contract" (Garner 2005, 441). This means a contract will be consummated and legally binding on the parties through email and website platforms.

Technology has dramatically changed the way we live, think, and do business. Advances in computer technology have revolutionized business, both nationally and globally. The internet is rapidly becoming a preferred source for business transactions. Amazon and eBay are prominent examples of successful internet businesses. Most traditional companies have established websites to provide product information and they also accept electronic business orders. Such websites provide technical support, ordering information, pay by phone options, and other customer services.

The internet is cheaper, faster, and more convenient than getting in your car and driving to traditional brick-and-mortar retail outlets. Unfortunately, the forgoing also creates problems with formation and enforcement of internet contracts.

One of these issues is **formation**. Contracts formed over the internet must still meet the basic elements of mutual assent, genuine assent, consideration, capacity, legality, and proper form. With computer generated contracts, difficulty may arise in determining existence of those elements, and consequently, enforcement can become a major challenge. How do you know who is sitting at the other end of the computer placing the order? Are they of proper age? Do they have the requisite mental capacity to understand the terms and conditions of the contract and its consequences? Do they have authority to enter into the contract? Was there a meeting of the minds? These are just some of the questions businesses and the courts have to resolve with e-contracts.

For example, assume you are the manager of a hotel and wish to order Direct TV for your guests. You access the Direct TV website and place an order. The website provides an informational presentation of costs, installation, order, and payment procedures. You place an order and schedule installation. After installation, you discover the service is not what you wanted or in your opinion not what was represented on the website.

The following important issues are present. Was there a fraudulent misrepresentation, or did you misread the information? Was there contractual authority to place the order? Did the website provide you with a copy of the agreement for your review prior to you placing an order? If an agreement was provided on the website, where was it positioned on the screen? Was it in the space immediately prior to the ordering button or in the space after the ordering button? Some courts will not enforce an internet agreement if the ordering button can be activated before a complete copy of the agreement is accessible.

PRACTICUM

Internet sellers can minimize contract disputes by doing the following:

- Ensure terms of the online offer are clear, in readable-sized font, and conspicuously placed for consumers to review.
- Place a hypertext link to a copy of the agreement before the consumer can click the order button.
- Ensure key terms of the agreement are highlighted in bold print, such as:
  - price
  - payment methods
  - return/cancellation policy
  - product disclaimers
  - company privacy policy
  - disputes resolution procedures
- Include an acceptance clause that clearly explains the legal consequence of clicking the order button (i.e., it creates a binding contract).
- Conversely, consumers of e-contracts can avoid making mistakes and entering onerous contracts by becoming familiar with the above points.

Adherence to the forgoing discussion of e-contracts will assist in reducing economic loss and anxiety caused by unnecessary litigation.

Enforcement

How to resolve a dispute becomes important, and this is referred to as **enforcement**. The best course of action is settling disputes without the need for a court trial is by way of a reasonable settlement between the parties or through formal alternative dispute resolution (ADR; see ADR discussion in Chapter 2). If a party settlement is not attainable, ADR should be considered.

A key issue for resolution is the proper forum for ADR. If the seller of a product is domiciled in New York and the customer is domiciled in California, where is the proper forum (i.e., state) for resolution of the dispute? Usually, jurisdiction exists where the contract was formed by the parties or where the obligations are to be performed.

In the above example, was the contract formed in New York or in California? Where did those little packets of information meet to create the agreement? If the internet signal originates from a headend in Nevada and is relayed into California, did the contract form in Nevada or California?

A reasonable solution to the forum question is to include a forum selection clause in the contract that both parties agree upon. The proper forum for the internet seller is usually the state where the seller is domiciled. The home state is closer, cheaper to litigate, and more efficient, especially if there is a high sales volume that originates from multiple states. The consumer will be at a disadvantage because of the distance and cost of litigation in a distant state.

Similar to the proper judicial forum is the question of which state law is applicable. That decision also should be agreed to in the contract agreement. Should it be California, New York, or Nevada? Because of the relative infancy of computers and e-contract business transactions, the law is unsettled in these areas. Accordingly, the parties need to be wary of e-contract consequences.

State contract laws may vary greatly, and a calculated decision must be made as to which state law is most favorable. In some instances the choice of law clause may be more important than the choice of forum clause. Most e-contracts have both forum selection and choice of law clauses included by the seller that greatly favor the seller.

Most e-contracts contain a contract provision that specifies which state the proper forum will be for litigation or for ADR, referred to as a **forum selection clause**. If both parties agree, there is no problem. However, more than likely the forum selection clause will favor the drafter of the contract, usually the seller of the product or service.

As mentioned previously, if the seller is in New York and the buyer is in California, the buyer is at a distinct disadvantage. The cost of traveling to New York to resolve a dispute is too costly and time consuming for most consumers. Accordingly, if you are a buyer, be sure to review the forum selection prior to signing a contract.

Similar to the forum selection clause is the **choice of law clause**. This clause specifies which state law will apply to a contract dispute. As mentioned previously, this decision may often be as important, or more so, than the forum selection clause. The law of one state may be so favorable to a party that where the case is litigated may be a secondary concern. Here is a suggested clause that combines both issues:

> All claims, controversies, disputes, suits, and matters of any kind whatsoever arising out of, concerned with, or incident to the contract entered into between the parties shall be resolved in the Superior Court of Los Angeles in Los Angeles, California. All legal issues shall be resolved under laws of the State of California.

As a general rule, courts usually enforce forum selection and choice of law clauses unless they are unconscionable (i.e., the clauses unreasonably favor the party with the strongest bargaining power, usually the drafter of the agreement).

Summary

Mutual assent is the first of the required six elements necessary for the formation of a contract. It is an agreement among two or more parties to specific terms and conditions enforceable in a court of law. Courts will focus on the objective intent of the parties, not the subjective intent that may differ substantially from what the objective facts indicate.

The formation of a contract commences with an offer from one party (offeror) to another party. The offer must be made with clear and unambiguous terms. It must be communicated to the other party (offeree), who must accept the offer without variation of any material terms. If material terms are varied, the courts will deem it rejected. It will then become a counteroffer.

Termination of an offer may be effectuated by the parties or by operation of law. If terminated by the parties, it could be revoked by the offeror any time before acceptance by the offeree. It can be rejected by the offeree or by way of a counteroffer.

Termination may be accomplished by operation of law through the following ways. It may be terminated by the lapse of a stated date in the offer. Also, an offer cannot be accepted if the subject of the offer is destroyed. Similarly, it may be terminated by death of either party or if either is unable to understand the terms and conditions of the contract because of mental incapacity. Finally, a superseding event, such as the passage of a statute that makes the contract illegal, qualifies for termination.

E-contracts are contracts formed over the internet. They must contain the same six elements of a conventional contract. However, because of its unique characteristics (i.e., negotiated and executed electronically), several significantly different problems arise with enforcement. Because the parties are often domiciled in different states, the issue of the proper forum and the choice of law to apply are difficult to determine. A useful method for resolving the aforementioned problems is for the parties to decide those questions in advance. This is done with inclusion of a forum selection clause and choice of law clause in the initial contract.

Comprehension Check

True/False

Directions: Look at each statement below. Based on what you learned in this chapter, decide if the statement is true or false.

1. The statutory source of law for contract issues is American common law, such as the Uniform Commercial Code.
2. The function of contract law is to help resolve any disputes regarding the intent of the contracting parties.
3. Contract disputes are analyzed by the subjective intent of the parties since that is the only sure way to understand the negotiations.
4. The objective intent of the parties is determined by what a reasonable person would have said or done.
5. What a party has said is not as important as what a party was truly thinking.
6. With respect to intent, the surrounding circumstances are irrelevant.
7. The term "meeting of the minds" is synonymous with mutuality.

8. The general rule of contract intent when a subsequent agreement amends a prior agreement and creates an ambiguity is that the last in time always prevails.
9. A contest or lottery is a unilateral offer to contract, and begins negotiations, but is not offered to bind the offeree.
10. The following is an objective intent to be bound in a contract: "The Hotel Regency has rooms available for $200–$400 per night. First Come First Served."
11. The intent of an implied contract may be determined by a tacit understanding of the parties.
12. Conduct of the parties may demonstrate intent to waive express terms of a contract.
13. If a person, such as a minor, has a voidable right, that person must show intent to exercise the right within a reasonable time.
14. A contract implied in law lacks intent of a party to contract; therefore, the court must create intent in order to avoid an unjust consequence.
15. The plain meaning rule may be employed to determine intent of the parties.

Multiple Choice

Directions: Use what you learned in this chapter to choose the best response to each of the prompts below.

1. All the following are true, except:
   a. An expression of an opinion is a valid offer.
   b. A statement of future intent is not an offer.
   c. An invitation to submit bids is not an offer.
   d. The offer must have a serious intent to be bound.

2. All the following are true, except:
   a. Offers made in obvious anger do not meet the objective intent test.
   b. Subjective intent is considered when assessing intent to be bound.
   c. Mutual assent is the same as an agreement.
   d. What a reasonable person outwardly expresses is the most important factor for intent to be bound.

3. All the following are situations that may lack intent to be bound, except:
   a. preliminary negotiations
   b. invitations to bid
   c. silence
   d. auctions

4. All the following are true of auctions, except:
   a. The seller is the offeror.
   b. A live auction may be with reserve.
   c. An online auction is automated.
   d. An online auction may be without reserve.

5. All the following are true of an offer, except:
   a. The parties must be identified clearly.
   b. proper identification of the subject matter
   c. consideration to be paid
   d. all of the above

6. An offer must have all the following, except:
   a. serious intent to be bound
   b. The terms must be reasonably certain.
   c. The offer must be accepted.
   d. The offer must be communicated to the offeree.

7. An offer may be terminated by all the following, except:
   a. by operation of law
   b. by revocation
   c. by reasonable notice
   d. by rejection

8. All the following are true, except:
   a. A counteroffer is not a rejection of the initial offer.
   b. An offer may be terminated by the parties.
   c. An acceptance is effective upon placement in the mailbox.
   d. Rejection by offeror terminates the offer.

9. Termination by operation of law includes all the following, except:
   a. destruction of the subject matter
   b. lack of objective intent
   c. lapse of time
   d. when either of the parties becomes mentally incapacitated

10. A contract can be created by all the following, except:
    a. mutual agreement
    b. an email
    c. misrepresentation
    d. silence

Scenarios

1. Restaurant has been purchasing supplies from Grocer for five years. The terms were always the same—deliver supplies to the restaurant every three months and payment within 30 days. On one occasion Grocer sent the restaurant a notice that due to a labor dispute it will take an additional 30 days for the next delivery. The notice also said Restaurant may otherwise pick up the supplies at Grocer's place

of business. Restaurant did not respond. Does Grocer have a valid legal claim for breach of contract? Explain your answer. Include a comparison of the legal position of each party.

2. Bill and Tim are neighbors. For three years Tim has been trying to purchase a vacant lot that separates their properties. Bill told Tim he would sell the lot for $100,000. They got together at Tim's house for dinner one evening, and both consumed large quantities of alcohol. Towards the end of the evening, Tim pulled out $80,000 in cash and handed Bill the money plus a contract for the sale of the vacant lot for Bill's signature. They quibbled over the price and made over a dozen changes to the terms. For example, Bill required Tim to grant him an easement over the property and also to pay "not a cent less than $90,000." Both parties signed the contract. Bill wakes up the next morning and realizes what he did. He calls Tim and tells him that he didn't know what he was doing, and he wants to rescind the contract. What will be the result? Explain your answer.

Decisional Review

1. Plaintiff built a home and leased it to Defendant. The agreement was executed on June 1, 2019, and possession was supposed to take place on August 1, 2019. On July 31, 2019, the day before the scheduled date for transfer of possession, Defendant ordered his bank to stop payment on his check. He no longer wished to lease the property, and Plaintiff filed suit for damages. Defendant asserted the contract was not effective until possession was transferred. Plaintiff asserted the contract became effective at the date of execution. What theory should the court use to resolve the issue? What should be the result, and why? See *Pan Handle Realty, LLC v. Olins*, 140 Conn.App. 556 59 A.3d 842 (2013).
2. An agreement entered into by Plaintiff and Defendant was modified by a subsequent agreement. A dispute arose regarding the intent of the agreements, so the court reviewed each contract separately to determine the intent of the parties.

   The agreements, according to Defendant, were based upon a requirement of tenure of Plaintiff, which was not awarded. Plaintiff was given an extension to achieve tenure, but that likewise was denied. There was an ambiguity between the two contracts as to whether tenure was assured or whether it had to be earned. Therefore, the court admitted extrinsic evidence to clear up the ambiguity. How should the court rule, and why? See *Weston v. Cornell University*, New York Supreme Court, Appellate Division, Third Department, 136 A.D.3d 1094, 24 N.Y.S.3.D 448 (2016).

Chapter 7

Absence of Genuine Assent

Introduction

Absence of genuine assent is often confused with mutual assent. Both elements concern the intent of the parties to be bound in contract. The issues differ because mutual assent is a voluntary agreement to be bound in a contract. Absence of genuine assent concerns an involuntary agreement to be bound in a contract, which means one of the parties was either coerced or tricked into acting involuntarily.

Absence of genuine assent refers to situations where one party does not wish to be bound to the contract but does so anyway. Typical examples are duress, undue influence, blackmail, mistakes, fraudulent misrepresentation, and equitable contracts created by the courts, such as contracts of adhesion and unconscionable contracts.

Chapter Objectives

Upon completion of this chapter, the student will understand:

- the nature of absence of genuine assent
- the concepts of duress, blackmail, and undue influence
- the difference between a unilateral and mutual mistake
- the impact of fraudulent misrepresentation on assent
- the nature of a contract of adhesion
- the nature of an unconscionable contract

Key Terms

Directions: Each of the terms below will be used in this chapter. Before reading, scan the chapter. The terms will appear in bold. Take a moment to see how the term is used so you can understand it in context. The terms are listed in the order in which they will appear in the chapter.

Absence of genuine assent (p. 142)
Duress (p. 142)
Undue Influence (p. 143)
Mistake (p. 145)
Mutual mistake (p. 146)
Unilateral mistake (p. 146)
Misrepresentation (p. 146)
Intentional misrepresentation (p. 146)
Negligent misrepresentation (p. 147)
Innocent misrepresentation (p. 148)
Contract of adhesion (p. 148)
Unconscionable contract (p. 148)

Absence of Genuine Assent

Generally, both mutual assent and genuine assent are contract elements, which concern the parties' intent to be bound in contract. Specifically, the question is, have they reached an agreement regarding the terms and conditions of the contract? Mutual assent is a determination that the parties to a contract know and understand the terms and conditions of a contract and voluntarily agree to them.

Absence of genuine assent concerns whether the agreement between the parties "is authentic or real; something that has the quality of what it is purported to be or to have" (Garner 2005, 570). It means the parties to an agreement may understand the terms and conditions but may not have voluntarily agreed to those terms and conditions. The absence of genuine assent means one or both parties did not understand the terms and conditions or did not knowingly and voluntarily agree to them. This element is affected by one or more of the following factors:

- duress
- undue influence
- mistake—bilateral or unilateral
- fraudulent misrepresentation
- contracts formed as a matter of law
- contracts of adhesion
- unconscionable contracts

Duress

Duress is "... a threat of harm made to compel a person to do something against his or her will or judgment; esp., a wrongful threat made by one person to compel a manifestation of seeming assent by another person to a transaction without real volition" (Garner 2005, 426). Genuine assent is absent when a party to a contract is coerced into agreeing to the terms and conditions, such as by harm or threats of harm. The threats must be illegal.

For example, the threat of a lawsuit is not duress. It is asserting the legal right under the law to sue. What may be duress is to intentionally delay the construction of a home in order to press for an increase in the contract price. This is referred to as economic duress. The owner of the future home may not have a viable option for living quarters and may pay the higher amount requested just to ensure a place to live.

For another example, assume Mary, the purchasing agent for a chain of hotels ("Luxury Suites"), decides to replace 1,000 beds at a cost of $500/bed for a total price of $500,000. Mary has used the same vendor, Classic Bed Technologies ("Classic Bed"), and salesman, Bob, for the last ten years. She is content with the prices and the quality of the product. Tim, the salesman for a competitive vendor, Modern Sleep Products ("Modern Sleep"), has been trying desperately to convince her to switch to his company for the last two years. His product line is comparable in quality but at a slightly lower cost. Mary steadfastly refuses to purchase from Modern Sleep.

Tim heard rumors that link Mary and Bob romantically, and he hires a private investigator to confirm the rumors. The private investigator followed the two leaving for lunch, but instead, they go to a local motel where they spent several hours. He captured the two on a video camera, hand in hand, entering the "no tell motel" and also exiting several hours later.

Tim threatened to reveal the video tapes to both Mary's supervisor and her husband unless she switched her purchases to Modern Sleep (i.e., blackmail). Because of the threat of disclosure, Mary agrees to the contract with Modern Sleep. If Luxury Suites subsequently learns of the blackmail by Modern Sleep, it can void the contract because it was signed by Mary, who lacked genuine assent.

Undue Influence

Often, people in a position of trust take advantage of their authority by exerting control over a person in a weakened state, such as dementia or a physical disability. This is accomplished by exerting undue influence over the person and controlling the person's free will.

Undue influence is defined as "the improper use of power or trust in a way that deprives a person of free will and substitutes another's objective. Consent to a contract, transaction, or relationship or [other such] conduct is voidable if the consent is obtained through undue influence" (Garner 2005, 1276). Such consent obtained from a person in a weakened state is vulnerable to a claim the contract is absent genuine assent.

Undue influence allegations surface when persons are placed in a fiduciary relationship, one of special trust imposed by law. Relationships between principal and agent, physician and patient, parent and child, husband and wife, and priest and parishioner are common fiduciary relationships.

Minors, elderly persons, and persons with mental deficiencies who are appointed a guardian by a court of law are typical targets for this pernicious form of control. For example, a person who is 90 years old, has dementia, and has a terminal disease may be convinced by a guardian to change a last will and testament in favor of the guardian or a family member of the guardian.

With fiduciary relationships, a high standard of proof is required to prevail in a court challenge of a fiduciary's decision making. The alleged undue influence must show by clear and convincing evidence the targeted person was not acting under their own free will. The policy for such a high burden is to encourage people to assume the fiduciary duty role with its attendant high level of responsibility.

Fear of a complicated, expensive, and time-consuming lawsuit would discourage many from assuming the responsibilities of a fiduciary relationship. Moreover, if persons with a fiduciary duty were personally sued and lost, notwithstanding the high standard of proof required, few would take the risk.

The following case explains that having a close relationship by itself is not enough to conclude that genuine assent did not exist.

---

273 VA. 262

Supreme Court of Virginia.
Gilbert R. BAILEY
v.
Linda D. TURNBOW, Executrix of the Estate of Annerbell Brewer.
Record No. 060713.
Jan. 12, 2007.

Synopsis

Background: Executrix of grantor's estate filed complaint to set aside deed conveying real property to grantor's nephew based on allegations of undue influence and other claims. The Circuit Court, City of Chesapeake, Russell I. Townsend, Jr., Judge Designate, set aside deed on grounds that it was obtained by undue influence, and nephew appealed.

Holding: The Supreme Court, Charles S. Russell, Senior Justice, held that close relationship between grantor and her nephew did not give rise to presumption of undue influence, as grounds for setting aside deed.

Opinion by Senior Justice CHARLES S. RUSSELL.

In this case, the chancellor held that a deed to real property had been procured by undue influence and set the deed aside. That holding was premised upon the chancellor's finding that a confidential relationship existed between the grantor and the grantee, giving rise to a presumption of undue influence, which the grantee had failed to rebut. This appeal questions the sufficiency of the evidence to support that finding.

Facts and Proceedings

***

Soon after she had left the nursing home, Mrs. Brewer went with Gilbert Bailey to the office of the Department of Motor Vehicles and transferred the title of her automobile to the joint ownership of herself and Bailey. Later, she told Bailey that she wanted to transfer the title of her house to him as well. He testified that she said that "she wanted to do her house just like she'd done the car so that she would have it, and then at her death, I would own it."

On September 4, 1997, Mrs. Brewer came into the house after a drive with Ann Bailey and asked him whether he had the deed. He showed it to her, read it in full to her, and asked her if it was what she wanted. She replied that it was "exactly what she wanted" and signed it in the presence of a notary public who was employed by the Baileys and was working in the office they maintained in the basement of their home. Bailey subsequently had the deed recorded.

After Mrs. Brewer's death, Linda Dee Turnbow qualified as executrix under Mrs. Brewer's will and filed this suit against Gilbert Bailey.... The chancellor ruled, however, that the Executrix had carried her burden to prove a confidential relationship between Bailey and Mrs. Brewer giving rise to a presumption of undue influence, which Bailey had failed to rebut, in the procurement of the challenged deed. The chancellor entered a final decree setting aside and canceling the deed. We awarded Bailey an appeal.

Analysis

A court of equity will not set aside a contract because it is "rash, improvident or [a] hard bargain" but equity will act if the circumstances raise the inference that the contract was the result of imposition, deception, or undue influence.

***

[W]here great weakness of mind concurs with gross inadequacy of consideration, or circumstances of suspicion, the transaction will be presumed to have been brought about by undue influence.

***

Because the chancellor found no evidence to support a finding of weakness of mind on Mrs. Brewer's part, his holding must rest entirely upon the second condition discussed by Fishburne: the existence of a "confidential relationship" between the parties to the deed. Although the law in other jurisdictions differs, in Virginia we have adhered to the view that a close family relationship, even the relationship of parent and child, will not, alone, give rise to a confidential relationship creating a presumption of undue influence. [Citations omitted.] Instead, for the presumption to arise, the party asserting it must establish, by clear and convincing evidence ... [that such a relationship exists].

***

The only evidence of financial advice or assistance to Mrs. Brewer by a family member was that given by Mary Crawford, not by Bailey. The chancellor expressly found that the transfer of title to Mrs. Brewer's car was free of undue influence. The only other business relationship between the parties to the deed shown by the evidence was the exchange of lands between them in 1963 and Bailey's construction of the Brewers' home. There was no evidence indicating that to have been anything other than an arms-length business transaction. A mere commercial relationship, even where the parties like and trust each other, is insufficient to establish a confidential relationship. Friendly Ice Cream Corp., 268 Va. at 34–35, 597 S.E.2d at 40. Because the complainant failed to present evidence sufficient to establish a confidential relationship, no presumption of undue influence arose to shift the burden of production to Bailey.

Conclusion

Reversed and final judgment.

Mistake

Regarding contracts, a **mistake** is defined as "the situation in which either (1) the parties to a contract did not mean the same thing, or (2) at least one party had a belief that did not correspond to the facts or law. As a result, the contract may be voidable" (Garner 2005, 839). If one or both parties to a contract make a mistake concerning the terms and conditions of the contract, genuine assent may be absent. The mistaken party will be expected to do something they didn't think they had to do, or they will be expected to accept something for which they didn't anticipate in the bargain.

Mistakes can be mutual (both parties make an error) or unilateral (one party makes an error). The law permits contract recession in certain situations, usually when there is a mutual mistake.

When both parties hold a different understanding of a material contract term, there may be an absence of genuine assent. **Mutual mistake** is defined as "(1) a mistake in which each party misunderstands the other's intent or (2) a mistake that is shared and relied on by both parties to a contract" (Garner 2005, 839). Under a mutual mistake, either party may rescind the contract; but in practice, it is usually the party most adversely affected that will attempt to do so.

For example, assume a large restaurant chain orders 1,000 pounds of prime rib steaks from a meat packer at $2.99/lb. The meat packer later discovers, due to a clerical error, the price should have been a market price of $3.99/lb. This was a mutual mistake because both parties were mistaken as to the proper price.

The restaurant had checked the market price and thought the price was a special price and a good bargain. Therefore, the restaurant would not likely want to rescind the contract. The meat packer of course will lose $1.00/lb. and will push for rescission. The court has the discretion to reform the contract or to rescind it, depending on the evidence presented.

PRACTICUM

In this scenario, the difference in price is $1,000 and not something that may be worth the time and cost of a lawsuit for either party, especially if the parties have a long-term, mutually beneficial relationship. The parties should either agree to rescind the contract or settle the dispute with a revised price, such as $3.50/lb.

A **unilateral mistake** occurs when there is "a mistake by only one party to the contract. A unilateral mistake is generally not as likely to be grounds for voiding the contract as is a mutual mistake" (Garner 2005, 839). An exception would be if the unilateral error was substantial and inadvertent.

In the example above, assume the restaurant was unaware the day before the order was placed that the market price of prime rib had dropped to $2.80/lb. The meat packer was aware of the price drop but left the price at $2.99/lb. The restaurant made a unilateral mistake by not verifying the market price. However, the difference in price, arguably, is not substantial, and a court would likely not grant rescission of the contract.

If the market price per pound of prime rib dropped substantially lower, such as $1.80/lb. and the order was for 10,000 lbs., the difference in price is substantial, and the court would likely reform the contract to reflect the lower price. Additionally, in this scenario, the fact that the meat packer was aware of the substantial price drop and did not unilaterally make the adjustment demonstrates a dishonest motive that most courts would not receive well.

Misrepresentation

Misrepresentation occurs when a party to a contract makes representations to another party of the contract that are not factually correct. A definition for it is "(1) The act of making a false or misleading assertion about something, usu. with the intent to deceive. (2) The assertion so made; an assertion that does not accord with the facts" (Garner 2005, 838). There are three types of misrepresentation: intentional, negligent, and innocent.

Intentional misrepresentation is defined as "a false statement that is known to be false or is made recklessly—without knowing or caring whether it is true or false—and that is intended to induce a party to detrimentally rely on it" (Garner 2005, 838–839). Genuine assent is absent if the person defrauded does not know the true set of facts at the time of the agreement. Had they known the truth, they probably would not have agreed to the contract.

The elements of intentional misrepresentation are:

- a misrepresentation of a material fact
- intent to deceive
- reasonable reliance by the defrauded party
- damages

In the example above regarding duress, assume the salesman for Modern Sleep promised a 20% discount to Mary, the purchasing agent, for, allegedly, a far superior product. The salesman knew the product was substantially inferior, and the total sale had a true value of $350,000. The purchasing agent agrees to order the beds because she believes the value of the beds is $500,000, and with the 20% discount, she was saving $100,000 for Luxury Suites. When the beds arrive, Luxury Suites determines they are obviously a lesser quality than what was represented by the salesman and it refuses to accept them. Applying the facts to the elements demonstrates a fraudulent misrepresentation has occurred:

- Material fact: The beds are of an inferior quality.
- Intent: The salesman promised a 20% discount, knowing the product was inferior and worth $350,000 instead of alleged true value of $500,000.
- Justifiable reliance: It is reasonable for a purchasing agent to rely on the promise of a salesman for a 20% discount on a superior product.
- Damages: Luxury Suites will be paying $400,000 after the 20% discount ($500,000 × 80% = $400,000) for inferior beds worth only $350,000, a net loss of $50,000 from the true value of $350,000.

Genuine assent was absent because Mary believed she was gaining a $100,000 net benefit for her company. Had she known the true facts, she probably would not have agreed to the purchase. The purchasing agent thought she was buying a superior quality bed at a 20% discount. In reality she was buying an inferior bed at a $50,000 inflated price over true value. Accordingly, lack of genuine assent is a defense to enforcement of the contract.

A misrepresentation may occur because a party may have been careless and forgot to include certain important terms in the contract. There is no intent to misrepresent the omitted important terms. This is **negligent misrepresentation**, and it is defined as "a careless or inadvertent false statement in circumstances where care should have been taken" (Garner 2005, 839).

Continuing the example of Luxury Suites above, assume the Modern Sleep salesperson heard prices were going to increase significantly within a week or so. Because of a desire to close this important purchase, the salesmen did not take the time to verify if the information was true and the extent of the increases. So he convinced Luxury Suites to buy at the current price of $500/bed. The prices in fact dropped $50.00/bed one week after the sale was executed.

Luxury Suites subsequently learns of the price drop and confronts the sales representative for a price reduction. The salesman attempts to get the reduced price, but Modern Sleep refuses because of the large ($50,000) price difference. Luxury Suites sues for the lower price and gets a court order for the difference because the court concludes it was a negligent misrepresentation.

Sometimes a party to a contract makes a false statement not knowing it is false. An **innocent misrepresentation** is "a false statement that the speaker or writer does not know is false; a misrepresentation that, though false, was not made fraudulently" (Garner 2005, 839). In the Luxury Suites case, that could occur if the salesman requested a price check from the accounting department and that department made a clerical error. This is a unilateral mistake, not a fraudulent misrepresentation, because there was no intent to deceive.

Courts may also use an equitable remedy to avoid a great injustice to a party in a contract. This occurs where one party has greater bargaining power than the other party and the former takes unfair advantage of the latter. This is referred to as absence of Genuine Assent as a matter of law. Examples are when one party to the contract is poorly educated or does not speak the language well.

The judicial rationale is the targeted party would not have agreed to the contract if they understood the consequences of the terms. Hence, there is an absence of genuine assent. The courts use two theories in order to rescind such a contract. They are a contract of adhesion or an unconscionable contract. The differences are explained below.

A **contract of adhesion** is "a standard-form contract prepared by one party, to be signed by another party, usu. a consumer, who adheres to the contract with little choice about the terms" (Garner 2005, 271). It is often referred to as a "take it or leave it" contract. It is characterized by use of a standard form, prepared by the party with overwhelming bargaining power, containing incomprehensible legalese, in fine print.

Key provisions are usually hidden on back pages at the end of the contract where unsophisticated consumers cannot locate them nor understand them if they did locate them. The provisions usually shift the risk in an unlawful or seriously unfair way. Typical examples of adhesion contracts are financing/loan agreements, insurance agreements, lease agreements (both auto and real estate), and employment agreements.

The aggrieved party to an adhesion contract must prove the superior bargaining power of the other party and show that it would be unfair or oppressive if the contract is enforced. For example, consider a case where a car dealer uses a standard sales agreement with unfair one-sided provisions. The contract retains access to the courts for the dealer but includes a mandatory arbitration clause and a voluntary relinquishment of statutory remedies for the consumer. The lawsuit claimed the dealership misrepresented the trade in value, artificially increased the price of the new vehicle, and failed to provide promised rebates (*Simpson v. MSA of Myrtle Beach, Inc.*, 644 SE, 2d 663 (2007)).

Some contracts are so unfair and oppressive courts will not enforce them. In addition, some provisions within a contract, as opposed to the entire contract, may be unconscionable. An **unconscionable contract** is defined as "an agreement that no promisor with any sense, and not under a delusion, would make, and that no honest and fair promisee would accept" (Garner 2005, 59). For more information, see U.C.C. § 2-302, which applies the doctrine to the sale of goods. There is an absence of genuine assent as a matter of law because there is no legal meeting of the minds.

Usually a court of law does not look to fairness of consideration and it assumes the parties understand their agreements. But some contracts are so unscrupulous that a court will not enforce them. For example, assume a person without a formal education and with a slight mental deficiency decides to buy a refrigerator. They sign a contract with a local retailor for an installment purchase.

The monthly payments total four times the value of the refrigerator, and the contract contains a provision that limits the purchaser to arbitration by the local retail association. The contract also requires the purchaser to pay all costs of collection, including costs of the arbitration if they lose the dispute. A court would likely rescind the contract because of the substantial advantage the retailer possesses and the resultant serious injustice upon the consumer (see, for example, *Wisconsin Auto v. Jones* below).

---

290 WIS.2D 514

Supreme Court of Wisconsin.
WISCONSIN AUTO TITLE LOANS, INC., Plaintiff–Appellant–Petitioner,
v.
Kenneth M. JONES, Defendant–Respondent.
No. 2003AP2457.
Argued Feb. 21, 2006. Decided May 25, 2006.

***

The arbitration provision broadly states that all disputes, controversies, or claims between the borrower and Wisconsin Auto … relating to the loan agreement shall be decided by binding arbitration. Nevertheless, the arbitration provision carves out for Wisconsin Auto … the right to enforce the borrower's payment obligations in the event of default by judicial or other process, including self-help repossession.

***

The circuit court held the arbitration provision unconscionable. The court of appeals granted Wisconsin Auto['s] … request to appeal the non-final order of the circuit court and affirmed the circuit court's order denying Wisconsin Auto['s] motion to compel arbitration.

***

We have made several attempts at delineating what is meant by unconscionability.

***

The factors to be considered include, but are not limited to, age, education, intelligence, business acumen and experience, relative bargaining power, who drafted the contract, whether the terms were explained to the weaker party, whether alterations in the printed terms would have been permitted by the drafting party, and whether there were alternative providers of the subject matter of the contract.

No single, precise definition of substantive unconscionability can be articulated. Substantive unconscionability refers to whether the terms of a contract are unreasonably favorable to the more powerful party.

***

Substantive unconscionability has usually been successfully raised against commercial interests dealing with consumers, especially poor and disadvantaged consumers. In many of the cases in which a contract provision has been held to be substantively unconscionable, a creditor has unduly restricted a debtor's remedies or unduly expanded its own remedial rights. The instant case seems to be one in which the creditor has unduly restricted the debtor's remedies relative to those available to the creditor.

The exception to the arbitration provision is far too broad and one-sided, granting Wisconsin Auto ... a choice of forum—arbitration or the circuit court—for its claims, while permitting the borrower to raise claims only before an arbitrator. The doctrine of substantive unconscionability limits the extent to which a stronger party to a contract may impose arbitration on the weaker party without accepting the arbitration forum for itself.

***

The unconscionable one-sidedness of the arbitration provision is sufficient to hold the arbitration provision substantively unconscionable, and we so hold.

***

We conclude that the broad, one-sided, unfair ... [arbitration clause] allowing Wisconsin Auto ... full access to the courts, free of arbitration, while requiring the borrower to arbitrate, renders the arbitration provision substantively unconscionable.

We thus conclude, as did the circuit court and court of appeals, that the arbitration provision is both procedurally and substantively unconscionable. We further conclude that there is a sufficient quantum of both procedural and substantive unconscionability to render the arbitration provision invalid.

ABSENCE OF GENUINE ASSENT

Mutual assent is a key element of an enforceable contract. It occurs when parties to a contract understand the contract and voluntarily agree to the terms. A contract may on its face appear to be voluntary, but when challenged in a court of law, an absence of genuine assent may be present for the following reasons.

Duress. This is a threat of harm made to compel a person to do something against that person's will. It must be an illegal or wrongful activity. It may be physical threats to a family member or economic threats to a person's business.

Undue influence. This is exertion of undue influence over a person by a substitution of another's free will. It usually exists in a fiduciary relationship where a person is weak, infirm, or disabled. Any contract entered into is voidable at the election of the victim.

Mistake. There are two types of mistakes. A mutual mistake occurs when both parties acted with a misunderstanding of key facts. Courts are more willing to rescind or reform a mutual mistake because of the absence of genuine assent. The other is a unilateral mistake, which courts are reluctant to remedy, unless there will **be an unjust result to the person who made the mistake.**

Misrepresentation. This is a representation that does not accord with the facts. There are three types of misrepresentation: intentional, negligent, and innocent. All three result in a person agreeing to a contract that they would not want to do if they knew the true facts.

EQUITABLE REMEDIES AT LAW

Contracts of adhesion are standard contracts prepared by someone with overwhelming bargaining power containing incomprehensible legalese in fine print. Such contracts shift the risk in an unlawful or seriously unfair way.

Unconscionable contracts are contracts so unfair and oppressive that courts refuse to enforce them. They target unsophisticated, uneducated persons or those who do not speak the language well or at all.

Summary

Absence of genuine assent is the opposite of mutual assent. With mutual assent the parties know and understand the terms and conditions and voluntarily agree to them. The parties want the contract to be executed (see Chapter 6). Absence of genuine assent means one party either is forced to agree or agrees because of a misrepresentation, and therefore, their assent is not genuine or voluntary. This may occur because the unwilling party may be threatened with physical force or be a victim of blackmail. Undue influence by a guardian or family member may likewise invalidate a contract.

In addition, a unilateral or bilateral mistake may have been made, so the contract may be rescinded or reformed, depending on the facts of each case. For one or both parties, an absence of genuine assent may be present. A court will more likely rescind a contract containing a mutual mistake rather than a unilateral mistake. Fraudulent misrepresentation, negligent misrepresentation, or innocent misrepresentation also create a false sense of what a party is bargaining for and show an absence of genuine assent.

Finally, certain contracts, such as a contract of adhesion and an unconscionable contract, as a matter of law and based upon public policy, may be so unfair that the courts will not enforce them. The policy is to prevent a serious miscarriage of injustice to one of the parties.

Comprehension Check

True/False

Directions: Look at each statement below. Based on what you learned in this chapter, decide if the statement is true or false.

1. Mutual assent can occur when the parties substantially understand the contract but cannot quite agree to all the material facts.
2. A contract of adhesion is one that primarily refers to unscrupulous businesses with overwhelming bargaining power who take advantage of uneducated consumers.
3. An unconscionable contract is one that is replete with legaleze hidden in long paragraphs of fine print.
4. Courts are more willing to rescind a contract for a unilateral mistake than one with a mutual mistake because the former will be easier to resolve.
5. Duress occurs when one party agrees to terms in a contract that as drafted is overly complicated.
6. A misrepresentation in a contract could lead to a court finding that there is an absence of genuine assent.
7. There is no substantive difference between a negligent misrepresentation and an innocent misrepresentation.

8. In the case *Wisconsin Auto v. Jones*, the court concluded the arbitration clause was operative because a notice in bold print indicated so.
9. If a seller of a product prevents a buyer from learning of a material negative fact, a contract of adhesion is usually created.
10. For a mutual mistake allegation, most courts do not require a showing of injury with mutual mistake, because both parties are returned to their original position.
11. With regard to mutual mistake, a court will likely rescind the contract if each party has reasonably relied on a different interpretation of material facts.
12. Fraudulent misrepresentation is tort; therefore, it is now applicable to a contract case.
13. Intent to deceive is also referred to as scienter.
14. In a case concerning a fiduciary relationship, a presumption of undue influence exists if the fiduciary benefits for a challenged transaction.
15. Unconscionability is applied to the U.C.C. § 2-302, which deals with the sale of goods.

Multiple Choice

Directions: Use what you learned in this chapter to choose the best response to each of the prompts below.

1. All the following are true, except:
   a. A mistake of fact is unilateral.
   b. Opinion is not a fact.
   c. A typographical error by one party warrants contract rescission.
   d. A bilateral mistake can be rescinded by either party.

2. All the following are true, except:
   a. If one party to a contract attaches a different but reasonable meaning to a contract term, a court may permit rescission.
   b. A mistake of the value of an article sold is not a mistake of fact, and therefore, rescission is not a remedy.
   c. Either party can rescind a contract when there is a mutual mistake of fact.
   d. A court will permit rescission of a contract if there was a substantial mathematical error.

3. The elements of fraudulent misrepresentation are all the following, except:
   a. material fact
   b. intent to deceive
   c. proximate cause
   d. justifiable reliance

4. All the following are true, except:
   a. Misrepresentation can occur when a party actively conceals a material fact.
   b. If a customer asks to see a sculpture by a specific person but is shown several that are not by that person, a misrepresentation has occurred.
   c. Statements of opinion, if greatly exaggerated, may be legally actionable.
   d. A misrepresentation must be an important factor in the deceived decision to be considered justifiable reliance.

5. All the following are true with regard to misrepresentation, except:
   a. Intent to deceive must show guilty knowledge.
   b. Innocent misrepresentation occurs when a person makes a statement based upon mistaken facts.
   c. A latent defect is one that can be readily ascertained.
   d. Defects that are obvious are not legally actionable.
6. All the following are true with regard to misrepresentation, except:
   a. Most courts require proof of injury for recovery for contract rescission.
   b. Recovery caused by fraud requires proof of harm.
   c. The harm must be a major injury.
   d. A comment in jest can't be legally actionable.
7. Lack of genuine assent can occur by all the following, except:
   a. misrepresentation
   b. duress
   c. presumption of undue influence
   d. factual misunderstanding
8. All the following are true of duress, except:
   a. It requires force or threats of force.
   b. Threatening to sue is a form of duress.
   c. Blackmail is a form of duress.
   d. Duress must be something that is illegal to do, such as physical violence.
9. All the following are true, except:
   a. A contract of adhesion is an equitable contract.
   b. An unconscionable contract is one filled with hidden, unfair provisions.
   c. An equitable contract can require repayment of money.
   d. Equitable contracts are created to avoid a serious injustice.
10. All the following are true, except:
    a. A contract formed as a matter of law is called a contract of adhesion.
    b. A contract formed as a matter of law is an equitable contract.
    c. An equitable contract requires payment of money.
    d. Absence of genuine assent means the targeted party may understand the terms and conditions but have not voluntarily agreed to them.

Scenarios

1. Mary and Bill were favorites of their grandfather. She cared for him when he was ill, when he was in assisted living, and when he entered a nursing home. Bill, an attorney, took care of all his financial and legal affairs. So it was a surprise that when he passed, he left his entire estate to Mary. Bill became

suspicious upon learning of his grandfather's bequest, especially when he learned Mary was alone with him the last time he updated his will, which was the day before he died. He now challenges the bequest, asserting Mary must have taken advantage of his weak mental condition. What should Bill allege in his legal challenge, and what is the likelihood he will prevail?

2. Peter owned a hotel located on the beach on the coast of Florida. It once was a very successful destination during the winter season for wealthy Canadians. The hotel deteriorated due to lack of maintenance and repair. The foundation was eroding, and the estimated cost of repair was $500,000. He decided to sell the property and retire. The sales listing for the property stated an annual net income of $5 million and that it was a turnkey operation. The last two winter seasons netted an average $75,000. A consortium of investors from New York purchased the property and after six months learned the property was declared unfit for habitation by the county. The consortium sues Peter for rescission of the purchase contract. What will be the result? Explain your answer.

Decisional Review

1. In order to obtain a commitment to join a dance studio, an instructor told a prospective student she had the potential to become a professional dancer. The instructor sold her over $30,000 worth of lessons. When the student realized she never would become a professional, she sued for misrepresentation. The studio countered with the defense of reasonable opinion, not a statement of fact. What will be the result, and why? See *Vokes v. Arthur Murray, Inc.*, 212 So. 2d 906 (Fla. Dist. Ct. App. 1968).
2. Plaintiff, an employee of Defendant hospital, signed a waiver of all claims required by the hospital. Upon separation of employment for early retirement from the hospital, the employee sued, alleging the hospital engaged in undue influence in obtaining the waiver. Defendant introduced evidence the waiver was signed in consideration of benefits provided to Plaintiff. Moreover, employee was provided 45 days to consult with an attorney and consider the effect of the waiver. See *Zepher v. Kaiser Foundation Hospital*, 687 Fed. Appx. 636. What will be the result? Explain your answer.

Chapter 8

Consideration

Introduction

In order for a contract to be enforceable in a court of law, the parties to a contract must exchange something of value. This something of value is called consideration. It can be a promise, action, forbearance, or some other tangible form of benefit to the other parties. Its purpose is to legally bind the parties to an enforceable contract. This chapter includes discussion of miscellaneous concepts, such as unforeseen difficulties, illusory contracts, and special issues like promissory estoppel and contract settlements.

Chapter Objectives

Upon completion of this chapter, the student will understand:

- the purpose of consideration
- the "value and bargained for exchange" concept
- miscellaneous concepts, such as adequacy, unforeseen difficulties, past consideration, and illusory contracts
- promissory estoppel
- concepts regarding settlement of contracts

Key Terms

Directions: Each of the terms below will be used in this chapter. Before reading, scan the chapter. The terms will appear in bold. Take a moment to see how the term is used so you can understand it in context. The terms are listed in the order in which they will appear in the chapter.

Consideration (p. 156)
Illusory contract (p. 156)
Value (p. 156)
Preexisting obligation (p. 156)
Agreement for a future activity (p. 157)
Agreement to forbear a legal right (p. 157)
Bargained-for exchange (p. 158)
Promissory estoppel (p. 158)
Adequacy of consideration (p. 159)
Unforeseen difficulties (p. 161)
Past consideration (p. 162)
Illusory contract (p. 162)
Contract settlements (p. 164)
Accord (p. 164)
Satisfaction (p. 164)
Unliquidated debt (p. 164)
Liquidated debt (p. 164)
Release (p. 164)
Novation (p. 165)

Consideration and Its Purpose

Consideration, in the context of contract law, is "something (such as an act, a forbearance, or a return promise) bargained for and received by a promisor from a promisee; that which motivates a person to do something, esp. to engage in a legal act" (Garner 2005, 256). Consideration is required to be exchanged before a contract is enforceable. It is the glue that binds the parties to the terms of a contract. It provides value and is the reason parties make a promise or perform an act for each other. It is referred to as the "bargained for exchange" of a contract that motives the parties to do business with each other.

Consideration is something of value, such as money, a promise, an act, an article of furniture, food, wearing apparel, service on a cruise, or a seat at a sporting event. For example, assume a hotel chain ("Hotel") orders 200 new beds from a manufacturer as part of a summer renovation. The general manager promises to pay $500 per bed if they are delivered by May 1, 2017, in time for the summer vacation period, and the manufacturer agrees.

Consideration for the manufacturer of the beds is the $100,000 purchase price. Consideration for the hotel is the 200 beds delivered by May 1, 2017. Each party receives something of value, which is the bargained for consideration of the contract.

Contrast an agreement for 200 beds at $500 per bed, delivery by May 1, 2017, subject to availability. The foregoing is not enforceable, because the manufacturer is not bound to deliver the beds. The manufacturer may find a hotel willing to pay $550 per bed and decide not to honor their agreement with Hotel, because "supplies are unavailable."

The above example is referred to as an **illusory contract** lacking legal consideration for the hotel to bind the manufacturer. The foregoing contingency is an escape valve for the manufacturer and negates an otherwise valid contract negotiated between the parties. Consideration requires two basic elements: It must have value, and it must be bargained for between the parties.

Value and Bargained-for Exchange

Value is "(1) The significance, desirability, or utility of something of value; (2) the monetary worth or price of something; the amount of goods, services, or money that something will command in an exchange" (Garner 2005, 1294). An intangible, such as love and affection, may also be valid consideration.

It may also be one of the following three general types of agreements concerning promises or actions: (1) a promise to do something a person is not under a preexisting obligation to do; (2) performance of a future act one is not under obligation to do; (3) the forbearance of an act one has a right to do.

The **preexisting obligation** rule is "the rule that if a party does or promises to do what the party is already legally obligated to do ... the party has not incurred detriment. This rule's result is that the promise does not constitute adequate consideration for contractual purposes" (Garner 2005, 988). If you are obligated to do such an act, it cannot be a bargained-for exchange, because you are already committed to do it. As a result, it lacks present value.

For example, hotels often use police officers to assist with security needs. Assume the general manager ("GM") of a hotel asks local "on-duty police officers" for a visible presence on the premises in the late evening hours as a deterrent to a recent crime spree in the area. In exchange, the GM promises to provide each police officer with a room and dinner one weekend each month they work for the hotel (commonly referred to as "payment in kind"). The police officers agree and provide the enhanced service.

If the hotel later decides not to honor the agreement, the police officers cannot enforce the agreement in court, because it lacks consideration. The police officers are on duty and obligated to the city for whom they work and get paid. They have a preexisting duty to provide service to the hotel and the public while on duty.

Agreement for a future activity refers to a contract in which a promise for a future act is made. If the agreement is for the police officers to work while off duty, consideration exists because the officers are not obligated to the police department during that time. Since the police officers are off duty, they will be giving up their spare time, a commodity that has value, in return for the payment in kind. This agreement is enforceable in court.

Agreement to forebear a legal right is "the act of refraining from enforcing a right, obligation, or debt. Strictly speaking, a forbearance denotes an intentional negative act" (Garner 2005, 537). In the above example, assume the off-duty police officers are injured in an altercation removing a combative, intoxicated guest from the hotel bar and they intend to sue the guest. The guest is a prominent member of the community, and the hotel wishes to protect the guest, as well as itself, from unflattering news.

The GM agrees to pay all medical expenses, lost wages, and a lump sum amount (i.e., a settlement) for the inconvenience and damages experienced by the off-duty officers. In return, the off-duty officers agree to forego their right to sue the guest. Under this agreement, the officers have given up the legal right to sue the guest in exchange for the GM's promise to compensate them for the inconvenience and damages they sustained. Both parties have given up something of value, which binds them in an enforceable contract. The text box that follows summarizes value.

VALUE AND CONSIDERATION

Value is something that both parties desire. Each party will give something the other wants. As mentioned, it can be many tangible things, such as money, service, or some article. It may also be an intangible, such as forbearance of a right and even love and affection. This text box explains different types of agreements that concern valid consideration. They are agreements that are burdened by a preexisting obligation, agreements that are for a future activity, and agreements to forbear a legal right.

Preexisting obligation. Once a party has given an article for consideration in a contract, it cannot be used again. Any attempt to do so renders the contract unenforceable. For example, assume a restaurateur uses the equity in the restaurant to finance business operations, such as purchasing supplies and costs of labor. The same equity cannot be used as collateral for the purchase of kitchen equipment. The equity is pledged for other purposes and cannot be used again until the associated debt has been paid. There is a preexisting obligation that makes any other pledge unenforceable.

Agreement for a future activity. Often, parties to a contract enter into an agreement to be performed in the future. For example, in the hypothetical unilateral contract whereby Beach Hotel offers to pay $8,000 to the first vendor to deliver 2,000 beach towels before June 1, nothing will take place until Beach Hotel receives 2,000 beach towels. At that time, the offer has been accepted, and consideration by the vendor complete. Also, the agreement is partially executed. Beach Hotel must pay $8,000 and when paid, the contract becomes fully executed.

Agreement to forbear a legal right. Consider the agreement in the case *Hammer v. Sidway,* 27 N.E. 256 (1891). In that case William Story's uncle offered to pay him $5,000 if he would refrain from drinking, swearing, and other questionable habits. Story did not provide any tangible consideration in return for the uncle's promise. The promise was later legally challenged with the assertion that it lacked consideration. The court concluded that forbearance of the activities he was legally entitled to do was a form of consideration. There was reliance by Story, which created a legal detriment to which he did not have to give up.

Bargained-for exchange concerns something of value, and it is defined as "consideration that is valid under the law; consideration that either confers a pecuniarily measurable benefit on one party or imposes a pecuniarily measurable detriment on the other" (Garner 2005, 258). It must be negotiated and bargained for as opposed to a unilateral promise of a gift.

In the above example concerning the off-duty police officers, the GM offered to provide a room and dinner ("in-kind payment") one night per month (the offer). The police officers agreed to provide a presence at the hotel while off duty in the evening hours to deter crime (the acceptance). This is a bargained-for exchange that each party negotiated, and each received something of value.

If the GM promised to give the police officers the in-kind payment because he was grateful for their consistent outstanding professional manner while on duty, the in-kind payment would not be bargained-for consideration binding the hotel. The police officers have performed their preexisting duty required by the police department for which they were employed. Since the officers have not given up some new consideration, the in-kind payment would be a gift, which could be retracted by the GM at any time without legal consequences. (Off-duty police work is subject to police department policy regarding the acceptance of gifts. See Practicum below.)

PRACTICUM

Many police departments, as a matter of policy, prohibit such off-duty work. In those jurisdictions, violation of such policy results in disciplinary actions of the police officers. Moreover, if the violation occurs while the officers are on duty, it could lead to a criminal and/or civil liability for the hotel, called "bribing a police officer." Tread carefully with this activity, and always contact city officials to ensure it is a permissible activity. Also, if there is a crime spree of activity in the area, contact city officials and ask for more police support. If additional on-duty police support is not possible, seek an exception to the policy prohibiting the hire of off-duty officers.

Promissory Estoppel

Promissory estoppel is "the principle that a promise made without consideration may nonetheless be enforced to prevent injustice if the promisor should have reasonably expected the promisee to rely on the promise and if the promisee did actually rely on the promise to his or her detriment" (Garner 2005, 471). Courts possess discretion to make such equitable decisions in the interest of fairness.

Just as a court may create an implied-in-law contract, a court may create consideration in situations where, technically, it does not exist. One such situation occurs when a party to a legally unenforceable contract justifiably changes position in reliance on representations or actions of the other party. The rationale is to achieve fairness and justice in unique circumstances. The elements for application of promissory estoppel are:

- There is a clear and definite promise.
- It is reasonable to expect the promisee to rely on the promise.
- The promisee reasonably relies.
- The reliance resulted in substantial detriment.
- Enforcement of the promise is required to avoid injustice.

Assume Old World Restaurant ("Old World"), unhappy with its current lease, negotiates a five-year lease in a shopping mall (lessor) for 4,000 sq. ft. of space at cost of $1.00/sq. ft. per month. Old World explained to the lessor it must renew its current lease within ten days or it must find other space. The negotiations were completed quickly because of the foregoing and because the lessor asserted the space was in high demand and others were lining up to sign a lease for the same location.

Old World explained to the lessor that it requires home office approval and that would take one additional week to obtain. Old World's current landlord has a new tenant ready to sign once Old World's lease expires. The lessor agrees to wait one week but indicates it will not sign the lease until the approval by Old World's home office is obtained. Old World signs the agreement to show good faith and because it does not want to lose the location. The lessor assures Old World it will wait one week without a problem.

Old World obtains the approval in nine days and attempts to finalize the new lease. At that time, based upon an alleged new market price in the area, the lessor explains the lease has been amended to a cost of $1.50/ sq. ft. Meanwhile, the lease at Old World's existing space expired, and new tenants have been secured. Old World has 30 days to vacate, so it signs the new lease because it has no other place to go. Old World then files a lawsuit arguing the first contract price, not the new contract price, is the proper one for contract enforcement.

Under these facts, the first contract does not technically exist, because only one of the parties, Old World, signed the lease (the statute of frauds requires a contract for an interest in land to be in writing by both parties), and it is also unenforceable because there was a lack of consideration. If Old World paid a fee to the lessor (i.e., some value that would have created an option clause), there would have been consideration to bind the parties.

Nonetheless, a court could decide to enforce the original agreement based upon the doctrine of promissory estoppel. A clear and definite promise was made. The lessor should have expected Old World to rely on $1.00/ sq. ft. cost because that was the amount it submitted for approval to its home office. Old World reasonably believed the price would not change in nine days.

The reliance was reasonable, and a substantial detriment will occur if Old World must pay $.50/sq. ft. for the five years of the new lease. Finally, it is clear the lessor knows of the urgency and appears to be taking advantage of Old World's predicament. The court could reasonably conclude it is unfair and an injustice to enforce the "new market price."

Miscellaneous Consideration Issues

As a general rule, courts tend to avoid rendering decisions based upon the adequacy of consideration. **Adequacy of consideration** is defined as "consideration that is fair and reasonable under the circumstances of the agreement" (Garner 2005, 256). Judicial policy defers the decision regarding the value of the bargained-for consideration to the parties. As some may say, one person's garbage may be another person's treasure.

More importantly, if the courts regularly decided whether a contract was a good or bad bargain, judicial caseloads would explode exponentially. Accordingly, judicial economy requires each party to decide for themselves the value of their contract consideration.

Similarly, a court will not dismiss a case for breach of contract because a party alleges inadequate consideration. The court in the following case overruled a previous court's decision to dismiss a case for that reason. It concluded that any consideration, as long as it has some value, is consideration enough.

UNITED STATES COURT OF APPEALS,

Ninth Circuit.
Dennis GALLAGHER; Shelly Gallagher, Plaintiffs—Appellants,
v.
Terry J. HOLT, now known as Terry Jan Mace; Jerri A. Wells, now known as Jerri A. Carsello, Defendants—Appellees.
No. 10–15784.
Argued and Submitted May 13, 2011. Filed June 6, 2011.
Before: O'SCANNLAIN and GOULD, Circuit Judges, and ST. EVE, District Judge.

MEMORANDUM

Plaintiffs Dennis and Shelly Gallagher appeal the district court's order granting Defendants' motion for summary judgment as to the Gallaghers' action for damages for breach of contract. We review a district court's grant of summary judgment de novo. [Citations omitted.] The district court erred in finding as a matter of California law that, to obtain damages for breach of contract, a plaintiff must prove adequate consideration. The California Civil Code ("the Code") provides that consideration is an essential element of a contract. Cal. Civ. Code § 1550. *It further provides that "[a]ny benefit conferred, or agreed to be conferred, upon the promisor, by any other person, to which the promisor is not lawfully entitled, or any prejudice suffered, or agreed to be suffered, by such person, other than such as he is at the time of consent lawfully bound to suffer, as an inducement to the promisor, is a good consideration for a promise." Id. at § 1605 (emphasis added).*

The adequacy of consideration is relevant to the question whether a promisee can compel a party to perform under a contract.

***

Section 3391, however, does not purport to limit a plaintiff's right to obtain common-law damages for breach of contract, for which good consideration exists. It is well established in California that, to maintain an action at law for breach of contract, one need only prove the existence of consideration, rather than its adequacy. See, e.g., Kremen v. Cohen, 337 F. 3d 1024, 1028 (9th Cir. 2003). *("The adequacy of consideration doesn't matter, but it must be 'something of real value.'") [Citations omitted.]*

***

The district court relied on the 1931 decision of the California Court of Appeals in Cushing v. Levi, 117 Cal. App. 94, 102–03, 3 P.2d 958 (1931), *for the proposition that a plaintiff must allege and prove adequate consideration to obtain damages for breach of contract. To the extent that Cushing purports to stand for this principle, it is no longer good law. This necessarily follows from the contrary precedent of the Supreme Court of California, other California case law, and the Code.*

Because the district court erred in granting Defendants' motion for summary judgment as to Plaintiffs' action for damages for breach of contract, we reverse.

Costs are awarded to Plaintiffs–Appellants.

REVERSED.

Moreover, it is not the court's duty to protect a person from making an imprudent contract. For example, assume environmentalists succeed in obtaining regulatory controls that drastically restrict fishing in the area, which will substantially decrease the available supply of seafood. The owner of a seafood restaurant, aware of the adoption of the regulatory controls, decides to sell because the cost of fish is projected to increase tenfold in the near future.

Assume a person unfamiliar with the restaurant business decides to purchase the seafood restaurant, historically very successful, for $950,000. The buyer did not research future availability of fish and naively purchased the restaurant based solely on historical revenue data. This turns out to be a very bad bargain for the buyer who was required to close its doors after only six months of operation.

If the buyer decides to sue the seller, it will have to be on some basis other than inadequate consideration. The buyer cannot reasonably argue the purchase price of the restaurant should have been less because the owner knew of the negative impact of the regulatory controls. The court will not undo the buyer's poor decision to buy the restaurant based upon the theory of inadequate consideration. A buyer is expected to conduct the due diligence required by best business practices.

There would be a cause of action for fraudulent misrepresentation if the seller represented that his research indicated a plentiful supply of fish well into the future. Such a representation might be viewed as reasonable for the buyer to believe, and it would be an inducement to purchase the restaurant (see discussion of misrepresentation in Chapter 3).

Unforeseen difficulties are another type of consideration issue. Often, two parties enter into an agreement and both believe they have a fair bargain, but some unforeseen event occurs that neither party could have reasonably expected. For example, suppose the owner of a hotel decides to build a pool for guests and negotiates a contract with a contractor to build a swimming pool. The negotiated cost is $125,000 for a completed pool and related pool equipment, with a completion date of June 1, 2016, in time for the summer vacation season.

Construction commences, and progress benchmarks are on schedule. On May 1, the contractor's workers hit a very large boulder that must be busted into smaller pieces and extracted. The estimated cost is an additional $30,000, which wipes out the contractor's entire profit and renders the contract worthless. The type of boulder encountered is not common to the area and is a surprise to all involved, especially the expert who performed soil tests.

Normally, courts will not interfere with a contract fairly negotiated at arm's length. In this example, the court may decide otherwise. It would treat the encounter with the very large boulder as an unusual, unforeseeable occurrence. That decision would permit the court to conclude the contract is not enforceable and thereby permit further negotiation for completion of the job.

Under several other scenarios, a court would likely enforce the contract. The first is when such boulders are frequently found in the area. The contractor should have known of that fact. The other is when evidence showed the contractor bid low just to get the contract and contemplated a subsequent contract amendment. This is referred to as contract extortion. Facts of the case are key to the court's decision, and pretrial discovery is very important to that end.

The policy for the unforeseen difficulties is to protect consumers from extortion by unscrupulous contractors. Such contractors commence a project and then stop work unless the consumer pays more money for an alleged unforeseen budget overrun. In these cases, the court will decide whether a true unforeseen difficulty is present.

PRACTICUM

Construction contracts are notoriously plagued with overruns, change orders, alleged "necessary safety revisions," and outright fraud. Such unpleasant facts of life are often referred to as "contract extortion." Great care must be exercised to be as specific, thorough, and accurate as possible in contract negotiations. Retention of a lawyer and/or an accountant with experience in the construction industry will be well worth the money spent.

Past consideration is "an act done or a promise given by a promisee before making a promise sought to be enforced [in a new contract]. Past consideration is not consideration for the new promise because it has not been given in exchange for this promise" (Garner 2005, 257). Assume, in the above example, the pool was finished on budget and on time. After several weeks' use, the hotel owner is extremely pleased with the results and in his euphoric state promised the contractor a week's complimentary stay anytime a room is available, including meals and alcohol. He tells the pool contractor, "I'm giving you a $5,000 value because of the excellent job you did with the pool."

Subsequently, there were minor but excessive equipment troubles and a few slight cracks developed in the plaster surface at the bottom of the pool. The contractor was under no legal obligation to correct them. When the hotel owner asked the contractor to make the necessary repairs, he became unavailable. When the pool contractor tried to reserve the room, the hotel owner adamantly refused to honor his promise.

The pool contractor does not have an enforceable contract, because the promise for the one-week stay is based upon past consideration. Without further consideration from the pool contractor, there is inadequate consideration for enforcement of the hotel owner's promise. If the contract contained a provision that required the contractor to make such minor repairs at his expense, consideration exists in the original contract price, but the contractor must make the repairs.

An **illusory contract** is "an agreement in which one party gives as consideration a promise that is so insubstantial as to impose no obligation. The insubstantial promise renders the agreement unenforceable"

(Garner 2005, 274). Upon initial reading of the contract, it may appear to be an enforceable contract. But upon analysis it may lack an essential element, such as binding consideration.

For example, suppose the owner of a restaurant chain hires a general manager ("GM") for $100,000 a year for five years. Profits for the first two years increase 10% each year, and the owner calls the general manager in for his annual review. The owner showers the GM with praise and says, "If you continue this *strong performance and continue to make me happy*, next year I will give you a 25% bonus." The next year is as profitable as the first two years. But when the GM asks about the bonus, the owner refuses to honor his promise.

The owner's promise is unenforceable because it is not a specific bargained-for exchange. The court does not know what the statement "strong performance and continue to make me happy" means. The consideration offered by the owner is vague and was not exchanged for some clear additional consideration in return.

Consequently, the contract is legally illusory. If the owner said to the GM, "You have increased sales by 10% each of your first two years, and if you increase sales the next year by 10% or more, I will give you a 25% bonus." This promise is a clearer, precise, unilateral offer that, if achieved by the GM's performance, is an acceptance that provides adequate consideration to bind the hotel.

SUMMARY OF MISCELLANEOUS TOPICS

Consideration is affected by several varied topics, summarized below.

Adequacy of consideration. As a matter of policy, a court will not challenge the adequacy of consideration, leaving that decision to the parties of contract. Value is a subjective matter that will vary by the parties through offer and acceptance. The courts feel that, absent duress, misrepresentation, and undue influence, it is not their province to decide what is a fair deal. Moreover, in the interests of judicial economy, the administration of justice is better served.

Unforeseen difficulties. The presence of unforeseeable events is a good reason for courts to intervene because such events prevent a true meeting of the minds. Without a meeting of the minds, the key element of mutual assent is absent.

Past consideration. Past consideration is no consideration at all and cannot bind the parties. It is a promise for actions that have occurred in the past and for which there is no present promise or act. Analytically, it is more of a gift because nothing was given in exchange.

Illusory promise. On the face of a contract, the language may appear to contain a reasonable promise to do an act, but upon analysis, there is slight if any consideration at all. The promise in a contract may contain an opportunity for not completing the promised act. Thus, it is illusory.

Settlement of Claims

If you are the litigant in a contract dispute, you are usually paying for an attorney by the hour. Consequently, the more you delay, the greater the financial cost and additional mental anguish you suffer. Lawyers, of course, are usually the main beneficiaries of protracted litigation because the hourly meter keeps running.

If you are the plaintiff in a tort lawsuit and hire counsel on a contingency fee basis (usual method in tort claims), around 30% to 40% of the award will go to plaintiff's counsel without the running of an hourly meter. The tort plaintiff does not pay for the attorney's time. But they must still pay for court costs, such as depositions and court fees. Nonetheless, despite the relative benefit of a contingency fee, the longer the litigation, the higher the reading on the scale of mental anguish. If you are a defendant in a tort case or either the plaintiff or the defendant in a contract case, you will be paying by the hour, and that will mean a drain on your cash flow as well as your peace of mind.

The best business decision is to try to settle your case without litigation. The following section describes the form of settlements most often used.

Contract settlements are used for contract claims that are settled prior to a lawsuit. This can be accomplished in several ways; all of which require a subsequent contract:

- accord and satisfaction
- release
- novation

Accord and Satisfaction

An accord and satisfaction is "an agreement to substitute for an existing debt some alternative form of discharging that debt, coupled with the actual discharge of the debt by the substituted performance" (Garner 2005, 14). It is a new, separate contract entered into by the parties that supplants an existing contract in the dispute. The parties decide to resolve the dispute with one party accepting an amount less or accepting some action different than promised in the original contract. The new contract is called an **accord.** The agreement to accept alternative consideration is called the **satisfaction** and is expressed in the accord.

The accord and satisfaction is used when the original contract amount is not a "fixed or settled" amount. The price will float up or down, depending on market value. This concept is referred to as an **unliquidated debt** and is defined as "a debt that has not been reduced to a specific amount, and about which there may be a dispute" (Garner 2005, 345).

For example, say a restaurateur orders all the lobster a distributor can provide (referred to as an output contract) at the distributor's market price per pound, up to a designated limit, such as 600 lbs. for the next three months. The amount is not settled; it may go up or down depending on the market price for lobster as well as the distributor's ability to provide available lobster. In the event a dispute develops regarding the market price, the parties could decide to enter an accord and satisfaction at a different price for any of the lobster delivered and accepted.

An accord and satisfaction is generally not available if the price in question is a fixed or settled amount easily determined. Assume, in the example above, the contract called for 600 lbs. of lobster at a price of $10.00/lb. for each of the next three successive months. In this case, the contract has a fixed price of $6,000.00 per month and is referred to as a liquidated debt. A **liquidated debt** is defined as "a debt whose amount has been determined by agreement of the parties or by operation of law" (Garner 2005, 344). Since the amount is for a fixed or settled price per pound, it is easily determined, and an accord and satisfaction is usually not the remedy for the problem.

Release

If a contract dispute occurs with a liquidated debt, the parties would probably enter into a new contract, referred to as a release. A **release** is a substitute for the existing contract that will settle their dispute and avoid litigation. A release is defined as "liberation from an obligation, duty or demand; the act of giving up a right or claim to the person against whom it could have been enforced" (Garner 2005, 1067). According to a release, the parties waive their right to sue based upon the terms and conditions in the release that bars any further recovery, except for that stated in the release. The elements of a release are:

- given in good faith
- expressed in writing (Some states do not require a writing, but it's always best to do so in order to avoid further misunderstandings.)
- consideration

Novation

A **novation** is "the act of substituting for an old obligation a new one that either replaces an existing obligation with a new obligation or replaces an original party with a new party" (Garner 2005, 900). It is a separate, new contract regarding the same subject matter of the original contract but with modified terms. The novation requires all the same elements as the original contract, and it is substituted for the old contract.

The main difference between a novation and the other two settlement methods (accord and satisfaction or the release) is that with a novation the parties decide to continue to do business with each other, based upon the terms of the original contract, as modified. With the other two types of settlements, the original contract ceases to exist, and the parties part ways disregarding the content of the original contract.

PRACTICUM

The author is an ardent proponent of settlement in lieu of litigation. Chapter 2 explains what a lengthy and expensive proposition may result from litigation and why an early settlement of a claim is important. Chapter 3 discusses ADR, such as mediation and arbitration, which also reduces the time and cost for a lawsuit. As discussed in Chapter 2, it does not matter when you settle a case; however, the sooner, the better.

Summary

Consideration is the value exchanged between parties to a contract. It must be something of value, such as money, service, a product, a promise to do something, or the forbearance to do something that a person has a legal right to do. It is characterized by creation of a legal detriment by the party offering to provide it as consideration. It is commonly referred to as a meeting of the minds, without which you do not have an enforceable contract.

Sometimes, consideration may be created by the courts to avoid a serious injustice to one party. It is called promissory estoppel, which occurs when a person reasonably relied on the promise and incurred a serious detriment.

The chapter discusses various special considerations that affect consideration. Included are adequacy of consideration. The courts will not interfere with the choice of consideration between the parties. To do so would open the floodgates of lawsuits. Plus, the courts will not attempt to enter the minds of the parties to determine their subjective intent.

Unforeseen difficulties can impact consideration in a particular case. The general rule is the courts refuse to get involved unless the activity is unforeseeable, which means there is no meeting of the minds. Therefore, the parties will be held to the contract terms.

If the consideration offered in a contract was used in a prior contract, it will not be allowed to be used again. A contract will not be enforceable without further consideration. This can occur when one party offers something of value to another because of gratitude for the outcome of a current contract. Unless further consideration is provided, the promise based upon gratitude for efforts of an existing contract is not enforceable. Finally, sometimes the value asserted by a party is not in existence, such as when the consideration is not well defined and in reality does not create a determent. The consideration in these cases are illusory.

Comprehension Check

True/False

Directions: Look at each statement below. Based on what you learned in this chapter, decide if the statement is true or false.

1. Consideration for a contract means the offer must be clear and definitive.
2. If the proponent of certain consideration changes its legal position, usually, consideration will be legally achieved.
3. Forbearance is not valid consideration, because it is an intangible.
4. Bargained-for exchange refers to the concept that creates a meeting of the minds.
5. Promissory estoppel occurs only with bilateral contracts.
6. A novation requires a party to step into the shoes of the other party to a modified contract.
7. A release of contract obligations is a court-ordered equitable remedy taken to avoid an extreme injustice.
8. An illusory contract contains consideration that is difficult to discern because of its clandestine origins.
9. An important purpose of contract settlements is to clear the court's calendar in the interests of judicial economy.
10. An accord is an agreement to modify a contract rather than have it dismissed because of a legal defect.
11. A liquidated debt is one that has been paid in full and that results in a mutual satisfaction.
12. In the case *Hammer v. Sidway*, the court concluded that the major defective was the lack of a legal detriment by Hammer.
13. In an accord and satisfaction, one party agrees to accept less of an amount than originally agreed upon or to accept something other than what was agreed upon.
14. A court can create consideration to a contract when it technically is not present.
15. A release of all claims is required by the statute of frauds to be in writing.

Multiple Choice

Directions: Use what you learned in this chapter to choose the best response to each of the prompts below.

1. All the following are true regarding a release, except:

   a. It must be an unliquidated debt.
   b. It must be in writing.
   c. It must demonstrate good faith.
   d. It requires the parties to enter into a new contract.

2. All the following are true of a novation, except:
   a. After a novation, the parties will no longer do business with each other.
   b. It substitutes a new obligation for the old obligation.
   c. The new obligation consists of a modification of the old terms.
   d. The subject matter is essentially the same as before.
3. All the following are true of an accord and satisfaction, except:
   a. It concerns only an unliquidated debt.
   b. The original contract amount is fixed.
   c. It consists of a separate new contract.
   d. It consists of two separate elements: an accord and satisfaction.
4. The elements of promissory estoppel include all the following, except:
   a. a clear and definite promise
   b. reasonable reliance
   c. The reliance was detrimental.
   d. Consideration must be reasonable.
5. The text box regarding miscellaneous topics concerns all the following, except:
   a. adequacy of consideration
   b. an express promise
   c. past consideration
   d. unforeseen difficulties
6. All the following are true of consideration, except:
   a. Once used, the same consideration cannot be used again.
   b. It must be something of value.
   c. A gift from a family member may be consideration for a contract.
   d. It can be nonaction, such as forbearance of a legal right.
7. All the following are true of unforeseen difficulties, except:
   a. They do not affect consideration of a contract.
   b. The difficulty must not be foreseeable.
   c. There is no meeting of the minds.
   d. The policy is to protect against unscrupulous contractors.
8. All the following are true of an illusory contract, except:
   a. There is slight or no consideration present.
   b. The absence of consideration makes the contract unenforceable.
   c. A term in a contract that requires the owner to be happy with an employee's efforts is sufficiently clear and enforceable.
   d. Failure to provide additional consideration for a gratuitous promise is an illusory contract.

9. Consideration may be all the following, except:
   a. money
   b. love and affection is not because it is intangible.
   c. service, such as painting a home
   d. forbearance

10. With regard to type of agreements, all the following are true of consideration, except:
    a. an agreement to forbear a legal right
    b. an agreement to something not under a preexisting obligation
    c. an agreement not to compete
    d. an agreement for a future act

Scenarios

1. Bill has three sons and a daughter. All of them but one, named Jerry, are extremely well off. Bill, in sympathy for Jerry's status, says, "In consideration for the fact that you are experiencing extreme financial hardship, I will pay you $1,000 every month until your status improves." Is Bill's promise to pay $1,000/month valid consideration? Why, or why not?
2. Assume you hire a contractor to build a small manufacturing plant for $1 million by June 8, 2020. It is needed to accommodate your current needs and also because of a new lucrative contract ($5 million) to build machinery due for delivery January 1, 2021. if that deadline is not met, you will have to pay a late fee of ten percent. After two months, the contractor demands $100,000 more for alleged necessary cost overruns. You cannot find anyone else to complete the project, and the contractor threatens to walk off the job. What would you argue to a court of law to remedy the situation? Do you think you will be successful, and why?

Decisional Review

1. Jeffrey and Kathryn Dow owned 125 acres of land. With the Dows' permission, their daughter Teresa installed a mobile home on the land. After Teresa married, the Dows promised to pay for construction of a house on the land for the couple. Teresa's husband died in a motorcycle accident. Teresa paid for the construction of the house with her husband's insurance proceeds. Later, Teresa requested a deed for the property so that she could obtain a mortgage. They refused, and Teresa sued for relief in court. What should be her argument, and what is the likely outcome? See *Harvey v. Dow* 11 A. 3d 303 (Me. 2011).
2. An appliance dealer induces a consumer to sign a contract that requires the consumer to pay an amount that significantly exceeds the market value of the appliance. The disparity in value is enough to cause a judge to inquire if the contract was entered into voluntarily. This is an unusual effort by the court since the consumer did not expressly allege the disparity in the value. What will be the result? Explain your answer. See *Orcilla v. Big Sur, Inc.*, 244 Cal. App. 4th 982, 198 Cal Rptr., 3d 715 (2016).

Chapter 9

Contract Capacity

Introduction

This chapter discusses capacity to enter into a contract. It concerns minors, persons who are mentally incapacitated, and persons under the influence of alcohol and/or drugs. The foregoing persons have certain defenses that may render a contract either void or voidable. A void contract is one that is unenforceable from its inception. A voidable contract is one that will be enforceable or disaffirmed upon the election of the incapacitated person.

The rationale for such defenses is based upon the inability of a person to understand the terms and conditions of a contract. Without the ability to understand, there is no meeting of the minds. Therefore, the contract is not enforceable.

Chapter Objectives

Upon completion of this chapter, the student will understand:

- the nature and importance of contract capacity
- the general defense of incapacity to contract
- age and its treatment in contract formation
- mental capacity and its treatment in contract formation
- intoxication and its treatment in contract formation
- the distinction between void and voidable contracts

Key Terms

Directions: Each of the terms below will be used in this chapter. Before reading, scan the chapter. The terms will appear in bold. Take a moment to see how the term is used so you can understand it in context. The terms are listed in the order in which they will appear in the chapter.

Contracting capacity (p. 170)
Valid contract (p. 170)
Voidable contract (p. 170)
Void contract (p. 170)
Disaffirmance (p. 170)
Necessaries of life (p. 173)
Emancipated minor (p. 174)
Mental capacity (p. 175)
Intoxication (p. 176)

Contracting Capacity

Chapter 6 discussed mutual assent between contracting parties. It is generally described as two or more parties agreeing to the terms of a contract. In order for contracting persons to reach agreement, the parties must be able to understand the terms of the contract and the consequences for failure to meet the terms of the contract. The ability to understand the terms of a contract is referred to as contracting capacity.

Contract capacity is "the power to create or enter into a legal relationship under the same circumstances in which a normal person would have the power to create or enter into such a relation" (Garner 2005, 171). A person's age, mental capacity, and level of intoxication are evaluated to determine if legal contract capacity was present at the time the contract was negotiated and executed. The following discussion explains the three major defenses to contract enforcement based upon incapacity: age, mental capacity, and intoxication.

Age

A person under the legal age set by state statute is presumed by law to lack contractual capacity and is referred to as a minor. In most states that age is 18. That means such a person may not legally enter into a **valid contract**, which is "a contract that is fully operative in accordance with the parties intent" (Garner 2005, 277).

If a minor enters into a contract, it will be unenforceable in a court of law. A minor's contract is considered a voidable contract as opposed to a valid or void contract. A **voidable contract** is "a contract that can be affirmed or rejected at the option of one of the parties" (Garner 2005, 277). "A contract is void as to the wrongdoer but not void as to the party wronged, unless that party elects to treat it as void" (Garner 2005, 277).

A **void contract** is "a contract that is of no legal effect, so that there is really no contract in existence at all" (Garner 2005, 277). "A contract may be void because it is technically defective, contrary to public policy or illegal" (Garner 2005, 277). The process for a minor attempting to reject a voidable contract is referred to as **disaffirmance**, which is defined as "(1) an act of denial; a repudiation, as of an earlier transaction; (2) a declaration that a voidable contract (such as one entered into by a minor) is void" (Garner 2005, 388).

For example, assume John, a seventeen-and-a-half-year-old, decides to purchase a cell phone for $1,000 at a local retail outlet. He decides to return the cell phone after three months of use. The retailer refuses to refund the purchase price because it has a "no refund policy" and because of the obvious physical wear of the cell phone. Because John is a minor, he may seek disaffirmance in a court of law, such as a small claims court.

Jurisdiction for small claims varies by jurisdiction but usually is for a maximum limit from $7,000–$10,000. Upon proof of age and upon John's disaffirmance, the court has several options. It may declare the contract void as to the retailer and order the entire $1,000 be refunded. It is a voidable contract at the request of John, which means John can honor the contract or disaffirm it.

John, as a matter of law, is incapable of entering into an enforceable valid contract. The retailer cannot allege John looked 18 or over; it's the retailer's responsibility to check John's identification for proof of age. Consequently, the retailer is considered the wrongdoer and must refund the retail price.

PRACTICUM

Retailers understand this requirement, but they make a business decision not to check identification, knowing some minors will take advantage of their age to disavow but most will not do so. Hence, they will generate more business than they lose. It is the cost of doing business.

There is a split in jurisdictions regarding how to treat underage contracts. For example, the ability for a minor to return a purchase may be limited, depending on the reasonableness of the time the item has been used. Assume the same facts as the above example, except John decides to keep the phone for one year, which means it is six months after reaching majority (the legal age).

Some jurisdictions will hold the contract voidable for a reasonable amount of time. A court in those jurisdictions may decide six months is still within the reasonable time frame and order the retailer to refund the $1,000. Some jurisdictions may require John to pay a reasonable sum for use of the phone. Finally, some jurisdictions may decide that six months past the age of majority is too long of a time and find that John impliedly ratified the contract resulting in no refund.

Finally, some jurisdictions refuse a minor's disaffirmance if the retailer presents evidence the minor misrepresented their age. Legislators are concerned about sending the wrong message to minors engaging in fraud. For example, a minor may have an altered driver's license indicating an age just over the statutory limit. As such, the likelihood of acceptance by a retailer may be increased.

The following case is a good example of the trend of judicial thought toward limiting a minor's ability to rescind a contract and receive full repayment. There is a growing effort to consider depreciation of the merchandise and for the value of use of the merchandise while in the minor's possession. Any evidence of overreaching by the seller likewise is considered. It appears to be a fair balancing of the interests.

---

824 S.W.2D 545

Supreme Court of Tennessee,
Joseph Eugene DODSON, a minor, by his next friend Gene DODSON, Plaintiff/Appellee,
v.
Burns SHRADER, Jr., and Mary Shrader, individually and d/b/a Shrader's Auto Sales, Defendant/Appellant.
Jan. 27, 1992

OPINION

O'BRIEN, Justice.

This is an action to disaffirm the contract of a minor for the purchase of a pick-up truck and for a refund of the purchase price. The issue is whether the minor is entitled to a full refund of the money he paid or whether the seller is entitled to a setoff for the decrease in value of the pick-up truck while it was in the possession of the minor.

In early April of 1987, Joseph Eugene Dodson, then 16 years of age, purchased a used 1984 pick-up truck from Burns and Mary Shrader. The Shraders owned and operated Shrader's Auto Sales in Columbia, Tennessee. Dodson paid $4,900 in cash for the truck, using money he borrowed from his girlfriend's grandmother. At the time of *the purchase there was no inquiry by the Shraders, and no misrepresentation by Mr. Dodson, concerning his minority. However, Mr. Shrader did testify that at the time he believed Mr. Dodson to be 18 or 19 years of age.*

In December 1987, nine (9) months after the date of purchase, the truck began to develop mechanical problems. ... Mr. Dodson did not want, or did not have the money, to effect these repairs. He continued to drive the truck despite the mechanical problems. One month later, in January, the truck's engine "blew up" and the truck became inoperable.

Mr. Dodson ... contacted the Shraders to rescind the purchase of the truck and requested a full refund. The Shraders refused to accept the tender of the truck or to give Mr. Dodson the refund requested.

***

... in an opinion by Mr. Justice McKinney, the modern rule that contracts of infants are not void but only voidable and subject to be disaffirmed by the minor either before or after attaining majority appears to have been favored.

***

He [the minor] is thus permitted to assume the burden of a contract, clearly disadvantageous to him, if he deems himself under a moral obligation to do so.

***

Thus the minor can secure the advantage of contracts advantageous to himself and be relieved of the effect of an injudicious contract.

***

As a result, two (2) minority rules have developed which allow the other party to a contract with a minor to refund less than the full consideration paid in the event of rescission.

***

The first of these minority rules is called the "Benefit Rule" [Citations omitted.] The rule holds that, upon rescission, recovery of the full purchase price is subject to a deduction for the minor's use of the merchandise. The other minority rule holds that the minor's recovery of the full purchase price is subject to a deduction for the minor's "use" of the consideration he or she received under the contract, or for the "depreciation" or "deterioration" of the consideration in his or her possession. [Citations omitted.]

***

We state the rule to be followed hereafter, in reference to a contract of a minor, to be where the minor has not been overreached in any way, and there has been no undue influence, and the contract is a fair and reasonable one, and the minor has actually paid money on the purchase price, and taken and used the article purchased, that he ought not to be permitted to recover the amount actually paid, without allowing the vender of the goods reasonable compensation for the use of, depreciation, and willful or negligent damage to the article purchased, while in his hands. If there has been any fraud or imposition on the part of the seller or if the contract is unfair, or any unfair advantage has been taken of the minor inducing him to make the purchase, then the rule does not apply.

Further, it does not appear consistent with practice of proper moral influence upon young people, tend to encourage honesty and integrity, or lead them to a good and useful business future, if they are taught that they can make purchases with their own money, for their own benefit, and after paying for them, and using them until they are worn out and destroyed, go back and compel the vendor to return to them what they have paid upon the purchase price. Such a doctrine can only lead to the corruption of principles and encourage young people in habits of trickery and dishonesty.

The case is remanded to the trial court for further proceedings in accordance with this judgment. The costs on appellate review are assessed equally between the parties.

REID, C.J. and DROWOTA, DAUGHTREY and ANDERSON, JJ., concur.

Necessaries

Exceptions to the age requirement exist for purchases that are necessaries of life and also for contracts incurred as an emancipated minor. **Necessaries of life** include "things that are indispensable to living" and include "whatever food, medicine, clothing, shelter and personal services usually essential for the preservation and enjoyment of life" (Garner 2005, 868). For a contract to qualify as one of necessaries, it must be needed to maintain the minor's subsistence, valued at the minor's current standard of living, and the minor must be under the present care of a parent or guardian.

For example, if a minor goes to a restaurant and orders a meal (the order is an offer) and the restaurant places the order (this is an acceptance), this creates a contract. Food is a necessity of life; therefore, disaffirmance of this contract will not be available to relieve the minor's obligation to pay. Instead, the minor's parents or guardian will be held responsible for the purchase.

It is generally against public policy to permit a minor to disaffirm a contract for necessaries of life. To do otherwise would discourage restaurants from serving minors if they order a meal without a parent or guardian present. Instead, public policy encourages restaurants to serve minors, especially if they do not presently have money and need a meal. The same analysis applies to a hotel room. In the example above concerning the cell phone (arguably not a necessity), a parent will only be liable if they have cosigned the contract.

PRACTICUM

When a minor declines to pay after consuming a meal, the restaurant has several options. It can call the police and create an unwanted scene at the restaurant, it can warn the minor not to return because they will not be served again, or it can try to determine the minor's residence or phone number and attempt to reach the minor's parents to pay for the meal. The decision is a matter of restaurant policy and not a matter of law. The author favors either option two or three, unless the minor is obnoxious or creates a scene; then option one should be taken.

Emancipation

An **emancipated minor** "is a minor who is self-supporting and independent of parental control, usually a result of a court order" (Garner 2005, 834). It occurs when a minor's parents or legal guardian relinquish the legal right to exercise control over the minor. A minor may also petition a court to declare emancipation.

It also occurs when minors marry, enter the military service, or leave home to support themselves. Once emancipated, a minor may enter into any contract an adult may legally make, except those the law expressly prohibits minors from legally doing, such as contracts for the purchase of alcoholic beverages (see the text box below).

GENERAL RULES OF DISAFFIRMANCE FOR MINOR'S CONTRACTS

General rule. Minors are not legally capable of entering into an enforceable contract. The law presumes minors are not mature enough to do so. A minor may disaffirm the contract and receive full repayment for the product.

Ratification. The minor must disaffirm within a reasonable amount of time, or the court may hold the contract was ratified by the minor. Ratification is more likely to occur after the minor has attained the statutory age of adulthood.

Minor misrepresentation. Courts in some jurisdictions refuse disaffirmance if the minor possessed fraudulent I.D. The rationale is public policy to deter other minors from doing likewise. However, a verbal misrepresentation will not suffice because that would pose evidentiary problems in a court of law.

Depreciation/use. A growing trend, jurisdictions will consider how long the minor had possession of the product, the physical condition it is in, and any calculable market value. Based upon the foregoing, the court will assess a reasonable sum to be deducted from the purchase price.

Vendor's bad acts. A mitigating factor for the two previous points is any unfair business practices of the vendor, such as misrepresentations and high-pressure sales tactics.

Necessaries. An exception to the general rule of disaffirmance. Public policy encourages vendors of food, medicine, and shelter to provide their product to minors. Hence, for necessaries a parent or guardian becomes liable for any such contract.

Emancipation. An emancipated minor is legally responsible for all contracts that an adult may execute, except those forbidden by statute to minors (e.g., alcohol purchases).

Mental Capacity

Mental capacity is "the mental ability to understand the nature and effect of one's acts" (Garner 2005, 171). If a person lacks mental capacity, the person cannot fully understand their actions or agreements. Accordingly, there can't be a meeting of the minds. Public policy encourages protection of those afflicted, and therefore, a contract entered into by a person who is mentally incapacitated will not be enforceable.

A defense for breach of contract based upon mental incapacity renders a contract either void or voidable. First, a contract will be void if there is past court action declaring the person to be incapacitated. This usually requires the court to appoint a guardian, create a transcript record, and enter an order in the record concluding the person is incapacitated. Such proof is hard to refute and should be so.

Second, if there is no prior court declaration, a court hearing of incapacity will be deemed voidable, which means the person's caretaker must prove mental incapacity existed when the contract was formed. The court treats the former situation as one that is void because the court decree is deemed constructive notice to all that such a person is incapable of entering into an enforceable contract. For example, if a person is under the supervision of a court-appointed guardian, that person is considered legally unable to enter into a contract.

Proof at trial of the court's declaration of incapacity will relieve the person of any liability. If there was not a prior court declaration, the contract is voidable. This means, depending on the circumstances and after a reasonable amount of time, the caretaker may decide to honor the contract, or they may decide to disaffirm the contract.

Also, a person may possess capacity when entering into a contract but subsequently lose mental capacity. In such a case, the contract may be voidable while the person is incapacitated subject to ratification and/or enforcement if mental capacity returns.

The obvious question for a retailer to ponder is, how do you know the person buying your product or service is incapacitated? In many instances the person who is mentally incapacitated may not exhibit any objective manifestation of a problem. Consequently, the retailer may not have a reason to suspect the incapacity exists, and the agreement will be consummated.

Unfortunately for the retailer, it will not matter in court, because the law is designed to protect those who can't understand what they are doing. Just as a minor is deemed unable to form a contract, so is the incapacitated person. Under the law, the retailer's inability to detect the mental incapacity at the time the contract is formed is irrelevant.

For example, assume a person with a prior court declaration of incapacity sneaks away from their guardian and goes to a hotel for a long weekend. That person has a credit card in their own name, and there are no obvious objective manifestations of mental incapacity (e.g., a mild case of dementia). The total charge for the weekend, including the room and meals, is $1,600. When the credit card statement is reviewed by the guardian, the charge is discovered and challenged.

The guardian may show proof of a court declaration of incapacity and demand a refund. If the hotel refuses, the guardian may seek redress in a small claims court and will likely get the court to order the refund because the contract is void. If there was not a prior court declaration of incapacity, the guardian may still go to court and prove that at the time of the contract the person was incapacitated. However, this will be difficult to do and it would probably be in all parties' best interest to settle the matter for a reasonable sum of money.

Intoxication

Intoxication is "a diminished ability to act with full mental and physical capabilities because of alcohol or drug consumption" (Garner 2005, 683). The law treats persons who are under the influence of alcohol/drugs similarly to minors and people who are mentally incapacitated. Persons intoxicated are unable to understand the terms of a contract or the consequences for failure to honor the contract terms.

Accordingly, if intoxication existed at the time of contract formation, the contract is voidable and, at the request of the intoxicated person, will not be enforceable. The intoxication must be extreme in order to be recognized as mentally disabling and is a condition difficult to prove in a court of law. Courts require proof of "clear and convincing" evidence that extreme intoxication existed, a high standard of proof in the courts. Moreover, both courts and juries are usually not sympathetic to persons incapacitated because of alcohol or drug use.

The following excerpt concerns an example of the standard for determining intoxication used in the *Lucy v. Zehmer* case discussed previously in Chapter 5.

> *Lucy took a partly filled bottle of whiskey into the restaurant with him for the purpose of giving Zehmer a drink if he wanted it. Zehmer did, and he and Lucy had one or two drinks together. Lucy said that while he felt the drinks he took he was not intoxicated, and from the way Zehmer handled the transaction he did not think he was either.*
>
> *In his testimony Zehmer claimed that he "was high as a Georgia pine," and that the transaction "was just a bunch of two doggoned drunks bluffing to see who could talk the biggest and say the most." That claim is inconsistent with his attempt to testify in great detail as to what was said and what was done. It is contradicted by other evidence as to the condition of both parties, and rendered of no weight by the testimony of his wife that when Lucy left the restaurant she suggested that Zehmer drive him home. The record is convincing that Zehmer was not intoxicated to the extent of being unable to comprehend the nature and consequences of the instrument he executed, and hence that instrument is not to be invalidated on that ground. 17 C.J.S., Contracts, § 133 b., p. 483; Taliaferro v. Emery, 124 Va. 674, 98 S.E. 627. It was in fact conceded by defendants' counsel in oral argument that under the evidence Zehmer was not too drunk to make a valid contract.*
>
> See *Lucy v. Zehmer*, 196 Va. 493 (1954)

A contract entered into when a person is extremely intoxicated is a voidable contract. Like a minor, the intoxicated person has a reasonable amount of time in which to disaffirm the contract or to ratify it. Disaffirmance may be express or implied, and any consideration must be returned. A court has discretion to order payment for the reasonable use of the product while in possession of the intoxicated person. The courts also apply an objective standard test to assist in the determination of intoxication.

Once the intoxicated person becomes sober, they must make a decision relatively quickly to disaffirm or ratify the contract. For example, assume a couple (both known to be heavy drinkers) decide to spend a weekend celebrating their anniversary. They spend most of the weekend drinking with friends and relatives at meals and at parties thrown in their honor. After three full days of drinking, they decide to have one final celebration at Sunday brunch.

They spend several hours drinking champagne and then decide to look at condominiums for a future purchase. They encounter a persuasive salesperson who convinces them to purchase one for a $750,000. They make the down payment of $7,500 with a personal check. The next morning, they awake to the unpleasant realization they purchased a condominium, and they want to rescind the deal.

The first thing they should do is talk with the realtor and explain that they were grossly intoxicated and did not fully understand what they were doing. They should try to rescind the contract and have their deposit returned. This is an express disaffirmance that may or may not work. If it does not work, they will have to hire an attorney and prove their intoxication through settlement negotiations or with litigation.

A lawsuit can be very expensive for both parties. A settlement should be pursued, such as the seller rescinding the contract but keeping the $7,500 deposit. If the couple waits more than several months to take action, it will be harder to disaffirm the contract. This is especially true if they take overt steps toward possession, such as accepting the keys and moving furniture and personal effects into the unit. The courts would likely find the delay and subsequent action was an implied ratification.

Proof a person is an alcoholic standing alone may not be sufficient to void a contract. There must be evidence they were under the influence of alcohol at the time they executed the contract. Moreover, the person was unable to understand the terms and conditions and its consequences. Proof the person seeking disaffirmance was sober at the time will defeat the attempt to void the contract.

The following case stands for the proposition that the relevant time for the disaffirmance of a contract based upon intoxication is at the time the contract was signed.

---

228 MICH. 152

Supreme Court of Michigan.
BURNS
v.
MISURA et al.
No. 105.
July 24, 1924.

In determining right to cancellation of conveyances on ground of intoxication, test is whether at time plaintiff executed same his understanding was clouded or reason dethroned by actual intoxication.

Opinion

SHARPE, J.

The defendants appeal from a decree setting aside certain conveyances by which plaintiff conveyed a farm in the county of St. Clair and certain personal property to defendant Misura in exchange for his equity in a parcel of real estate in Detroit. The trial court found that plaintiff executed the conveyances when so intoxicated that he did not realize what he was doing, and that his intoxication was procured, at least in part, by the defendant Misura.

***

The undisputed facts may be thus stated. In June, 1921, plaintiff listed his 80-acre farm with one John K. Denton for sale at the price of $8,500. On October 17th Denton, a real estate broker named Olyczynski, and Misura came to the home of plaintiff's brother, where he then was. Plaintiff went with them to his farm, and the four then drove to Misura's property in Detroit, arriving there after dark. They then went to the office of Mrs. Gaston, a notary public in Hamtramck. She prepared the conveyances in question.

***

It is the claim of plaintiff's counsel that he had been much intoxicated on October 16th, and that after the noon hour on the 17th he tumbled out of a chair in his brother's house, and was put to bed, "hopelessly drunk." That he was roused out of a drunken stupor by Denton, and told that he must go to Detroit to secure a deal for his farm for $14,500; that more drink was furnished him in Detroit that evening and the next morning; and that he was in such a "helplessly intoxicated condition" when he signed the papers that he had no understanding of the nature of the deal he was entering into.

***

It is defendants' claim that plaintiff was sober at the time the properties were visited and the papers prepared and executed. We are impressed that he was not. The trial court, after seeing the witnesses and hearing them testify, concluded that his condition then was such that he had no proper understanding of what he was doing. The conclusion reached by him is so much more likely to be in accord with the truth than that formed by us from reading the printed record that we are unwilling to reverse it.

***

We are in accord with the rule of law stated by defendant's counsel that the test is whether, at the time plaintiff executed the conveyances, "his understanding was clouded, or his reason dethroned, by actual intoxication." [Citations Omitted.]

Summary

In order to have an enforceable contract, the parties must possess the legal capacity to understand the terms and conditions of the contract and also the consequences for failure to adhere to the terms and conditions. This is referred to as contractual capacity. There are several defenses to contractual capacity to enforcement of a contact based upon lack of contractual capacity; they are age, mental incapacity, and gross intoxication.

Minors have a voidable right to rescind a contract and obtain a full repayment. The modern trend is to seek a fair balance of the interests between the parties. Depreciation and value of use concepts are considered as well as any overreaching by the seller of the merchandise.

Mental incapacity may make a contract either void or voidable. If a court hearing with a legal determination of mental incapacity has been held, the contract may be void. If there was no previous court hearing, a contract may be declared voidable at a current one.

A grossly intoxicated person has a voidable right to rescind the contract. This defense is not a popular one. Courts and jurors do not have much sympathy for a person who consumes too much alcohol or drugs.

The distinction between a void contract right and a voidable contract right is determined by the extent of the right. A void contract carries more legal power than a voidable right. For example, a formal court determination that a person is mentally incapacitated and requires a guardian is constructive notice to everyone who deals with that person, which means no contract that person enters can legally exist. A voidable right is one that provides an election by the incapacitated person. They may decide to keep the contract or void the contract.

Comprehension Check

True/False

Directions: Look at each statement below. Based on what you learned in this chapter, decide if the statement is true or false.

1. A voidable contract is one that is void from its inception.
2. Minors' contracts are void as a matter of law.
3. A formal court hearing with appointment of a guardian will create a legal right for a person who is incapacitated to accept or reject a contract.
4. In order to prove gross intoxication, a person must be able to prove they possessed all the objective symptoms of being under the influence of alcohol.
5. The trend in contracts with minors is for the court to deduct the reasonable value of the use of the merchandise from the purchase price.
6. A person attempting to rescind a contract on the basis of gross intoxication must do so soon after sobering up.
7. In the case *Lucy v. Zehmer*, the plaintiff's attempt to show gross intoxication was rejected by the court.
8. An emancipated minor will still be treated as a minor for contract purposes.
9. A minor who enters into a contract for necessities can't rely on their parents to pay unless the parents co-sign.
10. In the case *Dodson v. Schrader*, the court decided the minor was taken advantage of, and therefore, the contract should be rescinded.

11. A void contract is really no contract at all, and therefore, there is no need to respond to the contract.
12. A minor must disaffirm a contract by showing intent not to be bound.
13. The general rule is that a minor can enter into a contract that an adult may enter.
14. A minor who has reached the age of majority may ratify a contract expressly or by implication.
15. As a general rule, the parents of a minor are not liable for the contracts of a minor.

Multiple Choice

Directions: Use what you learned in this chapter to choose the best response to each of the prompts below.

1. With respect to a minor all the following are true, except:
   a. As a general rule, parents are not responsible for the contracts of a minor.
   b. Minors may disaffirm a contract at will.
   c. A minor's parents are responsible for any contracts concerning necessaries.
   d. Courts may reduce the refund a minor receives based upon depreciation of the product.
2. All the following are true, except:
   a. A general rule is that an emancipated minor may enter into any contract that an adult may enter.
   b. A person asserting intoxication when entering into a contract must do so within a reasonable time after sobering up.
   c. A court hearing is required to prove mental incapacity in order to rescind a contract.
   d. A minor has six months after attaining majority within to disaffirm a contract.
3. All the following are true regarding mental incapacity, except:
   a. It means a person is unable to understand the nature of one's acts.
   b. It means a contract entered into is void as a matter of law.
   c. It means a person may still be liable for a contract if that person can understand some of the consequences of that person's acts.
   d. It means a contract entered into is voidable at the person's discretion.
4. All the following relate to emancipation generally, except:
   a. It refers to a minor who is self-supporting.
   b. It occurs when a parent relinquishes legal right to exercise control.
   c. It requires a court declaration of emancipation.
   d. It affects the authority of a court-appointed guardian.
5. All the following apply to a minor's disaffirmance, except:
   a. Minors are presumed to be too immature to enter into contracts.
   b. A minor may disaffirm a contract and receive full value in return.
   c. A minor must disaffirm a contract before the statutory deadline; otherwise, it is deemed ratified.
   d. A court will consider a vendor's bad acts to determine disaffirmance.

6. All the following are included in Text Box regarding general rules for minors' disaffirmance, except:
   a. minor's misrepresentation
   b. guardianship authority
   c. depreciation/use of product
   d. necessaries
7. All the following are true regarding necessaries, except:
   a. They are an exception to the rule regarding disaffirmance.
   b. A parent may be liable for the contract.
   c. A guardian is exempt from payment.
   d. Public policy requires parents to pay for them.
8. All the following are true regarding use of intoxication as a defense, except:
   a. It refers to a diminished ability to act with full mental capability.
   b. The contract is voidable.
   c. Proof a person is an alcoholic is sufficient.
   d. The relevant time period for disaffirmance commences at the time the contract was signed.
9. All the following apply to a void contract, except:
   a. It may be enforced at the discretion of the protected person.
   b. It may be void based upon a technicality.
   c. It may be void as contrary to public policy.
   d. It literally means the contract never existed.
10. All the following are true regarding the case *Burns v. Misura*, except:
    a. It concerned an appeal by the defendant who granted plaintiff a decree setting aside a real estate conveyance.
    b. The trial court conceded that at some point in time the plaintiff was not intoxicated during negotiations.
    c. The facts in the trial court concluded that the plaintiff was "hopelessly intoxicated."
    d. Defendant claims Plaintiff was sober at all relevant times of the transaction.

Scenarios

1. Bill is 17 years old. He got married and joined the Marines. He purchased a car with a conventional bank loan. He defaulted, and the bank repossessed the car and sued him for breach of contract. He asserted his age qualified him as a minor and he disaffirmed the contract. Is Bill correct? Explain your answer.
2. John was a chronic alcoholic known to all in the community as such. He entered into an installment contract to purchase tools he needed for his job as mechanic. He was fired for working on the job while intoxicated. Without an income he defaulted on the installment contract. When sued for breach of contract, he asserted he lacked capacity at the time of entering into the contract. He also introduced

evidence of his many DUIs and his court-mandated Alcoholics Anonymous attendance to prove his chronic alcoholism. Do you think he has a meritorious defense? Explain your answer.

Decisional Review

1. A fifteen-year-old student joined the high school's Reserve Officer Training Corps. When attending a U.S. Marine Corps training facility, she had to sign a waiver that exempted the Marine Corps from liability for any injuries she might sustain during the visit. She was seriously injured and filed suit against the Marine Corps. The court ruled that a minor may disaffirm the waiver agreement. See *Kelly v. U.S.*, 809 F. Supp. 2d 429 (E.D.N.C. 2011).
2. Defendant inherited substantial real property from his parents. After their death his behavior became very erratic. He quit work and spent most of his time in local bars. He was rejected by the Army and subsequently was served with divorce papers. He entered into a contract to sell the property but later refused to convey it. He subsequently was declared mentally incompetent, and a guardian was appointed. He alleged that at the time of the sale he lacked contract capacity. The price for the sale of the property was substantially below market price. Defendant was sued for specific performance for the property. The court found his lack of capacity to contract despite his high intelligence. See *Star Realty Inc. v. Bower*, 17 Mich. App. 248.

Chapter 10

Legality

Introduction

It is understood and universally accepted that a contract entered into which has an illegal purpose is not enforceable in a court of law. Courts will not allow parties to such a contract to use taxpayer institutions, such as the court system, to resolve disputes. So any product that is illegal to purchase or sell will not have the protections of the law. There are many statutes that which prohibit illegal activities, such as usury laws, gambling, and pyramid schemes.

Regulatory power of government licensing activities is intended to ensure the public is protected from those unqualified to do business. Lawyers, doctors, and engineers are good examples. Moreover, the hospitality industry is one of the most regulated business activities in the country. Health, safety, advertising, menu content, and civil rights of patrons are just a few of the many regulatory targets.

Chapter Objectives

Upon completion of this chapter, the student will understand:

- the nature of contract illegality
- statutory illegality and exceptions
- licensing statutes
- the nature of contracts against public policy

Key Terms

Directions: Each of the terms below will be used in this chapter. Before reading, scan the chapter. The terms will appear in bold. Take a moment to see how the term is used so you can understand it in context. The terms are listed in the order in which they will appear in the chapter.

Unclean hands (p. 184)
Requirements contract (p. 184)
Usury (p. 185)
Factor (p. 185)
Gambling (p. 185)
Licensing statute (p. 186)
Noncompetition covenant (p. 188)
Sale of a business (p. 188)
Employment contracts (p. 190)
Exculpatory clause (p. 193)
Theft (p. 193)
Physical injury (p. 194)
Dangerous activities (p. 194)
Covenants not to compete (p. 194)
Franchising (p. 194)

The Nature of Illegality

In order for a contract to be enforceable in a court of law, the subject matter of a contract must have a legal purpose. A court of law will not permit parties to use the court's powers and taxpayers' money to resolve disputes concerning illegal contracts. That would be contrary to common sense and against public policy.

Historically, the courts used their inherent power through the common law equitable doctrine of **unclean hands** to deny jurisdiction in cases with an illegal subject matter. Assume a hotel owner planning to sell the hotel property offers an appraiser $20,000 to inflate the value of the property, and the appraiser accepts the offer. The subject matter of the contract, an intentionally inflated price, is fraud and is illegal.

Further assume the hotel owner subsequently sells the hotel for the inflated price but refuses to pay the $20,000 promised to the appraiser. The appraiser will not be able to enforce the contract in a court of law. It was a contract for an illegal purpose and prohibited by the equitable doctrine of unclean hands.

Today, legality is predominantly codified by local, state, and federal government law (collectively, "statutory law"). For example, in California fraud is defined in *West's Annotated California Codes*, § 1689.

Similarly, if the bargained-for consideration violates any statute or ordinance, courts will also deny jurisdiction. Assume a restaurant decides to adorn its foyer with "authentic" elephant tusks and it places an order through an importer of African artifacts. The importer promises to send the elephant tusks upon clearance of the restaurateur's check by the bank. Once that occurs the importer delivers realistic looking, but synthetic, tusks.

Upon discovery of the fraud, the restaurateur will be unable to sue the importer to obtain a refund of his payment or to have a court order delivery of authentic ivory tusks. It is illegal in the United States and many other countries to deal in authentic elephant ivory. The discussion of legality in this chapter concerns only the civil law implications and not the criminal law implications.

Statutory Law

General Rule

Statutes are laws passed by legislative bodies, such as Congress, state legislatures, counties, and municipalities (see previous discussion in Chapter 1). If the subject matter of a contract violates statutory law, it is unlawful and unenforceable by the courts. Typical statutory violations include usury laws, gambling laws, and pyramid schemes. They are discussed below.

A relatively recent example of statutory illegality is a ban on shark fins. California adopted a statute that prohibits the sale of shark fins, used predominantly by Asians to make shark fin soup, a traditional cultural delicacy for millennia. The California legislature adopted the ban because, among other things, it considered the method of killing sharks as cruelty to animals. Fishermen would catch sharks, harvest the fins, and throw live, helpless, finless sharks back into the ocean to certainly perish.

Assume a Chinese restaurant decides to continue the traditional sale of shark fin soup, and it contracts with a fisherman to provide shark fins on a requirements contract basis. A **requirements contract** is one based upon the needs of the party ordering the product, usually for a specified time (e.g., three months) or specified numerical limit (e.g., 100 lbs. at $100/lb.).

Further assume the fisherman, wary of violating the statute, decides to substitute dolphin fins for those of sharks. The restaurant pays the fisherman $10,000 in advance for 100 lbs. of shark fins, not an unreasonable amount since shark fin soup may retail for $400–$1,000 a bowl. The fins are delivered and accepted, but the true species is not determined until the master chef decides to prepare the soup.

Upon detection of the true species, the restaurant demands its money back from the fisherman, who refuses to do so. At this point there is a breach of contract normally resolved in a court of law. Unfortunately for the restaurant, the subject of the contract is in violation of a state statute and is illegal. As such, a court will not entertain jurisdiction, and the restaurant must find another way to resolve the breach.

Usury

Usury statutes are "law(s) that prohibits moneylenders from charging illegally high interest rates" (Garner 2005, 1290). They limit the interest rate permissible for business transactions such as bank loans, credit cards, auto loans, home financing, and so on. Contracts that contain an interest rate in excess of the statutory limit are deemed unlawful.

Most states have adopted usury statutes and impose criminal penalties, as well as civil penalties, for violations. However, exceptions to statutory limits for certain financial loans exist. For example, depending on the state, certain financial institutions are permitted to exceed the usury rate established by statute.

For example, a **factor** is a financial institution the state of California permits to offer short-term loans at rates much higher than the statutory limit. They are useful when a new business is unable to obtain a conventional loan or an existing company is experiencing a short-term cash flow problem. But the terms are onerous, and this type of loan should be one of last resort.

Assume the statutory usury rate is 12%, and a newly established restaurant is unable to secure a conventional business loan from a local bank. The restaurant may decide to borrow money from a factor at a rate of 25% to finance its payroll and inventory. Terms of a factoring contract vary widely, but a typical one permits the factor to control accounts receivable and accounts payable. The factor may require all money received from accounts receivable be sent directly to its office so that it can pay the major bills, including its monthly contract fee.

A percentage of accounts receivable is remitted to the business for officers' salaries and other minor expenses. In addition, the factor will take as much collateral, personal as well as business, as it possibly can to cover its loan in case the business defaults. After the loan has been paid in full, the factor releases its control of the accounts receivable and all collateral it obtained for the loan.

Gambling

The federal government and most states have statutes which prohibit gambling (see, for example, 18 U.S.C.A. § 1081 et. seq.). **Gambling** is generally defined as "the act of risking something of value, esp. money, for a chance to win a prize" (Garner 2005, 562). The challenge with prosecuting gambling violations is largely the failure of state legislatures to clearly and accurately define them so people can avoid committing a crime.

Games such as poker, craps, roulette, and bingo appear to fall within the definition of criminal gambling. Many states permit such activities with proper government regulation and if a business license is obtained. In other words, such activities are exempt from the statute. However, many of the same activities are regularly engaged in by nonexempt parties.

The legal question to resolve is, are these same activities criminal if nonprofit local schools, church groups, and charities employ them to raise money at a casino night? Can people invite friends to their home on a regular basis to play poker for money? Such nonexempt gambling activities are a favorite American past time and a losing cause for prosecutors. Juries are reluctant to find the above nonexempt parties guilty of a crime, even when apprehended with chips and currency on the table.

Some nonexempt activities popular with patrons at a restaurant or bar, such as betting on a sports pool, are not regulated. A sports pool consists of a matrix of boxes developed by the establishment that lists numbers, usually from one to ten, across the top of the matrix and the same numbers vertically down the side of the matrix. Patrons select a number in advance of a sporting event, such as a football game; pay a predetermined amount, such as $50; and hope the numbers they selected coincide with the eventual score at each quarter of the game and/or the final score of the game. If the game numbers selected fall within the selected boxes, the lucky patron will receive a predetermined lump sum of money.

Analytically, a sports pool seems to fit the definition of illegal gambling, but the statutory definition is not clear. Absent a statutory exception, establishments that offer sports pools and patrons who participate may be subject to criminal prosecution. It will depend on the policy of local prosecutors and the attitudes of jurors.

Enforcement of a sports pool may become a civil legal issue. A sports pool is a contract; the solicitation for participation is an offer to win money, and the patron's payment of the minimum amount is an acceptance of the offer. However, since the sports pool is a gambling event, without a statutory exception, it arguably is an illegal, unenforceable contract.

That means an unscrupulous bar owner/manager may decide not to honor a winner. Also, the pool money may be stolen by someone. If so, patrons who participate will not be able to seek judicial assistance to recover an amount they may have won or paid into the pool.

Licensing Statutes

A **licensing statute** is a government regulation adopted to protect the public interest. Government agencies are delegated authority by legislative bodies to enforce provisions of such statutes. The government regulatory oversight falls within the jurisprudence of administrative law. It affects all businesses and the life of every person, arguably, as much as any other form of law.

Typical areas of licensing statutes include certain professions (e.g., lawyers, doctors, engineers, and accountants). Business establishments are also regulated comprehensively (e.g., banks, construction, manufacturing, retailing, telecommunications, and energy are a short list of those scrutinized). The governmental purpose is to ensure they, among other things, operate safely and in the public interest.

The hospitality industry is no exception. Agency regulation in the hospitality industry is pervasive and comprehensive. To legally operate a hotel, motel, restaurant, bar, or food truck, you must, among other things, obtain a business license. The license permits one to operate according to state and local health and safety codes, operate according to zoning ordinances, and follow liquor laws.

The purpose of hospitality licensing is to protect the public interest, a moving target dependent upon where a business decides to operate. For example, a liquor license will be easier to obtain in San Francisco, New York, or Chicago than in Salt Lake City, Utah.

Other considerations include ensuring a business is operated with qualified personnel, protects the health and safety of guests and employees, and operates within the overall business plan of the community (e.g., zoning). For example, a bar or night club will likely be prohibited from operating in residential areas or close to schools or churches, especially if they offer an adult theme (e.g., scantily clad servers).

Local government may regulate the location of such establishments via its police power. But it can't prohibit such businesses without a compelling governmental interest, such as protecting the interest of children in the community.

A hotel, bar, or restaurant must obtain a business license in order to operate their establishments. A local government will require its licensees to follow its rules and regulations by way of ordinances. Failure to abide by the ordinances may result in fines, the loss of a license, and sometimes incarceration. Some valid issues local government may consider prior to granting such a license are:

- proximity to schools
- amount of vehicular and pedestrian traffic
- noise
- hours of operation
- adherence to building codes
- safety of the premises
- adherence to health codes
- frequency that patrons breach the peace
- number of DUI arrests

See Chapter 12 for further discussion of government regulation.

Contracts Against Public Policy

Public policy is defined broadly as "principles and standards regarded by the legislature or the courts as being of fundamental concern to the state and the whole of society" (Garner 2005, 1029). Public policy is promulgated in statutes or a local ordinance. "Courts sometimes use the term to justify their decisions, as when declaring a contract void because it is 'contrary to public policy'" (Garner 2005, 1029).

In other words, policy is what a legislature thinks is good for the people within its jurisdiction. If a statute is challenged in court, public policy is what a judge thinks it is, and that is largely in the court's discretion. Judges sometimes do not accept the stated legislative intent and decide public policy themselves.

Contracts are enforceable agreements between two or more private parties (see Chapter 5). Hence, their impact on society is generally not a relevant enforcement consideration. However, certain types of contracts do impact societal concerns and may be rendered unenforceable in court under public policy theory. Contracts in restraint of trade and exculpatory clauses included in contracts fall within the purview of this concept.

Contracts in Restraint of Trade

Our country was founded upon the principle of free trade and competition, commonly referred to as capitalism. The United States of America prospered because of capitalism, and most of the free world embraces some form of a competitive business society.

The pure communist world, which favors a state-run business society, has shrunk to just a few countries, such as North Korea and Cuba. China, once the world's largest communist state (it still professes to be), has decidedly moved toward capitalism, and it currently has the fastest growing economy in the world.

Congress and all states have adopted statutes which support free trade in the name of public policy. For example, at the federal level, Congress adopted Interstate Commerce Act, 49 U.S.C. § 501-526 (1887); the Sherman Antitrust Act, 15 U.S.C. § 1-7 (1890); and the Clayton Act, 15 U.S.C. § 12-27 (1914).

Virtually all states have adopted similar state statutes (see California Business and Professions Code § 17200). Both levels of government have also adopted numerous other statutes that protect free trade. Accordingly, capitalism is an important concept embodied in the societal interests of the United States.

The courts, through their decisions, vigorously enforce antitrust laws under public policy rationale. Anticompetitive agreements are generally struck down by the courts as against public policy. Covenants not to compete and franchising are notable exceptions to the rule.

The Noncompetition Covenant

The **noncompetition covenant**, more commonly referred to as a covenant not to compete, is "a promise, usu. in a sale-of-business, partnership, or employment contract, not to engage in the same type of business for a stated time in the same market as the buyer, partner, or employer" (Garner 2005, 312). They are upheld to protect goodwill in the sale of a company and promote the sale of business interests. The ultimate goal is to stimulate business enterprise.

In other contexts, they are generally disfavored as restraints of trade and unenforceable. Yet the courts will uphold such contracts if there is a legitimate business purpose and limited reasonable restrictions. The issue arises most often with two types of contracts: the sale of an ongoing business and employment contracts.

The **sale of a business** is one area relevant to noncompetition covenants. The seller of the business usually promises not to compete with the buyer of the business. If such an agreement is not entered into, the seller of the business would be in a position to undermine the sale. It could do so by immediately restarting the same business in close proximity to the purchased business and unfairly taking back all its former customers.

If agreements not to compete were disallowed, the market for the sale of ongoing businesses would diminish, and courts would be flooded with litigation. For those reasons, the courts conclude the public policy supports covenants not to compete.

However, the terms of covenants not to compete are construed strictly to prevent abuse. For example, assume John sells his successful restaurant in downtown Los Angeles to Mary for $200,000. Mary wants to protect her investment from John, so she demands he agree not to compete with her for ten years within a radius of 20 miles. Otherwise, she will not purchase the restaurant. After three years, John decides to open another restaurant within ten miles of the old restaurant. Mary is infuriated and sues John in court for breach of the covenant not to compete.

The courts would likely rule in favor of John because the covenant not to compete is too restrictive and is against public policy. Downtown Los Angeles is a high-density population center with numerous restaurants competing against each other. It is unlikely that John's decision to open a restaurant ten miles from the one he sold to Mary and within three years of the sale would have much effect on Mary's ongoing business.

Assume the terms of the foregoing covenant not to compete in Los Angeles was for three years and within four miles of the old restaurant, and John opened the restaurant two years after the sale and three miles away. The court may take a different view because the shorter duration in both time and geographical proximity appears more reasonable. Also, the competition from other restaurants for Mary may be less within the shorter distance.

For a further example, assume John's restaurant was located in a rural area, such as the Mojave Desert. The covenant not to compete contains the same terms as the Los Angeles covenant not to compete. Under this scenario, an agreement not to compete for ten years within a radius of 20 miles might be upheld as reasonable.

The Mojave Desert has fewer restaurants competing for local diners, and patrons may be willing to travel longer distances for a favorite meal. Accordingly, John's decision to open a competing restaurant within ten miles after only three years could be viewed as unfair competition and breach of the covenant not to compete (for further illustration, see Figure 10.1).

Covenant not to Compete
Sale of a Business

Diagram 10-1a

Mary purchases steakhouse located in Downtown Denver, CO

*Covenant 20 miles for 10 years

John opens new Steakhouse 3 years after sale within 10 miles

This is an obvious violation of the covenant. If Mary sues for breach, she might lose due to it being a dense metropolitan area.

Diagram 10-1b

Mary purchases steakhouse located in Arkadelphia, AK

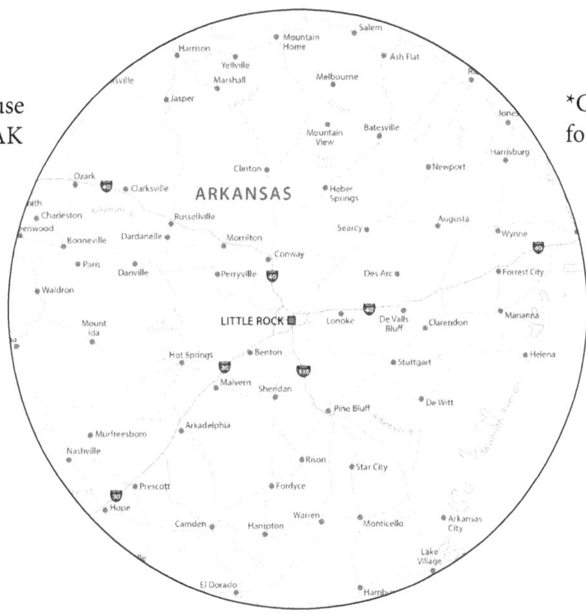

*Covenant 20 miles for 10 years

John opens new Steakhouse 3 years after sale within 10 miles

Mary would likely prevail if she sues John because the terms are more reasonable plus competition would be reduced substantially in a less metropolitan area.

FIGURE 10.1 Covenant Not to Compete—Sale of a Business

Other factors a court may decide relevant to enforcement of a covenant not to compete would be the type of new restaurant John may decide to open. For example, if John decided to open a seafood restaurant rather than a steak house, a court may view the seafood restaurant not sufficient competition within the purview of the covenant for a steak house. Similarly, a family restaurant that may serve many other items, such as pasta, pot roasts, hamburgers, and hot dogs as well as a steak item may not be sufficiently competitive to breach the covenant not to compete.

Employment Contracts

A talented employee is valued in any business, and employers will do what they can in order to ensure they stay on the job. Usually, that means a good salary plus benefits. In return for the generous compensation package, an employer may also expect the employee to sign an **employment contract** to work for a specified number of years. The contract may also contain a provision not to compete with the business for a number of years within a geographical radius after separation from the business.

For example, in the restaurant business, a talented chef may be the difference between success and failure. A talented chef's compensation is often relatively high compared to a general manager's compensation. Owners of restaurants pay high compensation in return for the chef agreeing to stay for a specified number of years and if the chef agrees to reasonable terms in a covenant not to compete. The terms are often similar to that for the sale of an ongoing business. Accordingly, the courts will use a similar reasonableness analysis to determine if the employee covenant not to compete is enforceable.

The following case discusses covenants not to compete for both the sale of a business and an employee contract. The same general principles apply to both. However, because a covenant not to compete can deprive a person of earning a livelihood, the court required a more stringent test to deny the enforceability of the employment covenant based upon public policy grounds.

---

13 NY2D 267

Court of Appeals of New York.
PURCHASING ASSOCIATES, INC., Respondent,
v.
Morton WEITZ, Defendant and Third-Party Plaintiff-Appellant; Albert J. KAPLAN, Third-Party Defendant.
Dec. 30, 1963.

Opinion

**269 FULD, Judge.*

This appeal, here by our leave, requires us to determine whether the covenant made by the defendant not to compete with the plaintiff is enforcible.

The defendant Morton Weitz was engaged for some years in data processing work in New York City as an employee of Grayson-Robinson Stores, a retail chain. In April of 1961, he and two other men formed a partnership known as Purchasing Associates to carry on the business of purchasing routine supplies for business organizations on a fee basis. About a month and a half later, on June 6, a contract was executed between that partnership and Associated Sales Analysts, Inc., whereby the former agreed in terms to "sell" its assets to the plaintiff, a newly formed wholly owned subsidiary of Associated, which was to engage, among other things, in the data processing business.

***

... the covenant was made "in connection with the sale of a business" ...

At one time, a covenant not to compete, basically an agreement in restraint of trade, was regarded with high disfavor by the courts and denounced as being "against the benefit of the commonwealth." [Citations omitted.] It later became evident, however, that there were situations in which it was not only desirable but essential that such covenants not to compete be enforced.

Where, for instance, there is a sale of a business, involving as it does the transfer of its good will as a going concern, the courts will enforce an incidental covenant by the seller not to compete with the buyer after the sale. [Citations omitted.] This rule is grounded, most reasonably, on the premise that a buyer of a business should be permitted to restrict his seller's freedom of trade so as to prevent the latter from recapturing and utilizing, by his competition, the good will of the very business which he transferred for value. [Citations omitted.]

***

The sole limitation on the enforceability of such a restrictive covenant is that the restraint imposed be "reasonable," that is, not more extensive, in terms of time and space, than is reasonably necessary to the buyer for the protection of his legitimate interest in the enjoyment of the asset bought. [Citations omitted.] Also enforceable is a covenant given by an employee that he will not compete with his employer when he quits his employ, and the general limitation of "reasonableness," to which we have just referred, applies equally to such a covenant.

***

Since there are powerful considerations of public policy which militate against sanctioning the loss of a man's livelihood, the courts have generally displayed a much stricter attitude with respect to covenants of this type. [Citations omitted.] Thus, a covenant by which an employee simply agrees, as a condition of his employment, not to compete with his employer after they have severed relations is not only subject to the overriding limitation of "reasonableness" but is enforced only to the extent necessary to prevent the employee's use or disclosure of his former employer's trade secrets, processes or formulae. If, however, the employee's services are deemed "special, unique or extraordinary," then, the covenant may be enforced by injunctive relief, if "reasonable," even though the employment did not involve the possession of trade secrets or confidential customer lists.

***

Although the plaintiff had the defendant sign a paper labeled "contract of sale," the present transaction may not be considered the sale of a "business" involving the transfer of its "good will."

***

What it really was, was a hiring of the defendant as an employee, plus the consequent elimination of the very short-lived partnership as a competitor.

***

Thus, the only thing which the defendant "gave" the plaintiff was his services as an employee and, accordingly, there was here no more of a transfer of "good will" than is present in any employment situation. The enforceability of the defendant's restrictive covenant is, therefore, necessarily governed by the rules applicable to covenants made in connection with contracts of employment.

When so viewed, it is clear that it is not enforceable [as to the employment aspect of the contract]. Since there is a finding below that no trade secrets are involved and since no claim is advanced that customers have been pirated or customer lists used, the plaintiff may prevail only if the defendant's services are "unique" or "extraordinary." More must, of course, be shown to establish such a quality than that the employee excels at his work or that his performance is of high value to his employer. It must also appear that his services are of such character as to make his replacement impossible or that the loss of such services would cause the employer irreparable injury. [Citations omitted.] We search the record before us in vain for any evidence which even points in such a direction. On the contrary, not only is there neither mention in the complaint nor proof upon the trial that the defendant's services are or were considered "unique" or "extraordinary." ... Since, then, there is no evidence to support a finding either that the defendant's services are "unique" or that the transaction under consideration constitutes a "sale" of the kind envisaged by the court when it announced the rule to govern the enforcement of restrictive covenants ancillary to the sale of a business, it follows that no basis exists for enjoining the defendant from pursuing his occupation.

The order appealed from should be reversed, with costs in all courts, and the complaint dismissed.

DESMOND, Chief Judge (dissenting).

Franchising

The franchise business model is a very popular and successful way to do business. It is premised on use of the intellectual property of another business. The franchise agreement consists of many different bargained-for benefits and liabilities of the parties. In the fast-food industry, the franchisor requires the franchisee to purchase all the important supplies of the franchisor. This is known in antitrust law as a tying arrangement, which is a classic antitrust violation.

In the fast-food industry, tying arrangements are exempt from antitrust laws in order to maintain quality and the identification of the franchisor. For example, McDonald's restaurants need to have their products all look alike and taste alike in order to preserve their reputation. Without a tying arrangement, a franchisee could substitute different and lesser quality meat, buns, fries, and other hallmark characteristics of McDonald's intellectual property.

Exculpatory Clause

A contract that contains an exculpatory clause may be unenforceable because of public policy considerations, depending on the terms of the agreement. An **exculpatory clause** is "a contractual provision relieving a party from liability resulting from a negligent or wrongful act" (Garner 2005, 483). This type of provision usually exists in contracts dealing with property damage, physical injury, or dangerous activities.

For example, public parking lots often have a clause printed on the claim ticket that states the owner of the parking lot is not responsible for any loss, such as physical injury, theft, or property damage, to the car. Such a clause is often unenforceable in court if recently there have been multiple break-ins and vandalism at the parking lot.

Such criminal activity places the owner of the parking lot on notice that there is a problem with safety of its premises. This notice creates a common law duty to take precautionary steps. Also, with proof of negligence or willful misconduct by the owner or the parking lot attendants, liability will likely be found. The discussion below provides other common situations.

Theft is one common situation concerning exculpatory clauses. Assume a hotel provides space for its guests to park and charges a fee for that privilege. The hotel issues a claim check that contains an exculpatory provision disclaiming liability for any loss incurred to the guest's car. If the hotel has experienced a recent rash of car break-ins, the hotel has noticed a problem exists. Notice creates a duty to take precautions to prevent further such occurrences. Perhaps improved lighting in the parking lot or provision of security guards would resolve the problem. If the hotel fails to take preventative action, a court may find that the hotel breached its duty and is therefore negligent and liable for the guest's loss.

Physical injury may also negate an exculpatory clause. Assume a restaurant includes an exculpatory clause in a chef's employment agreement excluding liability for injury from burns or cutlery wounds. The industry is plagued with a high frequency of this type of injury. Most states have stringent safety statutes that protect kitchen employees. Consequently, such an exculpatory clause in an employment agreement will likely be found to violate public policy and would be unenforceable.

Dangerous activities are the final example concerning exculpatory clauses. Consumers pay to engage in many discretionary activities that are regarded as dangerous, such as sky diving, scuba diving, horseback riding, parasailing, and attending sporting events. Exculpatory clauses are commonly included in such agreements (some with separate contracts or printed on the face of an entrance ticket) by the purveyors of the activity.

The courts often enforce such agreements because they are discretionary, and the consumer is deemed to have assumed the risk of the danger. For example, assume a person decides to take sky diving lessons. The school providing the lessons will require the student to sign an agreement with an exculpatory clause. Because learning to sky dive is highly dangerous and is discretionary, a court may find the clause enforceable absent proof of negligence (e.g., a faulty parachute that does not open).

However, an airline that offers public transportation to a traveler may not legally include an exculpatory clause with the purchase of a ticket. Air travel is perceived as a necessity in modern life and is heavily regulated by the government. Public policy encourages the public to use airline travel for both business and pleasure, and therefore, courts would deem them unenforceable.

CONTRACTS THAT VIOLATE PUBLIC POLICY

Contracts that violate public policy may be found to be illegal as a matter of law. They include those that concern the state and society as a whole. They are deemed to be in violation of the best interests of the people within the jurisdiction of the state. They include those that restrain trade and exculpatory contracts.

Contracts in Restraint of Trade

Covenants not to compete. These are normally an unlawful restraint of trade. Several exceptions have developed to protect certain interests and promote business activity.

- *Sale of a business.* When a business is sold, the buyer has a right to obtain a covenant not to compete for a reasonable time and distance. Otherwise, the vendor could unfairly compete and undermine the sale.
- *Employment.* Persons with special skills, unique attributes, or knowledge of trade secrets may be required to sign restrictive covenants to protect the employer. Such covenants are generally analyzed similar to the sale of a business for reasonable time and distance. One important difference is that public policy requires strict compliance of the above referenced attributes because a person may lose their livelihood.

Franchising. The unique nature of the business requires the franchisee to protect the quality of the product and reputation of the franchisor's intellectual property. Therefore, a tying arrangement otherwise in violation of antitrust laws is permitted.

Exculpatory Contracts

Contracts that require consumers to waive all liability irrespective of fault will not be enforced. Such contracts are usually required for personal injury, loss of property, and contracts for dangerous activities. A court will examine an exculpatory contract to check for fairness. If the court decides the contract unfairly favors the proponent, it will declare the contract in violation of public policy and unenforceable.

PRACTICUM

Lawyers representing business interests will include exculpatory clauses in the situations described above because such provisions are in their client's best interest. The vast majority of consumers are unaware of their legal rights and fail to consult an attorney. Consumers tend to accept the exculpatory clause since they had notice of it in writing. They assume it is applicable to their situation, and legal recourse is therefore precluded. Such a practice is the first line of defense for businesses and usually ends any possibility of a lawsuit.

Summary

An illegal contract is one that violates a statute, common law, or an administrative rule or regulation. Some contracts are illegal as violation of public policy. If any of the foregoing occur, courts will not entertain jurisdiction of a dispute between the parties. The concept commenced during the early days of common law when the courts developed the equitable doctrine of unclean hands. At that time, the courts concluded that a party agreeing to an illegal act in a contract was not welcome in a court of law. The courts and other legal institutions that utilize taxpayer dollars must not be misused by parties to a contract.

Contracts that engage in restraint of trade are some of the cases most often the subject of illegality. Contracts that violate the Sherman Antitrust Act and the Clayton Act that encourage free enterprise are examples. Exceptions to restraint of trade laws include covenants not to compete in a sale of a business or an employment contract. They are upheld as necessary to promote business enterprise. Franchising agreements that protect the reputation of a business that licenses its intellectual property are likewise exempt from some antitrust laws, such as tying arrangements.

Contracts and provisions of exculpation are violative of public policy and illegal in order to protect consumer interests. Exculpation contracts unfairly remove all liability for the actions of a business and place them on consumers. They concern personal injury, property loss, and contracts for dangerous activities.

Comprehension Check

True/False

Directions: Look at each statement below. Based on what you learned in this chapter, decide if the statement is true or false.

1. A contract that requires a person to refrain from competing with a former employee unfairly jeopardizes a person's livelihood.
2. Franchising agreements engage in illegal restraint of trade by requiring a franchisee to purchase all supplies from only the franchisor.
3. An exculpatory contract will be analyzed for legality by the "rule of reason" test under antitrust law.
4. State and local jurisdictions require persons to obtain licenses in order to practice a business profession.
5. Operating a business without a license is illegal by statute, and any contracts entered into by the business are void and unenforceable.
6. A key legal requirement in a sale of a business is the uniqueness of the skills the employees possess.

7. An airline that offers public transportation may include an exculpation provision within the ticket contract as a necessary dangerous activity liability protection.
8. Assumption of the risk is a valid defense for inclusion of an exculpation provision.
9. In the case *Purchasing Associates v. Weitz*, the court concluded that the employee covenant not to compete was valid as to time and space.
10. With a covenant not to compete in the sale of a business, the type of new restaurant matters as much as the time and space provisions.
11. Korea and Cuba are the only true communist countries in existence.
12. China professes to be a pure communist country, but it is one of the most successful capitalist countries on the planet.
13. If covenants not to compete were enforced, the business of selling companies would come to a screeching halt.
14. A noncompetition agreement is less stringent in its terms than a covenant not to compete.
15. Franchising has become a disfavored form of business model because of its antitrust requirements.

Multiple Choice

Directions: Use what you learned in this chapter to choose the best response to each of the prompts below.

1. All the following are true with regard to contract legality, except:
   a. Courts historically used an equitable doctrine referred to as unclean hands to deny jurisdiction.
   b. A contract concerning an illegal subject matter is unenforceable.
   c. Illegality is not applicable to consideration of a contract.
   d. Today, illegality is primarily regulated by statutory law.

2. All the following apply to statutory law regulating illegality, except:
   a. The use of shark fins for soup is illegal in California.
   b. Usury laws prevent unreasonable interest rates for consumer loans.
   c. California does not exempt local banks from usury laws.
   d. Gambling is expressly permitted in residential homes.

3. All the following are true, except:
   a. Football pools are permitted by statute in neighborhood bars.
   b. Health codes apply to hotels and restaurants.
   c. Safety codes apply to manufacturing businesses but not to hospitality businesses.
   d. Licensing statutes are designed to protect consumers from unskilled professionals.

4. All the following are issues a city normally raises when granting licenses for hospitality establishments, except:
   a. safety of the premises
   b. frequency of DUI arrests
   c. traffic congestion
   d. noise levels

5. All the following are true regarding public policy, except:
   a. It is what the legislature believes is of fundamental concern to society.
   b. Judges are bound by the legislative intent of the legislature.
   c. In general, business contracts are not a relevant public policy concern.
   d. Contracts in restraint of trade are against public policy.
6. All the following are true with regard to a violation of restraint of trade, except:
   a. Generally, a restraint of trade is a violation of antitrust law.
   b. A tying arrangement is always a restraint of trade.
   c. A covenant not to compete regarding the sale of a business is in the public interest.
   d. A covenant not to compete is difficult to enforce because it may deprive a person of their livelihood.
7. All the following are good examples of statutes which criminalize restraint of trade, except:
   a. Interstate Commerce Act of 1887
   b. Clayton Act of 1914
   c. California Unfair Business Practices Act
   d. The Sherman Antitrust Act.
8. All the following are true, except:
   a. Communism favors a state-run business society.
   b. Korea is a pure communist society.
   c. Cuba and China are pure communist societies.
   d. Most of the free world has embraced some form of capitalism.
9. All the following are true with regard to the franchise business model, except:
   a. It concerns the use of intellectual property of another business.
   b. Its predicate is to protect the reputation of the franchisor.
   c. In the fast-food industry, they use the antitrust tying arrangement.
   d. Without a tying arrangement, the quality of the product will diminish.
10. All the following are true with regard to an employee covenant not to compete, except:
    a. A talented chef's compensation is relatively high compared to restaurant managers.
    b. Proof the employee is unique and special is required to enforce one.
    c. The terms are very similar to the covenant not to compete with the sale of a business regarding time and distance.
    d. Courts use the objective facts interpretation test in their analysis for enforceability.

Scenarios

1. Bill was a franchisee of a fast-food chain. The franchise agreement required him to purchase all supplies from a supplier recommended by the franchisor. The supplies were delivered late and were of poor quality. He complained to the franchisor but was told to continue using the supplier. Bill sued under

antitrust laws, asserting the arrangement was an unlawful restraint of trade. What will be the result of the lawsuit? Explain your answer.

2. John, a licensed plastic surgeon, was suspended from practice for six months because he failed to take continuing education classes as required by state law. His practice results were exceptional: no complaints and hundreds of satisfied clients. After four months he continued his practice because of high demand for his services. The medical board held a hearing where it revoked his license and threatened criminal sanctions as required by law. He sues in the superior court for reinstatement, alleging his right to practice was irreparably damaged by an unconstitutional violation of due process of law. What will be the result? Explain your answer.

Decisional Review

1. Indemnification provision of contract between Owner of chain of convenience stores and Contractor in which Contractor agreed to defend Owner and hold it harmless against the store's own negligence was contrary to public policy. Contractor sued Owner for injuries contractor suffered while loading a freezer into a truck at one of Owner's stores. Court held since Contractor was in a clearly inferior bargaining position, one-sided contract burdened Contractor, a 55-year-old man with an eighth-grade education, with the requirements and restrictions of at-will employment by owner but with no employee-type benefits. See *Speedway v. Erwin* 250 S.W. 3d 339 (2008).
2. The provision in this case extends indefinitely and has no geographic limitation whatsoever. Covenants not to compete are valid if an employee obtained confidential information relevant to the employer's business. Defendant did not provide the court with any cases that indicate a covenant not to compete that protects trade secrets or other confidential information can apply to the entire world. The provision would prevent plaintiff from working for a beverage company in China or Germany. See *Bodemer v. Swanel Beverage, Inc.*, 884 F.Supp.2d 717 (2012).

Credits

Fig. 10.1a: Copyright © 2020 Depositphotos/aallm.
Fig. 10.1b: Copyright © 2016 Depositphotos/Lesniewski.

Chapter 11

Proper Form

Introduction

The general rule regarding proper from for contracts is that no special form is legally required. A contract may be oral or in writing as long as all the elements are present. There are some contracts specified by the statute of frauds which are required to be in writing. The exceptions to the statute of frauds are court admissions, promissory estoppel, full or partial performance, and U.C.C. requirements. There are others, such as wills, trusts, and real estate deeds, that also must be in writing and, in some cases, notarized.

The parol evidence rule is a common law rule, now codified, that restricts what evidentiary evidence is admissible to prove the existence of a contract. Generally, it prohibits the use of any extrinsic evidence that would contradict or explain contract terms, if the contract is clear and unambiguous on its face.

It permits evidence to clarify a contract, such as ambiguities, trade usage, and past practice among contracting parties. People often confuse the meaning of the parol evidence rule and think it applies only to oral evidence. However, written evidence may also be used to clarify a contract. Accordingly, the "extrinsic evidence rule" would be a more appropriate name.

Chapter Objectives

Upon completion of this chapter, the student will understand:

- the general rule for legally enforceable contracts
- The statute of frauds and its purpose
- types of contracts covered by the statute of frauds
- exceptions to the statute of frauds
- the parol evidence rule
- exceptions to the parol evidence rule

Key Terms

Directions: Each of the terms below will be used in this chapter. Before reading, scan the chapter. The terms will appear in bold. Take a moment to see how the term is used so you can understand it in context. The terms are listed in the order in which they will appear in the chapter.

Statute of Frauds (p. 200)
Meeting of the minds (p. 201)
Easement (p. 201)
Secondary promise (p. 204)
Primary promise (p. 204)
Primary obligation exception (p. 204)
Marital promises (p. 204)
Prenuptial agreement (p. 204)
Intramarital agreement (p. 204)

Proper Form

General rule: Unless required by law, there is no special form for a contract. It may be written or oral. All that is required is inclusion of all material terms of the agreement. The terms will vary, among other things, depending on the type of contract, where the contract was executed, and where the contract will be performed. The following list contains some of the more common material terms:

- names of the parties
- quantity and specifications of the product
- description of the product or service
- delivery terms
- procedure for returns and/or dispute resolution
- forum and choice of law clauses

There are several exceptions to the general rule for contracts covered by the statute of frauds: statutory requirements included in wills and trusts, birth certificates, and other special documents. Below is a discussion of the contracts required to be in writing.

PRACTICUM

Although an oral contract may be legally enforceable, it is a best practice to memorialize a contract in writing because a written contract is easier to interpret and enforce. An oral contract is harder to prove, and such a contract may encourage fraud. Unless you have credible witnesses to the negotiations, the debate centers on what the parties recall. After a period of time, memories fade, evidence is lost or destroyed, and people move and/or die. Consequently, unless the material terms are embodied in writing, an otherwise valid oral contract may be unenforceable in a court of law.

Statute of Frauds

The Statute of Frauds is "a 1667 English statute that declared certain contracts judicially unenforceable (but not void) if they were not committed to writing and signed by the party to be charged" (Garner 2005, 1179). Because of inherent problems with dishonesty and evidentiary proof associated with oral contracts, the statute of frauds was adopted "to prevent fraud and perjury by requiring certain contracts to be in writing" (Garner 2005, 1179).

The Statute of Frauds requires certain types of contracts be in writing and signed by the party to whom enforcement is sought. America inherited this statute when Great Britain seized the American colonies in the 1600s. The Statute of Frauds's importance endured throughout British rule, and it was adopted by the United States after its independence in 1776. The following types of contracts are required to be in writing:

- contracts involving an interest in land
- collateral promises
- contracts for the sale of goods over $500
- contracts that cannot by their terms be completed within one year
- contracts in consideration of marriage

Such contracts are usually complex, technical, and involve large sums of money. In addition, they are among the most voluminous occurring types of contracts in society. As such, unless they are written, they become difficult to prove and they would inundate courtrooms with time consuming litigation. Accordingly, requiring them to be in writing helps assist with judicial economy.

Without a written document, a contract dispute will be dismissed in a pretrial motion. The policy for the writing requirement is to ensure a written document is available as evidence of the agreement and to assist in determining the intent of the parties. Without a writing to evidence, a **meeting of the minds** may be difficult to prove, and the opportunity for dishonesty increases. Accordingly, if it is in writing, it will be easier and quicker for judicial resolution. All states have adopted a statute of frauds, but they may differ slightly in wording and their emphasis.

Contracts Involving an Interest in Land

An interest in land can be the purchase or sale of land, an easement, or the lease of land. Such contracts are complex, require a certain amount of expertise by the parties, and usually involve large sums of money. Accordingly, they are required to be in writing to be enforced.

An **easement** is "an interest in land owned by another person, consisting in the right to use or control the land ... for a limited purpose" (Garner 2005, 431). For example, a hotel may have a large parking lot with a large amount of unused parking available. A restaurant next door may lack sufficient space to accommodate all its patrons. The hotel may agree to allow the restaurant to use such space on a temporary basis for a fee and for a limited time. This limited use is an easement that is not permanent and may be revocable upon specified terms, such as the hotel eventually requiring more parking for its patrons.

Land is real property and all physical objects attached to the land. That includes buildings, sheds, garages, fences, trees, and growing crops. Once crops or trees are severed, they become personal property not subject to the statute of frauds unless they qualify as goods being sold for an amount more than $500.

Assume Sally, a restaurateur, decides to sell a successful restaurant for $1.2 million. The description of the sale includes the building, all fixtures, existing inventory, all kitchen equipment, dishware, customer/vendor lists, and linens. It is purchased by John, an inexperienced would-be restaurateur. No mention is made of the land in the contract negotiations or in the written contract.

The seller states verbally the land will be conveyed for its appraised value, after six months, if the same level of profitability continues. John agrees to pay rent of $3,000/month during that time. If the parties are satisfied after six months and the land is sold, no problem exists. However, the seller may later decide she would rather keep the land and continue to charge John rent. If John attempts to seek a judicial remedy for breach of contract, a court will likely deny the claim because the promise to convey the land was verbal.

---

153 GA. APP. 886

Court of Appeals of Georgia.
ROMANIK et al.
v.
BUITRAGO et al.

Synopsis

Owners of condominium sued vendees seeking damages allegedly sustained as a result of vendees' failure to close sale of the unit. The DeKalb State Court, Mitchell, J., rendered summary judgment for vendees, and vendors appealed. The Court of Appeals, Birdsong, J., held that: (1) where, in contract for sale of condominium located at 3229 Clairmont Road, property were described as "3200 Clairmont Road," which was address of the entire condominium complex, the description was sufficient to furnish a key by which the property could be identified and, thus, trial court did not err in allowing extrinsic proof to identify and connect the contract to the particular condominium, especially as there was no confusion that vendees understood they had contracted to purchase the individual unit at 3229 Clairmont Road, and (2) material fact issues existed as to whether identity of the property as shown by conduct and apparent knowledge of each party was sufficiently established, precluding summary judgment.

Judgment reversed.

Opinion

**886 BIRDSONG, Judge.*

Summary judgment. The evidence shows that Mr. and Mrs. Romanik were the owners of a condominium at 3229 Clairmont Drive which was in a condominium complex known as 3200 Clairmont Drive. ... The appellees, Mr. and Mrs. Buitrago offered to buy the condominium for $59,000. ... In the sales contract the condominium was described as being at 3200 Clairmont rather than at 3229. There was also evidence to indicate that the Buitragos went to Decatur Federal, applied for mortgage money for the purchase of the condominium, and were successful therein. The evidence showed that the Buitragos had been to the particular condominium at 3229 Clairmont on several occasions and during the month of November, moved some personal belongings into the condominium. Ultimately however, the Buitragos declined to close the sale before or after December 15, 1978. The Romaniks brought suit claiming as damages the mortgage payments they had been forced to pay after the closing date. ... The Buitragos answered denying the material allegations and filed a counterclaim seeking the return of the $210 paid together with costs of litigation and attorney fees. The Buitragos moved for summary judgment, apparently on the ground that the sales contract called for the sale of 3200 Clairmont Drive rather than the single condominium located at 3229 Clairmont Drive. The trial court granted the motion for summary judgment and the Romaniks bring this appeal enumerating that grant as error. Held: ...

The failure of the appellee to file a brief does nothing to the case except to admit the statement of facts by appellant, which may be accepted by this court as being prima facie true.

***

We are here confronted with the sufficiency of the description of a condominium by house number only. There can be no real contention that the parties were not fully aware of the exact condominium and location that was under contract of sale. Likewise, the parties made clear to the trial court that 3200 Clairmont Road was the address of the entire condominium complex, that the Romaniks were at least part owners of the entire condominium complex, and specifically owned that portion of the complex at 3229 Clairmont Road. There could be no confusion that the Buitragos understood they had contracted to purchase the condominium at 3229 Clairmont Road, for no reasonable person could believe that $59,000 could purchase an entire complex of homes.

The question of the sufficiency of description of property in a contract is one of law, for the court; that of the identity of the property is one of fact, to be decided by the jury. [Citations omitted.] ... It is sufficient if the description can be made certain by extrinsic evidence. [Citations omitted.] In this case we conclude that the description of the property to be sold was sufficient to furnish a key by which the property may be identified. Therefore the property was sufficiently described to the trial court to allow extrinsic proof to identify and connect the contract to the property desired to be sold. [Citations omitted.]There remained as a question of fact whether the identity of the property as shown by the conduct and apparent knowledge of each party to the contract was sufficiently established. [Citations omitted.] There remaining contested issues of material fact, the trial court erred in granting summary judgment to the appellees.

Judgment reversed.

DEEN, C. J., and SOGNIER, J., concur.

Contracts for the Sale of Goods

The Uniform Commercial Code (U.C.C.) governs the sale of goods in excess of $500. It has been adopted in all states and contains a statute of frauds provision (U.C.C. § 2-201(1)). Generally, a writing under the U.C.C. need only state the quantity, such as 300 bushels of avocados. Other terms may be introduced with testimony in court. But the contract will only be enforced to the extent of the quantity of goods stated in the writing (U.C.C. § 2-201(3) (b)). If the contract exceeds a value of $500, it must be in writing. A "writing includes printing, typewriting, or other intentional reduction to a tangible form" (U.C.C. § 1-201 (43)). Accordingly, it can be a purchase order, fax, letter, email, or perhaps a message branded on the side of a cow for delivery to the slaughterhouse.

Oral Contracts Performable Within One Year

Under this rule the contract by its express terms must be performable within one year. The rationale for this policy is to encourage a writing for long-term contracts. After one year there is a higher probability memories will fade, evidence may be lost, people may move or pass away, and fraud may occur.

Assume a hotel hires an experienced, highly sought chef for a term of nine months because the hotel closes during the summer season. This contract need not be in writing to be enforceable because it may be fully performed in nine months. If the agreement is for nine months in two or more successive years, the contract can't be fully performed in one year, and it would have to be in writing to be enforceable by either party.

Assume the chef is internationally renowned and insists on a long-term contract. The general manager of the hotel offers the chef a contract for the rest of his natural life. Theoretically, this contract need not be in writing because the chef might die in six months, and therefore, it is possible the contract may be fully performed within one year.

Promises to Pay Another Person's Obligation

A promise to pay another person's obligation is referred to as a **secondary promise.** The statute of frauds requires such a promise to be in writing. If the promise is to unconditionally pay for another person's promise, it is referred to as a primary promise. A **primary promise** does not need to be in writing because the legal obligation of promisor is directly to creditor. However, there is an exception to the foregoing rules referred to as the **primary obligation exception.**

Assume John owns a restaurant in a predominantly Hispanic neighborhood and has a large clientele of Spanish-speaking patrons. He requires his wait staff to speak Spanish to customers. He also agrees to reimburse his wait staff for attending Spanish language classes. Arguably, the promise to reimburse is for the benefit of the wait staff and is a secondary obligation which must be in writing. However, in this instance the court may assume the apparent secondary obligation is in reality for the direct benefit of John. It therefore is a primary obligation and need not be in writing to be enforceable against John (see Figure 11.1 for illustration).

Promises Made in Consideration of Marriage

Promises made in consideration of marriage fall into three categories. First is a promise to enter into marriage. The second is a promise to divide the property prior to marriage. The third is a promise that occurs during marriage to divide the property.

- **Marital promise**: is a promise by one person to make a monetary payment or a promise to purchase property intended as an inducement to marriage that is required to be in writing. For example, a father promises to purchase a home if his daughter and her fiancé decide to wed.
- **Prenuptial agreement**: is a promise to divide property before a couple weds in the event of a subsequent divorce. This agreement usually occurs when one or both parties have significant property holdings when entering the marriage and they agree to treat each other's property as separate property.
- **Intramarital agreement**: is a promise to divide property in a certain way entered into by the parties after marriage. This may occur in the event of a pending divorce or for other considerations, such as taxes or business interests. It also may occur when there is a prenuptial agreement, and the married couple decide that the marriage is secure, and all property should be shared as community property.

Contracts of Guarantee

Diagram 11-1a

Mexican restaurant in El Paso, TX requires all wait staff to speak Spanish to its Hispanic patrons.

Restaurant contracts with local university to pay for wait staff to take Spanish lessons.

*This is a primary obligation which need not be in writing.

Diagram 11-1b

Mexican restaurant in El Paso, TX requires all wait staff to speak spanish to its Hispanic patrons.

Restaurant promises to reimburse wait staff for taking Spanish lessons at the local university.

*This is a secondary obligation which is required to be in writing.

FIGURE 11.1

Exceptions to the Statute of Frauds

The following discussion concerns several frequent exceptions to the writing requirement of the statute of frauds. They include admissions, promissory estoppel, and full or partial performance of a contract.

Admissions

An admission against a party during a formal proceeding, under oath, such as a pleading, a deposition, or cross examination during trial may be used as evidence of a contract. Often, once a party is placed under oath and is confronted with the assertion that a contract exists, fear of committing perjury or loss of credibility with a judge or jury will encourage an admission. Such admissions may be used against the person denying a contract exists.

Promissory Estoppel

Promissory estoppel is an equitable doctrine that permits a judge to enforce a promise where some legal requirement like an element of a contract or a writing requirement is absent. The court may decide to enforce a promise if a great injustice is likely to occur.

For example, assume a 200-room hotel receives a request to reserve all of its rooms from XYZ Corporation, a subsidiary of Dell Corporation, for a two-week conference. The hotel sent Dell its standard form of a secondary promise to obtain a signature. Dell responded with an oral guarantee to pay for the rooms if XYZ Corporation defaults. They said their legal department would send the signed form after they reviewed and approved it.

The signed guarantee was never sent to the hotel. The conference takes place, and the final bill including meals is $800,000. XYZ failed to pay the bill because an unforeseen wildcat strike created financial insolvency. The hotel tried unsuccessfully for two months to collect from Dell Corporation and finally decided to file a lawsuit. Dell defends by asserting the statute of frauds as a defense.

A court could enforce the agreement without the signed agreement under the theory of promissory estoppel because of the serious injustice that the hotel would suffer. All elements of promissory estoppel are present. A promise was made. It arguably was reasonable to believe; therefore, reliance was justified, and a great injustice would otherwise occur. The court could also do so under the Primary Purpose Rule discussed above.

Partial Performance

Partial performance is another exception to writing requirement. Under the Uniform Commercial Code, any contract for the sale of goods in excess of $500 must be in writing. However, if a party accepts part of the consideration, a writing is not required. The acceptance is evidence that the parties intended to enter into a contract.

In the above example assume the parties agreed a down payment of 50% of the cost for the conference was required prior to any rooms being made available. That amount was paid by XYZ, with the balance due one week after the conference ends. Dell refuses to pay for the remainder because of the verbal guarantee asserting the statute of frauds writing requirement. A court could order the payment because a contract was clearly contemplated with assumption of the rooms and partial payment. The oral promise by Dell was reasonably relied upon and a great injustice could result.

Parol Evidence Rule

As we learned in the information age, communication now takes many different forms. Previously, a handwritten or typed letter was the obvious form of a writing. Now teletype, fax, emails, and electronic communications are considered sufficient to be a legal writing. Documents attached by staples, paper clips, or glue will also be sufficient to be considered one contract. Data stored in a computer may be a writing when retrieved in physical form, such as a printout.

The common law principle of parol evidence is defined as "a writing intended by the parties to be a final embodiment of their agreement cannot be modified by evidence of earlier or contemporaneous agreements that might add to, vary, or contradict the writing" (Garner 2005, 941). Parol evidence is commonly misunderstood to apply only to the exclusion of oral evidence that contradicts the contents of a writing. It also excludes written evidence that contradicts a writing.

A better description would be that parol evidence excludes any extrinsic evidence outside the four corners of the written contract. Accordingly, a more appropriate name would be the "extrinsic evidence rule." Under this rule the court will first decide whether the written contract represents the complete and final agreement of the parties. If the court concludes that it does, it most likely will exclude any oral or written evidence that contradicts the written agreement (see Restatement Second of Contracts § 213).

The parol evidence rule has several recognized exceptions. They include (1) contracts subsequently modified; (2) a contract formed due to mistake, fraud, or misrepresentation; (3) contracts made under duress; (4) incomplete contracts; and (5) contracts with prior course of dealing and trade usage issues, and gross clerical errors.

EXCEPTIONS TO THE PAROL EVIDENCE RULE

Contracts subsequently modified. Once a contract is finalized and executed, a meeting of the minds has occurred and it is an enforceable contract. However, it may be subsequently modified through an amendment because of changed circumstances. Evidence of the amendment is permitted because it adds to and does not contradict the original writing.

Evidence of mistake, fraud, or misrepresentation. Such evidence is admitted to show a meeting of the minds did not occur. The evidence shows one of the parties thought they were purchasing something other than what the contract states.

Evidence of duress. Such evidence is admitted to show that the agreement was not voluntary. If a person is threatened or blackmailed into agreeing to the contract, the agreement lacks genuine assent and is unenforceable.

Incomplete contracts. If a contract lacks some essential terms, a court may permit additions to complete the contract. It is permitted to advance public policy, which encourages business transaction and improves the economy. However, the court must believe a contract was intended by the parties. If any of the essential elements or a material term is missing, the evidence may not be allowed.

Prior course of dealing and trade usage. Courts will permit such evidence to be admitted if either or both prior course of dealing and trade usage are present. Those concepts, if proven, can show a party acted upon reasonable reliance a contract was in place.

Summary

An informal contract is one that is either oral or in writing. Such contracts are enforceable as long as other legal requirements are met, such as inclusion of the six elements of a contract. Despite the enforceability of an oral contract, it is strongly recommended a writing be obtained to clearly show the intent of the parties. A writing will dramatically improve the chances of enforceability. It will assist in providing the court with evidence showing a meeting of the minds. Memories fade, evidence is lost, and witnesses move away or pass away, but a writing should last indefinitely.

The statute of frauds is a legal law doctrine intended to prevent fraud. It is a carryover from English jurisprudence that America inherited from the English colonial rule. It identifies five types of contracts that must be evidenced with a writing. They are those concerning (1) an interest in real property, which is land and anything attached to the land, such as buildings and permanent fixtures, sheds, barns, and an easement associated with the property; (2) contracts for the sale of goods for a value that exceeds $500; (3) contracts not performable within one year; (4) promises to pay another's obligation unless the courts decide the promise is for the benefit of the promisor; and (5) contracts in consideration of marriage. Admissions, promissory estoppel, and partial performance are exceptions to the writing requirement.

The parol evidence rule is another doctrine intended to prevent fraud. It prohibits extrinsic evidence to be used to modify, deny, contradict, or explain a contract in a court of law. It permits evidence that will explain an ambiguity, trade usage, or past practice between the parties.

Comprehension Check

True/False

Directions: Look at each statement below. Based on what you learned in this chapter, decide if the statement is true or false.

1. The parol evidence rule prohibits oral evidence from contradicting a writing.
2. Under the statute of frauds, promissory estoppel is an exception to the writing requirement.
3. An easement need not be in writing because the holder of the easement does not acquire legal title to the property.
4. Partial performance of a contract in consideration of marriage is acceptable proof of intent to marry.
5. A secondary obligation requires a notarized contract, which will help prevent fraud.
6. A tree cut down and removed from the property for aesthetics purposes is not considered personal property.
7. The term "informal contract" refers only to a verbal contract not required to be in writing.
8. A course of prior dealing between parties is an exception to the parol evidence rule.
9. Contracts that cannot be completed within one year are informal contracts.
10. An incomplete contract must be dismissed because any extrinsic evidence introduced would be too unreliable to use.
11. An informal contract missing one of the six elements may still be enforceable under promissory estoppel.
12. The parol evidence rule is more appropriately called the extrinsic evidence rule.
13. Under the statute of frauds, full acceptance of the terms is not an exception to the writing requirement.
14. Documents attached to each other with paper clips is not a satisfactory writing because it is too easy to switch a forged document into the collective valid documents.
15. Under the statute of frauds, an admission during an informal discussion of the parties to a contract is not a satisfactory exception.

Multiple Choice

Directions: Use what you learned in this chapter to choose the best response to each of the prompts below.

1. All the following are true regarding proper form, except:
   a. Unless required by law, a contract may be either oral or in writing.
   b. The statute of frauds requires a writing as a matter of law.
   c. The purpose of a writing is more ceremonial than substantive.
   d. Contracts for the sale of goods for a value exceeding $500 require a writing.

2. All the following are true regarding the statute of frauds, except:
   a. It is an English common law doctrine.
   b. Its purpose is to ensure honesty and to prevent fraud and perjury.
   c. The United States adopted it after it declared independence from Great Britain.
   d. Without a writing, a contract dispute will be dismissed with a pretrial motion.

3. All the following are required to be in writing by the statute of frauds, except:
   a. contracts concerning an interest in land
   b. a license to enter the land of another person
   c. a contract that cannot be performed within one year
   d. a contract for marriage

4. All the following are true, except:
   a. A premarital agreement may be oral.
   b. A contract to pay another debt is required to be in writing.
   c. The primary obligation rule is an exception to a requirement for a writing.
   d. A primary obligation need not be in writing.

5. All the following are true with regard to marriage contracts, except:
   a. They must be in writing to be enforceable.
   b. A prenuptial agreement may be oral since there is no marriage yet.
   c. They may be for the purchase of real property as an inducement for someone to marry another.
   d. They may be a promise that occurs during marriage.

6. All the following are exceptions to the statute of frauds, except:
   a. an admission in a formal proceeding, such as a deposition
   b. The statute of frauds will not apply if promissory estoppel is asserted.
   c. if a party to a contract has accepted partial consideration
   d. if the parties expressly agree not to abide by the statute of frauds

7. All the following are true with regard to the parol evidence rule, except:
   a. It applies to oral evidence.
   b. It applies to written evidence.
   c. It does not apply to subsequent agreements.
   d. It should be called the admission of relevant evidence rule.
8. A writing, according to the statute of frauds, may be all the following, except:
   a. a note scribbled on toilet paper
   b. a fax
   c. a contract offer on Facebook
   d. an email
9. All the following apply to the parol evidence rule, except:
   a. It includes evidence that may add to, vary, or contradict a writing.
   b. The court must first decide whether the writing represents the final agreement between the parties.
   c. Data stored in a computer is a writing.
   d. Teletype is obsolete and therefore not a writing.
10. All the following are special documents that are required to be in writing as a matter of law, except:
    a. wills
    b. trusts
    c. bank agreements
    d. birth certificates

Scenarios

1. Bill and Mary were divorced after five years of marriage. During the fourth year, when things were starting to become difficult, they verbally negotiated a land sale contract for the purchase of their home by Mary in the case of divorce. After a bitter divorce, Bill refused to sell his interest in the property to Mary. She sues to enforce the verbal intramarital agreement as an exception to the statute of frauds. What will be the result? Explain your answer.
2. William purchased a lot from Bill containing a home, swimming pool, stand-alone theater complex, and five-car garage. Each structure was described in a separate document for ease of reference. All five documents were attached with tape. After payment of the full purchase price, Bill refused to convey title to the theater complex, saying it never was intended to be part of the deal. William asserts the fact of the attachment with tape demonstrates it was part of the deal. What will be the result? Explain your answer.

Decisional Review

1. Plaintiff, an insured of Defendant, was involved in a car accident. Defendant settled Plaintiff's claim for an amount less than the policy limits, which caused Plaintiff to be liable for any excess recovery amount above the policy limits. Plaintiff sued Defendant for cause of action for bad faith. Defendant presented evidence of a signed release of all claims by Plaintiff. Lower court precluded evidence of bad faith under

the parol evidence rule. Plaintiff countered that the release was ambiguous and applied only to contract claims and that a bad faith claim concerns a tort. Hence, extrinsic evidence was admissible. What will be the result? Explain your answer. See *Taylor v. State Farm*, 175 Ariz. 148.

2. Plaintiff, a former employee, sued Defendant, employer and CEO, for breach of employment contract. Plaintiff alleges he met with Defendant and relied on representations of certain terms in the contract. Plaintiff proffered a handwritten memorandum unsigned by Defendant containing the promises of Defendant. Trial court held the memorandum failed to meet the requirements of the statute of frauds, and therefore, it was inadmissible in court. Plaintiff appeals and asserts the memorandum should be admissible because of promissory estoppel and his detrimental reliance on the representations of Defendant. See *Hoffius v. Maestri*, 31 Ark. App. 13.

Credits

Chapter 12

Government Regulation

Introduction

Pursuant to the Tenth Amendment to the U.S. Constitution, states have all power not reserved to the federal government by Article I. Most important is police power, consisting of health, safety, and welfare. State and local governments use police power to regulate business, which is the main topic of this chapter. Under police power, state and local governments delegate power to agencies for implementation of local law. The hospitality industry (hereinafter "hospitality") is heavily regulated because of its direct impact on the safety and welfare of the public. The regulatory process is referred to as administrative law.

Chapter Objectives

Upon completion of this chapter, the student will understand:

- the nature of administrative law
- the government regulatory process
- the difference between the legislative and adjudicatory functions
- exhaustion of administrative remedies
- judicial deference to agencies
- the importance of government representation
- the basic government requirements for opening a business

Key Terms

Directions: Each of the terms below will be used in this chapter. Before reading, scan the chapter. The terms will appear in bold. Take a moment to see how the term is used so you can understand it in context. The terms are listed in the order in which they will appear in the chapter.

Administrative agencies (p. 214)
Statutory law (p. 214)
Delegation doctrine (p. 214)
Intelligible principles (p. 214)
Executive agencies (p. 214)
Secretary (p. 214)
Director (p. 214)
Independent agencies (p. 215)
Legislative function (p. 216)
Adjudicative function (p. 216)
Administrative law judge (p. 218)
Exhaustion of administrative remedies (p. 218)
Standing to appeal (p. 218)
Judicial deference (p. 218)
Government representation (p. 222)
Campaign contributions (p. 223)
Getting out the vote (p. 223)
Trade organizations (p. 223)
Attend legislative and administrative hearings (p. 223)
Direct democracy (p. 223)
Initiative (p. 223)
Recall (p. 224)
Referendum (p. 224)

The Need for Government Regulation

Whether you philosophically approve or not, government is a necessary institution. Government may be democratic, autocratic, communist, or tribal, but it is still government. Some form of government is necessary to organize a society. It becomes more important as life becomes more complex, when societies make advances in education, technology, and communications and world populations continue to grow. Today, you can fly across the ocean in five hours and drive across country in three days. It will become faster soon. Barriers to international business dwindle because of free trade agreements and instantaneous telecommunications, such as telephones, satellites, and the internet.

Government, among other things, supports education, negotiates treaties, invests in technology, promotes scientific research, ensures adequate housing, promotes business, and protects consumers. In times of crisis, such as war, pandemics, depressions, and recessions, it becomes vital. The contemporary way we live, work, travel, and do business requires careful organization, coordination, and oversight. Without government, society would collapse, and anarchy would flourish. The question to resolve is the extent of government oversight; business complains of too much, and consumers complain of not enough. We must achieve a fair, reasonable balance.

The Government Regulatory Process—Generally

Hospitality is one of the most highly regulated industries in the country because of its direct impact on public health and safety. Food must be safe to eat; hotels must be free from vermin and safe for travelers. Government regulates virtually every aspect of hospitality. Laws promulgated by government are implemented through **administrative agencies**.

Statutory law is "the body of law derived from statutes rather than from constitutions or judicial decisions" (Garner 2005, 1181). A statute is "a law passed by a legislative body, specif., legislation enacted by any lawmaking body, including legislatures" (Garner 2005, 1177). The foregoing includes, more specifically, Congress, state legislatures, and local government, such as county boards and city councils (hereinafter collectively referred to as "government").

With respect to hospitality, the process commences when government passes a law that regulates some portion of the industry. The regulation can be federal, state, or local law (see Figure 12.1 below, explaining how a law is adopted).

Delegation Doctrine

Neither the legislative branch nor the executive branch of government possesses the manpower, inclination, or the expertise to implement the high volume of laws adopted annually by all levels of government. In order to ensure implementation, the legislative branch creates a regulatory agency and delegates its authority to implement the law consistent with legislative intent. This is referred to as the **delegation doctrine**. As long as the delegation contains standards, referred to by courts as **intelligible principles**, to guide agency action, delegation is constitutionally permitted.

Executive Agencies

The legislative branch passes laws delegated to the executive branch of government for implementation. These agencies are referred to as **executive agencies**. Usually, at the federal level, an executive agency is run by a single person, referred to as a **secretary** (cabinet agencies) or a **director** (noncabinet agencies).

Executive agencies usually do not have an independent legislative function or an adjudicative function. The president appoints all secretaries and directors subject to a two-thirds vote of the Senate. They both serve at the pleasure of the president, who may dismiss them without cause.

Typical Sequence for Adoption of a Statute

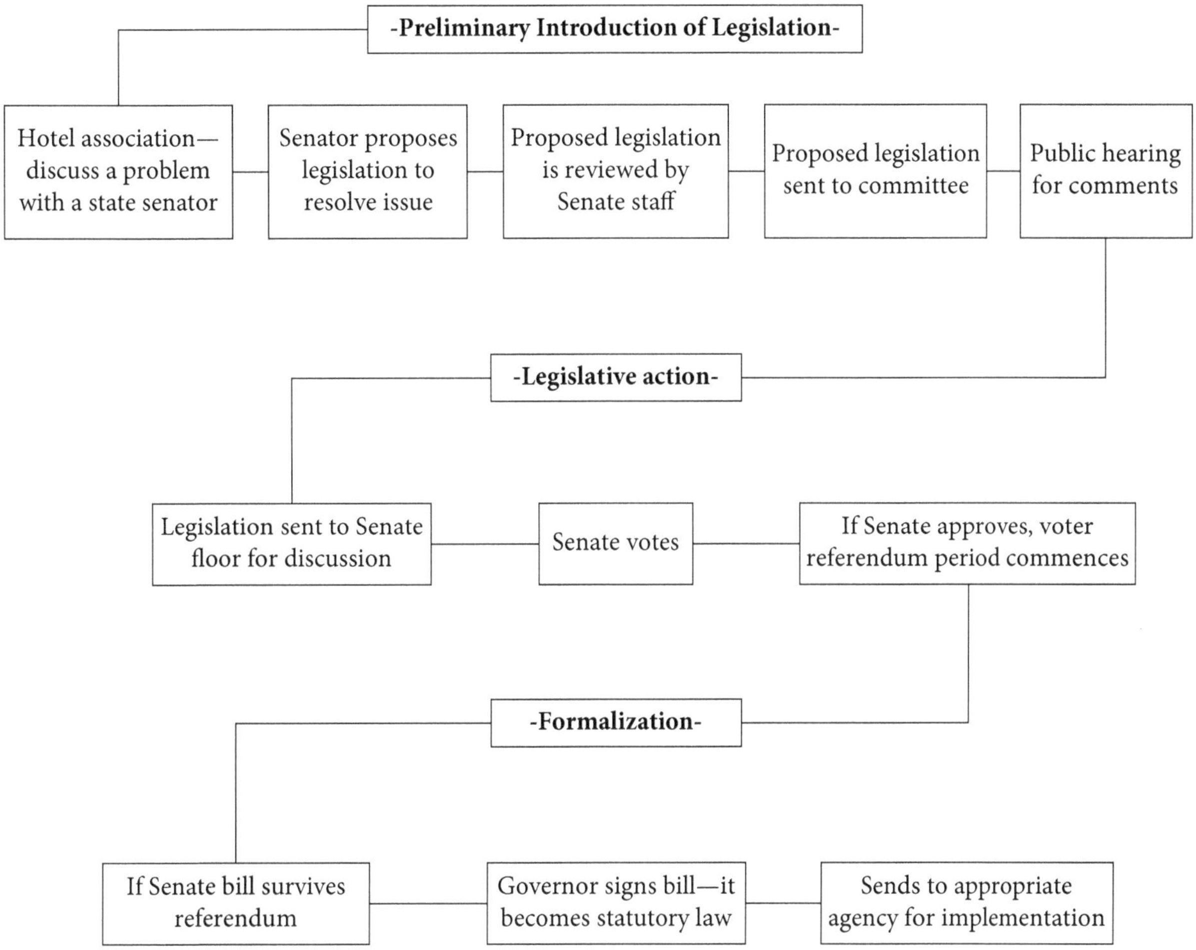

*Similar process for the assembly

*Total time varies depending on needs of the legislature, such as continuances, amendments, length of debate, gubernatorial veto, etc.

FIGURE 12.1 Typical Sequence for Adoption of a Statute

Sometimes the legislative branch delegates implementation authority to **independent agencies**. An independent agency usually possesses legislative and adjudication functions as well as its executive function. They usually are comprised of five member boards with one member serving as the chairperson.

The president appoints members to independent agencies subject to a two-thirds vote of the Senate. However, the president must have just cause to remove a member of an independent agency. As such, independent agencies are able to take action its members feel is in the best interests of the country, rather than a sitting president with a political agenda.

The **legislative function** is "(1) the duty to determine legislative policy; (2) the duty to form and determine future rights and duties" (Garner 2005, 752). Therefore, usually a statute will only become effective in the future. The **adjudicative function** is "an agency proceeding in which a person's rights and duties are decided after notice and an opportunity to be heard" (Garner 2005, 597). It permits retrospective enforcement of the agency's rules and regulations subsequent to their adoption. The adjudicative hearing is a similar but less formal proceeding than a court trial.

Many agencies possess power similar to all three separate constitutional branches of government. A troubling observation is the constitutional checks and balances are missing from the organizational structure of such administrative agencies. The agency's legislative and adjudicative functions are usually conducted through public hearings. But that alone is insufficient to inhibit an overzealous agency because of the time and cost to review and overturn an agency's decisions.

Figure 12.2 contrasts the three constitutional branches of government with an agency delegated similar constitutional powers. An alarming observation is that the agency has the identical powers of the three constitutional branches of government but not the identical constitutional checks and balances. Consequentially and regrettably, this means the agency is autocratic.

The Administrative Legislative Function

The administrative legislative function permits an agency to adopt rules and regulations to assist with agency implementation of the delegated statute. Government legislators delegate broad power to an agency to ensure government intent is accomplished.

For example, assume Congress passes a law that requires the federal minimum wage to increase from $7.00 an hour to $8.50 an hour. The National Labor Relations Board ("Labor Board"), the agency charged with the responsibility for enforcement of such laws, must decide how to implement the change. Will it be applied to all businesses across the board, or will it be phased in depending on whether a business is manufacturing, retailing, hospitality, banking, or the construction industry?

Valid reasons may exist to gradually implement the new law, depending on which businesses will likely have the most impact for congressional intent. The construction industry, which heavily relies upon union contracts, may have to be phased in after union contracts expire. In hospitality many hotels and restaurants operate with nonunion work forces, and the increase in the minimum wage may be introduced sooner.

The Board will hold public hearings, receive evidence, and make finding of fact in order to reach supportable legal conclusions. Such hearings are referred to as legislative hearings because they have a prospective effect. Also, the rules impact a large number of people and are based upon policy considerations that generally affect business operations as opposed to a single entity. Because of the foregoing, the traditional constitutional due process requirements are normally not required.

Generally, constitutional due process requirements include, among other things, the following rights: notice of a hearing, the right to participate in proceedings, adequate time to prepare, right to cross-examination of witnesses, right to counsel, and right to a fair hearing by an impartial trier of fact. It is not practical to apply such due process rights in legislative hearings because of the overwhelming cost and time requirements to do so.

Can you imagine all restaurants in a state or in the country asserting their due process rights at a public hearing every time an agency adopts a new rule? It would bring government to a screeching halt. Therefore, individual businesses may file comments with an agency, but they may not have the right to notice and an opportunity to be heard at the public hearing (see *Bi-Metallic Inv. Co. v. State Board of Equalization*, 239 U.S. 441, 36 S. Ct. 141 (1915)).

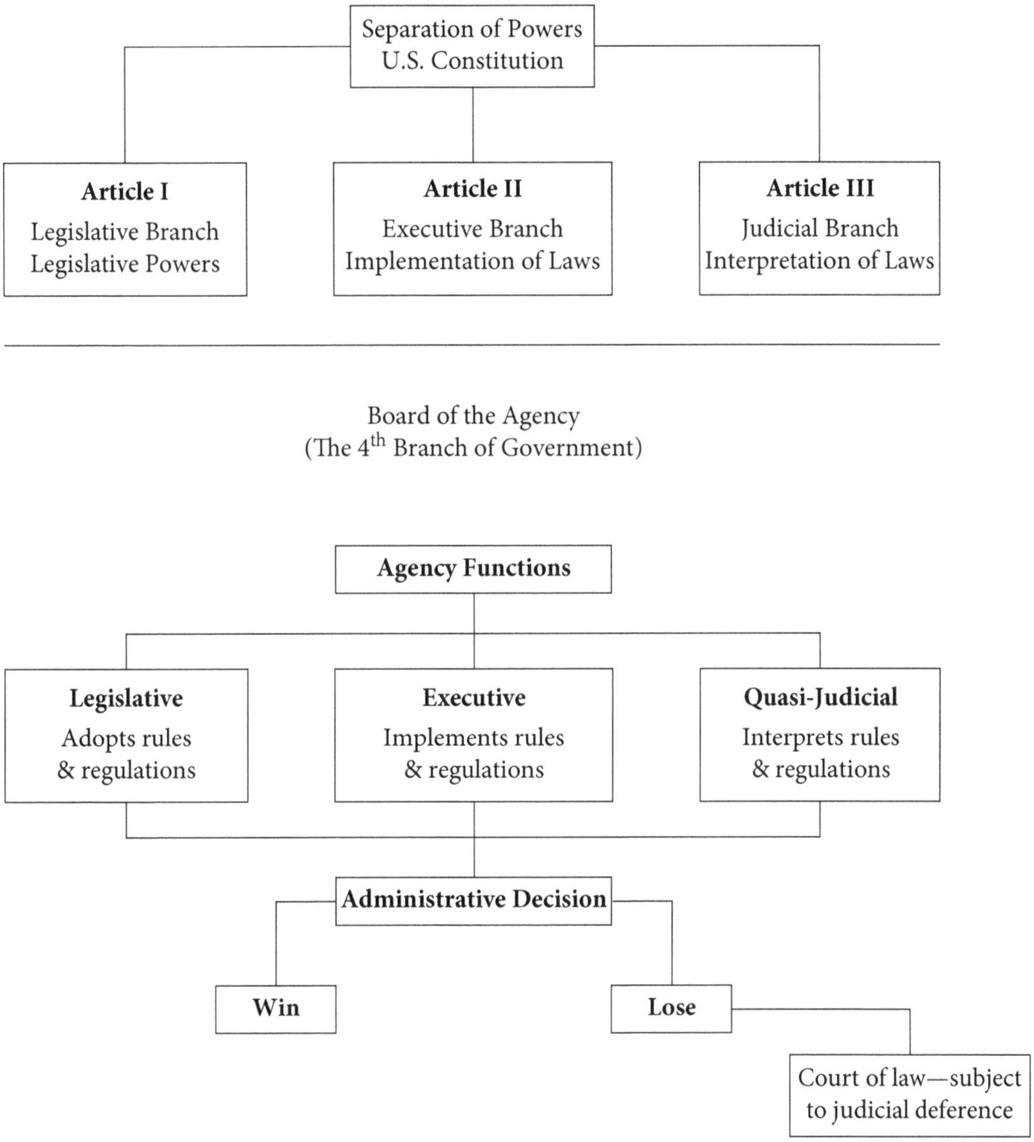

*All three functions are under jurisdiction of the agency.
*All three functions are handled by career employees of the agency.
*Supervision and appeals from each function is responsibility of the board.
*Consequence = no separation of powers.

FIGURE 12.2 Separation of Powers and Board of the Agency

The Administrative Adjudication Function

The adjudication function permits an agency to enforce the rules it promulgates to ensure compliance with the intent of the statute. In the above example, assume Labor Board, on September 1, 2019, passed a rule imposing the new minimum wage on hospitality before other industries because implementation is relatively easier to accomplish without union contracts. Further assume the deadline to implement the new minimum wage is January 1, 2020. McDonald's restaurant chain decides not to pay its employees the new minimum wage until March 1, 2020. It alleges it cannot meet the deadline, because administrative requirements for implementation would pose a serious hardship.

Assume on June 1, 2020, Labor Board imposes a $1,000,000 fine on McDonald's for violating the rule. McDonald's may either pay the fine or challenge the Labor Board's action. If it takes the latter course, the Labor Board will hold an adjudicative hearing to determine if the violation should stand, be modified, or be dismissed. The fine was imposed on McDonald's, a single entity, for a violation that occurred on January 1, 2020. Therefore, the Labor Board will be taking a retrospective look at the issue rather than a prospective look as it would in a legislative hearing.

The adjudication hearing is similar to a trial in a court of law but is substantially less formal, with an **administrative law judge** (ALJ) presiding. ALJs are not judges appointed by the executive branch to preside over a court of law. They are career bureaucrats, such as lawyers, accountants, engineers, or administrators of the agency, and preside in business attire. ALJs hear evidence submitted by Labor Board's investigative division and that submitted by McDonald's; then the ALJ will issue a proposed decision.

An ALJ will decide if McDonald's failure to comply with Labor Board's decision to increase the minimum wage on January 1, 2020, was justified. Because an agency violation may result in punitive consequences (e.g., fines, revocation, or suspension of a license), traditional due process requirements mentioned above are required for the adjudication hearing to ensure fairness.

Exhaustion of Administrative Remedies

Administrative action is reviewable by a court of law after all administrative remedies are exhausted. **Exhaustion of administrative remedies** is "the doctrine that, if an administrative remedy is provided by statute, a claimant must seek relief first from the administrative body before judicial relief is available" (Garner 2005, 488). It means the agency's appellate process must be completed before a litigant has standing to appeal to a court of law.

In the above example, assume the appellate procedure of Labor Board requires McDonald's to seek reconsideration for an adverse ALJ's decision. If reconsideration is denied, an appeal must then be filed with the full Labor board for its ruling on the matter. The Labor Board may reverse, modify, or uphold the decision of the ALJ. If the Labor Board upholds the ALJ, the administrative remedies are deemed exhausted. McDonald's may file a complaint with a court for resolution of the matter.

"The exhaustion doctrine's purpose is to maintain comity between the courts and administrative agencies and to ensure courts will not be burdened by cases in which judicial relief is unnecessary" (Garner 2005, 488). In the above example, it is possible Labor Board may modify or even reverse the ALJ decision. If McDonald's fails to appeal to Labor Board, the involvement of the courts prior to Labor Board's decision may be an unnecessary waste of judicial time.

Standing and Judicial Deference to Agency Decisions

Upon completion of the agency appellate process, standing to appeal to a court of law may be achieved. **Standing to appeal** refers to "a person's right to make a legal claim or seek judicial enforcement of a duty or right" (Garner 2005, 1172). Unfortunately, after exhaustion of administrative remedies, the administrative process has another pitfall, called judicial deference. **Judicial deference** means the courts will look to the agency for guidance on unfamiliar, highly technical matters. A key case for the judicial deference doctrine follows.

104 S.CT. 2778

Supreme Court of the United States
CHEVRON, U.S.A., INC., Petitioner,
v.
NATURAL RESOURCES DEFENSE COUNCIL, INC., et al.
AMERICAN IRON AND STEEL INSTITUTE, et al., Petitioners,
v.
NATURAL RESOURCES DEFENSE COUNCIL, INC., et al.
William D. RUCKELSHAUS, Administrator, Environmental Protection Agency, Petitioner,
v.
NATURAL RESOURCES DEFENSE COUNCIL, INC., et al.*
Nos. 82-1005, 82-1247 and 82-1591.
Argued Feb. 29, 1984. Decided June 25, 1984.

Opinion

Justice STEVENS delivered the opinion of the Court.

***

The basic legal error of the Court of Appeals was to adopt a static judicial definition of the term "stationary source" when it had decided that Congress itself had not commanded that definition.

***

When a court reviews an agency's construction of the statute which it administers, it is confronted with two questions. First, always, is the question whether Congress has directly spoken to the precise question at issue. If the intent of Congress is clear, that is the end of the matter; for the court, as well as the agency, must give effect to the unambiguously expressed intent of Congress. If, however, the court determines Congress has not directly addressed the precise question at issue, the court does not simply impose its own construction on the statute, as would be necessary in the absence of an administrative interpretation. Rather, if the statute is silent or ambiguous with respect to the specific issue, the question for the court is whether the agency's answer is based on a permissible construction of the statute.

***

"The power of an administrative agency to administer a congressionally created ... program necessarily requires the formulation of policy and the making of rules to fill any gap left, implicitly or explicitly, by Congress." [Citations omitted.] If Congress has explicitly left a gap for the agency to fill, there is an express delegation of authority to the agency to elucidate a specific provision of the statute by regulation. Such legislative regulations are given controlling weight unless they are arbitrary, capricious, or manifestly contrary to the statute. Sometimes the legislative delegation to an agency on a particular question is implicit rather than explicit. In such a case, a court may not substitute its own construction of a statutory provision for a reasonable interpretation made by the administrator of an agency.

***

Based on the examination of the legislation and its history which follows, we agree with the Court of Appeals that Congress did not have a specific intention on the applicability of the bubble concept in these cases, and conclude that the EPA's use of that concept here is a reasonable policy choice for the agency to make.

***

*After noting that the 1976 Ruling was ambiguous on the question "whether a plant with a number of different processes and emission points would be considered a single source," *** The use of offsets inside the same source is called the "bubble." EPA proposes use of the definition of "source" (see above) to limit the use of the bubble under nonattainment requirements in the following respects:*

Significantly, the EPA expressly noted that the word "source" might be given a plantwide definition for some purposes and a narrower definition for other purposes. It wrote:

"Source means any building structure, facility, or installation which emits or may emit any regulated pollutant. The EPA's summary of its proposed Ruling discloses a flexible rather than rigid definition of the term "source" to implement various policies and programs.

***

*In these cases, the Administrator's interpretation represents a reasonable accommodation of manifestly competing interests and is entitled to deference: the regulatory scheme is technical and complex, the agency considered the matter in a detailed and reasoned fashion, and the decision involves reconciling conflicting policies. *** and perhaps Congress was unable to forge a coalition on either side of the question, and those on each side decided to take their chances with the scheme devised by the agency. For judicial purposes, it matters not which of these things occurred.*

Judges are not experts in the field, and are not part of either political branch of the Government. Courts must, in some cases, reconcile competing political interests, but not on the basis of the judges' personal policy preferences. In contrast, an agency to which Congress has delegated policy-making responsibilities may, within the limits of that delegation, properly rely upon the incumbent administration's views of wise policy to inform its judgments.

***

We hold that the EPA's definition of the term "source" is a permissible construction of the statute which seeks to accommodate progress in reducing air pollution with economic growth. "The Regulations which the Administrator has adopted provide what the agency could allowably view as ... [an] effective reconciliation of these twofold ends. ..." [Citations omitted.] The judgment of the Court of Appeals is reversed.

It is so ordered.

Issues concerning the environment, nuclear energy, telecommunications, oil and gas exploration (e.g., fracking), safety of food and drugs, endangered species, and so on are just a few of the thousands of issues agencies regulate. Such technical issues are usually beyond the comprehension or experience of most judges. The agencies have career staff in the aforementioned areas who are bona fide experts. Accordingly, the doctrine of judicial deference emerged to bestow upon the agency experts the final say on many technical matters.

PRACTICUM

It is expensive and difficult to navigate the administrative process. In order to exhaust administrative remedies, an appellant must

- deal with unelected bureaucrats who are unaccountable to the public, unlike elected officials;
- confront time-consuming hearing processes with unclear procedures;
- interact with overworked or sometimes insensitive agency staff; and
- expend substantial time and money to vindicate their rights.

Unless it is clear a litigant was denied an important constitutional right and it possesses a generous litigation budget, resolution with a court may be elusive. Consequently, the time and expense of exhausting administrative remedies may be futile and unwise.

Government Regulation at the State and Local Level

A business is required to deal with administrative agencies at many levels in order to lawfully operate at the state and local level. In order to open a business, you must, among other things, obtain a business license, register a business name, register with the state tax authority, receive clearance from the local health department, and pass inspection with the fire department and local building authorities. The names and the requirements for each agency vary depending on what type of business you own, which state in which you decide to operate, and the reasonableness of locale within the state.

Most local governments require a public hearing to obtain a business license prior to the opening of certain hospitality establishments (e.g., hotels, restaurants, bars, nightclubs, and night clubs). The authority to require a business license is based upon local police power provided to the states by the Tenth Amendment to the U.S. Constitution. Some valid local considerations for hospitality establishments are:

- excessive traffic
- excessive noise
- proximity to schools, churches, residential areas, and other business establishments
- pollution
- potential for criminal activity and breach of the peace
- the number of similar establishments in the area
- premises safety

In addition to the business license requirements, hospitality establishments must follow government health and safety inspections. Restaurants and hotels must ensure their premises are free from insects, rodents, disease, and other harmful conditions. State governments usually defer to local governments to make routine inspections, and in many cases, cities and counties grade the establishment and publish the result for consumers.

The law of torts applicable to landowner premises is well established and is well regulated to ensure the public's safety. The rationale for premises liability is as follows.

If a business invites the public on to its premises to sell a product or provide a service, the business must ensure the safety of the patron. Since the business is making money off the patron, it should use some of its profits to make the premises safe. A business can buy insurance to pay for damages that may result from an accident. A government insurance requirement makes sure an injured patron will not be left without a remedy.

Most states have some form of comprehensive safety regulatory scheme modeled after the federal government's Occupational Safety Administration (e.g., California's Cal-OSHA). In addition, local governments have their own safety ordinances.

The Importance of Government Representation

Government representation is both necessary and legal. **Government representation** is the term presently used to define the pursuit to influence government action, formerly referred to as lobbying. Every person and entity has a constitutional right to encourage government to act in a manner they believe is best for their business or personal interests.

However, the manner in which one attempts to influence government can be problematic. In the past, lobbying was the term most often used by those attempting to influence government. That term now tends to carry a negative connotation, in part, because of unfortunate corruption and abuse by some lobbyists.

Provision of money, female escorts, expensive trips, gifts, and other gratuities became public headlines too often. This unfairly tarnished the industry and the majority of the honest professionals in the lobbying business. Many believe they can't influence government, and unfortunately, they make no attempt to do so. In reality there is much a local businessperson can and should do. Below are some of the participatory activities available to support government.

Local business owners and citizens may be active in their communities by contributing money to local campaigns, getting out the vote for their candidate of choice, joining and supporting trade organizations, attending legislative and administrative hearings to voice their opinions, and participating in direct democracy when necessary. These activities are explained more fully below:

- **Campaign contributions:** Candidates for political office require money to finance their campaigns. Money is the lifeblood of politicians, and successful businesses not only have a duty to support the candidate of their choice but it is also the smart thing to do. If a candidate believes it is important for society to ensure business prospers, then it makes sense for business owners to support that candidate. Important incentives for businesses, such as tax credits, zoning variances, and grants for facilities expansion or job creation, can be extremely valuable for the community as well as the local businessperson.
- **Getting out the vote:** If a monetary contribution is problematic, the provision of personnel to help get out the vote may be equally important to the candidate. Assisting with phone banks, walking the precincts, and handing out flyers will provide important manpower. It can make the difference between the success and failure of a political candidate.
- **Trade organizations:** Join trade organizations that are active in supporting candidates sympathetic to the groups' needs. They provide campaign contributions, assist candidates and legislators by providing technical support, such as drafting legislation and providing manpower to get out the vote, as discussed above.
- **Attend legislative and administrative hearings:** When legislators or administrative tribunals hold public hearings for proposed laws, rules, or regulations, attend and voice your opinion. Elected officials and administrative bureaucrats, albeit well intentioned, may not fully understand the problems their proposed laws or regulatory schemes may create. Local business input is invaluable and can make a great difference in the outcome of proposed laws and administrative regulations.
- **Direct democracy:** Direct democracy is an important component of the political process. Legislators sometimes don't listen to their constituents, and voters can't wait until the next election to vote them out. Direct democracy may be the answer. Direct democracy occurs without the traditional legislative process: "Democracy is government by the people, either directly or through representatives elected by the people" (Garner 2005, 366).

If it is government by the people, it is comprised of three tactical processes: initiative process, recall, and referendum. In all three, interested entities, such as citizen groups, business associations, trade groups, and public interest associations, must obtain a requisite number of signatures by qualified voters to place the issue on a ballot. If the requisite number of qualified signatures is obtained, the matter will be placed on the next election ballot. A winning vote by the electorate will make the matter law without the need for formal legislative action.

- **Initiative:** With an initiative, voters can amend the state constitution or pass a law they feel is important for society. This usually happens when legislative bodies are perceived to be unresponsive to the needs of voters. The constitutionality of same-sex marriage in California and other states proceeded with the initiative process.

- **Recall:** Recall is the process that permits elected officials to be removed prior to the completion of their term of office. Recent notable recalls occurred with the removal of Gray Davis as governor of California and the election of his replacement Governor Arnold Schwarzenegger in 2004; the failed attempt to recall Wisconsin Governor Scott Walker; and the recall of two Colorado legislators who spearheaded strict gun control legislation.
- **Referendum:** If a legislative body or city council passes an unpopular law, those opposed may overturn it by a direct vote of the people. The referendum process provides a statutory time period (usually 60–90 days) after passage of a law by the legislative body for citizens to obtain the necessary signatures of qualified voters to overturn the legislation.

New Owners and the Administrative Process

New owners often don't fully appreciate the administrative requirements necessary to open a business. The following information is from a case study of Lordsburg Taphouse and Grill in La Verne, California.

> *Relevant facts:*
>
> *LORDSBURG has 4,000 square feet of space and was purchased from an existing owner on February 15, 2013. The purchase included the building lease, a liquor license, a full kitchen, furniture and fixtures and existing inventory. It features an upscale menu, full bar and 60 beers on tap. The new owners made interior renovations, fortified a sagging floor and a sagging kitchen ceiling. Their initial target date for opening was March 30, 2013. Prior to opening, LORDSBURG was required to obtain the following government approvals:*
>
> *1. Obtain a business license with the city.*
> *(Filed on March 11, 2013, obtained March 12, 2013.)*
>
> *2. Pass a safety inspection by the La Verne Fire Department.*
> *(Requested March 11, 2013, Completed May 30, 2013.)*
>
> *3. Obtain approval for renovations with the City's Building Department.*
> *(Filed engineering plans April 17, 2013, Approval received May 31, 2013.)*
>
> *4. Obtain identical renovation approval from the County.*
> *(Filed identical engineering plans with the County May 5, 2013, Approval received on May 31, 2013.)*
>
> *5. Obtain a fictitious business name with the county.*
> *(Filed on March 17, 2013, received March 19, 2013.)*
>
> *6. Obtain a retail sales permit from the State Franchise Tax Board.*
> *(Filed March 12, 2013, obtained on March 25, 2013.)*

7. Obtain approval from the State Alcoholic Bureau Commission for the transfer of the liquor license.
(Filed March 11, 2013, Approval received on April 20, 2013.)

The Lordsburg case study was based upon interviews with the owners and is presented in Appendix C. The purpose of the interview was to obtain firsthand knowledge of the regulatory problems experienced when opening a restaurant. The owners explained what they thought they had to do, what they were required to do, and what they would have done differently had they known of, among other things, the substantial number of government requirements.

Summary

Government at all levels adopts laws applicable to business enterprise. The volume of new laws seems to be forever growing. Government does not have the time, manpower, or the inclination to implement the laws it adopts. Therefore, government created unelected agencies to do so. It provided the agencies with authority to create rules and regulations by way of the delegation doctrine. The courts have supported government by permitting such delegation as long as the delegation contains "intelligible principles" to guide the agencies.

Government agencies are either executive or independent. An executive agency reports to the executive branch of the government. At the federal level they are characterized by a single management person, referred to as a secretary (cabinet position) or director (noncabinet position). Executive agencies serve at the pleasure of the president.

Congress also creates independent agencies that possess legislative as well as adjudication functions. They are usually characterized by a five-member board led by a chairperson. They serve staggered terms and can only be removed with cause. This permits the board freedom to decide what is best for the country, not for the political agenda of the executive branch of government.

Government representation is an important right of the populace and businesses to influence government decision-making. They should support good government with political contributions and provide manpower to assist elected officials.

Comprehension Check

True/False

Directions: Look at each statement below. Based on what you learned in this chapter, decide if the statement is true or false.

1. The Tenth Amendment to the U.S. Constitution bestows power on state and local government to regulate business.
2. Police power concerns public safety at both federal and state levels of government.
3. Government creates agencies to adopt and implement laws to supplement the constitutional legislative powers of state and local governments.
4. Health and welfare responsibilities are implemented directly by state and local governments with valuable advice from existing agencies.

5. Administrative law refers to jurisprudence created by administrative agencies.
6. Rules and regulations adopted by administrative agencies have the same force and effect as statutes adopted by legislators.
7. The government regulatory process commences with agency adoption of a legislative rule.
8. Once a rule is adopted, the executive branch has 15 days to veto the rule; otherwise, it becomes an administrative law.
9. Exhaustion of one's administrative remedies means a litigant must navigate all levels of an agency's appellate process.
10. A court of law has authority to receive an appeal during any step of the agency appellate process with a showing of good cause.
11. Government representation is important to ensure laws are reasonable for society.
12. A legislative function is the creation of a rule or regulation for prospective application.
13. Adjudication is the prospective enforcement of a rule or regulation.
14. It is wise for a person starting a new business to be familiar with all relevant government agencies and their requirements.
15. Hospitality is unique because it has relatively less regulatory oversight from government than other industries.

Multiple Choice

Directions: Use what you learned in this chapter to choose the best response to each of the prompts below.

1. All the following are true, except:
   a. Regulation of hospitality is very extensive, especially at the federal level.
   b. The Tenth Amendment provides authority for local governments to regulate hospitality.
   c. Local agencies obtain their authority to regulate by legislative delegation.
   d. Delegated authority must contain "intelligible principles" to guide agencies.

2. All the following are true, except:
   a. An agency may have legislative authority.
   b. An agency may not have adjudication authority.
   c. An executive agency reports directly to the president.
   d. The Federal Communications Commission is an independent agency that does not answer to the president.

3. All the following are true with regard to government representation, except:
   a. It is a constitutional right.
   b. It provides an unfair advantage to big business relative to a citizen.
   c. States' and local governments' ethics commissions have successfully eradicated fraud and bribery of government officials.
   d. It will help a business obtain a building variance.

4. All the following are true regarding the exhaustion doctrine, except:
   a. It requires claimants to take all the necessary agency steps for appeal prior to seeking resolution in a court of law.
   b. An exception to the exhaustion doctrine occurs when it is clear that an appeal within the agency would be futile.
   c. A decision of an administrative law judge is never final.
   d. The full commission may override any decision that it disagrees with.
5. All the following are true with regard to a person starting a new business, except:
   a. Contribute to the campaigns for local elections.
   b. Become familiar with local rules and regulations of the government.
   c. Meet with the police and fire departments prior to deciding where to locate your business.
   d. It's best to hire a business consultant.
6. Police power includes all the following, except:
   a. It may be federally preempted, depending on the circumstances.
   b. It concerns the welfare of the community.
   c. It concerns public safety.
   d. It concerns water pollution.
7. All the following are true of local agencies, except:
   a. They possess the three functions similar to the constitutional functions of the three branches of federal government.
   b. The checks and balances are the same as the federal government.
   c. The due process rights are required for legislative rulemaking.
   d. An adjudicative hearing requires legal representation.
8. All the following are things a local business should do regularly, except:
   a. Join a trade association that provides business representation.
   b. Engage in direct democracy.
   c. Contribute monetary support to local candidates.
   d. Attend legislative and administrative hearings.
9. All the following refer to democracy by the people, except:
   a. initiative
   b. referendum
   c. government representation
   d. recall

10. All the following refer to federal government agencies, except:
    a. The president appoints and removes members at will.
    b. They may be either executive or independent.
    c. They may be either cabinet or noncabinet agencies.
    d. The head of a cabinet agency is referred to as a secretary.

Scenarios

1. A municipality passed an ordinance that required hotels to open their guest registers upon demand by government officials. The hotel association filed a lawsuit alleging the city ordinance was unconstitutional because it was a search without due process of law. What will be the result? Explain your answer.
2. A municipality conducted an unannounced inspection of a restaurant kitchen and cited the restaurant for numerous health violations. At an administrative hearing, the administrative law judge found the investigation was permitted by the police power of the city. The restaurant filed for an appeal with the city's health board of appeals, which affirmed the ALJ. The restaurant appealed to the county superior court. What will be the result? Explain your answer.

Decisional Review

1. U.S. Customs issued a tariff classification ruling challenged by a U.S. importer. The importer alleged the language in the statutory delegation did not contemplate deference for tariff classifications. The court agreed with the importer that Chevron deference was not available. Customs also alleged the statutory delegation could be treated as necessary for specialized experience and broader investigation/information with value in interests of uniformity. What will be the result? Please explain. See *U.S. v. Mead Corporation*, 121 S.Ct. 2164 (2001).
2. A city passed an ordinance that required restaurants to make minimum health care expenditures on behalf of the covered employees (payment directly to the city). Plaintiff, an association of local restaurants, sued, alleging the ordinance was preempted by a federal statute. What will be the result? Explain your answer. See *Golden Gate Restaurant Assoc. v. City and County of San Francisco*, 546 F3d 639.

Chapter 13

Negotiable Instruments

Introduction

This chapter is an introduction to negotiable instruments and some of their uses. It concerns requirements between banks and their customers for check deposits and withdrawals. Business activity in the United States relies heavily upon the use of negotiable instruments. They act as a substitute for cash and also provide a vehicle for obtaining credit. Negotiable instruments are safer than cash and are very flexible in business transactions. The form, method of transfer, and content of negotiable instruments is specified in Article 3 of the Uniform Commercial Code. In the event of a conflict between Article 3 and Article 4, Article 4 will govern. Also, regulations of the Board of Governors of the Federal Reserve System and operating circulars of the Federal Reserve Banks supersede inconsistencies with Article 3. (U.C.C. § 3-102 (c)).

Chapter Objectives

Upon completion of this chapter, the student will understand:

- the form and nature of negotiable instruments
- the most commonly used negotiable instruments
- the nature of an order to pay
- the nature of a promise to pay
- the requirements for negotiability

Key Terms

Directions: Each of the terms below will be used in this chapter. Before reading, scan the chapter. The terms will appear in bold. Take a moment to see how the term is used so you can understand it in context. The terms are listed in the order in which they will appear in the chapter.

Negotiable instrument (p. 230)
Draft (p. 233)
Drawer (p. 233)
Drawee (p. 233)
Payee (p. 233)
Bearer (p. 233)
Time draft (p. 233)
Sight draft (p. 233)
Check (p. 233)
Trade acceptance (p. 234)
Promissory note (p. 235)
Maker (p. 235)
Promisor (p. 235)
Promisee (p. 235)
Negotiation (p. 235)
Cashier's check (p. 236)
Certified check (p. 236)
Acceptance (p. 236)
Writing requirement (p. 238)
Signature requirement (p. 238)
Unconditional promise or order to pay (p. 238)
Collateral (p. 239)
Fixed amount of money (p. 239)

Negotiable Instruments—Generally

The Uniform Commercial Code (U.C.C.) provides statutory authority for negotiable instruments (U.C.C. § 3-102 (c)). Article 3 contains statutory rules for creation, endorsement, and transfer of negotiable instruments. An important purpose of a uniform law is to provide uniformity, predictability, and consistency of negotiable instruments among the states who have adopted it. As such, business enterprise should be stimulated. (Note: The author uses Black's Law Dictionary in some instances for a lay explanation and follows it with reference to the U.C.C. for a more technical explanation.)

A **negotiable instrument** is "a written instrument that (1) is signed by the maker or drawer, (2) includes an unconditional promise or order to pay a specified sum of money, (3) is payable on demand or at a definite time, and (4) is payable to order or to bearer" (Garner 2005, 873; U.C.C. § 3-104). Negotiable instruments are important to the business community because they serve as a substitute for cash and as a credit device. Negotiable instruments provide confidence, security, and predictability for business transactions. The following case is an early consideration of the requirements of a negotiable instrument and upholding the negotiability of an acceleration clause (see discussion below regarding accelerations clauses).

---

180 CAL. 1

Supreme Court of California.
UTAH STATE NAT. BANK
v.
SMITH et al.
L. A. 5791.
Feb. 24, 1919

Synopsis

In Bank.

Appeal from Superior Court, Orange County; Z. B. West, Judge.

Action by the Utah State National Bank, a corporation, against F. Owen Smith and another. From judgment for defendants, plaintiff appeals. Reversed.

Opinion

WILBUR, J.

Appellants, claiming to be bona fide purchasers for value of a negotiable promissory note, brought this action against the makers thereof to enforce its payment. The defendants, asserting that the note was nonnegotiable, interposed a defense valid against the payee therein.

***

The provision relied upon to establish nonnegotiability is the usual provision for accelerating the due date for default in the payment of interest, as follows:

"If the interest is not paid when due, then both principal and interest shall become due at the option of the holder of this note."

Negotiable Instruments ... An instrument to be negotiable must conform to the following requirements:

1. It must be in writing and signed by the maker or drawer;

2. Must contain an unconditional promise or order to pay a sum certain in money;

3. Must be payable on demand, or at a fixed or determinable future time;

4. Must be payable to the order of specified person or to bearer; and,

5. Where the instrument is addressed to a drawee, he must be named or otherwise indicated therein with reasonable certainty.

Time Payable. An instrument is payable at a determinable future time, within the meaning of this title, which is expressed to be payable:

1. At a fixed period after date or sight; or

2. On or before a fixed or determinable future time specified therein; or

3. On or at a fixed period after the occurrence of a specified event, which is certain to happen, though the time of happening be uncertain. An instrument payable upon a contingency is not negotiable, and the happening of the event does not cure the detect.

***

Before the enactment of this law [The Uniform Negotiable Instruments Law] the great weight of authority was that under the law merchant the clause accelerating the due date did not destroy its negotiability. [Citations omitted.] All the decisions based upon the uniform negotiable instrument law, so far as we are advised, hold that the clause in question does not destroy the negotiability of a promissory note.

***

The reasoning by which the courts have reached the conclusion that such a note is negotiable is not in each case the same.

***

There seems no reason for supposing that in this attempt to secure uniform legislation and decision it was intended to change a well-settled rule of the law merchant, by which in nearly every state such a note was negotiable. Construed in the light of such rule, and under the plain language of the statute, the note is clearly negotiable.

Respondent calls attention to the fact that the Utah negotiable instrument law differs from that of California and some other states.

***

If there is any decision of the Supreme Court of Utah bearing upon the construction of the statute, such decision was not proved in the case, and, it may be added, is not now called to our attention. The note was negotiable under the law of Utah. The instruction to the contrary was erroneous.

Judgment reversed.

We concur: ANGELLOTTI, C. J.; SLOSS, J.; LENNON, J.; SHAW, J.; MELVIN, J.; LAWLOR, J.

The rules for transfer and endorsement of negotiable instruments are contained in U.C.C. § 3-201. Confidence in reliability of the negotiation process encourages business entities to use negotiable instruments. The result will be a stimulation in commercial transactions. Businesses will increase production of goods and services, hire more employees who pay taxes, and public consumption of goods and services will increase. Hospitality is no exception and it likewise depends on negotiable instruments to conduct business. Figures 13.1 through 13.3 below discuss several important forms of negotiability and also a transfer of each form.

Commonly Used Negotiable Instruments

As stated above, a negotiable instrument is a signed writing with an unconditional promise to pay an exact amount on demand or at a specific time. As such, the instrument provides needed confidence for the business community to operate. As long as the statutory elements are met, businesses will accept a negotiable instrument as payment for value received.

The most common forms of negotiable instruments are drafts, checks, promissory notes, and certificates of deposits. Drafts and checks are orders to pay; promissory notes and certificates of deposit are promises to pay.

Orders to Pay

A **draft** "is an unconditional written order signed by one person (the **drawer**) directing another person (the **drawee**) to pay a sum certain of money on demand or at a definite time to a third person (the **payee**) or to **bearer**" (Garner 2005, 419; U.C.C. § 3-103 (6)). The person or entity who creates the draft and commits to pay its stated value is called the drawer. (Hereinafter, the term "person" includes both a person and a business entity.) The person obligated to pay the holder of the draft is referred to as the drawee (usually a bank), and the person who holds the rights to the draft is referred to as the payee.

Drafts may be categorized as time drafts, sight drafts, and trade acceptances. A **time draft** is one that is due and payable at a specific time, such as 90 days after receipt. A **sight draft** is one that is due and payable upon presentation to the drawee who is obligated to pay the amount due. A trade acceptance is discussed below.

A **check** is "a draft signed by the ... drawer, drawn on a bank, payable on demand, and unlimited in negotiability" (Garner 2005, 195; U.C.C. § 3-103 (f)). It is the most commonly used draft and consists of three parties. The drawer is the party who issues the check from funds contained in a checking account deposited in a financial institution, such as a bank. The drawer orders the drawee (the bank) to pay the amount specified to the payee on demand. That means whenever it is physically presented to the drawee. This is usually achieved through the electronic banking process (see banking process in Chapter 14. Also see Figure 13.1, below).

Check
(3 Party Instrument)

In this scenario, Bob wants to send his associate Richard a check for picking up costs on recent business related travel. Bob chooses to compensate Richard using a check.

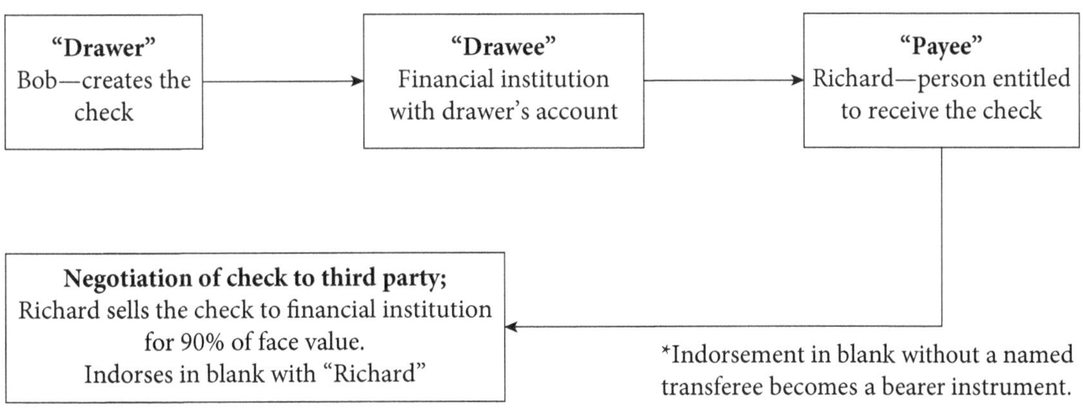

FIGURE 13.1 Check

Trade Acceptance

A **trade acceptance** is a special two-party draft used in the sale of goods. It is a credit device that permits the drawer to obtain credit from the payee for a specified time and at a specified interest rate. It differs from the usual draft in that the drawer is also the drawee. This arrangement eliminates the need for the time and expense of including a third party, like a bank (Figure 13.2).

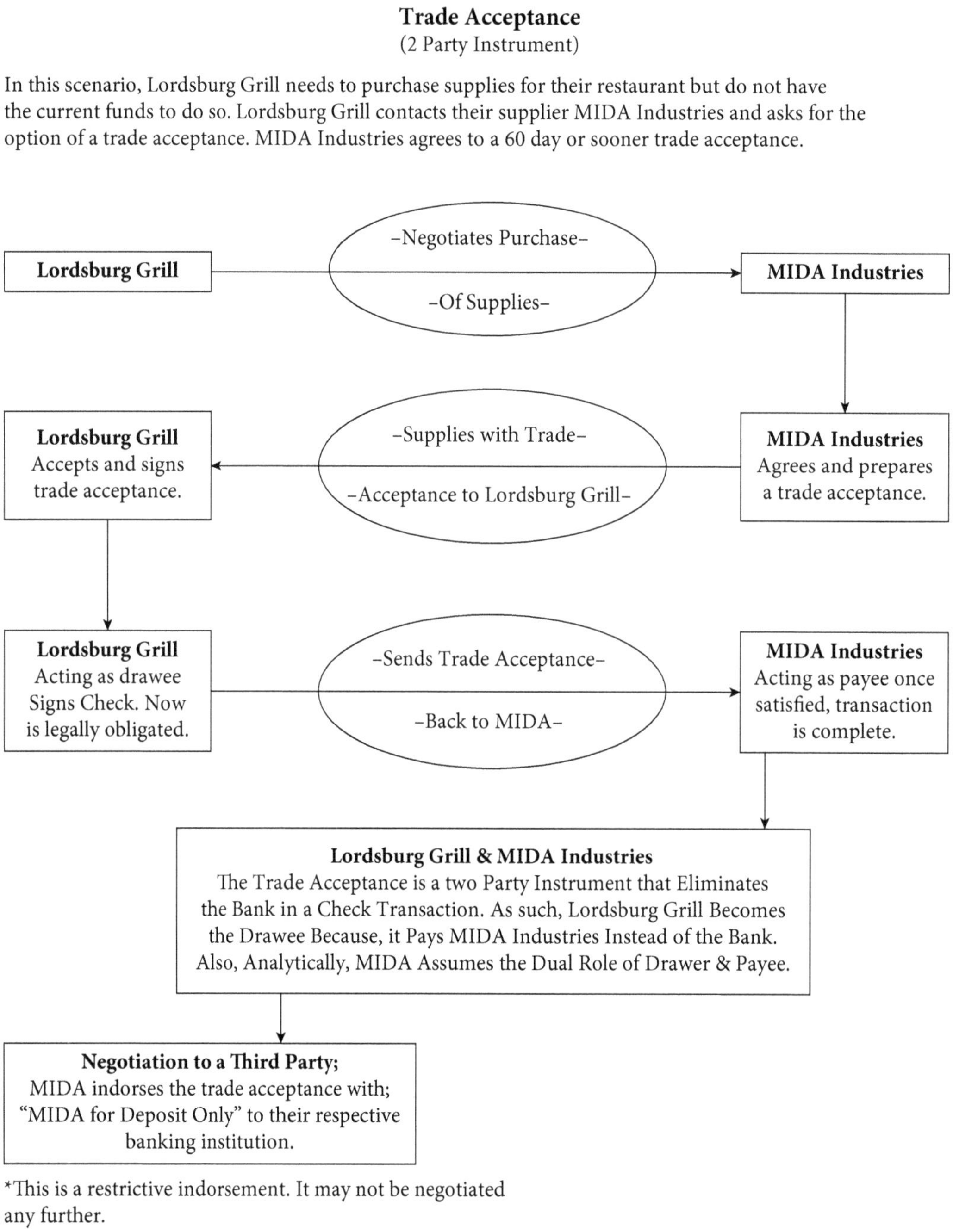

FIGURE 13.2 Trade Acceptance

Promissory Notes

A **promissory note** is a two-party instrument used to obtain credit. The promisor is the person seeking credit and is referred to as the **maker**. The person extending credit to the maker is referred to as the payee (Figure 13.3).

Promissory Note
(2 Party Instrument)

In this scenario, Cristina Marie needs to borrow money from Ed to purchase a vehicle. Ed requested that Cristina Marie sign a promissory note for the full value.

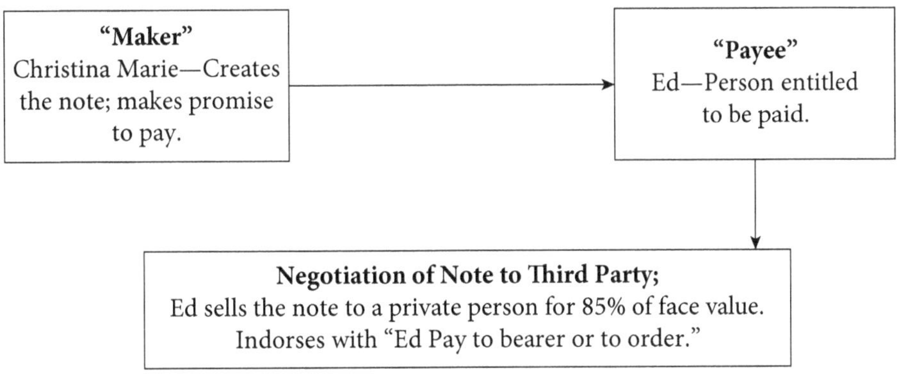

*Indorsement is to a named transferee, who can order it transferred to a subsequent transferee, or to that person's order. It is a special indorsement.

FIGURE 13.3 Promissory Note

A promissory note is "an unconditional written promise signed by the maker, to pay absolutely and in any event a certain sum of money either to, or to the order of, the bearer or a designated person" (Garner 2005, 895; U.C.C. § 3-103 (9)). It is a written promise made by a person to pay a specified sum of money. It involves two parties: the person who promises to pay the stated value of the note, referred to as the **promisor** or the maker of the note; and the person that has authority to collect on the note, referred to as the **promisee** or payee.

For a hospitality example, assume a restaurant purchases quantities of beef from a meat-packing house for $5,000. It may do so by issuing a promissory note for the amount of the beef, due and payable in 90 days at an interest rate of two percent. The promissory note creates the vehicle for several parties to create additional business otherwise not available. The restaurant obtains credit by paying for the beef in 90 days rather than at the time of purchase. The purchase encourages sales that benefit the packing house, making it easier for restaurants to purchase when they may not otherwise be able to do so. The packing house may have a need for immediate cash and may subsequently decide to negotiate the promissory note to a third party. This improves the cash flow of the packing house.

Negotiation means "to transfer (an Instrument) by delivery or indorsement, whereby the transferee takes the instrument for value, in good faith, and without notice of conflicting title claims or defenses" (Garner 2005, 874; U.C.C. § 3-201(a)). It is a process used by the holder of a negotiable note in order to obtain immediate cash by selling the note for less than face value. Assume, in the above example, the holder of the promissory note (the packing house) decides to sell the note for a discounted amount of $4,000.

The purchaser of the note (usually a financial institution that deals in purchases of negotiable instruments) becomes the legal owner and presents the note on the due date for its face value $5,000 plus interest at two percent, thereby generating a profit from the difference. In turn, the financial institution may also decide to discount the note to a third party, such as a private investor. Each party to the transfer of the note obtains rights and liabilities associated with the note. The foregoing illustrates the negotiation and the transfer of negotiable instruments.

Cashier's/Certified Checks

A **cashier's check** is "a check drawn by a bank on itself, payable to another person, and evidencing the payee's authorization to receive from the bank the amount of money represented by the check" (Garner 2005, 195; U.C.C. § 3-103 (g)). It is provided by a bank to ensure payment is made to a specified payee. The bank is both the drawer and the drawee.

A cashier's check is used to facilitate business transactions by providing a bank guarantee to the payee. The bank guarantee provides the requisite confidence the check will be honored, a condition that encourages business negotiations. For example, suppose John opens a new restaurant without a track record of success. Vendors may be reluctant to accept a business check or a personal check for payment. They also will not offer credit until John demonstrates success for a period of time.

Rather than paying vendors in cash (because of security concerns) and in order to gain the confidence of vendors, John may initially pay with a cashier's check. He would go to a bank and purchase a cashier's check for the specified amount naming the vendor as payee. He does not need to have an account with the bank he selects for purchase of the cashier's check. The bank issues a check on its account (not John's bank account), and since it has been paid in advance, the bank guarantees payment to the holder.

A **certified check** is "a depositor's check drawn on a bank that guarantees the availability of funds for the check" (Garner 2005, 195). Like a cashier's check, it also is guaranteed by the bank, but it is debited against the bank account of the drawer. In the above example, John (drawer) prepares a check on his bank account payable to the vendor and presents the check to its bank for acceptance.

In this context, the term **acceptance** means the bank segregates the stated amount of the check from John's account and earmarks it for payment to the holder of the check. The bank verifies sufficient funds exist in John's account, and if money is available, it stamps "ACCEPTED" on the face of the check. The bank will immediately debit John's account for the stated amount. The bank has the amount specified on the certified check segregated from John's account and available for future payment to the payee upon presentment. As with the cashier's check, this process provides the necessary confidence to a vendor the check will be honored.

Promises to Pay

Promises to pay come in two general forms: a promissory note or a certificate of deposit (CD).

Promissory Note

Unlike a draft, a promissory note does not have a bank or drawee as part of the original transaction. The promissory note may name a specific payee, or it may be designated as a bearer instrument. A bearer instrument is one held by a person "who possesses a negotiable instrument marked 'payable to bearer' or '[e]ndorsed in blank'" (Garner 2005, 125; U.C.C. § 3-109 (a)) rather than to the order of a specific named person.

For example, if a promissory note was endorsed by the payee and did not specify a person as transferee, it may be cashed by whoever has possession of the note. Assume Bill, a meat packer, receives a promissory note for $6,000 from a customer who purchased large quantities of beef. Also assume Bill just purchased some equipment for $6,000 from XYZ Company. Bill transfers the note to XYZ Company by endorsing it "pay to bearer" and delivering it to XYZ Company. XYZ Company may now deposit that check in its bank account for collection through the bank collection process (see the discussion of the banking process, Chapter 14).

For another example, assume a hotel enters into an agreement with a general contractor to have a tile floor installed in the hotel lobby. The hotel general manager signs the contract and signs a promissory note on June 1, 2013, that obligates the hotel to pay $20,000, with no interest, upon completion of the installation, currently scheduled for August 1, 2013. This arrangement permits the hotel to purchase the tile floor on 60 days credit, interest free. The contractor benefits because it will now have new business. The note must be paid on August 1, 2013, or the hotel is in default.

A promissory note is versatile, like most negotiable instruments, and it may be passed on to third parties through the negotiation process. In the above example, the general contractor may need immediate cash to purchase materials for the installation. He may sell the note to a bank or private investor at a discount to obtain the necessary working capital.

Assume a bank purchases the note from the general contractor on June 2, 2013, for $18,000 and redeems it August 1, 2013, from the hotel for the $20,000, as specified in the note. The general contractor immediately obtains the $18,000, and the bank nets $2,000 on the transaction in two months' time for advancing the $18,000.

Certificate of Deposit

A certificate of deposit (CD) is a banker's certificate acknowledging receipt of money and promising to repay the depositor. It is a promissory note issued by a bank to a party who deposits funds in the bank under special conditions. The CD binds the bank to repay the face amount of the CD, with a specified interest rate, after a specified length of time. A CD, unlike a conventional passbook savings account, is usually made in specified increments, such as $5,000, $10,000, or $25,000, and is required to be held for a specified period of time, such as six months or a year. The bank is the maker of the note, and the depositor is the payee.

A CD is a relatively safe way to save money at an interest rate usually higher than the local bank passbook rate. For example, a restaurant owner may wish to use a portion of restaurant profits to create a savings tool as a hedge for future financial needs. The restaurateur may purchase a $5,000 CD every six months at a rate of three percent interest, which will provide available cash semiannually with a good rate of return. If it is not needed at the time of maturity, the money may be reinvested in another CD. If it is reinvested, the CD will generate another three percent for the new six-month period. The annualized interest becomes six percent.

After several years of such purchases and with reinvestments, financial security may be achieved relatively soon. In case of emergency, a CD may be exchanged early, but that will reduce the applicable interest rate from the rate stated at maturity. As an alternative, a CD may also be discounted to a third party in order to obtain immediate cash.

Negotiability Requirements

The U.C.C. contains statutory requirements for an instrument to qualify as a negotiable instrument (see, generally, U.C.C. Article 3, et seq. at Appendix B). The agreement (1) must be in writing, (2) must be signed by the maker or drawer, (3) must contain an unconditional promise or order to pay, (4) state a fixed sum of money, (5) be payable on demand or at a definite time, and (6) be payable to order or bearer.

The first requirement is the **writing requirement**. Oral contacts are binding but are not recommended, because disputes over the terms are difficult to prove. Memories fade, evidence is lost, and witnesses are hard to locate and/or subsequently die. Moreover, oral contracts are vulnerable to fraud because some parties may just lie about the terms of the agreement. In a court of law, the plaintiff has the burden of proof by a preponderance of the evidence. Consequently, your word by itself may not be enough to prevail in a lawsuit.

An important benefit of negotiable instruments is its writing requirement and ease of transfer to third parties. An oral agreement transferred to several subsequent holders will probably be materially altered and become unrecognizable by the time of presentment. Remember the middle school exercise where students sit in a circle and pass a verbal message to the student to the left (i.e., "telephone" game). By the time it returns to the originator, the message is greatly distorted.

Accordingly, under the U.C.C., only a written contract will qualify as a negotiable instrument. The writing must also be in a relatively permanent, portable form easily transferred, such as paper or electronic data.

For example, carving an agreement on the side of a cow may help locate the agreement in question. However, negotiating such an agreement would be a challenge because it would be difficult to physically transfer the cow to a third party and any successive transferees. A cow is not very portable, and the message may become obscured over time with the growth of hair (not to mention this would be animal cruelty). Such an agreement would not be readily transferrable to meet the negotiability requirements.

The second requirement is a **signature requirement**. The instrument must be signed by the maker if it is a promissory note or the drawer if it is a check. An issue may surface regarding what qualifies as a signature. The U.C.C. defines a signature as "any symbol executed or adopted with the present intention to adopt or accept a writing" (U.C.C. § 1-201 (37)). In other words, if you agree to the terms of a written agreement, the mark you place on an instrument at the time of the agreement will be construed as your intent to be bound.

For example, suppose a cattle rancher decides to sell 100 cows to a meat packer. The meat packer requires time to sell the cows to a meat distributor. So the parties agree to a trade acceptance that permits the meat packer to pay for the cows within 90 days. The cattle rancher uses an inked rubber stamp containing its logo, trade name, or trademark on the trade acceptance to indicate agreement to the terms. Assuming adequate extrinsic evidence is present to support the intent (e.g., a witness to the signing), the imprint from the rubber stamp will be acceptable as a signature for purposes of negotiability. U.C.C. § 3-401 (b) states, "A signature may be made (i) manually or by means of a device or machine, and (ii) by the use of any name, or by a word, mark, or symbol."

The third requirement is an **unconditional promise or order to pay**. Under the Uniform Commercial Code, a negotiable instrument means "an unconditional promise or order to pay a fixed amount of money ... (1) if payable to bearer or to order, (2) is payable on demand or at a definite time; and (3) does not state any other undertaking or instruction by the person promising or ordering payment to do any other act in addition to the payment of money" (U.C.C. § 3-104 (a) (1)-(3)). In addition, "an instrument is a 'note' if it is a promise and [it] is a 'draft' if it is an order" (U.C.C. § 3-104 (e)). Both must be unconditional for purposes of negotiability.

The terms of the negotiable instrument must be stated on the face of the document, and the terms must be unconditional. An instrument with a precondition will not be readily accepted by a third party because of the uncertainty caused by the precondition. If third parties are reluctant to accept the document, its transferability is impaired, and the instrument will not be freely negotiated.

For example, assume John decides to sell his substantial real estate holdings to finance the purchase of a hotel and negotiates a loan with a bank for the purchase. The promissory note offered by John states his obligation to the bank is contingent on the sale of his real estate. The bank will not be able to discount or further negotiate the note, because of the uncertainty created by the sale of the real estate. Moreover, no reasonable third party would accept John's note as **collateral** or for payment for a subsequent transaction for the same reason.

The unconditional promise must be an affirmative, express promise or order to pay the amount stated on the face of the note. It is defined as "a promise that either is unqualified or requires nothing but the lapse of time to make the promise presently enforceable" (Garner 2005, 1015). Words of equivocation, such as "I understand I owe the amount stated in the note," do not meet the express promise requirement.

The fourth requirement is that a negotiable instrument must state a **fixed amount of money** on the face of the instrument that is easily understood and calculable at the time of payment. A description such as "twenty-five thousand dollars ($25,000), United States currency" is a fixed sum. It may include interest as long as the interest can be determined with certainty (e.g., adding the words "with interest in an amount of 10% per annum"). The U.C.C. states a negotiable instrument is "an unconditional promise or order to pay a fixed amount of money, with or without interest or other charges described in the promise or order" (U.C.C. § 3-104 (a)).

An interest rate referenced to a source not on the face of an instrument is acceptable if it is easily determined. For example, an interest rate based upon "the prime rate" published Monday, August 8, 2013, is not a fixed amount because many institutions publish prime rates comprised of varying components. The instrument fails to name which institution's prime rate should be applied. A prime rate based upon a named publication, like "*The Wall Street Journal*, published Monday, August 8, 2013," is easily determined and readily accepted in the financial community.

Reference to the "legal rate of interest" may appear to be vague, but it is easy to determine. A legal rate of interest is the amount a state legislature authorizes for various legal purposes, such as the amount to be imposed on court judgments. Each state sets the legal interest rate periodically by statute. All that is required for determination is for a person to access an internet search engine and enter the relevant state government website. The website will have a link to the legal interest rate for ease of a location.

The fixed sum must also be payable in money. Money is defined in the U.C.C. as "a medium of exchange currently authorized or adopted by a domestic or foreign government" (U.C.C. § 1-201 (24)). The term also includes a monetary unit of account established by an intergovernmental organization or by agreement between two or more countries (U.C.C. § 1-210 (24)). For example, a promissory note that requires payment in Mexican pesos is acceptable because the exchange rate for converting dollars to pesos is easily determined from banks, money exchanges, and governmental organizations.

The fifth requirement is that the agreement must be **payable on demand or at a definite time**. In order to create the requisite certainty and confidence for potential transferees, the time it is due and payable must be on the face of the instrument. Otherwise, it will not be clear when the maker must pay the holder of the instrument. Without such knowledge, few if any potential transferees would be willing to accept the instrument for discounting or for use as collateral. There are two options for this requirement:

- **Instruments payable on demand:** Demand instruments include those with words such as "upon presentment" or those that are typically payable upon sight, such as a personal check. Presentment means "the formal production of a negotiable instrument for acceptance or payment" (Garner 2005, 993). In addition, an instrument properly endorsed, but that does not state a specific date for payment, is considered a demand instrument (U.C.C. § 3-108(a)).

- **Payable at a definite time:** If an instrument does not fit the definition of a demand instrument, it must be payable at a definite time to be negotiable. For example, a promise to repay a lender a sum certain without specifying the due date destroys negotiability because the maker is not legally required to pay the note at a specified time. A potential transferee will not know when to present the instrument for payment and would also be less likely to accept the instrument in a business transaction. Examples of a definite time include the following:
- Payable on June 8, 2013.
- Payable upon the holder's next birthday.
- Payable upon sale of collateral in a secured transaction.
- Payable upon acceptance of promised merchandise.
- Payable in 30 calendar days.

For example, if a hotel executes a promissory note to a supplier of fixtures that says, "Hotel will pay the sum of $10,000 upon satisfactory installation of the fixtures," is not payable upon demand or at a definite time. The hotel may delay payment until it is fully satisfied, which could be a lengthy period if no time limit is specified. If the foregoing note specified "Hotel will pay the sum of $10,000 upon installation of the fixtures, but no later than two weeks after completion," a definite time is now discernible, and the note is negotiable.

The sixth requirement is that the agreement must be **payable to order or bearer**. The U.C.C. requires a negotiable instrument to be easily transferable. As part of the requirement, it must be payable to the maker's order (e.g., to the payee) or to bearer (e.g., the person in legal possession of the instrument), such as a transferee of an instrument endorsed in blank. An indorsement without naming a person is called an indorsement in blank. It is defined as "an indorsement that names no specific payee, thus making the instrument payable to the bearer and negotiable by delivery only" (Garner 2005, 642; U.C.C. § 3-205 (b)).

An order instrument is one that designates a payee. For example, a check that says, "Pay to the order of John Smith" or "Pay to John Smith or order." A bearer instrument is created when John Smith indorses the check without specifying another named person. After such an indorsement, the instrument becomes a bearer instrument, and any person in possession can demand payment according to its terms.

For example, suppose John, a restaurateur, pays West Coast Restaurant Supplies Co. (WCRS) $10,000 for napkins, aprons, cutlery, and tableware with a business check that reads, "Pay to WCRS or order." The check is an order instrument since the payee is named, including the instruction "or order." WCRS may indorse the check and deposit it in its bank account or indorse the check to one of its vendors in payment of an existing debt.

The same check could also be indorsed in blank by WCRS and delivered to the vendor as payment for a product or service without specifying a named party. Without specifying a named party, the instrument becomes a bearer instrument, which permits the holder to demand payment.

Special Rules

An **acceleration clause** permits the payee to demand full payment prior to the specified time for payment contained on the face of the instrument. For example, if a specified event occurs, such as default on a monthly payment, the payee of the note may demand full payment immediately. It is defined as "the shortening of the time for vesting in possession of an expectant interest" (Garner 2005, 10). Contracts for the sale of real estate usually contain an acceleration clause.

For further example, assume a restaurateur purchases an office building that includes space for a steak house. The purchase is financed by a local bank, and the terms of the loan include a monthly payment to the bank of $1,200. Also included is an acceleration clause for the full amount of the loan upon default. If the full payment is not made after default, the bank may foreclose on the loan and sell the property.

Acceleration clauses do not destroy negotiability, because they meet the fixed sum requirement. The amount due is easily calculable; it is the total purchase price less the amounts paid to date, including interest and applicable fees. It will also be payable at a time certain, which is the date of the default.

An **extension clause** is just the opposite of an acceleration clause, and it permits the date of maturity to be extended into the future. If the maker has the option to extend the maturity date, the note fails to contain a specific future date. This makes the note nonnegotiable under the U.C.C. A transferee will not know when the note will be paid.

If the holder has the option to extend, the specific future date need not be specified. The rationale for the difference concerns the transferability to a third party. If the maker controls the future date, a third-party transferee would not know if or when payment would be honored and would be less likely to accept such an instrument. When the holder has the option to extend, a third party would not be reluctant to accept the note, because a transferee steps into the shoes of the transferor, and it would control the future date.

Summary

Negotiable instruments are financial tools used to facilitate business transactions. They are flexible substitutes for cash and credit designed to increase confidence in commerce. The Uniform Commercial Code provides the rules for creation and use of negotiable instruments.

A negotiable instrument is a signed writing by a maker or drawer to unconditionally pay a sum certain to a promisee or payee on demand or at a specific time in the future. A maker is the creator of a promissory note. A drawer is the creator of a check drawn on a bank account. The most common types of negotiable instruments are drafts, checks, promissory notes, and certificates of deposit. The Uniform Commercial Code, Article contains rules for the form and transferability of negotiable instruments.

The writing must be for a fixed amount of money, defined as a medium of exchange by a domestic or foreign government. It must be signed by the obligor of the writing with a mark, symbol, or name with the present intent to adopt or accept the writing. An acceleration clause permits the holder to demand payment in advance of the specified date, usually upon default of the maker or drawer. An extension clause is the opposite and permits a holder to extend the payment date.

Review Questions

True/False

Directions: Look at each statement below. Based on what you learned in this chapter, decide if the statement is true or false.

1. A negotiable instrument must be endorsed by the drawee to permit a legal transfer.
2. A check is a two-party instrument consisting of the drawer and drawee.
3. A trade acceptance is a draft that permits the payee to control the outcome of the transaction.
4. Issue refers to the first delivery of a negotiable instrument to another person.
5. A promissory note is an order to the payee for transfer of the rights to the note.
6. For an instrument to be negotiable, it must be either written or oral in plain, unequivocal language.
7. A signature on a negotiable instrument may be placed anywhere on the face of the document.
8. A negotiable instrument may be conditional if the condition is easily attainable.
9. A negotiable instrument including "the legal rate of interest" is easily calculable and is therefore permissible for use in a legal transfer.
10. An acceleration clause permits the payment of the fixed amount earlier at the option of the payee.
11. An extension clause permits the maker of a note to control the payment for the payee.
12. An indorsement in blank creates a bearer instrument.
13. Antedating or postdating an instrument destroys its negotiability.
14. An instrument that states "with interest" will be interpreted as the legal judgment rate of the state of issue.
15. Unless the date of an instrument is necessary to determine a definite time for payment, its omission is not fatal to negotiability.

Multiple Choice

Directions: Use what you learned in this chapter to choose the best response to each of the prompts below.

1. The following are true of the special rules presented in the text, except:
   a. They cover acceleration clauses.
   b. They do not cover extension clauses unless both parties agree.
   c. An extension clause option held by the payee does not destroy negotiability.
   d. For an acceleration clause to be valid, it must describe with certainty the event that permits its application.

2. All the following apply to a pay to order or bearer, except:
   a. It must be payable to maker's order.
   b. It can be an indorsement without naming a future payee.
   c. A bearer instrument permits anyone the right to payment.
   d. It may be used to pay an existing debt.

3. All the following apply to a fixed amount of money, except:
   a. It must be located on the face of the instrument.
   b. It may include interest even if the interest rate is not presently known.
   c. It may be a source, such as the prime rate listed in *The Wall Street Journal* on August 8, 2021.
   d. The reference to the legal rate of interest is easily determinable.

4. The following all apply to a fixed sum, except:
   a. It must be a medium of exchange authorized by a domestic or foreign government.
   b. It can apply to a monetary unit established by an intergovernmental organization or by agreement between countries.
   c. An instrument that requires payment in Mexican pesos is not acceptable, because it's too vague.
   d. Use of rates set by banks and money exchanges are acceptable.

5. All the following apply to a definite time, except:
   a. It applies if an instrument fits the definition of a demand instrument.
   b. It must be payable at an exact time.
   c. Negotiability is not destroyed with a time certain, such as the holder's next birthday.
   d. Without a time certain, the potential transferee with not know when payment will occur.

6. All the following apply to an instrument payable on demand, except:
   a. It applies to a bank check.
   b. It applies upon presentment.
   c. It applies to an instrument without a specific definite time.
   d. It does not apply to an instrument "payable upon sight."

7. All the following area true, except:
   a. A negotiable instrument may be used as collateral for a loan.
   b. The words by a maker "I understand I owe the amount specified in the instrument" are acceptable.
   c. If the sum or date in an instrument is not clear, a transferee will not accept it.
   d. All material terms must be on the face of a negotiable instrument.

8. All the following are true with regard to an unconditional promise or order to pay, except:
   a. It includes payable to bearer or order.
   b. It is payable at a definite time.
   c. It does not refer to a draft, only to a check or note.
   d. It contains no other instruction than to pay the amount due.

9. All the following are true, except:
   a. A maker is the creator of a draft.
   b. A drawer is the creator of a check.
   c. A bank is the creator of a certificate of deposit.
   d. A negotiable instrument may be signed with any symbol as long as intent to pay is present.

10. All the following are true, except:
    a. Negotiable instruments are financial tools that facilitate business.
    b. U.C.C. Art. 4 provides the statutory requirements for negotiable instruments.
    c. The Federal Reserve Board provides oversight of some negotiable instruments.
    d. Negotiable instruments ae substitutes for cash.

Scenarios

1. Bill signed a promissory note to Chevy Lake Auto for the purchase of a used car. It stated that 12 monthly payments in the amount of $2,000, with interest, will be made until paid in full. Chevy discounted the note to First National Bank for $20,000. After eight months, Bill stopped paying. First National sued Bill for breach of contract. What will be the result? Explain your answer.
2. In May of 2020 Bill, a college student, purchased a state-of-the-art computer system that cost $3,600. He borrowed the money from his uncle. Payments were to be made in 12 equal installments, payment in full upon default. Bill's uncle immediately negotiated the note to a financial institution after the second installment. After the third installment, Bill paid late for the next four months. The financial institution filed suit to exercise the acceleration clause and collect the full amount due. What will be the result? Explain your answer.

Decisional Review

1. Plaintiff, a debtor in bankruptcy, files suit against a payday lender for violating a court-ordered 90-day stay on checks. Plaintiff borrowed $500 from Defendant and issued a check including interest and loan fee for an amount of $587.50. The check was prepared with the handwritten amount as five eighty-seven and fifty cents (the hundred-dollar word was omitted). Plaintiff argued the check was ambiguous and not negotiable. If Plaintiff was correct, it should not have been cashed, because that violates the automatic stay. Defendant asserts it was negotiable and therefore meets an exception to the automatic stay. What will be the result? Explain your answer. See *Blasco v. Money Services Center*, 352 B.R. 888.
2. Defendant was arrested for carrying certificates of deposit in excess of the $10,000 across the international border into the United States. Plaintiff, United States, alleges the certificates of deposit are negotiable instruments valued at $1.2 million. Defendant claims they are not negotiable instruments because they are not a sum certain. The bank agreement subjected the certificates to an offset for any amount owed against payee's account with the bank at the time of presentation. Therefore, the amount is not a sum certain. What will be the result? Explain your answer. See *United States v. Medina*, 797 F. 2d 1109, (5th Cir. 1986).

Chapter 14

Banking and the Hospitality Industry

Introduction

This chapter concerns the banking system as specified in Uniform Commercial Code, Article 4. Specifically, it concerns requirements for agreements between banks and customers for check deposits and withdrawals. In addition, Article 4 provides the rules for the Federal Reserve Bank check collection process.

As mentioned in Chapter 13, Article 3 of the U.C.C. concerns the form and content requirements for the transfer of negotiable instruments, referred to as negotiability. Both Article 3 and Article 4 have rules regarding checks. When a conflict arises between Article 3 and Article 4, Article 4 will control. The Board of Governors of the Federal Reserve System provides some oversight of Article 4.

The chapter discusses the nature and use of checks in the banking system. It explains the banking relationship created by a customer opening a checking account with a bank, such as the rights and duties both parties have relative to the banking relationship. Moreover, once a check is deposited into a bank account, the check collection process commences to ensure collection against the check.

Finally, the chapter provides background for the Check Clearing in the 21st Century Act ("Check 21"; 12 U.S.C. § 5010–5018) and explains its purpose. The act was adopted to implement an electronic check banking process. Previously, a manual check cashing system was in place. It was a slow, expensive, and labor-intensive system. Check 21 introduced digital checks, referred to as "substitute checks," to replace paper checks.

Chapter Objectives

Upon completion of this chapter, the student will understand:

- the nature and use of checks and the banking system
- the customer–bank relationship
- the Federal Reserve System collection process
- electronic fund transfers
- The Check Clearing in the 21st Century Act

Key Terms

Directions: Each of the terms below will be used in this chapter. Before reading, scan the chapter. The terms will appear in bold. Take a moment to see how the term is used so you can understand it in context. The terms are listed in the order in which they will appear in the chapter.

Drawer (p. 246)
Payee (p. 246)
Certified check (p. 247)
Drawee (p. 246)
Cashier's check (p. 247)
Traveler's check (p. 248)

Banking—Generally

The chapter explains the banking system and the responsibilities of both a bank and a depositor regarding electronic transfers through the banking system.

A bank is a business where customers make deposits for future use. Checks are used to access funds for payment to third parties. Banks accept the deposits and process checks though internal systems and through the Federal Reserve System. Banking relies on use of negotiable instruments, such as personal checks, cashier's checks, certified checks, and traveler's checks.

Banking is regulated by Article 3 and Article 4 of the Uniform Commercial Code. As discussed in Chapter 13, Article 3 governs form and content of negotiable instruments, their transfer, and the rights and responsibilities of parties to checks. Article 4 governs relationships among banks and between banks and their customers. Checks may fall within the purview of both Article 3 and Article 4. When a conflict arises between applications of the two aforementioned articles, Article 4 will usually prevail.

The statutory preference in favor of Article 4 demonstrates the power enjoyed by banks over consumers, in large part because the banking lobby wields substantial influence over Congress and state legislatures. The Great Recession is a case study of that power. Banks were a major culprit of the Great Recession because of risky financial and lending practices, their ability to block attempts at meaningful banking regulation, and heavy reliance on bailout largesse from government.

Checks

A check is a special kind of draft used by industry and consumers for everyday business. It minimizes potential loss due to theft and misplacement of cash. Restaurants, hotels, motels, resorts, and bars usually pay vendors, employees, and independent contractors with checks drawn on their local bank. Consumers use checks to pay their living expenses, such as mortgage payments, and point-of-sale transactions at hotels, restaurants, retail outlets, and supermarkets.

A check is an order by a depositor to its bank to pay a sum certain on demand. Banks are defined as "a financial establishment for the deposit, loan, exchange, or issue of money and for the transmission of funds; esp., a member of the Federal Reserve System" (Garner 2005, 117; U.C.C. § 4-105 (1)). As mentioned in Chapter 13, the person who writes the check is the **drawer**, and the person to whom the check is issued is called the **payee.** The bank that holds the deposits and on which the check is drawn is called the **drawee** (Figure 13.1).

Despite the historical value of checks as a safe substitute for cash, problems led to creation of several variations of checks. The banking industry developed cashier's checks, certified checks, and traveler's checks to further minimize the risk of loss, guarantee payment, and create additional revenue streams. The following discusses all three variations of a check.

As previously stated, checks are normally three-party instruments (see Chapter 13). However, sometimes a need arises for the drawer to guarantee payment to the payee during contract negotiation in order to secure performance. This can be accomplished with either a **cashier's check** or a **certified check** (see discussion in Chapter 13).

For example, assume a plumber negotiates a contract with a hotel to replace plumbing throughout the building. Materials for the job cost $50,000. The plumber is a new business without a credit history. The supplier of materials for the job may want assurances it will get paid. The plumber seeks an advance from the hotel to purchase supplies for the job. The hotel also has a concern (i.e., the advance may not be used for the intended purpose).

A solution for the above concerns is for the hotel to provide the advance with a cashier's check payable to the supplier, thereby circumventing the plumber and assuring the supplier will get the advance. The hotel will go to a bank and purchase a cashier's check in the amount of $50,500. The $500 is a bank fee for the cost of the cashier's check.

Banks create an in-house cashier's account for deposits of all money generated from customer purchases of cashier's checks. Payment of the face amount of the check is deposited in the bank's cashier's check account. The hotel need not have an account with the bank that issues the cashier's check since payment is made in full. The $50,000 is paid to the supplier for release of the supplies to the plumber. The supplier receives the $50,000 upon presentment of the cashier's check to the bank. The supplier thereby is guaranteed $50,000 payment for its supplies.

The cashier's check is drawn by the bank on its cashier's checking account. Analytically, the bank becomes both the drawer and drawee. The plumber would be outside the loop and unable to use the advance for other than the stated purpose. This arrangement protects both the hotel and the supplier and provides confidence that the project will be completed.

A **certified check** is a depositor's check drawn on its bank. The bank verifies the amount of the check is available in the depositor's checking account. The bank debts the depositor's bank account for the amount of the check and transfers the amount into its in-house certified checking account, similar to the bank's cashier's checking account mentioned above. Finally, the bank writes or stamps the word "ACCEPTED" on the face of the check.

The drawer gives the check to the payee for the amount due. Upon completion of the business transaction, the payee presents the certified check to the bank. When the check is presented for payment, the bank deducts the amount from its certified check account and remits that amount to the payee (U.C.C. § 3-409 (a) (d)). This arrangement provides the payee with assurance the drawer is paying with a check from an account with sufficient funds.

A bank is not obligated to agree to a depositor's request to "accept" a check, and its refusal to do so is not a dishonor of the check. A reason a bank may not agree to accept a check, even though adequate funds exist, may be the drawer's balance is below a stated policy level required by a bank or the drawer has been a problem account for the bank.

In the above example, assume the hotel decided to use its own account to issue the check rather than purchase a cashier's check for $500 dollars. The hotel would write the check payable to the supplier, go to its bank, and ask for acceptance. If the hotel is in good financial standing, the bank may accommodate the hotel with a "no charge acceptance" or a relatively smaller fee.

The face amount of the check is debited to the hotel's account and the word "ACCEPTED" placed on the face of the check. The hotel sends the check to the supplier, and the supplies are released to the plumber. All parties now have requisite confidence to proceed with the project.

A **traveler's check** is similar to a cashier's check. It is a negotiable instrument payable on demand. (U.C.C. § 3-104 (i)). As the name implies, such checks are used by persons traveling on vacations or for business purposes. Traveler's checks are a popular and safe substitute for cash. A person will go to a bank and purchase traveler's checks for a certain amount, usually in denominations of $50 or $100. If the purchaser has an account with the bank, it may purchase traveler's checks without payment of a fee; otherwise, a small fee will be charged.

The issuing bank will deposit the amount in its traveler's check account and pay the face amount of the traveler's checks as they are presented. The purchaser is required to sign a traveler's check twice to protect against theft or inadvertent loss, once at the time of purchase and then at the time of use (U.C.C. § 3-104 (i)). Hospitality is very familiar with traveler's checks. They are used to pay for, among other things, hotel rooms, dining expenses, airline tickets, car rentals, and merchandise.

A virtue of the check system is the relative procedural ease a holder must follow to obtain payment for a **lost or stolen check**. The claimant of the check may obtain a refund/replacement for the amount of the check by filing a claim describing the check with reasonable certainty before the check is cashed (U.C.C. § 3-312 (b)).

The claim must be filed by the drawer or payee of a certified check or the remitter or payee of a cashier's check who produces proper identification (U.C.C. § 3-312 (b) (i)). The claim must also be received at a time and in a manner affording the bank a reasonable time to act on it before the check is paid (U.C.C. § 3-312 § (b) (iii)). The claim becomes enforceable at the later of the time the claim is asserted (the 90th day of the date of the check in the case of a cashier's check or teller's check or the 90th day following the date of the acceptance in the case of a certified check; U.C.C. § 3-312 (b) (1)).

The Bank-Customer Relationship

The customer-bank relationship creates two basic types of relationships: contractual and creditor/debtor. The aforementioned relationships commence when the customer enters into a contractual agreement with a bank.

A **contract** is created when a customer opens a bank account with a deposit of a certain amount of money. The bank presents the customer with an informational packet describing the rights and duties of both parties and obtains the customer's signature to a bank agreement. The agreement is a binding contract that may vary depending on the type of relationship agreed to by the parties. The agreement can be for a passbook account, revolving line of credit, or some other financial arrangement for services.

The terms and conditions will vary by the financial institution based upon its policy and practices. It is important to distinguish between a bank's policy and banking laws. A bank policy may not always be consistent with the U.C.C. and it may not need to be in many instances. For example, banks will set a minimum deposit requirement for a customer to avoid a service charge. The U.C.C. does not require banks to set such a minimum deposit, but the law does not prohibit one.

When a customer deposits money in a bank account the bank becomes obligated to pay it back by way of withdrawals or to pay to the customer's order. The bank is the **debtor**, and the customer is the **creditor**.

Check Processing

When a bank provides checkbook services, it agrees to pay checks to the order of the customer and to collect amounts on checks deposited by the customer (see, generally, "Collection of Items: Payor Banks" in U.C.C.

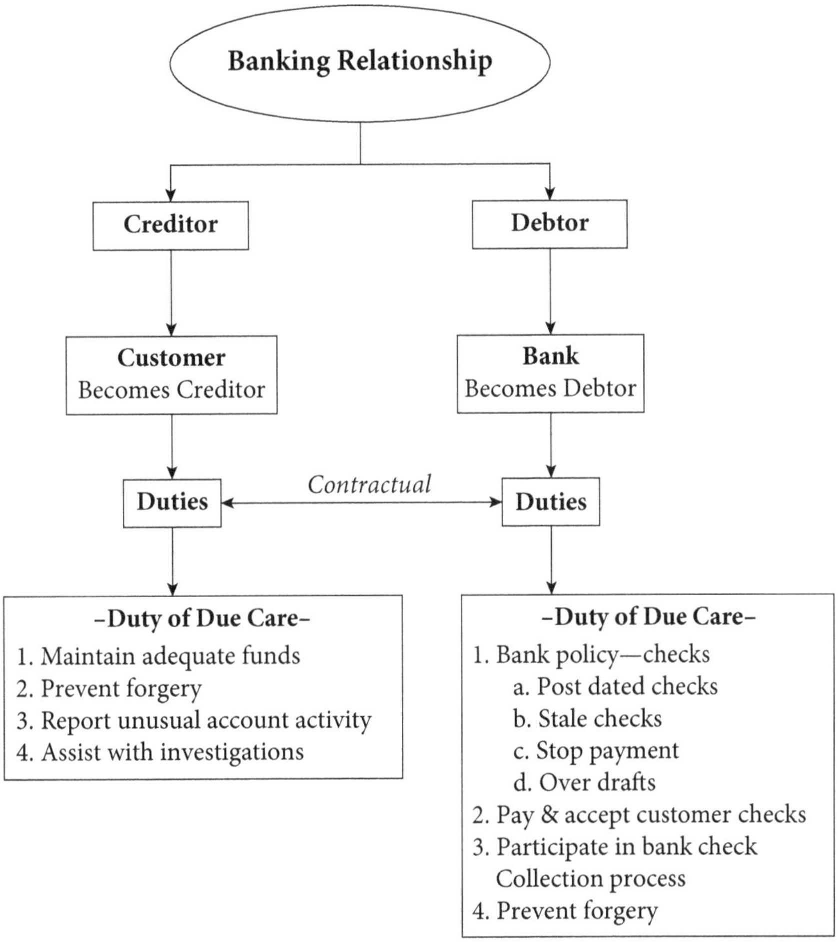

FIGURE 14.1 Banking Relationship

§ 4-301 (a)–(d)). The customer must maintain a balance sufficient to pay all checks that are issued. Lack of a sufficient balance may lead to dishonor of a check and the assessment of a banking fee.

If the customer writes checks with knowledge there are insufficient funds and the bank dishonors the check, the customer may be liable in a civil lawsuit by the payee of the dishonored check. If there is a consistent pattern of bad checks and a significant amount of money involved, a criminal prosecution may also be filed. Generally, prosecutors do not file a criminal complaint for bad check cases and instead consider them civil matters for resolution in small claims courts.

Most banks provide an overdraft service (for a fee) to avoid the dishonor of a check (U.C.C. § 4-401 (a)). If a bank wrongfully dishonors a check, it is liable to the customer for any damages (U.C.C. § 4-402 (a) (b)). Liability could relate to actual damages and any consequential damages proximately caused by the improper dishonor. Proximate cause refers to the legal cause determined by a court and for which the court may assess damages.

For example, assume Mary, the owner of a local restaurant, issues 15 checks to pay her vendors. The bank makes an error in her account by failing to credit her last deposit in the amount of $10,000. As a consequence, all 15 checks are dishonored, and she is assessed $35.00 for each dishonored check. The bank notifies the police of the situation and asks for a criminal investigation of Mary for writing checks with insufficient funds. They arrest Mary and commence an investigation. Her vendors stop providing supplies, and her restaurant is closed for a month.

Subsequently, police investigators and the bank's auditors discover the bank's error. Mary has been severely damaged as a result and sues the bank. She is entitled to recover the $35.00 fee for each check and any loss she can prove resulted from the closure of her restaurant, such as lost profits, payroll expenses, spoiled inventory, and so on. In addition, she should be able to recover damages to her reputation if she can show the bank error caused damage to her personal and business reputation. This latter consequence can lead to a very large sum in damages.

Bank Charges Against Customer's Account

The Uniform Commercial Code permits banks to charge customer accounts in the following important instances. The decision to do so is discretionary policy, not law, and so is the amount charged.

Overdrafts

Assuming the customer does not have overdraft protection, the bank has two options when the customer writes a check with insufficient funds in the account. It can either dishonor the check or pay the overdraft and charge the customer with an overdraft fee, consistent with bank policy and the banking agreement (U.C.C. § 4-401(a)). The bank may subtract the check amount from the next deposit by the customer or require full payment of the check to resume banking services.

Often, customers discover the discrepancy before they are notified by the bank and they make a subsequent deposit to cover the check. Many banks, as matter of policy, may permit the payee of a check rejected for insufficient funds at least one resubmission.

Postdated and Stale Checks

A postdated check is created when a customer makes a check payable at a future time. If it is cashed prior to the future date, the bank is not liable for any insufficiency in the account balance unless the customer has provided the bank with proper notice in a reasonable amount of time (U.C.C. § 4-401(c)).

The UC.C. (§ 4-404) defines a stale check as one presented for payment after six months has elapsed. A bank is not obligated to honor a stale check unless it is a cashier's check or a certified check (U.C.C. § 4-404). As a matter of policy, a bank may honor stale checks for long-term customers with large deposits and those with multiple business and personal accounts with the bank.

Stop-Payment Orders

A customer has the right to order a bank not to pay a check that may have been lost or stolen or if a customer has a legitimate basis to withdraw payment, such as a breach of contract. The stop order instruction must be given within a reasonable time for the bank to act, and the customer must follow proper bank procedures (U.C.C. § 4-403(a)). Usually, a written request is required to stop payment for a period of up to six months, which is renewable in writing for an additional six months (U.C.C. § 4-403 (b)). Many banks permit an oral stop payment if it is confirmed in writing within 14 days.

Liability for Stop-Payment Orders

A customer will be liable to the payee for damages if a stop-payment order is made without a legal basis for doing so. The customer has the burden of proof to establish the validity of the stop-payment order (U.C.C. § 4-403 (c)). A bank will be liable to the customer for damages if it fails to honor a valid stop-payment order. This will include the amount of the check and any consequential damages the failure to make the stop-payment may have caused (U.C.C. § 4-402 (b)).

For example, assume a hotel orders 500 new beds at a cost of $500 per bed, for a total cost of $250,000. In order to ensure timely delivery for a three-day conference that starts in one month, it pays the entire amount in advance. One week later, the manufacturer of the beds informs the hotel that it is insolvent and cannot comply with the deadline.

The check has not cleared the hotel's bank, so the hotel orders the bank, verbally and in writing, to stop payment. The bank loses the notification for the stop payment order, and the check clears the hotel's bank. The hotel is now without working capital to place a subsequent order with an alternative manufacturer in time for the conference.

The conference organizers learn of the problem and decide to cancel the event and find another venue. The hotel loses $500,000 in net revenue from the expected conference attendees, and its reputation is badly tarnished. The bank's failure to honor the stop payment could cost it compensatory damages in an amount of the $250,000 for the check to the insolvent manufacturer and $500,000 in lost net revenues. Consequential damages may also be recoverable by the hotel for loss of good will and damage to its reputation.

Forgery

Making false changes to a document is referred to as "forgery" and is defined as "the act of fraudulently making a false document or altering a real one to be used as if genuine" (Garner 2005, 542). A check may be altered in many ways, such as by changing a date, an amount, or a designated payee. Blank checks may be lost or stolen and made to look as if authentic. It is a serious problem for banks and their customers. The U.C.C. provides responsibility for both the banks and bank customers; each has a duty of due care to prevent forgery.

Bank's duty refers to the duty a bank has to verify signatures when a check is presented to an employee for cash. If the bank employee fails to do so, the bank will be liable for the amount of the check. If the check was intended to pay a bank customer's debt owed to a third party, consequential damages may result, and the bank will also be liable for that loss.

For example, assume a check was issued to a vendor of a restaurant in the amount of $20,000 for its banquet menu. The check was subsequently lost or was stolen. The payee designation was changed to an unknown third party and cashed at the drawee bank. The amount of the check was never recovered. The vendor never received payment and therefore refuses to ship the supplies. The banquet had to be canceled because the restaurant lacked sufficient funds to replace the $20,000.

Three possibilities may result from this scenario. First, the bank could be held liable for the amount of the check and any consequential damages for the loss of profit on the banquet. It had a duty of reasonable care to verify the signature. Second, the restaurant could be liable for the entire amount if the bank can show that the restaurant carelessly lost the check or did not take reasonable precautions to prevent the check from being lost or stolen. The bank customer has a similar duty of due care to manage its use of checks and safeguard its unused checks. Third, under the legal doctrine of comparative negligence, both the bank and the bank customer will share the loss by the assignment of "relative percentage of culpability" for the loss of the check (see discussion of comparative negligence).

The following case concerns a series of forged checks, and it discusses the duties and relative liability of the parties.

2010 WL 1712702

Court of Appeal, First District, Division 4, California.
Edward LITKE, Plaintiff and Appellant,
v.
CITY NATIONAL CORPORATION et al., Defendants and Respondents.
April 29, 2010.

Opinion

REARDON, J.

Over the course of six and a half years, appellant Edward Litke's bookkeeper embezzled close to $380,000 by forging makers' signatures on checks drawn against various accounts that Litke maintained at City National Bank. The trial court entered summary judgment against Litke on his action against the bank, correctly concluding he could not overcome multiple bars to the suit erected by the California Uniform Commercial Code, the applicable statute of limitations and the contract between Litke and CNB. Accordingly, we affirm the judgment.

I. BACKGROUND

A. The Forgeries

Litke operated sole proprietorships

***

Litke's bookkeeper at the time was Dahn Nguyen. He received the monthly bank statements for the accounts, maintained and reconciled the check register and maintained the accounts receivable. Nguyen forged makers' signatures on approximately 180 checks.... All totaled, Nguyen embezzled approximately $377,785.... Litke confirmed that the check[s] had been forged by Nguyen and so notified CNB. Thereafter, Litke discovered many more forged checks.

At each month's end, CNB would prepare bank statements on Litke's accounts. Early the next month it would mail the statements to Litke along with all cancelled checks paid for that reporting period. The first seven forged checks, totaling $21,063.46, were reflected on the June 30, 2000 bank statements which CNB sent to Litke in early July 2000.

***

B. The Accounts

Each of Litke's accounts was subject to an account agreement (hereafter, the signature card), which identified the authorized signators.

***

(Disclosures).

The Disclosures related the account holder's duty to examine each bank statement and promptly notify the bank of any unauthorized or forged transactions within 30 days of receipt.

***

Moreover, the bank might not be responsible for subsequent forgeries by the same wrongdoer if notice was not given within the 30 days. The Disclosures also stated that the customer was obligated to sue CNB on a forged or unauthorized item within one year of when CNB made the statement available to the customer.

***

Finally, the Disclosures reminded the customer of the risks of check fraud, especially internal fraud, and the importance of dividing financial responsibilities to minimize that risk.

C. Litigation

***

Opposing the motion for summary judgment, Litke maintained that CNB was equitably estopped from asserting the statute of limitations and that triable issues of material fact existed as to whether the bank was negligent. Litke submitted his own declaration, attesting that he was 83 years old and never read, in their entirety, CNB's "lengthy 'boilerplate' agreements, which are written in a small font size of approximately seven point."

In May 2007, CNB notified Litke that it would not honor his request for reimbursement for the forgeries because "the earliest forgeries were paid more than one year ago and your claim on the later forgeries is barred by your failure to timely discover the earliest forgeries. ..."

The trial court concluded that at law and under contract, Litke's suit was time-barred, his estoppel argument failed and CNB was not negligent in handling his accounts.

***

A. Governing Law

***

The customer must (1) "exercise reasonable promptness in examining the statement" or returned items to ascertain any unauthorized signature or alteration; and (2) promptly notify the bank of the pertinent facts if he or she reasonably should have discovered the unauthorized payment. (Id., subd. (c).)

***

[UCC] Section 4406 also establishes a rule of absolute preclusion of claims if the customer does not discover and report the forgery or alteration within one year of receiving the statement or items, regardless of either party's care or lack of care. (Id., subd. (f).)

***

B. Litke is Precluded or Time-barred from Pursuing his Claims

***

C. No Triable Issue of Fact as to CNB's Negligence

***

The concept of "ordinary care" in section 4406, subdivisions (d) and (e) "is a 'professional negligence' standard of care which looks at the procedures utilized in the banking industry rather than what a 'reasonable person' might have done under the circumstances." [Citation Omitted.]

***

Further, CNB's fraud detection filters "were equal to or more stringent than those of other peer banks in California." In fact, CNB reviewed a larger percentage of checks than other peer banks.

III. DISPOSITION

The judgment is affirmed.

The Check Collection Process

The **Federal Reserve System (Federal Reserve)** is "the central bank that sets credit and monetary policy by fixing the reserves to be maintained by depository institutions, determining the discount rate charged by Federal Reserve Banks, and regulating the amount of credit that may be extended on any security" (Garner 2005, 516). Banks involved in the collection process are designated according to function. A bank may be payor bank, collecting bank, depositary bank, or an intermediary bank, and sometimes a bank may be a combination of the foregoing (see below for definitions of the foregoing terms).

The Federal Reserve also acts as a national clearing house for the exchange of checks among banks. It was established by the Federal Reserve Act of 1913 (See 12 U.S.C. § 221). The Federal Reserve is "comprise[d] of 12 central banks supervised by a Board of Governors whose members [seven] are appointed by the president [14 year terms] and confirmed by the Senate" (Garner 2005, 516).

The check collection process is a main function within the purview of the Federal Reserve. It commences when a bank customer (drawer) issues a check to a person or entity (payee) in payment for a product or service. The check is a third-party draft that orders the drawer's bank (drawee) to transfer money from the drawer's account to the payee's bank for collection.

For example, assume Mary, an executive in a Los Angeles fast food chain, orders 7,000 pounds of beef from Prime Cut Meats ("Prime Cut"), a distributor of Angus beef in Kansas City, Kansas, for $1.00/lb. ($7,000). Once the order is placed, Prime Cut sends Mary the beef with an invoice describing the transaction and specifying the purchase price. Upon receipt of the beef and the invoice, Mary writes a check on her bank (payor bank) for the $7,000, payable to Prime Cut. A **payor bank** is the drawee of a draft (U.C.C. § 4-105 (3)).

Prime Cut deposits the check into its local bank (depositary bank). A **depositary bank** is the first bank to which an item is transferred for collection (U.C.C. § 4-105 (2)). The local bank is also concurrently a collecting bank. A **collecting bank** is any bank, other than a payor bank, that is involved in the collection process (U.C.C. § 4-105 (5)). The depositary bank initiates transfer of the check through the Federal Reserve System to the payor bank in Los Angeles. The collection process includes other banks, as discussed below. Mary is the drawer, her bank is the drawee, and Prime Cut is the payee (see Chapter 13, discussion of checks).

Prime Cut's bank forwards the check to the Kansas City Federal Reserve Bank. It is the first bank in the collection process, referred to as an "intermediary bank." An **intermediary bank** is any bank, other than the depositary bank or payor bank, designated to assist in the collection process (U.C.C. § 4-105 (4)). An intermediary bank is also a collecting bank since it is not a payor bank (U.C.C. § 4-105 (5)).

The Kansas City Federal Reserve Bank forwards the check to another intermediary bank in the process. The check will likely head from Kansas City to Chicago where the Federal Reserve Bank will process the check and forward it to another intermediary bank, probably in Denver. It will be further processed and forwarded to the Federal Reserve Bank in Los Angeles. The Los Angeles Federal Reserve Bank will forward the check to Mary's bank (payor bank) where the $7,000 amount will be debited to Mary's account.

The amount will also be electronically transferred by Mary's local bank to Prime Cut's local bank in Kansas City for deposit. Once Prime Cut's bank receives that electronic payment, it credits Prime Cut's account for the $7,000.

Note: The reason for transfers to several intermediary banks rather than directly from Kansas City to Los Angeles is predicated on a complex system for efficient check transfers (e.g., varying time of day volume of check transfers). A discussion of this subject is not relevant nor necessary for this course.

Electronic Check Presentment

The Check Clearing in the 21st Century Act ("Check 21"), enacted on October 28, 2004, is designed to supplant the historically cumbersome manually processed check system. Electronic processing was available before Check 21, but it initially was not embraced by the banking industry. Check 21 was designed to provide an impetus for conversion to the electronic system. As enacted, Check 21 requirements were not mandatory for banks. Congress recognized, among other things, the expense and disruption caused by conversion from the manual systems would fall hard on small local banks.

In recognition of the benefits from electronic processing of checks, large national banks took the lead and converted to Check 21. For example, manual check processing can take days, whereas electronic processing occurs within a day or less. Also, paper checks had to be transported from bank to bank in order to be cleared for proper crediting/debiting and ultimately stored somewhere. The foregoing is time consuming and very costly relative to electronic processing. Today, most banks have converted to the electronic system, and the era of manual check processing is now largely extinct.

With electronic processing, the pertinent bank information is encoded into a database for computer transfer. The physical check is usually stored at a depositary bank's location, and an image or description of the check is presented for payment (U.C.C. § 4-110 (a)). Check 21 permits a bank to create a paper reproduction of the original check, called a "substitute check," that contains the same information as the original check. The substitute check is proof of payment and thereby precludes the need for transfer of the original. The original may be stored locally and electronically retrieved when necessary, or the original may be destroyed and the data digitally stored. The savings in time, efficiency, and cost is obvious.

Another benefit of electronic processing is the reduction of time a bank may hold a check. Because of the inherent delay handling paper checks, referred to as "float time," parties were able to exploit the delay. For example, banks could make use of the value of the check for loan purposes during the processing time, which could be up to a week or more depending on the amount of the check.

The amount of free monetary use may be small for most checks, but collectively, the amount can be considerable. Depending on the volume of checks processed, for some banks it can be in the thousands or millions of dollars. Also, many savvy bank customers write checks with insufficient funds available because of the float time. They then make deposits prior to the submission date or seek a resubmittal of a check rejected for nonsufficient funds and ensure requisite funds are available the second time around. Check 21 and electronic processing minimizes the advantage derived from float time for both parties.

Summary

Banking is essential for both consumers and businesses (collectively, "customers"). Banking is a business that accepts deposits from customers and agrees to pay to their order. It is an essential tool for both business and consumers. The banking relationship creates duties for both the bank and the customer. The customer agrees to deposit a certain amount of money, to exercise due care in the maintenance of its account in order to prevent forgery, and to report any unusual activity within a reasonable time. The bank must honor all checks, pay checks upon presentation, and exercise due care with regard to its responsibilities. Failure by either a bank or its customers could make each responsible for damages that result, such as actual damages and consequential damages.

The Uniform Commercial Code regulates the banking industry through Article 3 and Article 4. Article 3 governs the form and content of negotiable instruments, their transfer, and the rights and responsibilities of the parties to checks. Article 4 provides the rules for the check collection process and for the content of the agreements between a bank and its customers. Since both Article 3 and Article 4 concern checks, on occasion a conflict may arise. If so, the conflict usually will be decided according to Article 4. The Board of Governors of the Federal Reserve System provides some oversight of Article 4.

Checks are a convenient and relatively safe substitute for cash. They are three-party instruments: the person who issues a check (drawer), the bank that pays the check when presented (drawee), and the person who is to be paid (payee). Several special types of checks have been developed over the years. They are cashier's checks and certified checks. They both are used in order to ensure that a person is not issuing a check with insufficient funds. A traveler's check is used by persons to pay for vacation expenses, hotel bills, dining expenses, airline tickets, and car rentals.

Checks can be negotiated by parties and transferred intrabank or interbank. If the checks are interbank, the check collection process does not require the Federal Reserve System to ensure proper collection. The Federal Reserve System is comprised of 12 Federal Reserve Banks across the country. The system is comprised of depositary banks, collection banks, intermediary banks, and payor banks.

Review Questions

True/False

Directions: Look at each statement below. Based on what you learned in this chapter, decide if the statement is true or false.

1. A bank is a government agency created to ensure checks are honored.
2. Article 3 of the Uniform Commercial Code regulates the intermediary banks.
3. Check 21 was created to convert paper checks to digital checks.
4. In the check collection process, the payor bank becomes the final collection bank in system.
5. Article 4 of the U.C.C. concerns the agreements between a customer and the bank.
6. There is a legal presumption in favor of U.C.C. Article 3 when there is a conflict with Article 4.
7. A check is a special draft that may be used as a substitute for cash and a credit device.
8. A depositary bank is the first bank in the collection process.
9. A certified check is purchased by a depositor in order to guarantee payment to a payee.

10. A cashier's check must be paid in full before a bank will stamp "ACCEPTED" on the face of the check.
11. A bank creates a cashier's checking account from which it pays all holders of a cashier's check upon presentment.
12. Before a bank will refund the amount of a lost or stolen check, the holder of the check must file a claim describing the check with reasonable certainty before the check is cashed.
13. A bank is required to pay checks to the order of its customer and to collect on the checks deposited by the customer.
14. A bank will only be liable for consequential damages if it dishonors a customer check.
15. A bank may pay an overdraft check and charge the customer with an overdraft fee without notice to the customer.

Multiple Choice

Directions: Use what you learned in this chapter to choose the best response to each of the prompts below.

1. All the following are true with regard to the Federal Reserve System, except:
   a. It includes depositary banks.
   b. It includes collection banks.
   c. It includes payor banks.
   d. It does not include intermediary banks.

2. All the following are true, except:
   a. Checks are a relatively safe substitute for cash.
   b. The Federal Reserve System contains 15 banks.
   c. In the collection process a bank can be both a collecting bank and an intermediary bank.
   d. If checks are issued interbank, the Federal Reserve collection process is not invoked.

3. All the following are true, except:
   a. The U.C.C. regulates banking though Article 3 and Article 4.
   b. Article 3 will concern negotiable instrument formation.
   c. Article 4 regulates banking relationships with customers.
   d. Article 3 will prevail if there is a conflict with Article 4.

4. All the following are true, except:
   a. Banks accept deposits and agree to pay to the order of its customers.
   b. The banking relationship creates duties for both the bank and its customers.
   c. If there is a dispute between the bank and its customer, the Federal Reserve Board will resolve it.
   d. Banks must honor all checks issued by its customers if their account contains sufficient deposits.

5. All the following are true with regard to banks' hold and float times, except:
   a. Electronic checking expedites payment of checks.
   b. Float times are no longer a negative issue.
   c. The Check 21 Act creates substitute digital checks.
   d. A substitute check must be confirmed with the original upon request.

6. All the following are true regarding Check 21, except:
   a. It replaces the historical paper processing system.
   b. Its speed reduces check processing from one week to one day.
   c. It requires storage of the paper checks.
   d. Congress enacted it as a voluntary measure for banks to implement.
7. All the following are true with regard to the Federal Reserve collection system, except:
   a. It commences with a check from the purchaser of a product to the vendor.
   b. The first bank to receive a check is the depositary bank.
   c. The depositary bank may also be an intermediary bank.
   d. A bank can be a collecting bank as well as an intermediary bank.
8. All the following are true of the Federal Reserve Bank, except:
   a. It is a clearing house for the exchange of checks among member banks.
   b. It was established by the Federal Reserve Act of 1913.
   c. It is comprised of seven members.
   d. The president appoints members with approval by both houses of Congress.
9. All the following are true with regard to a bank's duty, except:
   a. It must verify signatures when a check is presented for payment.
   b. The bank may be liable for consequential damages if it breaches its duty.
   c. The bank must honor all checks properly presented for payment.
   d. Damage to a customer's reputation is not compensable for breach of a bank's duty.
10. All the following are true, except:
    a. Banks agree to pay their customers' checks upon presentment.
    b. Banks agree to collect the amounts of checks deposited.
    c. A customer may be liable to third parties for a wrongly ordered stop-order payment.
    d. Bank regulations prohibit oral stop orders.

Scenarios

1. David, a traveling salesman, goes to commercial bank that offers cashier's checks for a fee. He pays the full amount of the check plus the bank fee. He uses the check to pay for repairs to his automobile and lists the auto repair shop as payee. The repairs are made, but the policy of the repair shop is to release the vehicle only after the bank clears the check. The bank dishonors the check because it fails to verify the identity of the payee. The auto repair shop refuses to release the vehicle to David unless they are paid. What potential liability does the bank have for dishonoring the check? Explain your answer.
2. Cristina issued a stop-payment order on a check written to her home mortgage company. She was informed the check was never received. She called her bank immediately upon notice by her mortgage company and she also sent it a written notice. The check was cashed at a pawn shop and it was endorsed "Cristina." What recourse does Cristina have, if any? Explain your answer.

Decisional Review

1. An American bank, on behalf of an American construction company, entered into a letter of credit with a Saudi bank and a foreign nation. It required the bank to guarantee progress payments for construction work in Saudi Arabia. The American bank claims it only guaranteed payments according to a "clean letter of credit," which does not provide control over the subject matter of the contract. A "documentary letter of credit" provides assurances on the subject matter of the contract and creates a fiduciary relationship in addition to honoring draws on the letter of credit. A dispute arose between the American construction company and the government of Saudi Arabia. The American construction company sued the American bank for breach of a fiduciary duty for not defending them. What should be the outcome of the lawsuit? See *McCormack v. Citibank*, 100 F. 3d 532 (8th Cir. 1956).
2. Appellant, Federal Reserve Board, appeals decision by Tenth Circuit granting summary judgment to appellees, several banks, challenging a board regulation and changing the definition of a bank. Appellees are nonbanks that do not provide commercial loans. Board's definition would include nonbanks under its regulatory authority. What will be the result? Explain your answer. See *Board of Governors of the Federal Reserve v. Dimension Financial Corp.*, 106 S. Ct. 681 (1985).

Chapter 15

International Business Considerations

Introduction

International business has become less novel and increasingly more important to the global economy. Technological advances with travel and communication is a key reason. International opportunities continue to increase, and global economies of the world have become more interdependent. International law is very different than national law because a global government, court system, and police force to legislate, interpret, and enforce laws is nonexistent. Accordingly, nations must cooperate voluntarily to create and abide by treaties, customs, and global norms, such as comity, traditions, and intergovernmental agreements.

This chapter explains how international business was created, has evolved, and how it currently operates. For example, four of the most popular international business models, export/import, licensing, franchising, and direct investment, are discussed and compared.

Chapter Objectives

Upon completion of this chapter, the student will understand:

- the sources of international law
- relevant U.S. constitutional and statutory law
- other international considerations, such as custom and comity
- the pros and cons of four popular business models
- important international business risks

Key Terms

Directions: Each of the terms below will be used in this chapter. Before reading, scan the chapter. The terms will appear in bold. Take a moment to see how the term is used so you can understand it in context. The terms are listed in the order in which they will appear in the chapter.

Treaty (p. 263)
Treaty power (p. 263)
Trade barrier (p. 263)
Tariff (p. 263)
Nontariff barrier (p. 263)
Quota (p. 263)
Executive agreement (p. 264)
Tariff and trade laws (p. 267)
Constitutional authority (p. 267)
Supremacy Clause (p. 267)
Preemption (p. 267)
Commerce Clause (p. 268)
Custom (p. 269)
Comity (p. 269)
International treaties and other agreements (p. 269)

Export/Import (p. 270)	Direct investment (p. 271)	Confiscation (p. 271)
Licensing (p. 270)	Nationalization (p. 271)	Financial risk (p. 272)
Franchising (p. 271)	Expropriation (p. 271)	Political risk (p. 272)

Considerations—Generally

The business world has expanded, among other reasons, due to many significant technological advances in travel and communications. In ancient times, sail boats permitted explorers to find new continents, civilizations, cultures, food, customs, languages, and philosophies. With each discovery humanity learned, adapted, and improved, and life evolved faster with the more sophisticated methods of travel and communication (for more on this, read *Future Shock* by Alvin Toffler).

Revolutionary technological innovations led to faster modes of travel, such as horses, trains, cars, aircraft, and now spacecraft. The world is experiencing an information revolution with communications constantly becoming faster and more accurate. Devices such as telephones, computers, smart phones, televisions, and satellites and facsimile machinery make global communications instantaneous.

The confluence of increased travel speed and improved communications makes globalization not only possible but also a mandatory global enterprise. It permits access to new sources of raw materials, labor pools, and markets for products and services. Those who fail to take advantage of this new dynamic will miss tremendous opportunities.

The hospitality industry is replete with international opportunities. Hotels, restaurants, entertainment venues, purveyors of culinary professions, and vendors of culinary equipment and supplies are flourishing across the globe. Sharing food and libations from various countries and different cultures has become a popular pastime for consumers and has created prosperity for entrepreneurs.

This chapter discusses several popular approaches to international investment, with its abundant opportunities and its significant political, financial, economic, and cultural risks. It also focuses on business models for international investment, such as export/import, licensing, franchising, and direct investment.

Sources of International Law

A good starting point for discussion is to review the source of law for international business. In the United States, the primary source of international law is the United States Constitution. As you may recall from Chapter 1, Article I of the Constitution enumerates powers of the federal government. It expressly provides Congress with authority over international business, such as the right to regulate commerce with foreign nations (U.S. Const. art. I, § 8, cl. 3). The Constitution may be found in Appendix A. Pursuant to the Constitution, Congress has enacted many statutes affecting international business law.

Generally, international business law is enforced in a country's national courts rather than in international courts. International courts, such as the International Court of Justice, located at The Hague, Netherlands, are voluntary forums, and disputes are limited to jurisdiction between nations, not individuals or business entities.

The executive branch of government negotiates international treaties with advice and consent of Congress (U.S. Const., art. II, § 2). The president has power to appoint and supervise ambassadors and to supervise all federal executive agencies that impact foreign affairs, such as the State Department, CIA, FBI, Commerce Department, and Treasury Department.

The president's role as commander in chief (U.S. Const., art. II, § 2, cl. 1) provides substantial power to the executive branch over international business. Also, Congress has delegated additional powers to the president for emergency purposes and protection of national security. For example, the president may order a ban on doing business with rogue countries, such as Iran and North Korea, in the interests of national security. The president may also impose tariffs, sanctions, and limited warfare when necessary to protect the interests of the United States.

A **treaty** is "an agreement formally signed, ratified, or adhered to between two nations or sovereigns; an international agreement concluded between two or more [foreign] states in written form and governed by international law" (Garner 2005, 1257.) A treaty must also be approved by the governmental entity or person in control of the signatory nation. In the United States, it is Congress. In Great Britain, it is the Parliament, and in China and Russia, it is the president.

The power to enter into international treaties and other agreements is the primary vehicle for exercising the government's authority over international business. This is referred to as **treaty power**, and it can be an agreement or contract between two or more nations or between a nation and an international organization.

A treaty usually affects a few nations and is limited to one major issue. For example, the North American Free Trade Agreement (NAFTA) was an agreement entered into by the United States, Mexico, and Canada to promote trade among the signatories. Certain **trade barriers**, such as **tariffs**, **nontariff barriers**, and **quotas**, were removed to encourage trade across common borders.

An international convention is a multilateral treaty and is defined as "an agreement or compact, esp. one among nations; a multilateral treaty" (Garner 2005, 281). It is an agreement among multiple nations and is broader than a treaty because it concerns global issues as well as regional issues. For example, The Montreal Convention, entered into by 142 nations, concerns the rights and remedies for persons injured or whose property is damaged in international air travel. It also concerns liability and limitations of liability for the foregoing (for purposes of this text, treaties and conventions will be collectively referred to as treaties).

As referenced above, in the United States, treaties are negotiated by the executive branch of government and require a two-thirds vote of approval by the Senate (U.S. Const., art. II, cl. 2). A treaty is considered the Supreme Law of the Land (U.S. Const., art. VI, § 1, cl. 2), and as such, states are bound to its terms. Since treaty power is enumerated in the U.S. Constitution, it is the sole power of the federal government. States are not able to enter into a treaty with a foreign nation.

For example, a state is bound by the requirements of NAFTA. A border state may not enter into an agreement with either Mexico or Canada regarding cross-border trade. Similarly, a state may not impose import fees, taxes, or duties on goods transported over international borders.

International treaties bind signatories to behave in a manner agreed to in the treaties. However, it is not easy to enforce treaties, because an international police or prosecutorial agency does not exist. Accordingly, compliance with treaties is largely voluntary, based upon the terms and conditions of the treaty and pressure from other signatories to do so.

For example, international treaties regarding intellectual property exist that require signatories to follow its requirements, such as honoring another country's trademark law. But if a signatory violates the treaty, no express treaty sanctions are available for other signatories to impose.

Consider the serious problem the United States has with exploitation of U.S. trademarks. China, as well as several other nations, permits its local manufacturers to use U.S. trademarks with impunity, costing American business billions of dollars annually.

If an American company files suit in a U.S. court and obtains an injunction against a Chinese company for such use, the injunction is meaningless unless the Chinese courts enforce it. If Chinese courts do not enforce the injunction, the only way to obtain compliance is diplomacy or sanctions, such as tariffs and quotas. We certainly are not going to declare war with them. To date, the United States has not been very successful obtaining cooperation enforcing U.S. intellectual property rights from the Chinese government. Russia, Ukraine, Indonesia, India, and Venezuela are some of the other countries that do not effectively enforce intellectual property rights.

An **executive agreement** is "an international agreement entered into by the President, without approval by the Senate, and usu. involving routine diplomatic or military matters" (Garner 2005, 485). It is similar to an executive order, which is "an order issued [without consent of the Senate] by or on behalf of the President, usu. intended to direct or instruct the actions of executive agencies or government officials, or to set policies for the executive branch to follow" (Garner 2005, 485–486).

It can be a contract executed by the United States and a foreign country or foreign agency. The power to enter into executive agreements is not expressed in the U.S. Constitution; rather, it is deemed implied as an inherent power of the president (U.S. Const., art. II, § 1, cl. 1 and § 3). Executive agreements (like executive orders) are widely used by all presidents. They are quicker to implement and often have the tacit approval of Congress, which enhances their credibility. The following case concerning the United States return of coronation regalia to Hungary is a good example.

UNITED STATES DISTRICT COURT, D. KANSAS.

Robert DOLE, Plaintiff,
v.
Jimmy CARTER, President of the United States of America, Defendant.
Civ. A. No. 77-2310.
Dec. 30, 1977.

United States Senator sued the President to enjoin him from returning the Hungarian coronation regalia to the People's Republic of Hungary. On the Senator's motion for a preliminary injunction, the District Court, O'Connor, J., held that: (1) there was no "tacit agreement" in the 1947 Paris Peace Treaty that the United States would retain custody of the coronation regalia until such time as Soviet troops were withdrawn from Hungary, and (2) the agreement to return the coronation regalia was not a treaty requiring ratification by the Senate.

***

O'CONNOR, District Judge.

***

The salient facts in this case, briefly summarized, are as follows: In approximately 1000 A.D., Pope Sylvester II donated to Stephen, then Duke of Hungary, a crown establishing Stephen as the first King of Hungary and declaring Hungary a state in the international system of Europe.

The Holy Crown apparently remained in Hungarian custody from 1000 A.D. until July 25, 1945, shortly after the surrender of all German forces in Europe at the conclusion of World War II.

***

At that time the Hungarian Commander of the Crown Guards entrusted to the United States for safekeeping the Holy Crown and other coronation regalia including the Coronation Robe, Orb, Sceptre and Sword. To date, the United States has secured said regalia in an undisclosed location with a view to its eventual return to the people of Hungary.

*On December 15, **1977**, the United States and Hungarian governments jointly announced that the President of the United States had determined it "appropriate and fitting" that the Hungarian coronation regalia be returned to the people of Hungary at ceremonies on January 6 and 7, 1978, and that it be thereafter placed on permanent public display in an appropriate historical location in Budapest for "the population of the country,*

***

Announcement of the proposed return of the Holy Crown generated not inconsiderable public controversy in various sectors, including groups of Hungarian nationals in the United States and elsewhere, members of the Roman Catholic Church, and certain members of the United States Senate and House of Representatives.

***

[That action] constitutes a violation of Article II, Section 2, of the Constitution of the United States. That constitutional provision, in relevant part, confers upon the President the power, "by and with the Advice and Consent of the Senate, to make Treaties, provided two thirds of the Senators present concur."

***

In determining whether the plaintiff here has established a reasonable probability of success on the merits of his claim, [The court must decide]

***

(2) whether the President's agreement to return the Hungarian coronation regalia constitutes a treaty obligation that must be ratified by the Senate.

***

It is well established, and even plaintiff admits, that the United States frequently enters into international agreements other than treaties. Indeed, as of January 1, 1972, the United States was a party to 5,306 international agreements, only 947 of which were treaties and 4,359 of which were international agreements other than treaties. [Citations omitted.]

***

[Implied powers of the President includes] (3) executive agreements executed pursuant to the President's own constitutional authority (hereinafter referred to as "executive agreements"). [Citations omitted.] Defendant contends that his agreement to return the coronation regalia to Hungary falls into the latter category, and the court agrees.

Section 121 of the Restatement (Second) of the Foreign Relations Law of the United States reads as follows:

"Scope of Executive Agreement Pursuant to President's Constitutional Authority.

An international agreement made by the United States as an executive agreement without reference to a treaty or act of Congress may, subject to the limitations indicated in s 117, deal with any matter that under the Constitution falls within the independent powers of the President."

***

The Supreme Court has long ago recognized that the President has the "power to make such international agreements as do not constitute treaties in the constitutional sense."

***

"(A)n international compact, as this was, is not always a treaty which requires the participation of the Senate. There are many such compacts, of which a protocol, a modus vivendi, a postal convention, and agreements like that now under consideration are illustrations." [Citations omitted.]

***

The United States' continued dominion over the Hungarian coronation regalia, in which this country claims no property interest, can reasonably be viewed as a serious "obstacle" which may impede the "rehabilitation of relations" between the United States and Hungary. The decision to remove such an obstacle appears to be well within the traditional powers of the President.

***

The President's agreement here involves no substantial ongoing commitment on the part of the United States, exposes the United States to no appreciable discernible risks, and contemplates American action of an extremely limited duration in time.

***

Finally, the agreement here encompasses no substantial reciprocal commitments by the Hungarian government. As a matter of law, the court is therefore persuaded that the President's agreement to return the Hungarian coronation regalia is not a commitment requiring the advice and consent of the Senate under Article II, Section 2, of the Constitution.

Congress enacted **tariff and trade laws** which provide the executive branch with authority to impose and collect tariffs. A tariff is "a schedule or system of duties imposed by a government on imported or exported goods" (Garner 2005, 1219). It is a form of tax adopted by congress for imports into the United States and can be an effective tool for reigning in a country that violates a treaty.

Trade laws adopted by Congress, such as the Omnibus Trade and Competitiveness Act of 1988, provide the president with authority to negotiate trade agreements for international business. For example, it provided President Clinton with the power to enter into NAFTA, a free trade agreement with Canada and Mexico. NAFTA was recently renegotiated in 2020 (see the United States, Canada, Mexico Trade Agreement July 1, 2020).

Constitutional authority refers to the power the U.S. Constitution delegated to the federal government to make treaties binding on the states (U.S. Const., Supremacy Clause, art. VI, § 2, cl. 3) as well as the power to regulate interstate commerce (U.S. Const., art. 1, § 8, cl. 3). For example, during the years of South Africa's apartheid policies, many states passed laws prohibiting businesses within their jurisdiction from doing business with South Africa. Enforcement of such state laws was deemed preempted by the U.S. Constitution under the **Supremacy Clause**. In constitutional law, **preemption** is "the principle (derived from the Supremacy clause) that a [valid] federal law can supersede or supplant any inconsistent state law or regulation. Also termed … federal preemption" (Garner 2005, 987).

Preemption is the legal doctrine used by the courts to implement the Supremacy Clause. In essence, the courts evaluate a state law alleged to conflict with a valid federal law. If courts conclude a conflict exists and the matter is a proper federal question, the state law will be deemed preempted. If the courts conclude the state law does not conflict or if the matter is a proper exercise of states' rights under the Tenth Amendment, there will be no preemption (see Chapter 1, "States' Rights").

In the above example, federal preemption does not mean the U.S. government approves of apartheid. It means the power over foreign trade must be made with one voice: that of the federal government. Otherwise, each of the 50 states could set their own international business laws, which would create havoc for the United States and its international business interests.

Under the **Commerce Clause**, the Constitution places all power over interstate commerce in the federal government (U.S. Const., art. 1, § 8, cl. 3). Therefore, a state government cannot enact a law that imposes an unreasonable burden on foreign trade. For example, 12 states have passed a law that prohibits the intrastate sale and use of shark fins (e.g., California adopted one in 2013). A common practice of many fisherman is to capture sharks, hack off their fins, and throw the live carcass back into the ocean.

Shark fins have been used by China and other Asian countries for inclusion in shark fin soup, a traditional delicacy. Proponents of shark fin soup assert it is a cultural heritage and allege the law is discriminatory. Opponents allege it is inhumane to cut off shark fins and throw the live shark back into the water to helplessly perish; plus, they assert the practice is driving sharks into extinction.

A related legal issue concerns whether Asian restaurants in California can legally import shark fins to be used in their traditional soup. Does the California statute outlaw such importation, and if so, does the law place an unconstitutional burden on foreign trade? If a court of competent jurisdiction decides such a law is an unreasonable burden on foreign commerce, the law will be unenforceable and preempted by the U.S. Constitution.

Similar issues arise with taxation of foreign property by more than one country. For example, if a Japanese international hotel chain decides to open hotels in several U.S. states through corporate subsidiaries, can the several states impose an income tax on the hotel proceeds? The outcome of such a tax will vary by the statutory law of the state.

For example, California passed an ad valorem tax on Japanese cargo containers docked in California ports for refueling. The cargo containers were used exclusively for transporting goods in international commerce. Japan Line, Ltd., the owner of Japanese cargo containers, contended the California tax was an unconstitutional double taxation because Japan initially taxed it and now the United States also imposed a tax. The U.S. Supreme Court agreed with Japan Line, Ltd. and held the California tax imposed an unreasonable burden on foreign trade (*Japan Line, Ltd. v. County of Los Angeles*, 441 U.S. 434 (1979)).

The importation of foreign food products, such as meat, fish, chicken, or grain, would draw the same scrutiny if states passed laws to regulate the imports. For example, assume a distributor of restaurant supplies imports fish from China for sale to California restaurants. The imported fish are raised in screened pools underneath open chicken coups. The fish feed off the chicken droppings and grow relatively large in size and have a savory taste.

The practice is common in China and other Asian countries, and a public health hazard has not been detected regarding this practice. Can a U.S. state prohibit the importation of such fish under its police power, or can it impose a licensing and label regulation for users of this fish and thereby deter consumer consumption? If the state can prove the fish is a health hazard, such a regulation could be constitutional; otherwise, it would be struck down as an unreasonable burden on foreign trade (see *Tupman Thurlow, Co. v. Moss*, 252 F. Supp. 641 (M.D. Tenn. 1961)).

Other Considerations

International law concerns other than a country's organic laws, such as the United States' constitutional or statutory law discussed above. They include custom, comity, and treaties/other agreements.

In primitive times people congregated together in small bands or groups, commonly referred to as tribes. A leader was selected, and councils of elders were selected to oversee the group's society. In order to coexist, informal rules, called customs, were adopted to provide structure for people to live, hunt, and defend themselves. For example, tribes would claim a certain territory in which to live and hunt. Other tribes would do the same, and each would respect their unofficial boundaries. This reciprocal adherence to unofficial boundaries is a custom.

A **custom** is "a practice that by its common adoption and long, unvarying habit has come to have the force of law" (Garner 2005, 330). It is a rule of conduct accepted by groups through consistent practice. International custom law evolved from that concept. For example, the customs of merchants in the mid-18th century led to "law merchant," which was the customary practice of nations to respect each other's commercial cargo on the high seas.

An important custom that exists today is the right of commercial ships to be free from capture as prizes of war (The Paquete Habana, 175 U.S. 677 (1900)). In this case, two Spanish fishing vessels were seized off the Florida coast by the U.S. Navy during the Spanish-American War and sold as prizes of war. The U.S. Supreme Court held that maritime custom prohibited the U.S. Navy's action. The custom accepted by the international community dictated that commercial fishing vessels not used in warfare were free from the military right of confiscation during war.

Comity is an important common law doctrine adopted because an international police force did not exist to resolve disputes among nations. It is premised on the theory that the international community needs to develop a way to peacefully coexist. A nation may grant comity to another nation expecting reciprocity from that nation. Comity is "a practice among political entities (as nations, states, or courts of different jurisdictions), involving esp. mutual recognition of legislative, executive and judicial acts" (Garner 2005, 223).

International treaties and other agreements are largely self-enforced. Nations follow the terms and conditions of treaties for which they agreed because it is their interests to do so. For example, under the Warsaw Convention, 146 countries signed an agreement to follow certain rules for air travel, such as the rights of air travelers to seek compensation for lost luggage.

Without an international agency in existence to enforce the Warsaw Convention, each signatory voluntarily enforces it within its territorial boundaries. For example, if a French traveler loses luggage at Kennedy Airport in New York, the Federal Aviation Agency will assist and oversee enforcement of the Warsaw Convention. The federal government cooperates because it wants the French government to assist American citizens who lose baggage at Orly Airport in Paris.

Such reciprocal conduct is also a form of comity. As used in the above example, comity means that absent a formal agreement like a treaty, countries will still protect the rights of foreign citizens, with the expectation its citizens will receive the same treatment by other foreign countries.

The decision to engage in international trade must be carefully weighed to minimize loss and maximize profits. An important decision is the selection of the proper business model. Some of the most popular international business models are export/import, licensing, franchising, and direct investment. Each has its benefits and risks, which are discussed below.

Export/import is the process whereby international businesses contract with each other to ship goods to a foreign country to sell (i.e., export). Export is defined as "a product or service created in one country and transported to another" (Garner 2005, 493). The converse, import, is defined as "a product brought into a country from a foreign country where it originated" (Garner 2005, 627).

Assume a Chinese producer of handcrafted jade figurines wishes to export to the United States retail market. The producer will contact a Chinese export company to find a buyer in the United States who will import the handcrafted jade figurines to the United States. The importer will then sell the imported product in the domestic marketplace.

The advantages are several-fold. If you export to a foreign business, you do not need to sell in the foreign market, and as such, the risk relative to the other business models is less. The importer in the host country knows the market, the price to charge, the local customs, and the government regulations. The exporter merely ships to the importer, and they pay for the product.

A downside is that you once you ship your product to a foreign country, you may not be paid as promised. Your only reasonable recourse is for a breach of contract lawsuit against the importer. International litigation can be very expensive and time consuming. For example, you need two lawyers: your lawyer and one in the foreign country. You must pay for interpreter expenses. You must pay travel expenses for you, your lawyer, and any potential witnesses. But your loss is usually only the value of the shipment, which relative to the other business models is small. Therefore, the best business decision may be to accept the loss.

Conversely, if you are the importer, the potential damage is greater. As mentioned above, an importer usually controls and may withhold payment if the exporter breaches the contract. The downside is that an importer may be sent an inferior product that could cause a loss in business or reputation.

For example, assume a large restaurant chain contracts for chicken from a foreign supplier. The product received may not meet U.S. government standards and it may be prohibited entry and/or distribution in the United States. In addition, if the chicken is of inferior quality, consumers may not like the taste, or worse, it may be contaminated with bacteria, and the customers become ill. The fast-food chain's reputation will be damaged, and those that become ill could file costly lawsuits.

A license is "a permission, usu. revocable, to commit some act that would otherwise be unlawful" (Garner 2005, 765). Under the **licensing** model, a business in a foreign country (licensee) signs an agreement to use another business's intellectual property (licensor) who resides in a different country. The agreement is very flexible in terms of duration, geography, and extent of the intellectual property use.

For example, suppose you operate a successful chain of steakhouses in the United States. You marinate your meat a very special way (a trade secret) that provides a unique, savory taste. Rather than make a financial investment by selling prepared frozen steaks (which diminishes the flavor), you enter into a licensing agreement with a foreign business. You grant the right to use your trademark, trade name, and trade secret (collectively, intellectual property) for a fee, referred to as a royalty. You are the licensor, and the foreign business is a licensee. The benefit is low financial risk and a potentially high return for the use of your intellectual property.

The financial risk is low because the licensor makes a very low out-of-pocket investment since all the licensor does is share its intellectual property. The licensee uses intellectual property to market its product pursuant to the license. In addition to the revenue stream, the agreement enhances your business reputation in the global market.

The business risk is that the licensee may not timely pay the agreed-upon royalty or may not pay at all. Moreover, the licensee may sell your intellectual property to others in the host country or sell an inferior product that damages your reputation. Your remedy for the foregoing risks will be an expensive lawsuit in a foreign country, which will be costly and the outcome questionable if the forum is not fair.

The **franchising** model has become a very popular business form, both internationally and nationally. Under this business model, the franchisor (owner of the intellectual property) sells the right to use its intellectual property for a one-time franchise fee and annual profit sharing for the term of the franchise. The amount of the franchise fee depends on the success of the franchisor's business. For example, a McDonald's franchise fee can cost over one million dollars or more, depending on the location.

The purchaser of the franchise is called the franchisee. The parties enter into a contract, called the franchise agreement, where the terms and conditions of the business arrangement are negotiated. The franchisor provides the franchisee with the use of its intellectual property, such as its trademark, logo, and trade dress. In addition, for a negotiated share of annual profits, the franchisor provides training, advertising, business advice, and product supplies to the franchisee.

The franchisee hires employees, obtains the necessary business licenses, deals with the local marketplace and government regulations, and essentially runs the business in the host country. This model has many of the same benefits of a licensing arrangement, but it permits greater control by the franchisor over its product than the license business model. Violation of the franchise agreement is grounds for termination of the franchise.

Franchising also provides an excellent opportunity for local persons to own their own business with relatively little or no experience. Creation of business opportunities for local citizens is an important policy welcomed and often demanded by the host country. The downside for this model is the franchisee may fail to live up to the franchisor's standards, such as safety, cleanliness, product quality, and hiring practices. This can damage the reputation and good will of the franchisor. In a foreign country, enforcement becomes a problem because of the distance from home and the difference in foreign law and regulations.

Under **direct investment** business model, a company will go to a host country and open a foreign business. It will purchase land and buildings; hire local staff and employees; manage its own business operations, such as purchasing its own supplies; and handle its own banking and government relations. It is a full commitment to doing business in the host country and can be very profitable in the right country.

The business model may be an operational foreign subsidiary, joint venture, acquisition of an existing business, or build a new business from the ground up. But it is very vulnerable, especially in developing countries, because some governments may decide to nationalize, expropriate, or confiscate foreign investment. Venezuela, Iran, and Cuba are some examples of countries where this has occurred.

Nationalization occurs when the host country takes over an entire industry, such as oil and gas, generally with payment at market value. **Expropriation** occurs when the host country only takes certain assets, such as land or factories, at the market value. **Confiscation** occurs when the host country takes the assets without compensation. Because of the aforementioned potential losses, a foreign direct investment is the riskiest model for international business.

In addition to the possibility of losing your investment, a **financial risk** that must be considered is currency and exchange risk. This risk occurs when an international business buys, sells, or accepts a foreign currency. The exchange rates may vary greatly because of government action or the swings in market values of currency. The international businessperson must be knowledgeable or retain an expert in currency and exchange rates to minimize this potentially debilitating risk.

Political risk occurs because of the unpredictable government action of many countries in the international community. Civil unrest, a change in government leaders, changes in government policy, war, and terrorism are a few examples of activity that can cripple international business. When governments change, so might their trade policy, tax structure, regulation of foreign businesses, and currency valuation. The recent tariff wars between the United States and other countries is precisely the type of political risk that stifles international trade.

For example, if there is a change in government leadership of the host country or its leaders are feuding with the U.S. government, retaliatory host country action may hurt foreign business. The confiscation of U.S. business interests by Cuba, Iran, and Venezuela are stark reminders of such risks, which remain unresolved.

The international businessperson must win the confidence of local government officials. It is important to explain exactly what type of business is intended and to present a credible business plan to achieve business goals. A local lawyer, banker, and businessperson familiar with government rules and regulations is a must. The objective is to meet with government officials and convince them there will be compliance with local law. A foreign business must also demonstrate how the business will benefit the host country.

Assume an international hotelier wishes to open a resort in a foreign country. Not only must there be scrupulous adherence to the law but the hotelier must also show the benefits to the local community. For example, jobs will be created; taxes will be paid; tourism will improve; and ancillary local businesses, such as restaurants, clothing apparel, souvenir shops, and local travel industry, will benefit from the project. If the project is in a developing part of the country, support for schools, charities, job training, hospitals, and improvements to local infrastructure should be offered to demonstrate corporate responsibility.

The diagram below compares and contrasts the risks and benefits of the four most popular forms of international business (Figure 15.1 and Figure 15.2).

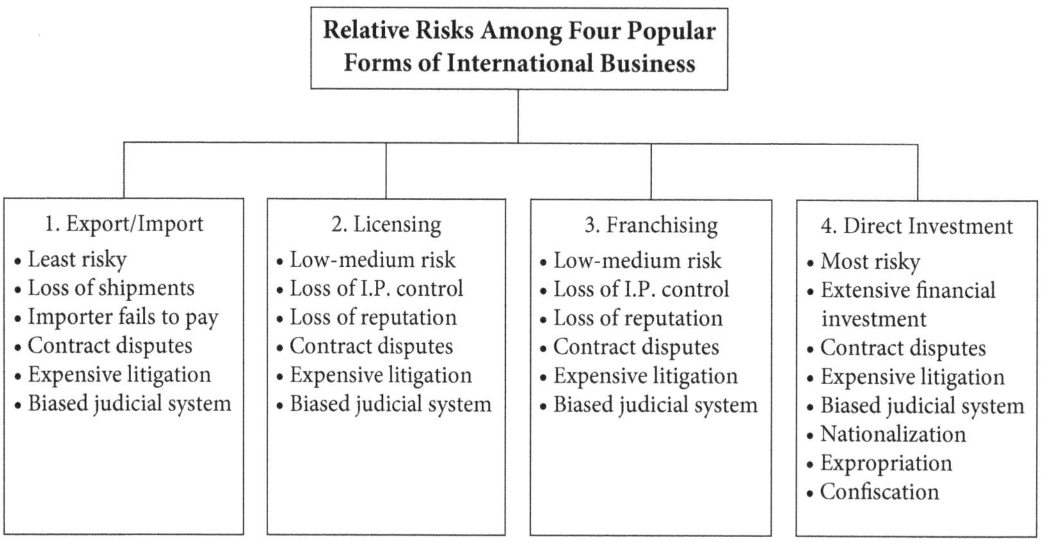

FIGURE 15.1 Relative Risks Among Four Popular Forms of International Busines

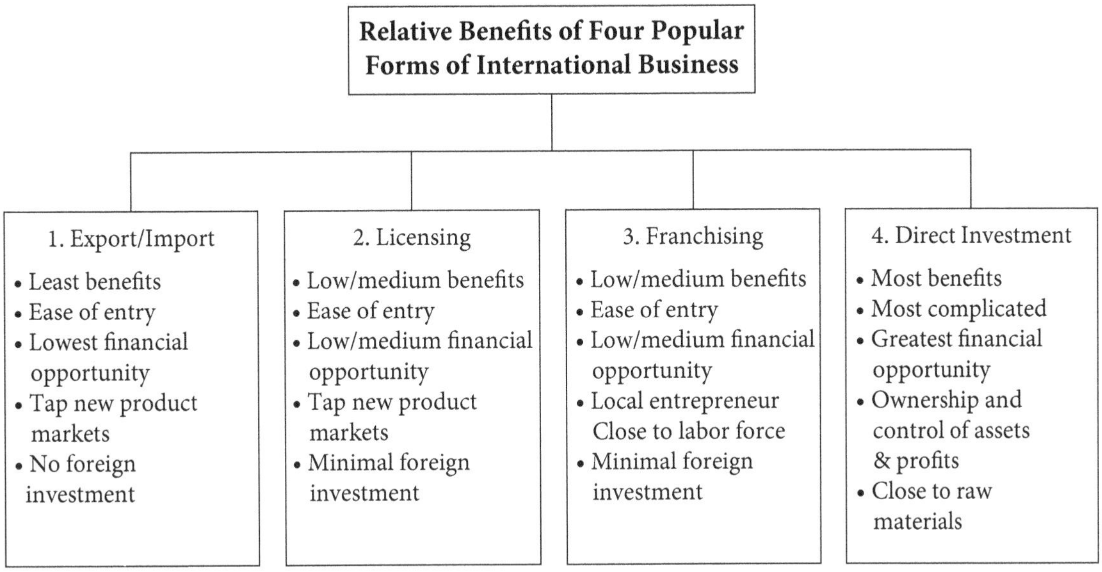

FIGURE 15.2 Relative Benefits of Four Popular Forms of International Business

Summary

International business has changed and continues to grow because of significant technological breakthroughs in travel and communications. It has become much easier for small business to participate. International business law is comprised of customs, treaties, and executive-branch trade agreements. Compliance with international business law is largely voluntary because of the absence of the three elements of a global government: a legislature body, a court system, and a police force.

International law is interpreted by a nation's court system rather than a global court system. National courts are not bound by the decisions of international tribunals, but they may use such decisions as persuasive arguments to guide them. Each nation will draw upon its own organic law, statutory law, and administrative law to resolve international disputes for which it has jurisdiction.

The chapter discusses four of the most popular forms of international business, which are export/import, licensing agreements, franchises, and direct investment. Each has merit and should fill the needs of practically any business interested in globalizing. The text compares and contrasts some of the more important risks and benefits of each.

Hospitality is a global industry. Hotels, restaurants, entertainment, and the culinary industry have mushroomed into profitable business enterprises. The future looks very good and should continue to do so.

Review Questions

True/False

Directions: Look at each statement below. Based on what you learned in this chapter, decide if the statement is true or false.

1. International business is a dynamic, expanding opportunity for just about any business enterprise.
2. Of the four most popular forms of international business, export/import is the riskiest because of the omnipresent threat of a tariff war.
3. International courts use the national organic and statutory law from the litigants' home countries to resolve disputes.
4. Interpol is the only international police enforcement agency, but it lacks sufficient personnel to be effective.
5. Comity is a typical doctrine used to enforce international customary law.
6. Hospitality is an industry very conducive to globalization.
7. Of the existing international business risks, the riskiest is political risk.
8. International business adds new product markets, sources of raw material, inexpensive labor, and enhancement of businesses' reputation.
9. Under U.S. law, a treaty may be negotiated, finalized, and signed by the president pursuant to constitutional implied power.
10. A convention must be approved by a two-thirds vote of the Senate.
11. Under the case *Dole v. Carter*, the U.S. Supreme Court concluded the agreement with the country of Hungary was a treaty and required Senate approval.
12. In *Dole v. Carter*, the court's rationale was that the significance of the Crown and Regalia was a significant consideration for its decision.
13. The form of direct investment may be a foreign branch, subsidiary, or joint venture.
14. Under the franchise model, a significant benefit is a local entrepreneur who knows the local market.
15. A congressional/executive agreement requires a two-thirds vote of approval, similar to a treaty.

Multiple Choice

Directions: Use what you learned in this chapter to choose the best response to each of the prompts below.

1. All the following are true of custom, except:
   a. It has been honored since primitive times.
   b. It is international law.
   c. A nation must formally adopt custom law.
   d. Law merchant is based upon custom.

2. All the following require a two-thirds vote by Congress, except:
   a. an ambassadorial appointment
   b. a convention
   c. comity
   d. a treaty

3. All the following are true of the *Dole v. Carter* case, except:
   a. It concerned the significance of the Crown Regalia.
   b. The senate approved the agreement.
   c. Hungary temporarily entrusted the jewel to the United States.
   d. The U.S. Supreme Court concluded the agreement was not a treaty.
4. The four most popular forms of international business models are all of the following, except:
   a. import/export
   b. franchise
   c. a subsidiary
   d. direct investment
5. All the following are true, except:
   a. Nationalization is the takeover of an entire industry.
   b. Expropriation occurs when certain assets of a business are taken.
   c. The market value is always paid according to international law.
   d. Confiscation occurs without compensation.
6. All the following are true with regard to international franchising, except:
   a. It is a negotiated agreement tailored to the parties' needs.
   b. It regards the use of someone's intellectual property.
   c. The use is only for an exclusive, one-time fee.
   d. The franchisee handles all local matters, such as labor and government regulations.
7. All the following are true of comity, except:
   a. It is international law.
   b. It is based upon reciprocity.
   c. It has developed over centuries of time.
   d. No legislation is required.
8. Under U.S. law regarding treaties, the president has all the following powers, except:
   a. to negotiate
   b. to sign
   c. to make final
   d. to enforce
9. Treaties are voluntary for all the following reasons, except:
   a. to assist with Interpol enforcement
   b. No legislative body exists.
   c. No international tribunals exist.
   d. No international jurisdiction exists.

10. All the following are true with regard to interpretation of international law, except:
    a. Every nation's domestic courts enforce international law.
    b. National courts are not bound by decisions of international tribunals.
    c. Each nation draws upon its own organic and statutory laws for enforcement.
    d. Decisions of international tribunals cannot be used as persuasive argument for outcomes in a nation's courts.

Scenarios

1. A successful event planning business is considering expansion into the international market. It has explored opportunities in the Philippines and seeks your advice for a proper business form. It is considering a license agreement with a local entity or a franchise model. Which would you recommend? Explain why.
2. An export/import company has experienced an explosion in foreign sales. It wishes to expand its market sales and is considering a franchise model and foreign direct investment. Which international business model would you recommend? Explain why.

Decisional Review

1. A fast food restaurant chain expanded into France and entered into a franchise agreement with a local entrepreneur. The franchise agreement contained the usual quality control terms to ensure the reputation of the franchisor remains untarnished. A quality control audit disclosed numerous health and safety violations. The franchisor sought termination of the franchise agreement. In its defense the franchisee argued the franchisor should have provided a French-speaking operations person to assist in translating the requirements for the local employees. What will be the result? See *Dayan v. McDonald's Corp.*, 466 N.E. 2d 958 (1984).
2. The inherent powers of a president of the United States are implied in the U.S. Constitution. It provides presidents broad power to do what is necessary to fulfill their constitutional duties. Assume a president decides to nationalize the steel industry during a contentious labor dispute in order to ensure a sufficient supply of steel for military purposes in an ongoing war. Is this permitted under a president's duties as commander in chief of the military? What will be the result? See *Youngstown Sheet & Tube v. Sawyer*, 343 U.S. 579 (1952).

Appendix A. The Constitution of the United States of America

We the People of the United States, in Order to form a more perfect Union, establish Justice, insure domestic Tranquility, provide for the common defence, promote the general Welfare, and secure the Blessings of Liberty to ourselves and our Posterity, do ordain and establish this Constitution for the United States of America.

Article I

Section 1

All legislative Powers herein granted shall be vested in a Congress of the United States, which shall consist of a Senate and House of Representatives.

Section 2

The House of Representatives shall be composed of Members chosen every second Year by the People of the several States, and the Electors in each State shall have the Qualifications requisite for Electors of the most numerous Branch of the State Legislature.

No Person shall be a Representative who shall not have attained to the Age of twenty five Years, and been seven Years a Citizen of the United States, and who shall not, when elected, be an Inhabitant of that State in which he shall be chosen.

Representatives and direct Taxes shall be apportioned among the several States which may be included within this Union, according to their respective Numbers, which shall be determined by adding to the whole Number of free Persons, including those bound to Service for a Term of Years, and excluding Indians not taxed, three fifths of all other Persons. (Note: changed by section 2 of the Fourteenth Amendment.) The actual Enumeration shall be made within three Years after the first Meeting of the Congress of the United States, and within every subsequent Term of ten Years, in such Manner as they shall by Law direct. The Number of Representatives shall not exceed one for every thirty Thousand, but each State shall have at Least one Representative; and until such enumeration shall be made, the State of New Hampshire shall be entitled to chuse three, Massachusetts eight, Rhode-Island and Providence Plantations one, Connecticut five, New-York six, New Jersey four, Pennsylvania eight, Delaware one, Maryland six, Virginia ten, North Carolina five, South Carolina five, and Georgia three.

When vacancies happen in the Representation from any State, the Executive Authority thereof shall issue Writs of Election to fill such Vacancies.

The House of Representatives shall chuse their Speaker and other Officers; and shall have the sole Power of Impeachment.

"The Constitution of the United States of America," 1789.

Section 3

The Senate of the United States shall be composed of two Senators from each State, chosen by the Legislature thereof, (Note: changed by the Seventeenth Amendment.) for six Years; and each Senator shall have one Vote.

Immediately after they shall be assembled in Consequence of the first Election, they shall be divided as equally as may be into three Classes. The Seats of the Senators of the first Class shall be vacated at the Expiration of the second Year, of the second Class at the Expiration of the fourth Year, and of the third Class at the Expiration of the sixth Year, so that one third may be chosen every second Year; and if Vacancies happen by Resignation, or otherwise, during the Recess of the Legislature of any State, the Executive thereof may make temporary Appointments until the next Meeting of the Legislature, which shall then fill such Vacancies. (Note: changed by the Seventeenth Amendment.)

No Person shall be a Senator who shall not have attained to the Age of thirty Years, and been nine Years a Citizen of the United States, and who shall not, when elected, be an Inhabitant of that State for which he shall be chosen.

The Vice President of the United States shall be President of the Senate, but shall have no Vote, unless they be equally divided.

The Senate shall chuse their other Officers, and also a President pro tempore, in the Absence of the Vice President, or when he shall exercise the Office of President of the United States.

The Senate shall have the sole Power to try all Impeachments. When sitting for that Purpose, they shall be on Oath or Affirmation. When the President of the United States is tried, the Chief Justice shall preside: And no Person shall be convicted without the Concurrence of two thirds of the Members present.

Judgment in Cases of Impeachment shall not extend further than to removal from Office, and disqualification to hold and enjoy any Office of honor, Trust or Profit under the United States: but the Party convicted shall nevertheless be liable and subject to Indictment, Trial, Judgment and Punishment, according to Law.

Section 4

The Times, Places and Manner of holding Elections for Senators and Representatives, shall be prescribed in each State by the Legislature thereof; but the Congress may at any time by Law make or alter such Regulations, except as to the Places of chusing Senators.

The Congress shall assemble at least once in every Year, and such Meeting shall be on the first Monday in December, (Note: changed by section 2 of the Twentieth Amendment.) unless they shall by Law appoint a different Day.

Section 5

Each House shall be the Judge of the Elections, Returns and Qualifications of its own Members, and a Majority of each shall constitute a Quorum to do Business; but a smaller Number may adjourn from day to day, and may be authorized to compel the Attendance of absent Members, in such Manner, and under such Penalties as each House may provide.

Each House may determine the Rules of its Proceedings, punish its Members for disorderly Behaviour, and, with the Concurrence of two thirds, expel a Member.

Each House shall keep a Journal of its Proceedings, and from time to time publish the same, excepting such Parts as may in their Judgment require Secrecy; and the Yeas and Nays of the Members of either House on any question shall, at the Desire of one fifth of those Present, be entered on the Journal.

Neither House, during the Session of Congress, shall, without the Consent of the other, adjourn for more than three days, nor to any other Place than that in which the two Houses shall be sitting.

Section 6

The Senators and Representatives shall receive a Compensation for their Services, to be ascertained by Law, and paid out of the Treasury of the United States. They shall in all Cases, except Treason, Felony and Breach of the Peace, be privileged from Arrest during their Attendance at the Session of their respective Houses, and in going to and returning from the same; and for any Speech or Debate in either House, they shall not be questioned in any other Place.

No Senator or Representative shall, during the Time for which he was elected, be appointed to any civil Office under the Authority of the United States, which shall have been created, or the Emoluments whereof shall have been encreased during such time; and no Person holding any Office under the United States, shall be a Member of either House during his Continuance in Office.

Section 7

All Bills for raising Revenue shall originate in the House of Representatives; but the Senate may propose or concur with Amendments as on other Bills.

Every Bill which shall have passed the House of Representatives and the Senate, shall, before it become a Law, be presented to the President of the United States; If he approve he shall sign it, but if not he shall return it, with his Objections to that House in which it shall have originated, who shall enter the Objections at large on their Journal, and proceed to reconsider it. If after such Reconsideration two thirds of that House shall agree to pass the Bill, it shall be sent, together with the Objections, to the other House, by which it shall likewise be reconsidered, and if approved by two thirds of that House, it shall become a Law. But in all such Cases the Votes of both Houses shall be determined by yeas and Nays, and the Names of the Persons voting for and against the Bill shall be entered on the Journal of each House respectively. If any Bill shall not be returned by the President within ten Days (Sundays excepted) after it shall have been presented to him, the Same shall be a Law, in like Manner as if he had signed it, unless the Congress by their Adjournment prevent its Return, in which Case it shall not be a Law.

Every Order, Resolution, or Vote to which the Concurrence of the Senate and House of Representatives may be necessary (except on a question of Adjournment) shall be presented to the President of the United States; and before the Same shall take Effect, shall be approved by him, or being disapproved by him, shall be repassed by two thirds of the Senate and House of Representatives, according to the Rules and Limitations prescribed in the Case of a Bill.

Section 8

The Congress shall have Power To lay and collect Taxes, Duties, Imposts and Excises, to pay the Debts and provide for the common Defence and general Welfare of the United States; but all Duties, Imposts and Excises shall be uniform throughout the United States;

To borrow Money on the credit of the United States;

To regulate Commerce with foreign Nations, and among the several States, and with the Indian Tribes;

To establish an uniform Rule of Naturalization, and uniform Laws on the subject of Bankruptcies throughout the United States; To coin Money, regulate the Value thereof, and of foreign Coin, and fix the Standard of Weights and Measures;

To provide for the Punishment of counterfeiting the Securities and current Coin of the United States; To establish Post Offices and post Roads;

To promote the Progress of Science and useful Arts, by securing for limited Times to Authors and Inventors the exclusive Right to their respective Writings and Discoveries;

To constitute Tribunals inferior to the supreme Court;

To define and punish Piracies and Felonies committed on the high Seas, and Offences against the Law of Nations; To declare War, grant Letters of Marque and Reprisal, and make Rules concerning Captures on Land and Water; To raise and support Armies, but no Appropriation of Money to that Use shall be for a longer Term than two Years; To provide and maintain a Navy;

To make Rules for the Government and Regulation of the land and naval Forces;

To provide for calling forth the Militia to execute the Laws of the Union, suppress Insurrections and repel Invasions;

To provide for organizing, arming, and disciplining, the Militia, and for governing such Part of them as may be employed in the Service of the United States, reserving to the States respectively, the Appointment of the Officers, and the Authority of training the Militia according to the discipline prescribed by Congress;

To exercise exclusive Legislation in all Cases whatsoever, over such District (not exceeding ten Miles square) as may, by Cession of particular States, and the Acceptance of Congress, become the Seat of the Government of the United States, and to exercise like Authority over all Places purchased by the Consent of the Legislature of the State in which the Same shall be, for the Erection of Forts, Magazines, Arsenals, dock-Yards, and other needful Buildings;—And

To make all Laws which shall be necessary and proper for carrying into Execution the foregoing Powers, and all other Powers vested by this Constitution in the Government of the United States, or in any Department or Officer thereof.

Section 9

The Migration or Importation of such Persons as any of the States now existing shall think proper to admit, shall not be prohibited by the Congress prior to the Year one thousand eight hundred and eight, but a Tax or duty may be imposed on such Importation, not exceeding ten dollars for each Person.

The Privilege of the Writ of Habeas Corpus shall not be suspended, unless when in Cases of Rebellion or Invasion the public Safety may require it.

No Bill of Attainder or ex post facto Law shall be passed.

No Capitation, or other direct, Tax shall be laid, unless in Proportion to the Census or Enumeration herein before directed to be taken. (Note: see the Sixteenth Amendment.)

No Tax or Duty shall be laid on Articles exported from any State.

No Preference shall be given by any Regulation of Commerce or Revenue to the Ports of one State over those of another: nor shall Vessels bound to, or from, one State, be obliged to enter, clear, or pay Duties in another.

No Money shall be drawn from the Treasury, but in Consequence of Appropriations made by Law; and a regular Statement and Account of the Receipts and Expenditures of all public Money shall be published from time to time.

No Title of Nobility shall be granted by the United States: And no Person holding any Office of Profit or Trust under them, shall, without the Consent of the Congress, accept of any present, Emolument, Office, or Title, of any kind whatever, from any King, Prince, or foreign State.

Section 10.

No State shall enter into any Treaty, Alliance, or Confederation; grant Letters of Marque and Reprisal; coin Money; emit Bills of Credit; make any Thing but gold and silver Coin a Tender in Payment of Debts; pass any Bill of Attainder, ex post facto Law, or Law impairing the Obligation of Contracts, or grant any Title of Nobility.

No State shall, without the Consent of the Congress, lay any Imposts or Duties on Imports or Exports, except what may be absolutely necessary for executing it's inspection Laws: and the net Produce of all Duties and Imposts, laid by any State on Imports or Exports, shall be for the Use of the Treasury of the United States; and all such Laws shall be subject to the Revision and Controul of the Congress.

No State shall, without the Consent of Congress, lay any Duty of Tonnage, keep Troops, or Ships of War in time of Peace, enter into any Agreement or Compact with another State, or with a foreign Power, or engage in War, unless actually invaded, or in such imminent Danger as will not admit of delay.

Article II

Section 1

The executive Power shall be vested in a President of the United States of America. He shall hold his Office during the Term of four Years, and, together with the Vice President, chosen for the same Term, be elected, as follows

Each State shall appoint, in such Manner as the Legislature thereof may direct, a Number of Electors, equal to the whole Number of Senators and Representatives to which the State may be entitled in the Congress: but no Senator or Representative, or Person holding an Office of Trust or Profit under the United States, shall be appointed an Elector.

The Electors shall meet in their respective States, and vote by Ballot for two Persons, of whom one at least shall not be an Inhabitant of the same State with themselves. And they shall make a List of all the Persons voted for, and of the Number of Votes for each; which List they shall sign and certify, and transmit sealed to the Seat of the Government of the United States, directed to the President of the Senate. The President of the Senate shall, in the Presence of the Senate and House of Representatives, open all the Certificates, and the Votes shall then be counted. The Person having the greatest Number of Votes shall be the President, if such Number be a Majority of the whole Number of Electors appointed; and if there be more than one who have such Majority, and have an equal Number of Votes, then the House of Representatives shall immediately chuse by Ballot one of them for President; and if no Person have a Majority, then from the five highest on the List the said House shall in like Manner chuse the President. But in chusing the President, the Votes shall be taken by States, the Representation from each State having one Vote; A quorum for this Purpose shall consist of a Member or Members from two thirds of the States, and a Majority of all the States shall be necessary to a Choice. In every Case, after the Choice of the President, the Person having the greatest Number of Votes of the Electors shall be the Vice President. But if there should remain two or more who have equal Votes, the Senate shall chuse from them by Ballot the Vice President. (Note: changed by the Twelfth Amendment.)

The Congress may determine the Time of chusing the Electors, and the Day on which they shall give their Votes; which Day shall be the same throughout the United States.

No Person except a natural born Citizen, or a Citizen of the United States, at the time of the Adoption of this Constitution, shall be eligible to the Office of President; neither shall any Person be eligible to that

Office who shall not have attained to the Age of thirty five Years, and been fourteen Years a Resident within the United States.

In Case of the Removal of the President from Office, or of his Death, Resignation, or Inability to discharge the Powers and Duties of the said Office, the Same shall devolve on the Vice President, and the Congress may by Law provide for the Case of Removal, Death, Resignation or Inability, both of the President and Vice President, declaring what Officer shall then act as President, and such Officer shall act accordingly, until the Disability be removed, or a President shall be elected. (Note: changed by the Twenty-Fifth Amendment.)

The President shall, at stated Times, receive for his Services, a Compensation, which shall neither be encreased nor diminished during the Period for which he shall have been elected, and he shall not receive within that Period any other Emolument from the United States, or any of them.

Before he enter on the Execution of his Office, he shall take the following Oath or Affirmation:—"I do solemnly swear (or affirm) that I will faithfully execute the Office of President of the United States, and will to the best of my Ability, preserve, protect and defend the Constitution of the United States."

Section 2

The President shall be Commander in Chief of the Army and Navy of the United States, and of the Militia of the several States, when called into the actual Service of the United States; he may require the Opinion, in writing, of the principal Officer in each of the executive Departments, upon any Subject relating to the Duties of their respective Offices, and he shall have Power to grant Reprieves and Pardons for Offences against the United States, except in Cases of Impeachment.

He shall have Power, by and with the Advice and Consent of the Senate, to make Treaties, provided two thirds of the Senators present concur; and he shall nominate, and by and with the Advice and Consent of the Senate, shall appoint Ambassadors, other public Ministers and Consuls, Judges of the supreme Court, and all other Officers of the United States, whose Appointments are not herein otherwise provided for, and which shall be established by Law: but the Congress may by Law vest the Appointment of such inferior Officers, as they think proper, in the President alone, in the Courts of Law, or in the Heads of Departments.

The President shall have Power to fill up all Vacancies that may happen during the Recess of the Senate, by granting Commissions which shall expire at the End of their next Session.

Section 3

He shall from time to time give to the Congress Information of the State of the Union, and recommend to their Consideration such Measures as he shall judge necessary and expedient; he may, on extraordinary Occasions, convene both Houses, or either of them, and in Case of Disagreement between them, with Respect to the Time of Adjournment, he may adjourn them to such Time as he shall think proper; he shall receive Ambassadors and other public Ministers; he shall take Care that the Laws be faithfully executed, and shall Commission all the Officers of the United States.

Section 4

The President, Vice President and all civil Officers of the United States, shall be removed from Office on Impeachment for, and Conviction of, Treason, Bribery, or other high Crimes and Misdemeanors.

Article III

Section 1

The judicial Power of the United States, shall be vested in one supreme Court, and in such inferior Courts as the Congress may from time to time ordain and establish. The Judges, both of the supreme and inferior Courts, shall hold their Offices during good Behaviour, and shall, at stated Times, receive for their Services, a Compensation, which shall not be diminished during their Continuance in Office.

Section 2

The judicial Power shall extend to all Cases, in Law and Equity, arising under this Constitution, the Laws of the United States, and Treaties made, or which shall be made, under their Authority;—to all Cases affecting Ambassadors, other public Ministers and Consuls;—to all Cases of admiralty and maritime Jurisdiction;—to Controversies to which the United States shall be a Party;—to Controversies between two or more States;—between a State and Citizens of another State; (Note: changed by the Eleventh Amendment.)—between Citizens of different States,—between Citizens of the same State claiming Lands under Grants of different States, and between a State, or the Citizens thereof, and foreign States, Citizens or Subjects. (Note: changed by the Eleventh Amendment.)

In all Cases affecting Ambassadors, other public Ministers and Consuls, and those in which a State shall be Party, the supreme Court shall have original Jurisdiction. In all the other Cases before mentioned, the supreme Court shall have appellate Jurisdiction, both as to Law and Fact, with such Exceptions, and under such Regulations as the Congress shall make.

The Trial of all Crimes, except in Cases of Impeachment, shall be by Jury; and such Trial shall be held in the State where the said Crimes shall have been committed; but when not committed within any State, the Trial shall be at such Place or Places as the Congress may by Law have directed.

Section 3

Treason against the United States, shall consist only in levying War against them, or in adhering to their Enemies, giving them Aid and Comfort. No Person shall be convicted of Treason unless on the Testimony of two Witnesses to the same overt Act, or on Confession in open Court.

The Congress shall have Power to declare the Punishment of Treason, but no Attainder of Treason shall work Corruption of Blood, or Forfeiture except during the Life of the Person attainted.

Article IV

Section 1

Full Faith and Credit shall be given in each State to the public Acts, Records, and judicial Proceedings of every other State. And the Congress may by general Laws prescribe the Manner in which such Acts, Records and Proceedings shall be proved, and the Effect thereof.

Section 2

The Citizens of each State shall be entitled to all Privileges and Immunities of Citizens in the several States. A Person charged in any State with Treason, Felony, or other Crime, who shall flee from Justice, and be found in another State, shall on Demand of the executive Authority of the State from which he fled, be delivered up, to be removed to the State having Jurisdiction of the Crime.

No Person held to Service or Labour in one State, under the Laws thereof, escaping into another, shall, in Consequence of any Law or Regulation therein, be discharged from such Service or Labour, but shall be delivered up on Claim of the Party to whom such Service or Labour may be due. (Note: changed by the Thirteenth Amendment.)

Section 3

New States may be admitted by the Congress into this Union; but no new State shall be formed or erected within the Jurisdiction of any other State; nor any State be formed by the Junction of two or more States, or Parts of States, without the Consent of the Legislatures of the States concerned as well as of the Congress.

The Congress shall have Power to dispose of and make all needful Rules and Regulations respecting the Territory or other Property belonging to the United States; and nothing in this Constitution shall be so construed as to Prejudice any Claims of the United States, or of any particular State.

Section 4

The United States shall guarantee to every State in this Union a Republican Form of Government, and shall protect each of them against Invasion; and on Application of the Legislature, or of the Executive (when the Legislature cannot be convened) against domestic Violence.

Article V

The Congress, whenever two thirds of both Houses shall deem it necessary, shall propose Amendments to this Constitution, or, on the Application of the Legislatures of two thirds of the several States, shall call a Convention for proposing Amendments, which, in either Case, shall be valid to all Intents and Purposes, as Part of this Constitution, when ratified by the Legislatures of three fourths of the several States, or by Conventions in three fourths thereof, as the one or the other Mode of Ratification may be proposed by the Congress; Provided that no Amendment which may be made prior to the Year One thousand eight hundred and eight shall in any Manner affect the first and fourth Clauses in the Ninth Section of the first Article; and that no State, without its Consent, shall be deprived of its equal Suffrage in the Senate.

Article VI

All Debts contracted and Engagements entered into, before the Adoption of this Constitution, shall be as valid against the United States under this Constitution, as under the Confederation.

This Constitution, and the Laws of the United States which shall be made in Pursuance thereof; and all Treaties made, or which shall be made, under the Authority of the United States, shall be the supreme Law of the Land; and the Judges in every State shall be bound thereby, any Thing in the Constitution or Laws of any State to the Contrary notwithstanding.

The Senators and Representatives before mentioned, and the Members of the several State Legislatures, and all executive and judicial Officers, both of the United States and of the several States, shall be bound by Oath or Affirmation, to support this Constitution; but no religious Test shall ever be required as a Qualification to any Office or public Trust under the United States.

Article VII

The ratification of the conventions of nine states, shall be sufficient for the establishment of this Constitution between the states so ratifying the same.

Amendments

Bill of Rights: Amendments I–X (Ratified December 15, 1791).

Amendment I

Congress shall make no law respecting an establishment of religion, or prohibiting the free exercise thereof; or abridging the freedom of speech, or of the press; or the right of the people peaceably to assemble, and to petition the Government for a redress of grievances.

Amendment II

A well regulated Militia, being necessary to the security of a free State, the right of the people to keep and bear Arms, shall not be infringed.

Amendment III

No Soldier shall, in time of peace be quartered in any house, without the consent of the Owner, nor in time of war, but in a manner to be prescribed by law.

Amendment IV

The right of the people to be secure in their persons, houses, papers, and effects, against unreasonable searches and seizures, shall not be violated, and no Warrants shall issue, but upon probable cause, supported by Oath or affirmation, and particularly describing the place to be searched, and the persons or things to be seized.

Amendment V

No person shall be held to answer for a capital, or otherwise infamous crime, unless on a presentment or indictment of a Grand Jury, except in cases arising in the land or naval forces, or in the Militia, when in actual service in time of War or public danger; nor shall any person be subject for the same offense to be twice put in jeopardy of life or limb; nor shall be compelled in any criminal case to be a witness against himself, nor be deprived of life, liberty, or property, without due process of law; nor shall private property be taken for public use, without just compensation.

Amendment VI

In all criminal prosecutions, the accused shall enjoy the right to a speedy and public trial, by an impartial jury of the State and district wherein the crime shall have been committed, which district shall have been previously ascertained by law, and to be informed of the nature and cause of the accusation; to be confronted with the witnesses against him; to have compulsory process for obtaining witnesses in his favor, and to have the Assistance of Counsel for his defence.

Amendment VII

In Suits at common law, where the value in controversy shall exceed twenty dollars, the right of trial by jury shall be preserved, and no fact tried by a jury, shall be otherwise re-examined in any Court of the United States, than according to the rules of the common law.

Amendment VIII

Excessive bail shall not be required, nor excessive fines imposed, nor cruel and unusual punishments inflicted.

Amendment IX

The enumeration in the Constitution, of certain rights, shall not be construed to deny or disparage others retained by the people.

Amendment X

The powers not delegated to the United States by the Constitution, nor prohibited by it to the States, are reserved to the States respectively, or to the people.

Amendment XI (Ratified February 7, 1795)

The Judicial power of the United States shall not be construed to extend to any suit in law or equity, commenced or prosecuted against one of the United States by Citizens of another State, or by Citizens or Subjects of any Foreign State.

Amendment XII (Ratified June 15, 1804)

The Electors shall meet in their respective states, and vote by ballot for President and Vice-President, one of whom, at least, shall not be an inhabitant of the same state with themselves; they shall name in their ballots the person voted for as President, and in distinct ballots the person voted for as Vice-President, and they shall make distinct lists of all persons voted for as President, and of all persons voted for as Vice-President and of the number of votes for each, which lists they shall sign and certify, and transmit sealed to the seat of the government of the United States, directed to the President of the Senate;—The President of the Senate shall, in the presence of the Senate and House of Representatives, open all the certificates and the votes shall then be counted;—The person having the greatest number of votes for President, shall be the President, if such number be a majority of the whole number of Electors appointed; and if no person have such majority, then from the persons having the highest numbers not exceeding three on the list of those voted for as President, the House of Representatives shall choose immediately, by ballot, the President. But in choosing the President, the votes shall be taken by states, the representation from each state having one vote; a quorum for this purpose shall consist of a member or members from two-thirds of the states, and a majority of all the states shall be necessary to a choice. And if the House of Representatives shall not choose a President whenever the right of choice shall devolve upon them, before the fourth day of March next following, then the Vice-President shall act as President, as in the case of the death or other constitutional disability of the President. (Note: superseded by section 3 of the Twentieth Amendment.)—The person having the greatest number of votes as Vice-President, shall be the Vice-President, if such number be a majority of the whole number of Electors appointed, and if no person have a majority, then from the two highest numbers on the list, the Senate shall choose the Vice-President; a quorum for the purpose shall consist of two-thirds of the whole number of Senators, and a majority of the whole number shall be necessary to a choice. But no person constitutionally ineligible to the office of President shall be eligible to that of Vice-President of the United States.

Amendment XIII (Ratified December 6, 1865)

Section 1

Neither slavery nor involuntary servitude, except as a punishment for crime whereof the party shall have been duly convicted, shall exist within the United States, or any place subject to their jurisdiction.

Section 2

Congress shall have power to enforce this article by appropriate legislation.

Amendment XIV (Ratified July 9, 1868)

Section 1

All persons born or naturalized in the United States, and subject to the jurisdiction thereof, are citizens of the United States and of the State wherein they reside. No State shall make or enforce any law which shall abridge the privileges or immunities of citizens of the United States; nor shall any State deprive any person of life, liberty, or property, without due process of law; nor deny to any person within its jurisdiction the equal protection of the laws.

Section 2

Representatives shall be apportioned among the several States according to their respective numbers, counting the whole number of persons in each State, excluding Indians not taxed. But when the right to vote at any election for the choice of electors for President and Vice-President of the United States, Representatives in Congress, the Executive and Judicial officers of a State, or the members of the Legislature thereof, is denied to any of the male inhabitants of such State, being twenty-one years of age, and citizens of the United States, or in any way abridged, except for participation in rebellion, or other crime, the basis of representation therein shall be reduced in the proportion which the number of such male citizens shall bear to the whole number of male citizens twenty-one years of age in such State.

Section 3

No person shall be a Senator or Representative in Congress, or elector of President and Vice-President, or hold any office, civil or military, under the United States, or under any State, who, having previously taken an oath, as a member of Congress, or as an officer of the United States, or as a member of any State legislature, or as an executive or judicial officer of any State, to support the Constitution of the United States, shall have engaged in insurrection or rebellion against the same, or given aid or comfort to the enemies thereof. But Congress may by a vote of two-thirds of each House, remove such disability.

Section 4

The validity of the public debt of the United States, authorized by law, including debts incurred for payment of pensions and bounties for services in suppressing insurrection or rebellion, shall not be questioned. But neither the United States nor any State shall assume or pay any debt or obligation incurred in aid of insurrection or rebellion against the United States, or any claim for the loss or emancipation of any slave; but all such debts, obligations and claims shall be held illegal and void.

Section 5

The Congress shall have power to enforce, by appropriate legislation, the provisions of this article.

Amendment XV (Ratified February 3, 1870)

Section 1

The right of citizens of the United States to vote shall not be denied or abridged by the United States or by any State on account of race, color, or previous condition of servitude.

Section 2

The Congress shall have power to enforce this article by appropriate legislation.

Amendment XVI (Ratified February 3, 1913)

The Congress shall have power to lay and collect taxes on incomes, from whatever source derived, without apportionment among the several States, and without regard to any census or enumeration.

Amendment XVII (Ratified April 8, 1913)

The Senate of the United States shall be composed of two Senators from each State, elected by the people thereof, for six years; and each Senator shall have one vote. The electors in each State shall have the qualifications requisite for electors of the most numerous branch of the State legislatures.

When vacancies happen in the representation of any State in the Senate, the executive authority of such State shall issue writs of election to fill such vacancies: Provided, That the legislature of any State may empower the executive thereof to make temporary appointments until the people fill the vacancies by election as the legislature may direct.

This amendment shall not be so construed as to affect the election or term of any Senator chosen before it becomes valid as part of the Constitution.

Amendment XVIII (Ratified January 16, 1919)

Section 1

After one year from the ratification of this article the manufacture, sale, or transportation of intoxicating liquors within, the importation thereof into, or the exportation thereof from the United States and all territory subject to the jurisdiction thereof for beverage purposes is hereby prohibited.

Section 2

The Congress and the several States shall have concurrent power to enforce this article by appropriate legislation.

Section 3

This article shall be inoperative unless it shall have been ratified as an amendment to the Constitution by the legislatures of the several States, as provided in the Constitution, within seven years from the date of the submission hereof to the States by the Congress. (Note: This amendment was repealed by the Twenty-First Amendment.)

Amendment XIX (Ratified August 18, 1920)

The right of citizens of the United States to vote shall not be denied or abridged by the United States or by any State on account of sex. Congress shall have power to enforce this article by appropriate legislation.

Amendment XX (Ratified January 23, 1933)

Section 1

The terms of the President and Vice President shall end at noon on the 20th day of January, and the terms of Senators and Representatives at noon on the 3d day of January, of the years in which such terms would have ended if this article had not been ratified; and the terms of their successors shall then begin.

Section 2

The Congress shall assemble at least once in every year, and such meeting shall begin at noon on the 3d day of January, unless they shall by law appoint a different day.

Section 3

If, at the time fixed for the beginning of the term of the President, the President elect shall have died, the Vice President elect shall become President. If a President shall not have been chosen before the time fixed for the beginning of his term, or if the President elect shall have failed to qualify, then the Vice President elect shall act as President until a President shall have qualified; and the Congress may by law provide for the case wherein neither a President elect nor a Vice President elect shall have qualified, declaring who shall then act as President, or the manner in which one who is to act shall be selected, and such person shall act accordingly until a President or Vice President shall have qualified.

Section 4

The Congress may by law provide for the case of the death of any of the persons from whom the House of Representatives may choose a President whenever the right of choice shall have devolved upon them, and for the case of the death of any of the persons from whom the Senate may choose a Vice President whenever the right of choice shall have devolved upon them.

Section 5

Sections 1 and 2 shall take effect on the 15th day of October following the ratification of this article.

Section 6

This article shall be inoperative unless it shall have been ratified as an amendment to the Constitution by the legislatures of three-fourths of the several States within seven years from the date of its submission.

Amendment XXI (Ratified December 5, 1933)

Section 1

The eighteenth article of amendment to the Constitution of the United States is hereby repealed.

Section 2

The transportation or importation into any State, Territory, or possession of the United States for delivery or use therein of intoxicating liquors, in violation of the laws thereof, is hereby prohibited.

Section 3

This article shall be inoperative unless it shall have been ratified as an amendment to the Constitution by conventions in the several States, as provided in the Constitution, within seven years from the date of the submission hereof to the States by the Congress.

Amendment XXII (Ratified February 27, 1951)

Section 1

No person shall be elected to the office of the President more than twice, and no person who has held the office of President, or acted as President, for more than two years of a term to which some other person was elected President shall be elected to the office of the President more than once. But this Article shall not apply to any person holding the office of President, when this Article was proposed by the Congress, and shall not prevent any person who may be holding the office of President, or acting as President, during the term within which this Article becomes operative from holding the office of President or acting as President during the remainder of such term.

Section 2

This article shall be inoperative unless it shall have been ratified as an amendment to the Constitution by the legislatures of three-fourths of the several States within seven years from the date of its submission to the States by the Congress.

Amendment XXIII (Ratified March 29, 1961)

Section 1

The District constituting the seat of Government of the United States shall appoint in such manner as the Congress may direct: A number of electors of President and Vice President equal to the whole number of Senators and Representatives in Congress to which the District would be entitled if it were a State, but in no event more than the least populous State; they shall be in addition to those appointed by the States, but they shall be considered, for the purposes of the election of President and Vice President, to be electors appointed by a State; and they shall meet in the District and perform such duties as provided by the twelfth article of amendment.

Section 2

The Congress shall have power to enforce this article by appropriate legislation.

Amendment XXIV (Ratified January 23, 1964)

Section 1

The right of citizens of the United States to vote in any primary or other election for President or Vice President, for electors for President or Vice President, or for Senator or Representative in Congress, shall not be denied or abridged by the United States or any state by reason of failure to pay any poll tax or other tax.

Section 2

The Congress shall have power to enforce this article by appropriate legislation.

Amendment XXV (Ratified February 10, 1967)

Section 1

In case of the removal of the President from office or of his death or resignation, the Vice President shall become President.

Section 2

Whenever there is a vacancy in the office of the Vice President, the President shall nominate a Vice President who shall take office upon confirmation by a majority vote of both Houses of Congress.

Section 3

Whenever the President transmits to the President pro tempore of the Senate and the Speaker of the House of Representatives his written declaration that he is unable to discharge the powers and duties of his office, and until he transmits to them a written declaration to the contrary, such powers and duties shall be discharged by the Vice President as Acting President.

Section 4

Whenever the Vice President and a majority of either the principal officers of the executive departments or of such other body as Congress may by law provide, transmit to the President pro tempore of the Senate and the Speaker of the House of Representatives their written declaration that the President is unable to discharge the powers and duties of his office, the Vice President shall immediately assume the powers and duties of the office as Acting President.

Thereafter, when the President transmits to the President pro tempore of the Senate and the Speaker of the House of Representatives his written declaration that no inability exists, he shall resume the powers and duties of his office unless the Vice President and a majority of either the principal officers of the executive department or of such other body as Congress may by law provide, transmit within four days to the President pro tempore of the Senate and the Speaker of the House of Representatives their written declaration that the President is unable to discharge the powers and duties of his office. Thereupon Congress shall decide the issue, assembling within forty-eight hours for that purpose if not in session. If the Congress, within twenty-one days after receipt of the latter written declaration, or, if Congress is not in session, within twenty-one days after Congress is required to assemble, determines by two-thirds vote of both Houses that the President is unable to discharge the powers and duties of his office, the Vice President shall continue to discharge the same as Acting President; otherwise, the President shall resume the powers and duties of his office.

Amendment XXVI (Ratified July 1, 1971)

Section 1

The right of citizens of the United States, who are 18 years of age or older, to vote, shall not be denied or abridged by the United States or any state on account of age.

Section 2

The Congress shall have the power to enforce this article by appropriate legislation.

Amendment XXVII (Ratified May 7, 1992)

No Law, varying the compensation for the services of the Senators and Representatives shall take effect, until an election of Representatives shall have intervened.

Appendix B. Uniform Commercial Code

ARTICLE I—GENERAL PROVISIONS

PART I—SHORT TITLE, CONSTRUCTION, APPLICATION AND SUBJECT MATTER

§ 28:1—101. Short title

This subtitle shall be known and may be cited as Uniform Commercial Code.

§ 28:1—102. Purposes; rules of construction; variation by agreement

1. This subtitle shall be liberally construed and applied to promote its underlying purposes and policies.
2. Underlying purposes and policies of this subtitle are
   a. to simplify, clarify and modernize the law governing commercial transactions;
   b. to permit the continued expansion of commercial practices through custom, usage and agreement of the parties;
   c. to make uniform the law among the various jurisdictions.
3. The effect of provisions of this subtitle may be varied by agreement, except as otherwise provided in this subtitle and except that the obligations of good faith, diligence, reasonableness and care prescribed by this subtitle may not be disclaimed by agreement but the parties may by agreement determine the standards by which the performance of such obligations is to be measured if such standards are not manifestly unreasonable.
4. The presence in certain provisions of this subtitle of the words "unless otherwise agreed" or words of similar import does not imply that the effect of other provisions may not be varied by agreement under subsection (3).
5. In this subtitle unless the context otherwise requires
   a. words in the singular number include the plural, and in the plural include the singular;
   b. words of the masculine gender include the feminine and the neuter, and when the sense so indicates words of the neuter gender may refer to any gender.

§ 28:1—103. Supplementary general principles of law applicable

Unless displaced by the particular provisions of this subtitle, the principles of law and equity, including the law merchant and the law relative to capacity to contract, principal and agent, estoppel, fraud, misrepresentation, duress, coercion, mistake, bankruptcy, or other validating or invalidating cause shall supplement its provisions.

§ 28:1—104. Construction against implicit repeal

This subtitle being a general act intended as a unified coverage of its subject matter, no part of it shall be deemed to be impliedly repealed by subsequent legislation if such construction can reasonably be avoided.

"Uniform Commercial Code," 1952.

§ 28:1—105. Territorial application of this subtitle; parties' power to choose applicable law

1. Except as provided hereafter in this section, when a transaction bears a reasonable relation to the District and also to a state or nation the parties may agree that the law either of the District or of such state or nation shall govern their rights and duties. Failing such agreement this subtitle applies to transactions bearing an appropriate relation to the District.
2. Where one of the following provisions of this subtitle specifies the applicable law, that provision governs and a contrary agreement is effective only to the extent permitted by the law (including the conflict of laws rules) so specified:

   Rights of creditors against sold goods. Section 28:2-402. Applicability of the article on bank deposits and collections. Section 28:4-102.

   Bulk transfers subject to the article on bulk transfers. Section 28:6-102.

   Applicability of the article on investment securities. Section 28:8-106.

   Policy and scope of the article on secured transactions. Sections 28:9-102 and 28:9-103.

§ 28 :1—106. Remedies to be liberally administered

1. The remedies provided by this subtitle shall be liberally administered to the end that the aggrieved party may be put in as good a position as if the other party had fully performed but neither consequential or special nor penal damages may be had except as specifically provided in this subtitle or by other rule of law.
2. Any right or obligation declared by this subtitle is enforceable by action unless the provision declaring it specifies a different and limited effect.

§ 28:1—107. Waiver or renunciation of claim or right after breach

Any claim or right arising out of an alleged breach can be discharged in whole or in part without consideration by a written waiver or renunciation signed and delivered by the aggrieved party.

§ 28:1—108. Severability

If any provision or clause of this subtitle or application thereof to any person or circumstances is held invalid, such invalidity shall not affect other provisions or applications of this subtitle which can be given effect without the invalid provisions or application, and to this end the provisions of this subtitle are declared to be severable.

§ 28:1—109. Section captions

Section captions are parts of this subtitle.

PART 2—GENERAL DEFINITIONS AND PRINCIPLES OF INTERPRETATION

§ 28:1—201. General definitions

Subject to additional definitions contained in the subsequent articles of this subtitle which are applicable to specific articles or parts thereof, and unless the context otherwise requires, in this subtitle:

1. "Action" in the sense of a judicial proceeding includes recoupment, counterclaim, set-off, suit in equity and any other proceedings in which rights are determined.
2. "Aggrieved party" means a party entitled to resort to a remedy.

3. "Agreement" means the bargain of the parties in fact as found in their language or by implication from other circumstances including course of dealing or usage of trade or course of performance as provided in this subtitle (sections 28:1—205 and 2—208). Whether an agreement has legal consequences is determined by the provisions of this subtitle, if applicable; otherwise by the law of contracts (section 28:1-103). (Compare "Contract".)
4. "Bank" means any person engaged in the business of banking.
5. "Bearer" means the person in possession of an instrument, document of title, or security payable to bearer or indorsed in blank.
6. "Bill of lading" means a document evidencing the receipt of goods for shipment issued by a person engaged in the business of transporting or forwarding goods, and includes an airbill. "Airbill" means a document serving for air transportation as a bill of lading does for marine or rail transportation, and includes an air consignment note or air waybill.
7. "Branch" includes a separately incorporated foreign branch of a bank.
8. "Burden of establishing" a fact means the burden of persuading the triers of fact that the existence of the fact is more probable than its non-existence.
9. "Buyer in ordinary course of business" means a person who in good faith and without knowledge that the sale to him is in violation of the ownership rights or security interest of a third party in the goods buys in ordinary course from a person in the business of selling goods of that kind but does not include a pawnbroker. "Buying" may be for cash or by exchange of other property or on secured or unsecured credit and includes receiving goods or documents of title under a preexisting contract for sale but does not include a transfer in bulk or as security for or in total or partial satisfaction of a money debt.
10. "Conspicuous": A term or clause is conspicuous when it is so written that a reasonable person against whom it is to operate ought to have noticed it. A printed heading in the capitals (as: Non-Negotiable Bill of Lading) is conspicuous. Language in the body of a form is "conspicuous" if it is in larger or other contrasting type or color. But in a telegram any stated term is "conspicuous". Whether a term or clause is "conspicuous" or not is for decision by the court.
11. "Contract" means the total legal obligation which results from the parties' agreement as affected by this subtitle and any other applicable rules of law. (Compare "Agreement".)
12. "Creditor" includes a general creditor, a secured creditor, a lien creditor and any representative of creditors, including an assignee for the benefit or creditors, a trustee in bankruptcy, a receiver in equity and an executor or administrator of an insolvent debtor's or assignor's estate.
13. "Defendant" includes a person in the position of defendant in a cross-action or counterclaim.
14. "Delivery" with respect to instruments, documents of title, chattel paper or securities means voluntary transfer of possession.

14a."District" means the District of Columbia; and "state" includes the District.

15. "Document of title" includes bill of lading, dock warrant, dock receipt, warehouse receipt or order for the delivery of goods, and also any other document which in the regular course of business or financing is treated as adequately evidencing that the person in possession of it is entitled to receive, hold and dispose of the document and the goods it covers. To be a document of title a document must purport to be issued by or addressed to a bailee and purport to cover goods in the bailee's possession which are either identified or are fungible portions of an identified mass.
16. "Fault" means wrongful act, omission or breach.

17. "Fungible" with respect to goods or securities means goods or securities of which any unit is, by nature or usage of trade, the equivalent of any other like unit. Goods which are not fungible shall be deemed fungible for the purposes of this subtitle to the extent that wider a particular agreement or document unlike units are treated as equivalents.
18. "Genuine" means free of forgery or counterfeiting.
19. "Good faith" means honesty in fact in the conduct or transaction concerned.
20. "Holder" means a person who is in possession of a document of title or an instrument or an investment security drawn, issued or indorsed to him or to his order or to bearer or in blank.
21. To "honor" is to pay or to accept and pay, or where a credit so engages to purchase or discount a draft complying with the terms of the credit.
22. "Insolvency proceedings" includes any assignment for the benefit of creditors or other proceedings intended to liquidate or rehabilitate the estate of the person involved.
23. A person is "insolvent" who either has ceased to pay his debts in the ordinary course of business or cannot pay his debts as they become due or is insolvent within the meaning of the federal bankruptcy law.
24. "Money" means a medium of exchange authorized or adopted by a domestic or foreign government as a part of its currency.
25. A person has "notice" of a fact when
    a. he has actual knowledge of it; or
    b. he has received a notice or notification of it; or
    c. from all the facts and circumstances known to him at the time in question he has reason to know that it exists.

A person "knows" or has "knowledge" of a fact when he has actual knowledge of it. "Discover" or "learn" or a word or phrase of similar import refers to knowledge rather than to reason to know. The time and circumstances under which a notice or notification may cease to be effective are not determined by this subtitle.

26. A person "notifies" or "gives" a notice or notification to another by taking such steps as may be reasonably required to inform the other in ordinary course whether or not such other actually comes to know of it. A person "receives" a notice or notification when
    a. it comes to his attention; or
    b. it is duly delivered at the place of business through which the contract was made or at any other place held out by him as the place for receipt of such communications.
27. Notice, knowledge or a notice or notification received by an organization is effective for a particular transaction from the time when it is brought to the attention of the individual conducting that transaction, and in any event from the time when it would have been brought to his attention if the organization had exercised due diligence. An organization exercises due diligence if it maintains reasonable routines for communicating significant information to the person conducting the transaction and there is reasonable compliance with the routines. Due diligence does not require an individual acting for the organization to communicate information unless such information is part of his regular duties or unless he has reason to know of the transaction and that the transaction would be materially affected by the information.
28. "Organization" includes a corporation, government or governmental subdivision or agency, business trust, estate, trust, partnership or association, two or more persons having a joint or common interest, or any other legal or commercial entity.

29. "Party", as distinct from "third party", means a person who has engaged in a transaction or made an agreement within this subtitle.
30. "Person" includes an individual or an organization (see section 28:1—102).
31. "Presumption" or "presumed" means that the trier of fact must find the existence of the fact presumed unless and until evidence is introduced which would support a finding of its nonexistence.
32. "Purchase" includes taking by sale, discount, negotiation, mortgage, pledge, lien, issue or re-issue, gift or any other voluntary transaction creating an interest in property.
33. "Purchaser" means a person who takes by purchase.
34. "Remedy" means any remedial right to which an aggrieved party is entitled with or without resort to tribunal.
35. "Representative" includes an agent, an officer of a corporation or association, and a trustee, executor or administrator of an estate, or any other person empowered to act for another.
36. "Rights" includes remedies.
37. "Security interest" means an interest in personal property or fixtures which secures payment or performance of an obligation. The retention or reservation of title by a seller of goods notwithstanding shipment or delivery to the buyer (section 28:2—401) is limited in effect to a reservation of a "security interest". The term also includes any interest of a buyer of accounts, chattel paper, or contract rights which is subject to article 9. The special property interest of a buyer of goods on identification of such goods to a contract for sale under section 28:2—401 is not a "security interest," but a buyer may also acquire a "security interest" by complying with article 9. Unless a lease or consignment is intended as security, reservation of title thereunder is not a "security interest" but a consignment is in any event subject to the provisions on consignment sales (section 28:2—326). Whether a lease is intended as security is to be determined by the facts of each case; however, (a) the inclusion of an option to purchase does not of itself make the lease one intended for security, and (b) an agreement that upon compliance with the terms of the lease the lessee shall become or has the option to become the owner of the property for no additional consideration or for a nominal consideration does make the lease one intended for security.
38. "Send" in connection with any writing or notice means to deposit in the mail or deliver for transmission by any other usual means of communication with postage or cost of transmission provided for and properly addressed and in the case of an instrument to an address specified thereon or otherwise agreed, or if there be none to any address reasonable under the circumstances. The receipt of any writing or notice within the time at which it would have arrived if properly sent has the effect of a proper sending.
39. "Signed" includes any symbol executed or adopted by a party with present intention to authenticate a writing.
40. "Surety" includes guarantor.
41. "Telegram" includes a message transmitted by radio, teletype, cable, any mechanical method of transmission, or the like.
42. "Term" means that portion of an agreement which relates to a particular matter.
43. "Unauthorized" signature or indorsement means one made without actual, implied or apparent authority and includes a forgery.

44. "Value". Except as otherwise provided with respect to negotiable instruments and bank collections (sections 28:3—303, 28:4—208 and 28:4—209) a person gives "value" for rights if he acquires them
    a. in return for a binding commitment to extend credit or for the extension of immediately available credit whether or not drawn upon and whether or not a charge-back is provided for in the event of difficulties in collection; or
    b. as security for or in total or partial satisfaction of a preexisting claim; or
    c. by accepting delivery pursuant to a pre-existing contract for purchase; or
    d. generally, in return for any consideration sufficient to support a simple contract.
45. "Warehouse receipt" means a receipt issued by a person engaged in the business of storing goods for hire.
46. "Written" or "writing" includes printing, typewriting or any other intentional reduction to tangible form.

§ 28:1—202. Prima facie evidence by third party documents

A document in due form purporting to be a bill of lading, policy or certificate of insurance, official weighers or inspector's certificate, consular invoice, or any other document authorized or required by the contract to be issued by a third party shall be prima facie evidence of its own authenticity and genuineness and of the facts stated in the document by the third party.

§ 28:1—203. Obligation of good faith

Every contract or duty within this subtitle imposes an obligation of good faith in its performance or enforcement.

§ 28:1—204. Time; reasonable time; "seasonably"

1. Whenever this subtitle requires any action to be taken within a reasonable time, any time which is not manifestly unreasonable may be fixed by agreement.
2. What is a reasonable time for taking any action depends on the nature, purpose and circumstances of such action.
3. An action is taken "seasonably" when it is taken at or within the time agreed or if no time is agreed at or within a reasonable time.

§ 28:1—205. Course of dealing and usage of trade

1. A course of dealing is a sequence of previous conduct between the parties to a particular transaction which is fairly to be regarded as establishing a common basis of understanding for interpreting their expressions and other conduct.
2. A usage of trade is any practice or method of dealing having such regularity of observance in a place, vocation or trade as to justify an expectation that it will be observed with respect to the transaction in question. The existence and scope of such a usage are to be proved as facts. If it is established that such a usage is embodied in a written trade code or similar writing the interpretation of the writing is for the court.
3. A course of dealing between parties and any usage of trade in the vocation or trade in which they are engaged or of which they are or should be aware give particular meaning to and supplement or qualify terms of an agreement.
4. The express terms of an agreement and an applicable course of dealing or usage of trade shall be construed wherever reasonable as consistent with each other; but when such construction is unreasonable

express terms control both course of dealing and usage of trade and course of dealing controls usage of trade.

5. An applicable usage of trade in the place where any part of performance is to occur shall be used in interpreting the agreement as to that part of the performance.
6. Evidence of a relevant usage of trade offered by one party is not admissible unless and until he has given the other party such notice as the court finds sufficient to prevent unfair surprise to the latter.

§ 28:1—206. Statute of frauds for kinds of personal property not otherwise covered

1. Except in the cases described in subsection (2) of this section a contract for the sale of personal property is not enforceable by way of action or defense beyond five thousand dollars in amount or value of remedy unless there is some writing which indicates that a contract for sale has been made between the parties at a defined or stated price, reasonably identities the subject matter, and is signed by the party against whom enforcement is sought or by his authorized agent.
2. Subsection (1) of this section does not apply to contracts for the sale of goods (section 28:2—201) nor of securities (section 28:8—319) nor to security agreements (section 28:9—203).

ARTICLE 2—SALES

§ 28:2—104. Definitions: "merchant"; "between merchants"; "financing agency"

1. "Merchant" means a person who deals in goods of the kind or otherwise by his occupation holds himself out as having knowledge or skill peculiar to the practices or goods involved in the transaction or to whom such knowledge or skill may be attributed by his employment of an agent or broker or other intermediary who by his occupation holds himself out as having such knowledge or skill.
2. "Financing agency" means a bank, finance company or other person who in the ordinary course of business makes advances against goods or documents of title or who by arrangement with either the seller or the buyer intervenes in ordinary course to make or collect payment due or claimed under the contract for sale, as by purchasing or paying the seller's draft or making advances against it or by merely taking it for collection whether or not documents of title accompany the draft. "Financing agency" includes also a bank or other person who similarly intervenes between persons who are in the position of seller and buyer in respect to the goods (section 28:2—707).
3. "Between merchants" means in any transaction with respect to which both parties are chargeable with the knowledge or skill of merchants.

§ 28:2—105. Definitions: transferability; "goods"; "future" goods; "lot"; "commercial unit"

1. "Goods" means all things (including specially manufactured goods) which are movable at the time of identification to the contract for sale other than the money in which the price is to be paid, investment securities (article 8) and things in action. "Goods" also includes the unborn young of animals and growing crops and other identified things attached to realty as described in the section on goods to be severed from realty (section 28:2—107).
2. Goods must be both existing and identified before any interest in them can pass. Goods which are not both existing and identified are "future" goods. A purported present sale of future goods or of any interest therein operates as a contract to sell.

3. There may be a sale of a part interest in existing identified goods.
4. An undivided share in an identified bulk of fungible goods is sufficiently identified to be sold although the quantity of the bulk is not determined. Any agreed proportion of such a bulk or any quantity thereof agreed upon by number, weight or other measure may to the extent of the seller's interest in the bulk be sold to the buyer who then becomes an owner in common.
5. "Lot" means a parcel or a single article which is the subject matter of a separate sale or delivery, whether or not it is sufficient to perform the contract.
6. "Commercial unit" means such a unit of goods as by commercial usage is a single whole for purposes of sale and division of which materially impairs its character or value on the market or in use. A commercial unit may be a single article (as a machine) or a set of articles (as a suite of furniture or an assortment of sizes) or a quantity (as a bale, gross, or carload) or any other unit treated in use or in the relevant market as a single whole.

§ 28:2—106. Definitions: "contract"; "agreement"; "contract for sale"; "sale"; "present sale"; "conforming" to contract; "termination"; "cancellation"

1. In this article unless the context otherwise requires "contract" and "agreement" are limited to those relating to the present or future sale of goods. "Contract for sale" includes both a present sale of goods and a contract, to sell goods at a future time. A "sale" consists in the passing of title from the seller to the buyer for a price (section 28: 2—401). A "present sale" means a sale which is accomplished by the making of the contract.
2. Goods or conduct including any part of a performance are "conforming" or conform to the contract when they are in accordance with the obligations under the contract.
3. "Termination" occurs when either party pursuant to a power created by agreement or law puts an end to the contract otherwise than for its breach. On "termination" all obligations which are still executory on both sides are discharged but any right based on prior breach or performance survives.
4. "Cancellation" occurs when either party puts an end to the contract for breach by the other and its effect is the same as that of "termination" except that the cancelling party also retains any remedy for breach of the whole contract or any unperformed balance.

§ 28:2—107. Goods to be severed from realty: recording

1. A contract for the sale of timber, minerals or the like or a structure or its materials to be removed from realty is a contract for the sale of goods within this article if they are to be severed by the seller but until severance a purported present sale thereof which is not effective as a transfer of an interest in land is effective only as a contract to sell.
2. A contract for the sale apart from the land of growing crops or other things attached to realty and capable of severance without material harm thereto but not described in subsection (1) is a contract for the sale of goods within this article whether the subject matter is to be severed by the buyer or by the seller even though it forms part of the realty at the time of contracting, and the parties can by identification effect a present sale before severance.
3. The provisions of this section are subject to any third party rights provided by the law relating to realty records, and the contract for sale may be executed and recorded as a document transferring an

interest in land and shall then constitute notice to third parties of the buyer's rights under the contract for sale.

PART 2—FORM, FORMATION AND READJUSTMENT OF CONTRACT

§ 28:2—201. Formal requirements; statute of frauds

1. Except as otherwise provided in this section a contract for the sale of goods for the price of $500 or more is not enforceable by way of action or defense unless there is some writing sufficient to indicate that a contract for sale has been made between the parties and signed by the party against whom enforcement is sought or by his authorized agent or broker. A writing is not insufficient because it omits or incorrectly states a term agreed upon but the contract is not enforceable under this paragraph beyond the quantity of goods shown in such writing.
2. Between merchants if within a reasonable time a writing in confirmation of the contract and sufficient against the sender is received and the party receiving it has reason to know its contents, it satisfies the requirements of subsection (1) against such party unless written notice of objection to its contents is given within ten days after it is received.
3. A contract which does not satisfy the requirements of subsection (1) but which is valid in other respects is enforceable.
   a. if the goods are to be specially manufactured for the buyer and are not suitable for sale to others in the ordinary course of the seller's business and the seller, before notice of repudiation is received and under circumstances which reasonably indicate that the goods are for the buyer, has made either a substantial beginning of their manufacture or commitments for their procurement; or
   b. if the party against whom enforcement is sought admits in his pleading, testimony or otherwise in court that a contract for sale was made, but the contract is not enforceable under this provision beyond the quantity of goods admitted; or
   c. with respect to goods for which payment has been made and accepted or which have been received and accepted (section 28:2—606).

§ 28:2—202. Final written expression: parol or extrinsic evidence

Terms with respect to which the confirmatory memoranda of the parties agree or which are otherwise set forth in a writing intended by the parties as a final expression of their agreement with respect to such terms as are included therein may not be contradicted by evidence of any prior agreement or of a contemporaneous oral agreement but may be explained or supplemented

a. by course of dealing or usage of trade (section 28:1—205) or by course of performance (section 28:2—208); and
b. by evidence of consistent additional terms unless the court finds the writing to have been intended also as a complete and exclusive statement of the terms of the agreement.

§ 28:2—203. Seals inoperative

The affixing of a seal to a writing evidencing a contract for sale or an offer to buy or sell goods does not constitute the writing a sealed instrument and the law with respect to sealed instruments does not apply to such a contract or offer.

§ 28:2–204. Formation in general

1. A contract for sale of goods may be made in any manner sufficient to show agreement, including conduct by both parties which recognizes the existence of such a contract.
2. An agreement sufficient to constitute a contract for sale may be found even though the moment of its making is undetermined.
3. Even though one or more terms are left open a contract for sale does not fail for indefiniteness if the parties have intended to make a contract and there is a reasonably certain basis for giving an appropriate remedy.

§ 28:2–205. Firm offers

An offer by a merchant to buy or sell goods in a signed writing which by its terms gives assurance that it will be held open is not revocable, for lack of consideration, during the time stated or if no time is stated for a reasonable time, but in no event may such period of irrevocability exceed three months; but any such term of assurance on a form supplied by the offeree must be separately signed by the offeror.

§ 28:2–206. Offer and acceptance in formation of contract

1. Unless otherwise unambiguously indicated by the language or circumstances
   a. an offer to make a contract shall be construed as inviting acceptance in any manner and by any medium reasonable in the circumstances;
   b. an order or other offer to buy goods for prompt or current shipment shall be construed as inviting acceptance either by a prompt promise to ship or by the prompt or current shipment of conforming or non-conforming goods; but such a shipment of non-conforming goods does not constitute an acceptance if the seller seasonably notifies the buyer that the shipment is offered only as an accommodation to the buyer.
2. Where the beginning of a requested performance is a reasonable mode of acceptance an offeror who is not notified of acceptance within a reasonable time may treat the offer as having lapsed before acceptance.

§ 28:2–207. Additional terms in acceptance or confirmation

1. A definite and seasonable expression of acceptance or a written confirmation which is sent within a reasonable time operates as an acceptance even though it states terms additional to or different from those offered or agreed upon, unless acceptance is expressly made conditional on assent to the additional or different terms.
2. The additional terms are to be construed as proposals for addition to the contract. Between merchants such terms become part of the contract unless:
   a. the offer expressly limits acceptance to the terms of the offer;
   b. they materially alter it; or
   c. notification of objection to them has already been given or is given within a reasonable time after notice of them is received.
3. Conduct by both parties which recognizes the existence of a contract is sufficient to establish a contract for sale although the writings of the parties do not otherwise establish a contract. In such case

the terms of the particular contract consist of those terms on which the writings of the parties agree, together with any supplementary terms incorporated under any other provisions of this subtitle.

§ 28:2—208. Course of performance or practical construction

1. Where the contract for sale involves repeated occasions for performance by either party with knowledge of the nature of the performance and opportunity for objection to it by the other, any course of performance accepted or acquiesced in without objection shall be relevant to determine the meaning of the agreement.
2. The express terms of the agreement and any such course of performance, as well as any course of dealing and usage of trade, shall be construed whenever reasonable as consistent with each other; but when such construction is unreasonable, express terms shall control course of performance and course of performance shall control both course of dealing and usage of trade (section 28:1—205).
3. Subject to the provisions of the next section on modification any waiver, such course of performance shall be relevant to show a waiver or modification of any term inconsistent with such course of performance.

§ 28:2—209. Modification, rescission and waiver

1. An agreement modifying a contract within this article needs no consideration to be binding.
2. A signed agreement which excludes modification or rescission except by a signed writing cannot be otherwise modified or rescinded, but except as between merchants such a requirement on a form supplied by the merchant must be separately signed by the other party.
3. The requirements of the statute of frauds section of this article (section 28:2—201) must be satisfied if the contract as modified is within its provisions.
4. Although an attempt at modification or rescission does not satisfy the requirements of subsection (2) or (3), it can operate as a waiver.
5. A party who has made a waiver affecting an executory portion of the contract may retract the waiver by reasonable notification received by the other party that strict performance will be required by any term waived, unless the retraction would be unjust in view of a material change of position in reliance on the waiver.

§ 28:2—210. Delegation of performance; assignment of rights

1. A party may perform his duty through a delegate unless otherwise agreed or unless the other party has a substantial interest in having his original promisor perform or control the acts required by the contract. No delegation of performance relieves the party delegating of any duty to perform or any liability for breach.
2. Unless otherwise agreed all rights of either seller or buyer can be assigned except where the assignment would materially change the duty of the other party, or increase materially the burden or risk imposed on him by his contract, or impair materially his chance of obtaining return performance. A right, to damages for breach of the whole contract or a right arising out of the assignor's due performance of his entire obligation can be assigned despite agreement otherwise.
3. Unless the circumstances indicate the contrary a prohibition of assignment of "the contract" is to be construed as barring only the delegation to the assignee of the assignor's performance.

4. An assignment of "the contract" or of "all my rights under the contract" or an assignment, in similar general terms is an assignment of rights and unless the language or the circumstances (as in an assignment for security) indicate the contrary, it is a delegation of performance of the duties of the assignor and its acceptance by the assignee constitutes a promise by him to perform those duties. This promise is enforceable by either the assignor or the other party to the original contract.
5. The other party may treat any assignment which delegates performance as creating reasonable grounds for insecurity and may without prejudice to his rights against the assignor demand assurances from the assignee (section 28:2—609).

PART 3—GENERAL OBLIGATION AND CONSTRUCTION OF CONTRACT

§ 28:2—301. General obligations of parties

The obligation of the seller is to transfer and deliver and that of the buyer is to accept and pay in accordance with the contract.

§ 28:2—302. Unconscionable contract or clause

1. If the court as a matter of law finds the contract or any clause of the contract to have been unconscionable at the time it was made the court may refuse to enforce the contract, or it may enforce the remainder of the contract without the unconscionable clause, or it may so limit the application of any unconscionable clause as to avoid any unconscionable result.
2. When it is claimed or appears to the court that the contract or any clause thereof may be unconscionable the parties shall be afforded a reasonable opportunity to present evidence as to its commercial setting, purpose and effect to aid the court in making the determination.

§ 28:2—313. Express warranties by affirmation, promise, description, sample

1. Express warranties by the seller are created as follows:
   a. Any affirmation of fact or promise made by the seller to the buyer which relates to the goods and becomes part of the basis of the bargain creates an express warranty that the goods shall conform to the affirmation or promise.
   b. Any description of the goods which is made part of the basis of the bargain creates an express warranty that the goods shall conform to the description.
   c. Any sample or model which is made part of the basis of the bargain creates an express warranty that the whole of the goods shall conform to the sample or model.
2. It is not necessary to the creation of an express warranty that the seller use formal words such as "warrant" or "guarantee" or that he have a specific intention to make a warranty, but an affirmation merely of the value of the goods or a statement purporting to be merely the seller's opinion or commendation of the goods does not create a warranty.

§ 28:2—314. Implied warranty: merchantability; usage of trade

1. Unless excluded or modified (section 28:2—316), a warranty that the goods shall be merchantable is implied in a contract for their sale if the seller is a merchant with respect to goods of that kind. Under this section the serving for value of food or drink to be consumed either on the premises or elsewhere is a sale.

2. Goods to be merchantable must be at least such as
   a. pass without objection in the trade under the contract description; and
   b. in the case of fungible goods, are of fair average quality within the description; and
   c. are fit for the ordinary purposes for which such goods are used; and
   d. run, within the variations permitted by the agreement, of even kind, quality and quantity within each unit and among all units involved; and
   e. are adequately contained, packaged, and labeled as the agreement may require; and
   f. conform to the promises or affirmations of fact made on the container or label if any.
3. Unless excluded or modified (section 28:2—316), other implied warranties may arise from course of dealing or usage of trade.

§ 28:2–315. Implied warranty: fitness for particular purpose

Where the seller at the time of contracting has reason to know any particular purpose for which the goods are required and that the buyer is relying on the seller's skill or judgment to select or furnish suitable goods, there is unless excluded or modified under the next section an implied warranty that the goods shall be fit for such purpose.

ARTICLE 3—COMMERCIAL PAPER

PART 1—SHORT TITLE, FORM AND INTERPRETATION

§ 28:3–101. Short title

This article shall be known and may be cited as Uniform Commercial Code—Commercial Paper.

§ 28:3–102. Definitions and index of definitions

1. In this article unless the context otherwise requires
   a. "Issue" means the first delivery of an instrument to a holder or a remitter.
   b. An "order" is a direction to pay and must be more than an authorization or request. It must identify the person to pay with reasonable certainty. It may be addressed to one or more such persons jointly or in the alternative but not in succession.
   c. A "promise" is an undertaking to pay and must be more than an acknowledgment of an obligation.
   d. "Secondary party" means a drawer or endorser.
   e. "Instrument" means a negotiable instrument.
2. Other definitions applying to this article and the sections in which they appear are:

   "Acceptance". Section 28:3—410.
   "Accommodation party". Section 28:3—415.
   "Alteration". Section 28:3—407.
   "Certificate of deposit". Section 28:3—104.
   "Certification". Section 28:3—411.
   "Check". Section 28:3—104.
   "Definite time". Section 28:3—109.
   "Dishonor". Section 28:3—507.
   "Draft". Section 28:3—104.

"Holder in due course". Section 28:3—302.
"Negotiation". Section 28:3—202.
"Note". Section 28:3—104.
"Notice of dishonor". Section 28:3—508.
"On demand". Section 28:3—108.
"Presentment". Section 28:3—504.
"Protest". Section 28:3—509.
"Restrictive Indorsement". Section 28:3—205.
"Signature". Section 28:3—401.

3. The following definitions in other articles apply to this article.
"Account". Section 28:4—104.
"Banking day". Section 28:4—104.
"Clearing house". Section 28:4—104.
"Collecting bank". Section 28:4—105.
"Customer". Section 28:4—104.
"Depositary bank". Section 28:4—105.
"Documentary draft". Section 28:4—104.
"Intermediary bank". Section 28:4—105.
"Item". Section 28:4—104.
"Midnight deadline". Section 28:4—104.
"Payor bank". Section 28:4—105.
4. In addition article 1 contains general definitions and principles of construction and interpretation applicable throughout this article.

§ 28:3—103. Limitations on scope of article

1. This article does not apply to money, documents of title or investment securities.
2. The provisions of this article are subject to the provisions of the article on bank deposits and collections (article 4) and secured transactions (article 9).

§ 28:3—104. Form of negotiable instruments; "draft"; "check"; "certificate of deposit"; "note"

1. Any writing to be a negotiable instrument within this article must
   a. be signed by the maker or drawer; and
   b. contain an unconditional promise or order to pay a sum certain in money and no other promise, order, obligation or power given by the maker or drawer except as authorized by this article; and
   c. be payable on demand or at a definite time; and
   d. be payable to order or to bearer.

2. A writing which complies with the requirements of this section is
   a. a "draft" ("bill of exchange") if it is an order;
   b. a "check" if it is a draft drawn on a bank and payable on demand;
   c. a "certificate of deposit" if it is an acknowledgment by a bank of receipt of money with an engagement to repay it;
   d. a "note" if it is a promise other than a certificate of deposit.

3. As used in other articles of this subtitle, and as the context may require, the terms "draft", "check", "certificate of deposit" and "note" may refer to instruments which are not negotiable within this article as well as to instruments which are so negotiable.

§ 28:3—105. When promise or order unconditional

1. A promise or order otherwise unconditional is not made conditional by the fact that the instrument
   a. is subject to implied or constructive conditions; or
   b. states its consideration, whether performed or promised, or the transaction which gave rise to the instrument, or that the promise or order is made or the instrument matures in accordance with or "as per" such transaction; or
   c. refers to or states that it arises out of a separate agreement or refers to a separate agreement for rights as to prepayment or acceleration; or
   d. states that it is drawn under a letter of credit; or
   e. states that it is secured, whether by mortgage, reservation of title or otherwise; or
   f. indicates a particular account to be debited or any other fund or source from which reimbursement is expected; or
   g. is limited to payment out of a particular fund or the proceeds of a particular source, if the instrument is issued by a government or governmental agency or unit; or
   h. is limited to payment out of the entire assets of a partnership, unincorporated association, trust or estate by or on behalf of which the instrument is issued.
2. A promise or order is not unconditional if the instrument
   a. states that, it is subject to or governed by any other agreement; or
   b. states that it is to be paid only out of a particular fund or source except as provided in this section.

§ 28:3—106. Sum certain

1. The sum payable is a sum certain even though it is to be paid
   a. with stated interest or by stated installments; or
   b. with stated different rates of interest before and after default or a specified date; or
   c. with a stated discount or addition if paid before or after the date fixed for payment; or
   d. with exchange or less exchange, whether at a fixed rate or at the current rate; or
   e. with costs of collection or an attorney's fee or both upon default.
2. Nothing in this section shall validate any term which is otherwise illegal.

§ 28:3—107. Money

1. An instrument is payable in money if the medium of exchange in which it is payable is money at the time the instrument is made. An instrument payable in "currency" or "current funds" is payable in money.
2. A promise or order to pay a sum stated in a foreign currency is for a sum certain in money and, unless a different medium of payment is specified in the instrument, may be satisfied by payment of that number of dollars which the stated foreign currency will purchase at the buying sight rate for that currency on the day on which the instrument is payable or, if payable on demand, on the day of demand. If such an instrument specifies a foreign currency as the medium of payment the instrument is payable in that currency.

§ 28:3–108. Payable on demand

Instruments payable on demand include those payable at sight or on presentation and those in which no time for payment is stated.

§ 28:3–109. Definite time

1. An instrument is payable at a definite time if by its terms it is payable—
   a. on or before a stated date or at a fixed period after a stated date; or
   b. at a fixed period after sight; or
   c. at a definite time subject to any acceleration; or
   d. at a definite time subject to extension at the option of the holder, or to extension to a further definite time at the option of the maker or acceptor or automatically upon or after a specified act or event.
2. An instrument which by its terms is otherwise payable only upon an act or event uncertain as to time of occurrence is not payable at a definite time even though the act or event has occurred.

§ 28:3–110. Payable to order

1. An instrument is payable to order when by its terms it is payable to the order or assigns of any person therein specified with reasonable certainty, or to him or his order, or when it is conspicuously designated on its face as "exchange" or the like and names a payee. It may be payable to the order of
   a. the maker or drawer; or
   b. the drawee; or
   c. a payee who is not maker, drawer or drawee; or
   d. two or more payees together or in the alternative; or
   e. an estate, trust or fund, in which case it is payable to the order of the representative of such estate, trust or fund or his successors; or
   f. an office, or an officer by his title as such in which case it is payable to the principal but the incumbent of the office or his successors may act as if he or they were the holder; or
   g. a partnership or unincorporated association, in which case it is payable to the partnership or association and may be indorsed or transferred by any person thereto authorized.
2. An instrument not payable to order is not made so payable by such words as "payable upon return of this instrument properly indorsed".
3. An instrument made payable both to order and to bearer is payable to order unless the bearer words are handwritten or typewritten.

§ 28:3–111. Payable to bearer

An instrument is payable to bearer when by its terms it is payable to—
   a. bearer or the order of bearer; or
   b. a specified person or bearer; or
   c. "cash" or the order of "cash", or any other indication which does not purport to designate a specific payee.

§ 28:3—112. Terms and omissions not affecting negotiability

1. The negotiability of an instrument is not affected by—
   a. the omission of a statement of any consideration or of the place where the instrument is drawn or payable; or
   b. a statement that collateral has been given to secure obligations either on the instrument or otherwise of an obligor on the instrument or that in the case of default on those obligations the holder may realize on or dispose of the collateral; or
   c. a promise or power to maintain or protect collateral or to give additional collateral; or
   d. a term authorizing a confession of judgment on the instrument if it is not paid when due; or
   e. a term purporting to waive the benefit of any law intended for the advantage or protection of any obligor; or
   f. a term in a draft providing that the payee by indorsing or cashing it acknowledges full satisfaction of an obligation of the drawer; or
   g. a statement in a draft drawn in a set of parts (section 28:3—801) to the effect that the order is effective only if no other part has been honored.
2. Nothing in this section shall validate any term which is otherwise illegal.

PART 2—TRANSFER AND NEGOTIATION

§ 28:3—201. Transfer: right to indorsement

1. Transfer of an instrument vests in the transferee such rights as the transferor has therein, except that a transferee who has himself been a party to any fraud or illegality affecting the instrument or who as a prior holder had notice of a defense or claim against it cannot improve his position by taking from a later holder in due course.
2. A transfer of a security interest in an instrument vests the foregoing rights in the transferee to the extent of the interest transferred.
3. Unless otherwise agreed any transfer for value of an instrument not then payable to bearer gives the transferee the specifically enforceable right to have the unqualified indorsement of the transferor. Negotiation takes effect only when the indorsement is made and until that time there is no presumption that the transferee is the owner.

§ 28:3—202. Negotiation

1. Negotiation is the transfer of an instrument in such form that the transferee becomes a holder. If the instrument is payable to order it is negotiated by delivery with any necessary indorsement; if payable to bearer it is negotiated by delivery.
2. An indorsement must be written by or on behalf of the holder and on the instrument or on a paper so firmly affixed thereto as to become a part thereof.
3. An indorsement is effective for negotiation only when it conveys the entire instrument or any unpaid residue. If it purports to be of less it operates only as a partial assignment.
4. Words of assignment, condition, waiver, guaranty, limitation or disclaimer of liability and the like accompanying an indorsement do not affect its character as an indorsement.

§ 28:3—203. Wrong or misspelled name

Where an instrument is made payable to a person under a misspelled name or one other than his own he may indorse in that name or his own or both; but signature in both names may be required by a person paying or giving value for the instrument.

§ 28:3—204. Special indorsement; blank indorsement

1. A special indorsement specifies the person to whom or to whose order it makes the instrument payable. Any instrument specially indorsed becomes payable to the order of the special indorsee and may be further negotiated only by his indorsement.
2. An indorsement in blank specifies no particular indorsee and may consist of a mere signature. An instrument payable to order and indorsed in blank becomes payable to bearer and may be negotiated by delivery alone until specially indorsed.
3. The holder may convert a blank indorsement into a special indorsement by writing over the signature of the indorser in blank any contract consistent with the character of the indorsement.

§ 28:3—205. Restrictive indorsements

An indorsement is restrictive which either

a. is conditional; or
b. purports to prohibit further transfer of the instrument; or
c. includes the words "for collection", "for deposit", "pay any bank", or like terms signifying a purpose of deposit or collection; or
d. otherwise states that it is for the benefit or use of the indorser or of another person.

§ 28:3—206. Effect of restrictive indorsement

1. No restrictive indorsement prevents further transfer or negotiation of the instrument.
2. An intermediary bank, or a payor bank which is not the depositary bank, is neither given notice nor otherwise affected by a restrictive indorsement of any person except the bank's immediate transferor or the person presenting for payment.
3. Except for an intermediary bank, any transferee under an indorsement which is conditional or includes the words "for collection", "for deposit", "pay any bank", or like terms (subparagraphs (a) and (c) or section 28:3—205) must pay or apply any value given by him for or on the security of the instrument consistently with the indorsement and to the extent that he does so he becomes a holder for value. In addition such transferee is a holder in due course if he otherwise complies with the requirements of section 28:3—302 on what constitutes a holder in due course.
4. The first taker under an indorsement for the benefit of the indorser or another person (subparagraph (d) of section 28:3—205) must pay or apply any value given by him for or on the security of the instrument consistently with the indorsement and to the extent that he does so he becomes a holder for value. In addition such taker is a holder in due course if he otherwise complies with the requirements of section 28:3—302 on what constitutes a holder in due course. A later holder for value is neither given notice nor otherwise affected by such restrictive indorsement unless he has knowledge that a fiduciary or other person has negotiated the instrument in any transaction for his own benefit or otherwise in breach of duty (subsection (2) of section 28:3—304).

§ 28:3–207. Negotiation effective although it may be rescinded

1. Negotiation is effective to transfer the instrument although the negotiation is
   a. made by an infant, a corporation exceeding its powers, or any other person without capacity; or
   b. obtained by fraud, duress or mistake of any kind; or
   c. part of an illegal transaction; or
   d. made in breach of duty.
2. Except as against a subsequent holder in due course such negotiation is in an appropriate case subject to rescission, the declaration of a constructive trust or any other remedy permitted by law.

§ 28:3–208. Reacquisition

Where an instrument is returned to or reacquired by a prior party he may cancel any indorsement which is not necessary to his title and reissue or further negotiate the instrument, but any intervening party is discharged as against the reacquiring party and subsequent holders not in due course and if his indorsement has been cancelled is discharged as against subsequent holders in due course as well.

   a. the burden of establishing it is on the party claiming under the signature; but
   b. the signature is presumed to be genuine or authorized except where the action is to enforce the obligation of a purported signer who has died or become incompetent before proof is required.
1. When signatures are admitted or established, production of the instrument entitles a holder to recover on it unless the defendant establishes a defense.
2. After it is shown that a defense exists a person claiming the rights of a holder in due course has the burden of establishing that he or some person under whom he claims is in all respects a holder in due course.

PART 4—LIABILITY OF PARTIES

§ 28:3–401. Signature

1. No person is liable on an instrument unless his signature appears thereon.
2. A signature is made by use of any name, including any trade or assumed name, upon an instrument, or by any word or mark used in lieu of a written signature.

§ 28:3–402. Signature in ambiguous capacity

Unless the instrument clearly indicates that a signature is made in some other capacity it is an indorsement.

§ 28:3–403. Signature by authorized representative

1. A signature may be made by an agent or other representative, and his authority to make it may be established as in other cases of representation. No particular form of appointment is necessary to establish such authority.
2. An authorized representative who signs his own name to an instrument
   a. is personally obligated if the instrument neither names the person represented nor shows that the representative signed in a representative capacity;
   b. except as otherwise established between the immediate parties, is personally obligated if the instrument names the person represented but does not show that the representative signed in a

representative capacity, or if the instrument does not name the person represented but does show that the representative signed in a representative capacity.
3. Except as otherwise established the name of an organization preceded or followed by the name and office of an authorized individual is a signature made in a representative capacity.

§ 28:3—404. Unauthorized signatures

1. Any unauthorized signature is wholly inoperative as that of the person whose name is signed unless he ratifies it or is precluded from denying it; but it operates as the signature of the unauthorized signer in favor of any person who in good faith pays the instrument or takes it for value.
2. Any unauthorized signature may be ratified for all purposes of this article. Such ratification does not of itself affect any rights of the person ratifying against the actual signer.

§ 28:3—405. Impostors; signature in name of payee

1. An indorsement by any person in the name of a named payee is effective if
   a. an imposter by use of the mails or otherwise has induced the maker or drawer to issue the instrument to him or his confederate in the name of the payee; or
   b. a person signing as or on behalf of a maker or drawer intends the payee to have no interest in the instrument; or
   c. an agent or employee of the maker or drawer has supplied him with the name of the payee intending the latter to have no such interest.
2. Nothing in this section shall affect the criminal or civil liability of the person so indorsing.

§ 28:3—406. Negligence contributing to alteration or unauthorized signature

Any person who by his negligence substantially contributes to a material alteration of the instrument or to the making of an unauthorized signature is precluded from asserting the alteration or lack of authority against a holder in due course or against a drawee or other payor who pays the instrument in good faith and in accordance with the reasonable commercial standards of the drawee's or payor's business.

§ 28:3—407. Alteration

1. Any alteration of an instrument is material which changes the contract, of any party thereto in any respect, including any such change in
   a. the number or relations of the parties; or
   b. an incomplete instrument, by completing it otherwise than as authorized; or
   c. the writing as signed, by adding to it or by removing any part of it.
2. As against any person other than a subsequent holder in due course
   a. alteration by the holder which is both fraudulent and material discharges any party whose contract is thereby changed unless that party assents or is precluded from asserting the defense;
   b. no other alteration discharges any party and the instrument may be enforced according to its original tenor, or as to incomplete instruments according to the authority given.
3. A subsequent holder in due course may in all cases enforce the instrument according to its original tenor, and when an incomplete instrument has been completed, he may enforce it as completed.

§ 28:3—408. Consideration

Want or failure of consideration is a defense as against any person not having the rights of a holder in due course (section 28:3—305), except that no consideration is necessary for an instrument or obligation thereon given in payment of or as security for an antecedent obligation of any kind. Nothing in this section shall be taken to displace any statute outside this subtitle under which a promise is enforceable notwithstanding lack or failure of consideration. Partial failure of consideration is a defense pro tanto whether or not the failure is in an ascertained or liquidated amount.

§ 28:3—409. Draft not an assignment

1. A check or other draft does not of itself operate as an assignment of any funds in the hands of the drawee available for its payment, and the drawee is not liable on the instrument until he accepts it.
2. Nothing in this section shall affect any liability in contract, tort or otherwise arising from any letter of credit or other obligation or representation which is not an acceptance.

§ 28:3—110. Definition and operation of acceptance

1. Acceptance is the drawee's signed engagement to honor the draft as presented. It must be written on the draft, and may consist of his signature alone. It becomes operative when completed by delivery or notification.
2. A draft may be accepted although it has not been signed by the drawer or is otherwise incomplete or is overdue or has been dishonored.
3. Where the draft is payable at a fixed period after sight and the acceptor fails to date his acceptance the holder may complete it by supplying a date in good faith.

§ 28:3—411. Certification of a check

1. Certification of a check is acceptance. Where a holder procures certification the drawer and all prior indorsers are discharged.
2. Unless otherwise agreed a bank has no obligation to certify a check.
3. A bank may certify a check before returning it for lack of proper indorsement. If it does so the drawer is discharged.

§ 28:3—412. Acceptance varying draft

1. Where the drawee's proffered acceptance in any manner varies the draft as presented the holder may refuse the acceptance and treat the draft as dishonored in which case the drawee is entitled to have his acceptance cancelled.
2. The terms of the draft are not varied by an acceptance to pay at any particular bank or place in the United States, unless the acceptance states that the draft is to be paid only at such bank or place.
3. Where the holder assents to an acceptance varying the terms of the draft each drawer and indorser who does not affirmatively assent is discharged.

§ 28:3—413. Contract of maker, drawer and acceptor

1. The maker or acceptor engages that he will pay the instrument according to its tenor at the time of his engagement or as completed pursuant to section 28:3—115 on incomplete instruments.

2. The drawer engages that upon dishonor of the draft and any necessary notice of dishonor or protest he will pay the amount of the draft to the holder or to any indorser who takes it up. The drawer may disclaim this liability by drawing without recourse.
3. By making, drawing or accepting the party admits as against all subsequent parties including the drawee the existence of the payee and his then capacity to indorse.

§ 28:3—414. Contract of indorser; order of liability

1. Unless the indorsement otherwise specifies (as by such words as "without recourse") every indorser engages that upon dishonor and any necessary notice of dishonor and protest he will pay the instrument according to its tenor at the time of his indorsement to the holder or to any subsequent indorser who takes it up, even though the indorser who takes it up was not obligated to do so.
2. Unless they otherwise agree indorsers are liable to one another in the order in which they indorse, which is presumed to be the order in which their signatures appear on the instrument.

§ 28:3—415. Contract of accommodation party

1. An accommodation party is one who signs the instrument in any capacity for the purpose of lending his name to another party to it.
2. When the instrument has been taken for value before it is due the accommodation party is liable in the capacity in which he has signed even though the taker knows of the accommodation.
3. As against a holder in due course and without notice of the accommodation oral proof of the accommodation is not admissible to give the accommodation party the benefit of discharges dependent on his character as such. In other cases the accommodation character may be shown by oral proof.
4. An indorsement which shows that it is not in the chain of title is notice of its accommodation character.
5. An accommodation party is not liable to the party accommodated, and if he pays the instrument has a right of recourse on the instrument against such party.

ARTICLE 4—BANK DEPOSITS AND COLLECTIONS

PART 2—COLLECTION OF ITEMS: DEPOSITARY AND COLLECTING BANKS

§ 28:4—201. Presumption and duration of agency status of collecting banks and provisional status of credits; applicability of article; item indorsed "pay any bank"

1. Unless a contrary intent clearly appears and prior to the time that a settlement given by a collecting bank for an item is or becomes final (subsection (3) of section 28:4—211 and sections 28:4—212 and 28:4—213) the bank is an agent or sub-agent of the owner of the item and any settlement given for the item is provisional. This provision applies regardless of the form of indorsement or lack of indorsement and even though credit given for the item is subject to immediate withdrawal as of right or is in fact withdrawn; but the continuance of ownership of an item by its owner and any rights of the owner to proceeds of the item are subject to rights of a collecting bank such as those resulting from outstanding advances on the item and valid rights of setoff. When an item is handled by banks for purposes of presentment, payment and collection, the relevant provisions of this article apply even though action of parties clearly establishes that a particular bank has purchased the item and is the owner of it.

2. After an item has been indorsed with the words "pay any bank" or the like, only a bank may acquire the rights of a holder
   a. until the item has been returned to the customer initiating collection; or
   b. until the item has been specially indorsed by a bank to a person who is not a bank.

§ 28:4—202. Responsibility for collection; when action seasonable

1. A collecting bank must use ordinary care in
   a. presenting an item or sending it for presentment; and
   b. sending notice of dishonor or non-payment or returning an item other than a documentary draft to the bank's transferor or directly to the depositary bank under subsection (2) of section 28:4—212 after learning that the item has not been paid or accepted, as the case may be; and
   c. settling for an item when the bank receives final settlement; and
   d. making or providing for any necessary protest; and
   e. notifying its transferor of any loss or delay in transit within a reasonable time after discovery thereof.
2. A collecting bank taking proper action before its midnight deadline following receipt of an item, notice or payment acts seasonably; taking proper action within a reasonably longer time may be seasonable but the bank has the burden of so establishing.
3. Subject to subsection (1) (a), a bank is not liable for the insolvency, neglect, misconduct, mistake or default of another bank or person or for loss or destruction of an item in transit or in the possession of others.

PART 3—COLLECTION OF ITEMS: PAYOR BANKS

§ 28:4—301. Deferred posting; recovery of payment by return of items; time of dishonor

1. Where an authorized settlement for a demand item (other than a documentary draft) received by a payor bank otherwise than for immediate payment, over the counter has been made before midnight of the banking day of receipt the payor bank may revoke the settlement and recover any payment, if before it has made final payment (subsection (1) of section 28:4—213) and before its midnight deadline it
   a. returns the item; or
   b. sends written notice of dishonor or nonpayment if the item is held for protest, or is otherwise unavailable for return.
2. If a demand item is received by a payor bank for credit, on its books it may return such item or send notice of dishonor and may revoke any credit given or recover the amount thereof withdrawn by its customer, if it acts within the time limit and in the manner specified in the preceding subsection.
3. Unless previous notice of dishonor has been sent an item is dishonored at the time when for purposes of dishonor it is returned or notice sent in accordance with this section.
4. An item is returned:
   a. as to an item received through a clearing house, when it is delivered to the presenting or last collecting bank or to the clearing house or is sent or delivered in accordance with its rules; or
   b. in all other cases, when it is sent or delivered to the bank's customer or transferor or pursuant to his instructions.

§ 28:4—302. Payor bank's responsibility for late return of item

1. In the absence of a valid defense such as breach of a presentment warranty (subsection (1) of section 28:4—207), settlement, effected or the like, if an item is presented on and received by a payor bank the bank is accountable for the amount of
   a. a demand item other than a documentary draft whether properly payable or not if the bank, in any case where it is not also the depositary bank, retains the item beyond midnight of the banking day of receipt without settling for it or, regardless of whether it is also the depositary bank, does not pay or return the item or send notice of dishonor until after its midnight deadline; or
   b. any other properly payable item unless within the time allowed for acceptance or payment of that item the bank either accepts or pays the item or returns it and accompanying documents.

§ 28:4—303. When items subject to notice, stop-order, legal process or setoff; order in which items may be charged or certified

1. Any knowledge, notice or stop-order received by, legal process served upon or setoff exercised by a payor bank, whether or not effective under other rules of law to terminate, suspend or modify the bank's right or duty to pay an item or to charge its customer's account for the item, comes too late to so terminate, suspend or modify such right or duty if the knowledge, notice, stop-order or legal process is received or served and a reasonable time for the bank to act thereon expires or the setoff is exercised after the bank has done any of the following:
   a. accepted or certified the item;
   b. paid the item in cash;
   c. settled for the item without reserving a right to revoke the settlement and without having such right under statute, clearing house rule or agreement;
   d. completed the process of posting the item to the indicated account of the drawer, maker or other person to be charged therewith or otherwise has evidenced by examination of such indicated account and by action its decision to pay the item; or
   e. become accountable for the amount of the item under subsection (1)(d) of section 28:4—213 and section 28:4—302 dealing with the payor bank's responsibility for late return items.
2. Subject to the provisions of subsection (1) items may be accepted, paid, certified or charged to the indicated account of its customer in any order convenient to the bank.

PART 4—RELATIONSHIP BETWEEN PAYOR BANK AND ITS CUSTOMER

§ 28:4—401. When bank may charge customer's account

1. As against its customer, a bank may charge against his account any item which is otherwise properly payable from that account even though the charge creates an overdraft.
2. A bank which in good faith makes payment to a holder may charge the indicated account of its customer according to
   a. the original tenor of his altered item; or
   b. the tenor of his completed item, even though the bank knows the item has been completed unless the bank has notice that the completion was improper.

§ 28:4—402. Bank's liability to customer for wrongful dishonor

A payor bank is liable to its customer for damages proximately caused by the wrongful dishonor of an item. When the dishonor occurs through mistake liability is limited to actual damages proved. If so proximately caused and proved damages may include damages for an arrest or prosecution of the customer or other consequential damages. Whether any consequential damages are proximately caused by the wrongful dishonor is a question of fact to be determined in each case.

§ 28:4—403. Customer's right to stop payment; burden of proof of loss

1. A customer may by order to his bank stop payment of any item payable for his account but the order must be received at such time and in such manner as to afford the bank a reasonable opportunity to act on it prior to any action by the bank with respect to the item described in section 28:4—303. No such order shall be valid, however, unless it shall be in writing specifically describing the item to which it relates by stating the amount, date and payee thereof.
2. Anything in this section 28:4—403 to the contrary notwithstanding, any stop payment order transmitted by telephone by a customer to an officer of a bank, while such officer is on the premises thereof, shall be accepted by such bank, upon such identification that will insure the order has been transmitted by such customer, as an effective order for a period of twenty-four hours, after which time it shall no longer be valid unless followed by a written order as provided in this section 28:4—403. A written order is effective for only six months unless renewed in writing. The bank may, at its option and without liability, stop payment of an item after the expiration of a stop payment order or any renewal thereof relating to such item.
3. The burden of establishing the fact and amount of loss resulting from the payment of an item contrary to a binding stop payment order is on the customer.

§ 28:4—404. Bank not obligated to pay check more than six months old

A bank is under no obligation to a customer having a checking account to pay a check, other than a certified check, which is presented more than six months after its date, but it may charge its customer's account for a payment made thereafter in the absence of an effective stop payment order in accordance with section 28:4—403.

§ 28:4—405. Death or incompetence of customer

1. A payor or collecting bank's authority to accept, pay or collect an item or to account for proceeds of its collection if otherwise effective is not rendered ineffective by incompetence of a customer of either bank existing at the time the item is issued or its collection is undertaken if the bank does not know of an adjudication of incompetence. Neither death nor incompetence of a customer revokes such authority to accept, pay, collect or account until the bank knows of the fact of death or of an adjudication of incompetence and has reasonable opportunity to act on it.
2. Even with knowledge a bank may for ten days after the date of death pay or certify checks drawn on or prior to that date unless ordered to stop payment by a person claiming an interest in the account.

§ 28:4—406. Customer's duty to discover and report unauthorized signature or alteration

1. When a bank sends to its customer a statement of account accompanied by items paid in good faith in support of the debit entries or holds the statement and items pursuant to a request or instructions

of its customer or otherwise in a reasonable manner makes the statement and items available to the customer, the customer must exercise reasonable care and promptness to examine the statement and items to discover his unauthorized signature or any alteration on an item and must notify the bank promptly after discovery thereof.

2. If the bank establishes that the customer failed with respect to an item to comply with the duties imposed on the customer by subsection (1) the customer is precluded from asserting against the bank
   a. his unauthorized signature or any alteration on the item if the bank also establishes that it suffered a loss by reason of such failure; and
   b. an unauthorized signature or alteration by the same wrongdoer on any other item paid in good faith by the bank after the first item and statement was available to the customer for a reasonable period not exceeding fourteen calendar days and before the bank receives notification from the customer of any such unauthorized signature or alteration.
3. The preclusion under subsection (2) does not apply if the customer establishes lack of ordinary care on the part or the bank in paying the item(s).
4. Without regard to care or lack of care of either the customer or the bank a customer who does not within one year from the time the statement and items are made available to the customer (subsection (1)) discover and report his unauthorized signature or any alteration on the face or back of the item or does not within three years from that time discover and report any unauthorized indorsement is precluded from asserting against the bank such unauthorized signature or indorsement or such alteration.
5. If under this section a payor bank has a valid defense against a claim of a customer upon or resulting from payment of an item and waives or fails upon request to assert the defense the bank may not assert against any collecting bank or other prior party presenting or transferring the item a claim based upon the unauthorized signature or alteration giving rise to the customer's claim.

§ 28:4—407. Payor bank's right to subrogation on improper payment

If a payor bank has paid an item over the stop payment order of the drawer or maker or otherwise under circumstances giving a basis for objection by the drawer or maker, to prevent unjust enrichment and only to the extent necessary to prevent loss to the bank by reason of its payment of the item, the payor bank shall be subrogated to the rights

a. of any holder in due course on the item against the drawer or maker; and
b. of the payee or any other holder of the item against the drawer or maker either on the item or under the transaction out of which the item arose; and
c. of the drawer or maker against the payee or any other holder of the item with respect to the transaction out of which the item arose.

Appendix C. Lordsburg Taphouse and Grill

Introduction

My wife and I were interested in purchasing a restaurant. Neither I nor she ever owned one before. My background was in the oil industry, and her background was in retail. We had little idea of what to expect. Friends of ours owned a restaurant bar and grill called T-Phillips in La Verne, CA. It offered a variety of items on its menu, accompanied by a 60-tap-beer selection. They offered it for sale, and we decided to purchase it. The price in our view was very reasonable.

The building is leased and had some obvious structural deficiencies. We had to make structural improvements in order to operate in the manner we preferred. Although obvious, this issue proved to be difficult for two reasons. The first reason was because city officials required complicated additions to the improvements we wanted to make. Instead of permitting us to repair the problem, the city made us remove and remodel. This cost significantly more and caused delay in our opening. A satisfactory $30,000 repair became a $130,000 remodel. The regulatory timeline we were required to meet was oppressive (see Chapter 12).

Secondly, dealing with a landlord posed other difficulties we were not expecting nor mentally prepared to confront. Landlords will try to maximize lease provisions in their favor, and of course, we wanted to do the same. Experience in lease negotiations is a real talent for a lessee. We managed and eventually obtained a reasonable lease over time with annual amendments.

Another tough issue was the operational challenges with the wait staff and food quality. Resolution of the food quality was straightforward because we retained a very talented and smart chef. All he needed was creative freedom and a budget to purchase quality ingredients, which we wisely provided.

The wait-staff issues also seemed easily rectified in the beginning, but they turned out to be very tricky and nuanced. We tried to implement a paradigm shift in attitude and execution. Ultimately, replacing employees was more effective than retraining them. Within two years only three of 30 original employees remained with us. We are very happy with the group as presently constituted and believe we have the best wait staff in the area.

Conclusion

It has been a rocky road at times but well worth the effort. The required structural improvements were costly but manageable. The government regulation was daunting and is an ongoing issue for the business. As the timeline indicates, administrative requirements were time demanding and sometimes redundant. Regulatory agencies required much of the same information without sharing and coordinating among themselves.

A newcomer to the restaurant business must review local regulations to determine the most business friendly city government. A decision to buy a restaurant because you enjoyed patronizing it can be dangerous. Without prior experience, government regulations may be your most challenging issue. Have plenty of cash to meet the unexpected problems, such as our structural ones. Make no mistake; there will always be unexpected problems.

We are pleased to have a successful business. Now that we are veterans of the hospitality industry, we are planning our next venture. We plan to open an upscale frankfurter restaurant in the same area.

www.ingramcontent.com/pod-product-compliance
Ingram Content Group UK Ltd.
Pitfield, Milton Keynes, MK11 3LW, UK
UKHW051453290926
15471UKWH00008B/1182

9 781793 515520